I WANT TO DISTURB
MY NEIGHBOUR

'I WANT TO DISTURB MY NEIGHBOUR':

LECTURES ON SLAVERY, EMANCIPATION AND POSTCOLONIAL JAMAICA

Verene A. Shepherd

For Dianne
Best wishes
VAShepherd
19/4/07

Ian Randle Publishers
Kingston • Miami

First published in Jamaica, 2007 by
Ian Randle Publishers
11 Cunningham Avenue
Box 686
Kingston 6
www.ianrandlepublishers.com

National Library of Jamaica Cataloguing in Publication Data

Shepherd, Verene A.
 "I want to disturb my neighbour" : lectures on slavery, emancipation and postcolonial
Jamaica / Verene A. Shepherd.

    p. ; cm.

    Bibliography : p.   .– Includes index

    ISBN 978-976-637-255-2 (pbk)
        976-637-255-1

1.   Slavery - Jamaica. 2.   Emancipation – Jamaica.   3.   Jamaica – Culture.
4.   Jamaica – History. 5. Haiti – History.

I.   Title

    326.97292   dc 21

Cover and book design by Ian Randle Publishers
Printed in the United States of America

TABLE OF CONTENTS

LIST OF TABLES

PREFACE

The primary responsibilities of the University academic are to teach and advise graduate and undergraduate students, attend to examination duties, conduct research and publish the findings of such research. However, few confine themselves to their core mandate. Many assume leadership positions and administrative responsibilities (including sitting on committees, sub-committees and the inevitable task forces), engage in public and professional service and outreach activities, and form links with the international academy through the delivery of conference papers and public lectures. Historians at the University of the West Indies (UWI) are among those who refuse to imprison themselves within the walls of academia, becoming heavily involved in public service, schools' and community outreach; and delivering public lectures locally, regionally and internationally. In this regard, we have continued a tradition long established by such activist scholars as Kamau Brathwaite, Elsa Goveia, C.L.R. James, Lucille Mathurin Mair, Walter Rodney and Eric Williams. In fact, many Caribbean scholars have long shunned the path of the classic intellectual, associated traditionally with 'ivory tower' and 'snobbishness'.[1] They adhere to the Gramscian view that 'all men are intellectuals';[2] that in Julian Benda's terms, they are engaged individuals, not 'other worldly, ivory-towered thinkers, devoted to abstruse subjects';[3] not people who detest the rise of mass societies and the 'common man'. They share the views articulated so well by Edward Said that: the intellectual is an individual in society that confronts orthodoxy and dogma; who cannot be reduced simply to being a faceless professional, a competent member of a class going about his/her business [but] an individual endowed with a faculty for representing, embodying, articulating a message, a view, an attitude, philosophy or opinion *to*, as well as *for*, a public.[4]

I have had the pleasure of contributing to this heritage, and like other colleagues in the Mona History and Archaeology Department, have accepted invitations to speak on a variety of historical issues in disparate locations.

This present collection consists of a selection of 21 lectures and speeches (some never before published), delivered locally and internationally in the period 1998–2005. I wish now to share these lectures with a wider audience, especially those unexposed to the history of the Caribbean and to undergraduates who will benefit from these summaries and interpretations. They are arranged thematically and sometimes chronologically, and not necessarily in the order in which they were delivered. They cover issues relevant to Jamaica's colonial past: conquest, colonization, slavery and anti-slavery, post-slavery society and the project of decolonization. Predictably, the overwhelming focus is on slavery, migration and gender issues as these are my major research interests.

One presentation is focused on Haiti, representing my modest contribution to the celebration of the bicentenary of Haitian independence in 2004. While by no means a specialist in Haitian history (and we are all aware of the phenomenon of academic territoriality), I subscribe to the view that the Haitian anti-slavery struggle and its impact on the Americas as well as Haiti's post-1804 political history cannot be the sole preserve of the so-called 'specialists' but must be the concern of all historians and all Caribbean people. In any event, Haiti has been of interest to me ever since I read C.L.R. James's *Black Jacobins* as an undergraduate student many decades ago, and then proceeded to research and teach comparative slavery. Interest in Haiti was, predictably, heightened in the bicentenary year when specialists in Caribbean history were kept busy responding to calls for guest lectures and conference/workshop presentations on Haiti. UNESCO also declared 2004 the 'International Year for the Commemoration of the Struggle against Slavery, and its Abolition' and established a National Task Force to plan events in celebration of the year; and I was honoured to have been a member of that committee (as well as of the Mona Campus' Planning Committees in 2004 and again in 2005). Celebrations and commemorative activities were, of course, marred by the deposing and eventual exiling to South Africa of President Jean Bertrand Aristide. Subsequently South Africa opened up a discursive space for Haiti and the wider Caribbean in its country and I was pleased to have shared in the discussions.

A few of the lectures and speeches address current issues such as the fight for reparation from slavery, the need to honour the island's 'Glorious Dead' through the construction of War Memorials, and the failure of postcolonial regimes to deliver on the promise of emancipation and independence. For while we mark annually the anniversaries of the abolition of slavery and the transatlantic trade in Africans, we are also conscious that the battle for true mental liberation and for respect for Black identity continues — making the Jamaican social landscape a truly 'contested terrain'. The lectures are intended to inform and educate students and the general public, many of whom are still grappling with the complexities of the Caribbean's historical past and its relationship with the international community; with the enduring plantation-type rule that characterizes so much of our institutions and everyday interaction with the power-holders in our society. One or two might even be amusing especially to a Jamaican audience. Several are deliberately activist, intended to (and here I borrow from Bob Marley), 'disturb my neighbour', following the legacy and tradition of other activist Caribbean historians. Bob Marley has provided other writers with the titles of their books and for me, 'I Want to Distrub My Neighbour' seemed the logical one, although there are many Marley lines that I like, including 'Get up, Stand up; Stand up for Your Rights'.

Endnotes have been added where there were none to ensure consistency in the publication. Of course, the very nature of the topics and the disparate contexts in which they were delivered make the overlap of some material inevitable. But they have mostly been left in the time and place in which they were delivered rather than subjected to too much retrospective analysis.

I wish to emphasize that the lectures were delivered to a wide variety of audiences, including academic specialists, undergraduates in the United States, school children, college graduates and sections of the Jamaican public that have not had access to formal education, especially at the post-primary level. In the case of the lecture delivered in South Africa, the audience knew very little about Haiti and as such the collection contains a wide variety of styles and levels as I adjusted my talks to suit my audience. Predictably, what academics refer to as 'the quality of content and presentation', varies. So, themes that were familiar and old to academics, especially students of history, were, as Jamaicans would say 'news' to nonspecialists and the general public at the time of delivery. This aspect of the publication will not please some readers but was a deliberate choice on my part (and my publisher concurred), since the alternative would have been three different collections, each suitable to a particular level.

I express my gratitude to the staff and students of the various colleges, schools, universities and other educational institutions and organizations who invited me to deliver these lectures and hosted me so graciously. They provided me with great opportunities to express my opinion in non-confrontational environments, present the results of my research to a wider audience as well as indicate the state of the historiography on topics outside of my own area of research. In this regard I thank, collectively, the history fraternity which provided me with data for some of these talks.

More specifically (at the international level) I thank Beloit College in Wisconsin; the University of the Netherlands Antilles in Curaçao; the University of Mauritius and the Mahatma Gandhi Institute in Mauritius; Sarah Lawrence College, New York; the University of South Africa (Centre for African Renaissance Studies); Queen's University, Belfast and York University, Toronto. Aspects/versions of the lectures included were also presented at the 37th Annual Association of Caribbean Historians' Conference in Colombia; the 3rd Text and Testimony Collective Conference in Limón, Costa Rica; the Australian National University; the College of Charleston; Colgate University; the University of London (ICS); the University of Michigan (CAAS); the University of Nottingham (ICHOS); Christchurch University, New Zealand; CODESRIA, Senegal; the University of Suriname; the University of Sussex; Syracuse University; the University of Vienna, Austria; the University of Warwick; and the University of Kwazulu-Natal in Durban. Travel to these states and countries allowed me to sample new cultures, make new friends (some from places outside those I was visiting, like Bolivia, Botswana, Ecuador, Ghana, India, Peru, Réunion, Uganda, Zimbabwe) and engage in political debates that are not often at the forefront of the Western media. It was particularly wonderful to meet Caribbean people settled in far-flung places and to benefit from the positive image that Jamaica has among some communities abroad, especially in Africa. Of course, this positive image is not shared by many immigration officers who construct, and act on, stereotypical images of the Black Jamaican woman — as I learned from encounters with some of these officers in Toronto, New Zealand and some countries in Latin America. As far as some of these immigration officers are concerned, the Black, female, Jamaican intellectual travelling to deliver guest lectures is an unfamiliar, even disturbing, phenomenon!

Locally and regionally, I thank the United Nations Educational, Scientific and Cultural Organization (UNESCO), Jamaica Office; the Mona Campus' 2004 Commemoration Planning Committee; the Institute of Jamaica (IOJ); and the Organizing Committees of the annual Churches' Emancipation Lecture in Kingston and Montego Bay. I especially thank the Cave Hill Campus and the UNESCO Slave Routes Project for giving me an opportunity to unveil my project on War Memorials to Caribbean heroes and heroines at their task force meeting in Barbados in December 2003. Versions of this lecture were also presented to the Jamaica Historical Society, the 2003 All African Students' Conference at the Mona Campus and formed the context of the 6th Walter Rodney Memorial Lecture hosted by the Institute of Caribbean Studies. Brown's Town Community College, the Latin American and Caribbean Centre (LACC) at the UWI's Mona campus, the Jamaica National Heritage Trust (JNHT), the Jamaica Reparation Movement, the Jamaica Cultural Development Commission (JCDC), the Marcus Garvey Movement at the Mona campus, the Planning Institute of Jamaica (PIOJ), Shortwood Teachers' College and the St. Mary Parish Library must also be recognized for hosting some or versions of these lectures.

I thank my family for their support (and sometimes company) as I travelled to near, but oftentimes more distant locations to deliver some of these lectures. I am also grateful to Cay Mullings and Karen Porteous-Granston for their hospitality and writing spaces in New York and London; and to graduate students Dalea Bean and Kerry-Ann Morris as well as IT specialists at Mona and other lecture venues for providing research and technical assistance respectively, especially as I ventured into the sometimes technologically perilous world of Power Point presentations. I thank Ian Randle Publishers for their patience as deadlines became more difficult for me to me

JNHT

adr

r

¹e to the staff and Board Members of the

the National Housing Trust (which

, and the Mona Campus' Heritage

mation Team for taking my 'War Memorial

nising to see that some alternative memorials

— the bicentenary of the passing of the Act to

c trade in Africans to Jamaica and other former

nk the reviewers for the useful comments that helped

me of the chapters. Finally, I owe a debt of gratitude to

a for its financial support in the form of research, study and

`                ).`

Verene A. Shepherd
May 2006

SECTION I

HISTORIOGRAPHY AND KNOWLEDGE PRODUCTION IN JAMAICA AND THE WIDER CARIBBEAN

Introduction

Like Africa, the Caribbean has been affected by a historically constructed image that still influences self-identity as well as global attitudes towards its citizens. This image was constructed by generations of writers from the North Atlantic System, from Christopher Columbus through Edward Long to Lowell J. Ragatz[1] and beyond. The machinery of knowledge production was fed by several factors that opened up a discursive space for its 'producers' including the European colonization of the region, the subordination of the indigenous peoples, the expropriation of Caribbean resources for the development of Europe, rivalry among imperial powers, the continued migration to and settlement of Europeans in the region, the forced relocation of Africans to provide labour for European economic enterprises, the indentureship of Asians and the creation of a racist sociopolitical regime that dichotomized blackness and whiteness.

This 'knowledge' was powerful enough to have a lasting impact on Caribbean, African and Indian diasporic identity, imagination and consciousness. However, what colonial writers presented as knowledge about Caribbean people was not allowed to go unchallenged. Caribbean scholars, many products of the University of the West Indies (UWI), have engaged in an opposite project of reconstruction, constructing indigenous interpretations of the Caribbean experience, fashioned by explicit formulations and theoretical constructs and offering the antithesis to the imperialist view of the Caribbean world.

The lectures and speeches in this section address the issue of knowledge production, explain its rationale and demonstrate the strides made by scholars in destabilizing traditional (mis)representations of Africans, Asians and Creoles. In the process, we get a glimpse of the scholars who are writing and 'righting' Caribbean history.

1

KNOWLEDGE PRODUCTION IN THE CARIBBEAN: Contemporary Writings, the Construction of 'Africa(n)' and the Task of Reconstruction[1]

Delivered at the University of South Africa's Centre for Renaissance Studies, June 2005

Historically, Europeans have dominated knowledge production on the colonial Caribbean. They appropriated the project of producing knowledge on the Caribbean, essentially for overseas audiences, introducing the Caribbean and its people to a wider public.

The early writings produced on the Caribbean, especially descriptive accounts of Africa and Africans, were not necessarily the result of careful research. This is because the knowledge produced, had a discrete political purpose: to support European imperialism and 'dislodge and disorient' the Caribbean in a similar way that it did Africa and the Orients, following Dani Nabudere's and Edward Said's formulations.[2] In other words, 'knowledge about the distant "other" served the purpose of dominating it and exercising power and authority over it.'[3] In the specific context of slavery, as some of the works sampled in this lecture will illustrate, the purpose of the production of knowledge about Africa and Africans was to prolong slavery and colonialism, and discourage self-confidence among Black people by demonizing blackness and the geographical origins of African diasporic peoples and promote whiteness (or even Creolité/hybridity) as the ideal.

Colonial writers' presentation of knowledge about Africa and diasporic Africans was not allowed to go unchallenged. As I will show, Caribbean scholars have engaged in an opposite project of reconstruction, constructing indigenous interpretations of the Caribbean experience, fashioned by explicit formulations and theoretical constructs and offering the antithesis to the

3

imperialist view of the Caribbean world. Even before Africans entered Caribbean space, the groundwork had already been laid in the historiography for the demonization of the colonial 'Other', manifested in the writings about the indigenous peoples.

Overview of the Knowledge Produced by Contemporary and Modern Writers

The project of knowledge production on the Caribbean has a long history dating back to the period of European conquest and colonization in the late fifteenth century. The inherently conquistadorial accounts of the first years of conquest were followed in the sixteenth and seventeenth centuries by more detailed descriptions of the progress of colonization in the Spanish Caribbean and the consequences of the encounter with the indigenous peoples. For the most part, the fifteenth- to eighteenth-century works engaged in the project of mis/representation of the indigenes, dichotomizing Tainos and Kalinago (Caribs) into peaceful/docile and cannibalistic respectively. Their objective was to demonize the people of the Caribbean and project them as immoral, uncivilized and barbaric in order to justify their military and spiritual subjugation. In the aftermath of the conquest, these works exhibited a tendency to negate or minimize the role of the indigenous peoples in the advance of Caribbean modernity, presenting both text and sub-text that projected perceptions of the indigenous Caribbeans as a 'problem' for colonial development and an obstacle to the European march to progress.

Interest in the colonies intensified as exclusive Spanish hegemony gave way to the incursion of other European colonizers and as English, Dutch and French writers generated their own literature. The seventeenth and eighteenth centuries saw the emergence of texts by those, many resident planters and missionaries, who claimed first-hand knowledge of the Caribbean. The narratives of Richard Ligon, Charles Leslie, Jean Baptiste du Tertre and Edward Long are good examples.[4] These contemporary works focused on aspects of the settlement history of particular territories in the region, with some attention to geography, flora and fauna, economic resources, trade, imperial rivalries, the progress of colonization, the diverse experiences of the early settlers, buccaneers and indigenous peoples, law and liberty, and the subject of slavery. The effects of conquest have been followed in the works of several historians like David Henige and Alvin Thompson who have not only recounted the quantitative dimensions of the 'genocidal' consequences of colonization, but also the complex commercial, political and social relations established between 'Amerindians' and Europeans.[5] The ways in which colonization was made effective through military conquests, and settlements made permanent through economic 'development' (following the European rather than the indigenous people's model) have been followed in the works of several authors. Those who have studied the labour history of the early colonial period have shown that white servitude was not an exclusive male enterprise and that white working-class women played fundamental roles in colonization as agricultural labourers, domestic servants and wives/concubines.[6]

Other historical works appeared in the eighteenth century dealing with the colonies' general development and social evolution, with several local histories and special studies, for example on the Maroons, being published. Arguably the three most influential works of the eighteenth century were those by Guillaume [Abbé] Raynal, Edward Long, and Bryan Edwards.[7] The eighteenth century was the height of African enslavement and the trade in African captives as well as of wars for empire and these themes are amply reflected in the works of the period. Various authors have examined several levels of engagement with the financial system of colonialism. All agree that the planters' aim in the global mobilization of productive resources was to realize a surplus from the transfer of money into the purchase of land, labourers and machinery. The eighteenth-century wars of empire and the struggle of Maroon men and women (like the quintessential rebel woman, Nanny) for social, economic and political terrain are themes targeted for analysis by later accounts of this period.

The nineteenth century was the age of the classical school of British historians, some of whom targeted the Caribbean for their discourses. Most supported the idea of the British empire and Britain's continued domination of so-called 'inferior' races. Thomas Carlyle (1849), for example, of whom Eric Williams said the idea of liberty made him mad and the idea of equality made him frantic, 'vituperated the free negro'.[8] Many late nineteenth-century writers, like Anthony Trollope and James Anthony Froude, inveighed against emancipation and the liberty conveyed on the African and African-

Caribbeans.[9] They were decidedly imperialist in their view of post-slavery resistance, for example, of the 1865 Morant Bay Rebellion in Jamaica which signalled the end of representative government and the intensification of Crown rule. The nineteenth century also saw the proliferation of local histories, which provided various perspectives on post-slavery society in individual territories. Pan-Caribbean or regional histories which went beyond narrow geographical boundaries, and micro-studies of special themes such as migration and population growth, labour conditions and the condition of the plantocracy also emerged.

The dominant note in the writings from around 1880 to 1945 was imperialism: the justification, encouragement, defence and apology for colonies. At the end of the nineteenth century the literature was still mainly from amateurs writing from an imperial perspective. Even in the early twentieth century, authors like Charles Lucas and A.P. Newton, Rhodes Chair of Imperial History at London, were still writing in the Eurocentric, imperial mode; and few challenges were forthcoming.[10] Change only became noticeable in the post-World War II period. One post-1945 trend was that the Eurocentric, imperialist tendencies of the works originating in the late eighteenth, nineteenth and early twentieth centuries were increasingly overtaken by revisionist works of a newer generation of scholars like Eric Williams and C.L.R. James who grounded their work in solid archival research.[11] The end of World War II, the escalation of the decolonization movement, the globalization of Western culture and the re-empowerment of non-Western states, all signalled a new intellectual age. The new writers questioned the essentialism of the traditional historiography and the master narrative imposed on former colonized peoples and introduced their own discursive practices. In the post-1970s in particular, there were renewed attempts, not always successful, to dethrone the old intellectual absolutisms and introduce new 'sociologies of knowledge'.

Imaging Africa and Africans

Of the works produced by contemporary and modern writers, it is perhaps the subject of slavery that has attracted the most attention, and the existence of enslaved and free Africans within a white supremacist social order fuelled a spate of writing that painted a less than empowering image of Blacks. A sampling of some of the works produced about Africa and Africans demonstrates this. In the contemporary writings of Edward Long, Maria Nugent, M.G. Lewis, Cynric Williams, A.C. Carmichael, Thomas Carlyle, Anthony Trollope, James Anthony Froude, Frank W. Pitman, and Lowell J. Ragatz, originates the negative representations of Africa, which are still embedded deeply within the consciousness of Caribbean people.[12]

These works had several common features. First, they tried to essentialize Africans, ascribing ethnic characteristics to the various groups forcefully transported to the Caribbean via the transatlantic trade that brought over 15 million Africans to the Americas, about 42 per cent to the Caribbean alone. Philip Curtin has shown that a diverse mix of African ethnicities were taken from Senegambia, Guinea-Biassau, Sierra Leone, the Cape Mount to Cameroon and Congo-Angola regions, and Southern and South Eastern Africa.[13] The colonialists were profoundly ignorant about the cultural attributes of Africans and were perhaps not even interested in supposedly mundane cultural accuracy. Instead, they maintained prejudices and stereotypes that served their purposes. For example, their 'knowledge' indicated that the Papaws from the so-called 'Slave Coast' made docile and agreeable enslaved people; the Nagoes and Whydahs developed into good field hands and had sunny dispositions; the Coromantees from the Gold Coast were proud, brave but rebellious; the Akans were clannish and rebellious; the Senegalese were bright and were suitable for skilled trades and domestic service but not field labour; the Mandingoes were gentle, unfit for prolonged labour and were born thieves; and the Ibos from the Niger delta were timorous and despondent. The Bantu-speaking Angolans were given the reputation of being rebellious and lazy.[14]

Colonial era writers portrayed Africans as uncivilized, irrational, deceitful and cunning (symbolized by the Ashanti Anancy figure in Jamaican folk tales); thoughtless, improvident, ugly, perverse, immoral, promiscuous, poor parents and lacking in intelligence. They equated familiarity with agriculture in Africa with 'suitability' to perform agricultural labour. Ignoring conveniently the period of white servitude in the Caribbean, they developed the dichotomy of strong black labourers and feeble white labourers. Within this context, Blacks were 'natural slaves', Whites supposedly unable to withstand tropical conditions and perform agricultural labour. The knowledge producers used tropical origins to argue that Africans would acclimatize quickly to Caribbean conditions and survive the rigours of chattel enslavement. The demographic disaster that was the reality of Caribbean slavery would eventually prove them wrong. Enslavers in the Caribbean were caught in the web of a major dilemma. As rational entrepreneurs they sought to maximize profits by reducing the cost of productive inputs. Expenditures on those enslaved were suppressed to subsistence levels. At the same time, however, the protection of property rights in chattel was a top priority that required careful policy formulation and implementation. The effective social maintenance of the enslaved then, meant that the daily management of subsistence and health care could not be left to chance. Those enslaved had to be properly nourished and assisted medically if they were to be productive workers. At the same time the impact of class and race prejudice upon economic thinking oftentimes led to subsistence levels being located below what was required to maintain general health and population growth. The planter M.G. Lewis attributed the failure of Jamaica's enslaved population to increase by natural means partly to female strategies of reproductive resistance, noting in the early nineteenth century that 'I really believe that the negresses can produce children at pleasure; and where they are barren, it is just as hens will frequently not lay eggs on shipboard, because they do not like their situation.'[15]

Edward Long provided detailed accounts of the structure of slavery and the sugar plantation system in the Caribbean. He also produced the most racist account of diasporic Africans in the Caribbean, inveighing against miscegenation, deriding the impact of Blacks on Creole white women and painting a negative image of the physical attributes of black women.[16]

The misrepresentations of Africans in the Caribbean intensified after 1791 and the outbreak of the Haitian revolution, and were geared towards maintaining slavery and avoiding the Haitian experience. Slavery and its systematic brutalities had long engendered a deep-seated insecurity among Whites in the Caribbean, but such fears intensified after 1791 and the news of violence against the white population in Haiti during the emancipation and independence struggles. Such fears and the actions taken to quell them are evident in the 1801–05 entries in Maria Nugent's journal. Maria Nugent was the American-born wife of the Governor of Jamaica, George Nugent, whose governorship lasted from 1801–06. Nugent and others became extra suspicious of Black people in Jamaica after 1800. They saw impudence and lack of respect in every grin, every face, every failure to bow; every instance in which Blacks looked directly at them instead of turning away. In 1805, after she had taken her children by boat to Port Royal, she then decided to take them for a walk and recounted that,

> We met a horrid looking black man, who passed us several times, without making any bow, although I recollected him as one of the boatmen of the canoe we used to go out in, before we had the Maria. He was then very humble, but tonight he only grinned, and gave us a sort of fierce look, that struck me with terror I could not shake off.[17]

M.G. Lewis, while overturning stereotypes such as Africans having no religious beliefs, also contributed to the misrepresentation of the African. For him, they were habitual liars; '[U]nless a Negro has an interest in telling the truth, he always lies — in order to keep his tongue in practice.'[18] The most outstanding description in his book is that of the African being content with enslavement. He described those in Jamaica as people who were always laughing and singing; 'who seem to perform their work with so much nonchalance, taking up their baskets and as if it were perfectly optional whether they took them up or left them there.... The Negro might well say, on arrival in England — "massa, in England everything work!" for here nobody appears to work at all.'[19] He was not indicating laziness but the lack of coercion to labour; a contentment and leisure uncharacteristic of the English working class. Lewis was however writing after the abolition of the trade in enslaved Africans when the threat of lack of labour petrified planters whose economic welfare depended on slavery. Here then, the colonial project required knowledge about slavery in the Caribbean and the treatment of labourers within the slave relations of production as a way to defeat the emancipationists.

Cynric Williams and A.C. Carmichael had similar intentions. For Williams, Africans had traditionally been content with their condition and only the anti-slavery movement in Britain had reversed this situation. Even so, they were merry; and based on the evidence of some planters he had met, better off than the English and Irish working classes. They lived

9

in a society of mostly benevolent masters, where even runaways (for two years) could receive free pardon. They had made religious progress because of the influence of the Christian missionaries, many of whom had tried to eradicate African religious tradition, including the Muslim tradition; but in his view, their religious progress '[did] not seem to improve their morality' as they still displayed the tendency to lie and cheat. He cited cases in which Africans had used their conversion to Christianity and the new names they had been given to evade debts, they claimed had been contracted by the unconverted versions of themselves![20]

Some writers demonized Africa and produced 'knowledge' that gave the impression that Africa's citizens were loath to return to their homeland. Mrs A.C. Carmichael, wife of a British planter, who spent the 1820s in Trinidad and St. Vincent in the British Caribbean and produced two volumes, published in 1833, is a good example of a writer who gave the impression that Africa was a place to which those who had left did not wish to return. Her ventriloquized dialogue with an enslaved 'Ebo' woman in St. Vincent, whom she called 'Q' and described as 'in manner a perfect savage, yet not rude', illustrates:

AC: What nation are you of, Q?
Q: An Ebo
AC: Would you like to go to Africa?
Q: Misses, me hope never to see dat country no more
AC: And you are now happier than you ever were in Africa?
Q: Yes, misses, Africa one bad country[21]

Carmichael recorded similar conversations with other enslaved people in St. Vincent. The conversations usually went the same way with the enslaved expressing gratitude to be in the Caribbean and denigrating Africa for one reason or another, from cruel 'massas', inadequate food and clothes, to unsavoury characters in Africa. The examples from Trinidad were remarkably similar to those she conducted in St. Vincent.

AC: Do you remember Africa?
S: (head boilerman, and a Coromantee): A little, misses
AC: Would you like to return there and see it again?

S: No misses, me country nigger very wicked — me no wish
            to see 'em again
AC: Do you think them more wicked than Negroes here —
            do they steal and lie more, and are they apt to quarrel and
            fight?
S: Misses, white lady know noting of Africa. In my part, dey
            bad too much; me cannot tell you how bad[22]

Carmichael's project was clear. It was to prove that 'native Africans do
not at all like it to be supposed that they retain the customs of their country;
and consider themselves wonderfully civilized by their being transplanted
from Africa to the West Indies.'[23] Carmichael's writings imply that it was
the planters' wives who were enslaved as they were forced to endure the
tardiness and sauciness of domestic women.

Years later Anthony Trollope, himself a supporter of the stereotypical
image of the African — fit for manual labour, intellectually deficient, anxious
to be white and despising himself, unable to understand western religion,
unambitious, lazy and willing to laugh, make merry and sleep through
life[24] — would write about the consequences of this negative representation
of Africa for the West Indian Creole. Thus in the mid 1850s he wrote, 'the
West Indian Negro knows nothing of Africa except that it is a term of
reproach.' He even supported the Carmichaelean notion of lack of attachment
to 'home', this time in relation to the Creole Blacks who had neither country
of their own nor country of adoption; who '[had] no idea of country, and
no pride of race; for even among themselves, the word "nigger" conveys
their worst term of reproach'.[25]

Thomas Carlyle, in his proslavery essay entitled 'The Nigger Question'
gave political imagery to the concept of 'Quashie' as a 'Black mind and
body that was unprepared for freedom.'[27] He did not 'hate the Negro',
stereotyped by him as 'a merry-hearted, grinning, dancing, singing,
affectionate kind of creature' who 'alone of wild men can live among men
civilized'. But he hated his alleged 'laziness'. As Trollope did years later,
ignoring the evidence of a workforce that had produced commodities that
energized the English industrial revolution, he insisted on categorizing the
Caribbean black person as someone who emerged out of slavery unable to
rouse him/herself to continue to work. On the contrary, 'sunk to the ears

in pumpkin, imbibing saccharine juices, and much at ease in the Creation, he can listen to the less fortunate white man's "demand" [for labour] and take his own time in supplying it.'[27] A century and a half later, Jamaican poet Lorna Goodison, armed with a battery of metaphorical representations, reacted to the epistemic violence of the imperial project by calling for a renegotiation of such 'bad words' to create an internal liberating narrative of self.[28]

The late nineteenth-century writings of James Anthony Froude and the twentieth-century works of Ragatz and Pitman were equally responsible for imagining the African and constructing knowledge that perpetuated damaging myths and stereotypes. For Froude, like many of his predecessors, Africans and their West Indian progeny were lacking in morals. With no knowledge of the idea of sin and the law, however, they could not be held accountable for their actions. Nakedness was natural and not a cause for emotions such as shame; and in the post-slavery era, they lived a happy, content life, with no ambitions or 'aspirations to make them restless'.[29] For Ragatz, the West Indian Black [who enjoyed in the Caribbean a better state than he had known in his African home], had all the characteristics of his race. He stole, he lied, he was simple, he was suspicious, inefficient, irresponsible, lazy, superstitious, and loose in his sex relations; ... [O]verdress and aping the manners of their betters [was an action they] freely indulged in.[30]

Pitman endorsed contemporary stereotypes of Black people, such as was held by Governor Trelawny of Jamaica, who believed that absenteeism of planters was inimical to the sugar plantation system since Blacks tended toward stupidity, slacking, real and feigned illness, thieving, lack of interest, malicious sabotage and marronage. They needed constant supervision because 'as primitive and lazy people, they would often try to avoid work'. They were irrational beings whose religious beliefs constituted primitive animism of a very low order.[31]

Prejudices were also evident in the writings about the family life of enslaved people. Contemporary observers like Thomas Atwood had denied the existence of enslaved families and the ability of enslaved women in particular, to establish and maintain families on account of their pathological promiscuity.[32] This negative approach carried over into works that appeared in the 1950s and 1960s. For example, the anthropologist, M.G. Smith suggested that it would have been impossible for the enslaved to establish stable marriage because they lacked the kinship and lineage groups to sanction and give permanence to unions.[33] Structuralists, like Orlando Patterson, as Marrietta Morrisey emphasized, regarded enslaved women as promiscuous, arguing that 'the breakdown of sexual mores and the institution of marriage among Negroes occured all over the New World'.[34] His 1982 work also suggested that the symbolic estrangement from kin and corresponding social illegitimacy of the enslaveds' natal ties precluded family formation.[35] Elsa Goveia argued for the British Leeward Islands that the African custom of polygamy gave way to promiscuity, though she blamed the institution of slavery for this condition. Such references to promiscuity, however, are deeply offensive to African-Caribbean women who continue to be painted with that particular brush of slavery.[36]

Negative representations of Africa and Africans were manifested in the behaviour of colonizers. For example, over time enslavers in the Caribbean tried to discipline and transform Africans into New World Creoles, placing them in a dialectical relationship to Africa(n) by rendering invisible the African ingredients of the cultural mix that became Creole. They attempted to decentre 'nation' or African ethnic identification and shift the enslaved's allegiance from Akan, Igbo, Yoruba, et cetera to 'Creole', assigning cultural meaning to Creole that went beyond a linguistic term meaning born in the Americas.[37] Certain social characteristics were attached to Creole which constructed the African as 'savage' and 'barbaric' and the Creole as more sensible and able to assume positions of responsibility in the slave hierarchy. While 'Creole' in the sense of being 'Caribbean' could imply unity and solidarity, 'Creole', as Percy Hintzen has observed, could also be inserted into a discourse of exclusion,[38] in the context of slavery African being the excluded category. A.C. Carmichael noted: 'Creole Negroes invariably consider themselves superior people and lord it over the native Africans.'[39]

Alternative Knowledge Systems: Colonization, Slavery, Africa and Africans

Modern scholars have sought to correct some of the misrepresentations and inaccuracies in the early works as well as to present new unexplored issues, beginning with representations of the indigenes. A few of the newer works project the role of the indigenous Caribbeans in the economic development of the region, in colonization, and in resistance to the land appropriation designs of the colonizers. Philip Boucher's 1992 work for example, cast great doubts on the accuracy of the term 'cannibal' traditionally used by writers such as Breton, du Tertre and Labat to describe the Eastern Caribbean Kalinago [Carib] people and focused readers' attention during the Columbus quincentenary on the misinformation which had previously been used to construct the 'history' of the indigenous peoples.[40] J. Paul Thomas and Hilary Beckles have also reminded us that the indigenous peoples, men and women, fought wars of resistance and did not accept European colonization willingly.[41] On the contrary, they must be credited with pioneering that radical tradition which was carried on by enslaved and indentured peoples thereafter. The more modern accounts of Beckles and Seaman also reveal that indigenous women were targeted for sexploitation and that nevertheless, these women were crucial in the social and economic evolution of the seventeenth- and eighteenth-century Caribbean; and they were a part of the struggle for terrain that characterized the relationship between colonizer and colonized in the seventeenth-century Eastern Caribbean.[42]

As Helen Seaman observes, in general there are very few studies that seek to theorize or specify the contributions and significance of the Kalinago/Carib role in the social history of colonial and postcolonial societies. Instead the tendency is to keep the indigenous peoples within the confines of conquistadorial perceptions and models, grounded in an uncritical acceptance of European enlightenment agendas.

More recent works on slavery cover its sociology and economics, illustrating the dynamic relations between modes of production and social life. The superstructures of slave systems have fascinated scholars perhaps to a greater degree than their economic substructures and as such the debates on race and colour relations, health and mortality, religion, recreational culture, women, family organization and kinship patterns, as well as the endemic problems of social reproduction are represented in a number of works. Research on slavery has also generated the most gender-differentiated data from that of historians of Caribbean history.

In terms of critical re-examination of early writers, Edward Long, the most overtly racist of the contemporary works on slavery has understandably been subject to the most intense scrutiny by historians, even as they continue to use his work for its wealth of empirical data on Jamaica. Goveia and Brathwaite problematize its essential racism; and scholars such as Lucille Mathurin Mair and Veronica Gregg have launched attacks on Long's sexism.[43]

The colonial project with its predominant male nature has also been criticized. Recent scholarship, attempting to compensate for past discursive shortsightedness, has emphasized that there was no homogeneous slave experience and that analyses of the conditions of the enslaved, and, indeed, of the slave system, must take gender differentiation into consideration. The greater focus has been on the experience of women, though a few recent studies have taken on board the issue of male marginalization and the ways in which black men had their masculinity negated under slavery as a way of keeping white males dominant.[44]

The conclusions from researchers, such as Kamau Brathwaite, Lucille Mathurin Mair, Barry Higman, Michael Craton, Hilary Beckles and Barbara Bush, have been instructive.[45] They emphasize that women did not live the way men did, and that slavery as a social system of oppression impacted on them differently. Enslaved women, for example, despite being under-represented in the transatlantic trade, formed the majority of the field gangs and worked as hard as men did. The experiences of women varied sharply between particular colonies but less so across imperial lines, as works by Arlene Gautier and Bernard Moitt for the French Caribbean and Digna Castañeda and Félix Matos Rodrígues for the Spanish Caribbean reveal when placed in comparative perspective with the British Caribbean.[46]

The quantitative study of the trade in African captives has predictably created an explosion of scholarship in the demographic history of slavery. In particular, concerns over fertility, mortality, and population growth and decline have attracted the attention of scholars. It was the 1970s and 1980s which saw the emergence of an impressive array of demographic bio-histories, that widened the empirical base of knowledge on the internal demographic characteristics of Caribbean enslaved populations. Much of this was generated in response to the need to explain the differential demographic experiences of the enslaved in the Caribbean and North America; for while the enslaved population in the US grew by natural means, with the exception of Barbados, The Bahamas and the Dutch Antilles, that of the Caribbean was not self-sustaining. Caribbean historians have been less concerned with the Tannenbaum-Freyre thesis, which focuses on treatment as an explanation for demographic features of the enslaved population.[47] They have been more focused on poor health and nutrition, as well as colour, sex ratio, work regime, age, gender, lactation practices and child-spacing, medical treatment, planter attitude (pro- vs anti-natalist), origins (Creole vs African born), family structure and the resistance strategies of women. Works by Kenneth and Virginia Kiple, Higman, Sheridan and Meredith John demonstrate that these factors contributed to the general inability of Caribbean enslaved populations, in particular those engaged in the sugar culture, to reproduce themselves naturally until the closing years of the slavery system.[48] Scholars have also shown that the pro-natalist policies of the post-1807 ameliorative period were doomed to fail as long as the majority of enslaved women laboured in the field. Women's productive capacity was not to be sacrificed for reproduction; thus there was a clear incompatibility between production and reproduction.

While the demographic historians mostly agree on the differential roles of diet, other material conditions and the work environment on the fertility and mortality experiences, skepticism still abounds over the feminist claim of 'gynaecological' resistance. Nevertheless the references to abortion and women's reluctance to reproduce cannot be ignored.

Women's experiences have been highlighted in the study of the cultural life of the enslaved, their ability to recreate and maintain family within the restrictions of chattel enslavement, their relationship with owners, their contribution through interracial sex to what Brathwaite has described as 'Creole society', and their attempt to become autonomous economic agents. As Mintz, Hall and Sheridan, among others show, the culture of marketing emerged among Blacks as a common expression, and material and social conditions on the plantations as well as in the towns made it particularly attractive.[49] Marketing symbolized a spirit of independence and was central to the process of non-violent protest and resistance which characterized day-to-day anti-slavery behaviour. The right to possession and open engagement in the market as autonomous buyers and sellers was aggressively demanded. Forms of collective bargaining, usually associated with industrial wage workers, emerged among the enslaved as Bolland, Turner, and others demonstrate; and some owners acquiesced to the enslaved's demand rather than relying always on the coercive power of the whip.[50]

Research into the family of the enslaved has also expanded since the 1960s, with differences in perspectives and interpretations emerging between structuralists, who claim that totalistic systems like slavery constrain cultural expression, including family formation, and class theorists whose view is that slavery allowed the enslaved some autonomy in constructing kinship and other forms of culture. Higman and Michael Craton basing their conclusions on solid quantitative analysis rather than on racist and sexist notions, argued that family, even the nuclear type, was prevalent in the later years of slavery in the British Caribbean.[51] Higman has stressed also that fresh analysis of the slave family requires a reorientation of perspective and redefinition of terms. Their conclusions have been reinforced by more recent researchers who stress the multidimensional nature of the family types among the enslaved and discount early perceptions of the enslaveds' inability to sustain lasting unions.

Slavery has been most closely associated with agricultural labour in the Caribbean. The urban dimension of slavery has received attention in the published works of Higman, Lorna Simmonds, Welch and Beckles.[52] They show that enslaved people in the urban areas were in the minority in all British Caribbean colonies. The enslaved urban population in the Caribbean was predominantly female, indicating that most were domestics. Urban enslaved people also worked as skilled labourers, sellers, transport and wharf workers, fishermen and general labourers. Women had a narrower range of occupations than men, working, in addition to domestic servants, as washerwomen, seamstresses and sellers. The importance of non-sugar economic activities and social contexts for slave life are topics also explored.

The final issues that have attracted the energies of historians of the slavery period are slavery and capitalist globalization, and emancipatory processes. Eric Williams, C.L.R. James and Walter Rodney have argued, against the tide, that the European trade with Africa and the Caribbean generated that surplus capital that propelled England and France into industrial development.[53] Far from being lazy, as Carlyle and others argued, Africans and African-Caribbean people were industrious and contributed to capital accumulation in the core. Three new trends in the study of resistance are firstly, the incorporation of women's resistant behaviour into the discourse of anti-slavery; secondly, the attempt to identify texts written or narrated by the enslaved which would provide more accurate versions of resistance; and thirdly, the broadening of the discussion of resistance to include those enslaved on non-sugar properties like livestock farms. The focus on women and resistance is based on the belief that the ideology of anti-slavery was not gender-free. While the struggles of the slavery period were inherently collective in that they were conceived in the consciousness of the communities inhabited by the enslaved, the gender relations of slavery determined actions in many ways. The system of slavery sought to degrade women and womanhood in ways which forced aspects of their resistance to assume specific forms. The use of rape as a brutal form of control and punishment, for example, targeted women more than men, as far we know. Certainly most of those like Hall and Beckles who have studied the journals of Thomas Thistlewood cannot help but be confronted by the violence of this enslaver towards women.[54] Maternity and fertility were also placed at the core of strategies for plantation survival, and so women's resistance to these policies meant that their opposition to slavery was probably more broadly based. Urban enslaved and those enslaved on non-sugar properties also used various strategies to undermine slavery.

Finally, what knowledge about Africa and being African did Africans in the Caribbean themselves produce? Given the paucity of first-hand sources, it is difficult to study the products of the mind of the enslaved. We know that they had an anti-slavery stance, manifested in strategies ranging from marronage to armed revolt. Indeed, resistance effectively indicates how most Africans felt about their entrapment and enslavement. African voices filtered through their writings and trial testimonies tell us about the brutality of slavery and the attempts to overthrow the slave systems despite the harsh punishments following revolt.

The evidence of resistance has been recounted by scholars like Brathwaite, Mair, Craton, Barry Gaspar, Beckles, Bush and Carey who have shown that instability, largely as a result of slave resistance, made the Atlantic World an unstable place;[55] for the 'Black Atlantic' was dichotomously opposed to the 'White Atlantic'. In fact very little, apart from transnational trade and finance and perhaps common imperial relationships and experiences, held this world together — albeit loosely. There was no such designation as an Atlantic world citizen. On the contrary, deep division, inequality and instability characterized the 'Atlantic World', and not all of the people who inhabited this 'world' were equally committed to its ideals. The exploited regions in this world of partners that were not really partners, as Walter Rodney has long noted, subverted the ideals of the Atlantic World.[56]

But while resistance is important, as it is an aspect of the power relationship through which the subaltern expressed its distinct and autonomous identity (though Monica Schuler and Douglas Chambers suggest that this identity was ethnic, not 'African', Akan and Igbo respectively represent an obvious paradigmatic form of signifying identity and difference)[57] and because its study is a methodological procedure by which one can obtain access into the consciousness of the subaltern, as Ranajit Guha has noted,[58] our grasp of the slavery period is still not informed by sources that would help us to know unambiguously what the enslaved thought about living in the Caribbean and about becoming Creole.

Conclusion

In conclusion, it must be admitted that of all the representations (and misrepresentations) surveyed in this lecture, it was, arguably, the representations of Africa and Africans that seemed to have done the most lasting damage, seeping into the consciousness of Caribbean people and determining the way that Africa and its diasporic citizens are still viewed and treated globally. Nevertheless, it is equally obvious that Caribbean scholars have attempted to destabilize the hegemonic European knowledge paradigms and discourses, and produced knowledge about the region that is designed to anchor its citizens to a more empowering past. The liberation by 'Creole interpreters' of Caribbean history of Black mind and body from the dis-empowering language and actions of colonizers is seen as essential to Black identity.

While much of the new knowledge produced resides in academic publications, Caribbean scholars also produce works that are accessible to students and the public at large. In this regard, textbook writing projects and public lectures have become standard activities of activist Caribbean scholars who have shunned the path of the classic intellectual, associated traditionally with 'ivory tower' and 'snobbishness'.[59] They adhere to the Gramscian view that 'all men are intellectuals';[60] that in Julian Benda's terms, they are engaged individuals, not 'other worldly, ivory-towered thinkers, devoted to abstruse subjects';[61] not people who detest the rise of mass societies and the 'common man'.

> They share the views articulated so well by Edward Said that the intellectual is an individual in society that confronts orthodoxy and dogma; who cannot be reduced simply to being a faceless professional, a competent member of a class going about his/her business [but] an individual endowed with a faculty for representing, embodying, articulating a message, a view, an attitude, philosophy or opinion *to*, as well as *for*, a public.[62]

A modified version of this lecture was presented as the 13th Shortwood Teachers' College's Founders' Day Lecture, The Hilton Hotel, September 29, 2005.

2

CULTURE, CREOLIZATION AND MARRONAGE IN THE CARIBBEAN: Engaging with the Writings of Rex Nettleford

Delivered at the Launch of the Second Edition of Rex Nettleford's Caribbean Cultural Identity: The Case of Jamaica. An Essay in Cultural Dynamics, *The Institute of Jamaica, November 25, 2003*

Caribbean Cultural Identity: The Case of Jamaica: An Essay in Cultural Dynamics by Professor the Hon Rex Nettleford, Vice Chancellor of the University of the West Indies, claims to be an essay. But this is no mere essay of the type to which University lecturers have become accustomed; imagine receiving an essay of four parts plus an introduction and epilogue! On the contrary this is a sophisticated exposition and analysis of the complex and ubiquitous problem of identity; of the dynamics of cultural evolution in postcolonial Jamaican and wider Caribbean societies. So, just in case those who have not yet read the book have plans to flip through it quickly, let me tell you that a quickie is impossible in this case. Like other pleasurable activities in life, to be truly enjoyed — especially to appreciate its lyrical content and passion — this book has to be read slowly so that the senses can be fully stimulated. I experienced the pleasure of reading this book three times: the first edition twice — first in the 1980s when I was reading for my MPhil degree in History and again in 2001 as I prepared for my Inaugural Lecture; and I read this new edition in preparation for this evening — though it took me longer this time around simply because the imagery on the cover detained me. In fact, I am still trying to deconstruct the art.

Having read the book in its various manifestations, however, I can say that Prof Nettleford's interventions in the discourses surrounding cultural identity and diversity are as relevant to contemporary society as when the first edition was published by the Institute of Jamaica in 1978 — maybe even more so now. It is even relevant to our future development; because as the author rightly points out, 'an appreciation of the history of Jamaica and the wider region is critical to a fuller understanding of contemporary realities and the challenges of a future which it is the task of the present generation to (quoting Earl Lovelace), "rescue".'[1]

The four parts of the book take us through key issues such as cultural pluralism and national identity; the preservation and further development of cultural values; the cultural dimension of development; and the possibility of cultural integration and cooperation between the territories of the Anglophone Caribbean on the one hand and the wider Caribbean and Latin America on the other. The blurb sums up a central value of the book rather well; for apart from providing us with a valuable historical record of the development of the arts in Jamaica and the wider Caribbean, and introducing us to important cultural workers critical to that development, *Caribbean Cultural Identity* constructs a convincing argument for 'the validity of that persistent quest by the Jamaican and Caribbean people for place and purpose in a globalised world of continuous change'. The author recognizes the successes of Caribbean peoples, despite obvious challenges, in indigenizing Caribbean culture and creating some degree of unity out of cultural diversity. Above all, convinced that culture is a key ingredient in national and social development, the author, centring the Jamaican experience, posits that cultural action is central to effective social change.

One of the things that struck me as I re-read this book was that it is written by a supremely self-confident Caribbean man; someone who has no struggle with his own identity; no ambiguities; no agonizing turmoil over the issue of 'double consciousness' in Paul Gilroy's formulation.[2] But then, Prof Nettleford is part of that generation of Caribbean scholars that has found creative ways to construct indigenous interpretations of Caribbean history, fashioned by explicit formulations and theoretical constructs that have had important implications for scholarly debates in the international academy. His work, like that of other cultural workers, has offered the antithesis to the imperialist view of the Caribbean world; the counter-discourse to the empowered 'bad words' of racist narrators such as Edward Long, James Anthony Froude and Thomas Carlyle.[3] Carlyle, we know, in his proslavery essay entitled 'The Nigger Question' gave political imagery to the concept of 'Quashie' as 'Black mind and body that was unprepared for freedom.' It was no wonder that a century and a half later, Jamaican poet Lorna Goodison, armed with a battery of metaphorical representations, reacted to the epistemic violence of the imperial project by calling for a renegotiation of such 'bad words' to create an internal liberating narrative of self.[4] I would locate this book precisely within that project in which so many postcolonial writers are engaged — that of creating an internal liberating narrative of self. The book offers creative representations of Caribbean history and culture and provides direction to young students and all who confront in the historiography, literature and society the legacies of colonialism, slavery and indentureship: the 'Otherization' of the Caribbean, as indeed of Africa and India; the tyranny of the Western intellectual tradition; the donmanship phenomenon evident in academic discourse — legacy of the dispensation of that first don, don Cristóbal Colón.

The book however is not only relevant for the study of Jamaican and wider Caribbean history and culture. I wish to suggest that it can be located within the larger study of the Atlantic World. In November 2003, the Cunliffe Centre for Atlantic Studies at the University of Sussex held a Colloquium on the theme 'Conceptualizing the Atlantic World'. Part of the discussion centred on the absence of a discrete Atlantic identity that was distinguishable from a burgeoning imperialist mentality. The view was expressed that the cultural experiences and interaction of Africans and Europeans did not determine the creation of a Creole vision that ultimately became the symbol of a homogeneous Atlantic identity. Even though Creole societies emerged, there was still an identifiable 'Black Atlantic' in the South Atlantic system that was dichotomously opposed to a 'White Atlantic' in the North Atlantic.

Obviously those who coined the term Atlantic World did so because they discerned common threads that seemed to have given a recognizable pattern and sense of community to the civilizations that developed and maintained intercontinental interconnections. As City University of New York (CUNY) Professor of History, Michael Kraus, observed in, arguably, one of the earliest works to conceptualize what he termed at the time the 'Atlantic Civilization', 'out of the play of influences crossing the sea westward and eastward emerged a sense of community sufficiently distinctive to be called the Atlantic Civilization.' This 'civilization', he said, embraced 'the whole Western Hemisphere and much of Europe (and even African Negro culture)',[5] he added almost as an afterthought. The linkages facilitated by colonialism, imperialism, trade, slavery and migration also facilitated the transfer and exchange of political systems, ideologies, religions, mentalities and social culture. Despite differences of location, imperial economic and political zone, origin, class, gender, ethnicity, colour and status, the argument goes, common ideologies, loyalties and institutions developed in various parts of the Atlantic World.

But critics maintain that very little apart from transnational trade and finance and perhaps common imperial relationships and experiences held this world together — albeit loosely. There was no such designation as an Atlantic world citizen. On the contrary, deep division, inequality and instability characterized the 'Atlantic World' as not all of the people who inhabited this 'world' were equally committed to its ideals. The exploited regions in this world of partners that were not really partners as Walter Rodney has long reminded us — much as critics of globalization are doing today — subverted the ideals of the Atlantic World: the export production of staples; the import of inputs, bilateral trading relationships; and what Charles Mills has described as the 'racial contract' founded on white supremacy, and Eurocentrism — the political philosophy or *raison d'être* of the Atlantic World. As this contract was one between the socially dominant whites of the North Atlantic, it was predictably contested by those who were not 'signatories' but were nevertheless deeply affected — mostly negatively.[6]

One of the most rebellious parts of the Atlantic World was the Caribbean. In this part of the world, we honed the practice of marronage, used here in René Depestre's broader sense of a historical process resulting from 'maroon activity' outside of the plantation system that 'engendered new modes of thinking, of acting, of feeling, of imagining'.[7] To illustrate, even at the height of the plantation system, the Caribbean and the Americas in general pursued a divergent economic path, even worldview. While the dominant trade routes during slavery led from the Caribbean to Europe and North America, intra-Caribbean links, which pre-date conquest, though not as developed, were not complete casualties of colonization and the monopolistic tendencies of empire (CARICOM would do well to publicize this history in defense of its call for regional integration). In other words, regional interconnectedness was not lost in the 'making of the Atlantic

World'; and an understanding of the emergence of the larger Atlantic World must take greater cognizance of intra-American resource exchange that operated within the panoramic context of what Immanuel Wallerstein has described as the world system.[8] So on this side of the Atlantic, we were building intra-Caribbean bridges, regardless of imperial economic and political zones, long before we were told it was okay to do so.

As I read this book fresh from my own engagement with the other scholars invited to the Sussex Colloquium, I could not help thinking that the book is about cultural marronage much as my intervention was about economic marronage; for Prof Nettleford sees the process of indigenization as intensely cultural.[9] He writes:

> In this part of the world people engaged in a "process of shaping an indigenous Caribbean lifestyle and a new, viable, worldview born out of the collective experience of a long-dominated but rebellious people — now enslaved, now brutalized, now indentured, now pressured into cultural submission, now colonized, but never defeated".[10]

So while, as the author observes,

> The Caribbean shares in the great drama of the Americas of which it is an integral part, whereby new societies are shaped, new and delicately tuned sensibilities are honed, and appropriate designs for social living are crafted through the cross-fertilisation of disparate elements. The process has resulted in a distinguishable and distinctive entity called "Caribbean".[11]

This Caribbeanness is evident even in still-to-be independent territories, a sure sign that not even imperialism and neo-imperialism can affect this process of cultural change.

In the Caribbean we know that there is need to counter essentialist concepts of ethnicity, nationality and identity when theorizing about the Atlantic World. Different modes of production co-existed; and imperial, universalist dictates had to yield to localizing and creolizing reality. Indeed, the book intervenes in the ongoing debates about creolization — that 'syncretic process of transverse dynamics that endlessly reworks and transforms the cultural patterns of varied social and historical experiences and identities.' Nettleford rehearses the debates, from M.G. Smith to Brathwaite and beyond,[12] about what holds together this society in which different cultures have collided. But this book is not only about creolization as *métissage, mestizaje, miscegenation* and what some see as 'cultural mutation'; it is also about how the African dimension of Creole culture (which some see as the one in the motto) struggles for cultural legitimacy within a tendency to dichotomize culture into high and low. But the prejudices of Eurocentrism are not dead;[13] and even though we know the dangers of binary opposites, it is not only the Europeans who have tried to construct this dichotomy. Even those whose anatomies are firmly Creole, to quote George Lamming, often display a pejorative attitude towards Creole. Patricia Mohammed reminds us in her analysis of the locational identities of the Indo-Caribbean woman that creolization is a troublesome term — 'perhaps even an offensive word to use in reference to Indian women in Trinidad' — because it sometimes signifies 'disindianization'.[14]

Perhaps this is why the author warns against any unedited use of the term 'multi-cultural society', since 'the "multi" could well speak to a pluralism which secures for each ingredient in the mix an unassailable corner of exclusivity'.[15] If one peels away the social hypocrisy (or what a colleague of mine calls diplocracy), we will find 'ranking', a metaphor for social ordering, social and cultural hierarchizing in so-called multicultural societies. In our own context 'ranking' represents the linguistic, oral and literary aspects of social culture that is the ritualized and politicized codes and consciousness of difference. Stuart Hall is correct to assert that the persistence of such colonial creations as ranking contradicts the cultural desire of postmodern mentalities for the celebration of difference in an egalitarian fashion rather than hierarchically.[16] As such we still adhere to boundary-maintaining mechanisms.

When during the intensely charged racial atmosphere of mid-twentieth century Jamaica the Organizer-General of the Afro-West Indian League stated in an article in the *Jamaica Times* that 'simply being born in Jamaica does not make one a Jamaican, ... in the same way that a chicken hatched in an oven cannot be called a bread',[17] he was entering the debate over who had cultural legitimacy in a multicultural society that rested on the ideology

26

of racial and ethnic inequality. His statement showed clearly that while 'Creole' in the sense of being 'Jamaican' could imply unity and solidarity, 'Creole', as Percy Hintzen has observed, could also be inserted into a discourse of exclusion.[18]

I wonder though if we have been successful, 53 years on in overcoming the side-by-sideness tendency and the ranking game to truly deal with the dilemma of difference? Prof Nettleford thinks that we have largely managed to do so, despite the hiccups along the way; that 'at the subliminal level, [the region] understands and trades on the unity which underlie the differences'.[19] Perhaps it is that long historical tradition of subverting mercantilism that is saving us. The physical/geographical fragmentation has never been an obstacle — the history of maritime marronage testifies to that. Our people have always found a way to build bridges across 'floating island spaces' in Nettleford's words, overcoming the legacy of a heritage of separation and fragmented identities. Culture — dance, music, art, literature —the outcome of the creative imagination of cultural workers has been a central part of the foundation of those connecting bridges.

But what about this social space; this piece of the ground we call home?; for Prof Nettleford cautions that before we can even think of regionalism and a Caribbean identity, we must look into our own backyard. Have we truly expunged the tendency to lessen the claim on citizenship by those whose ancestral homes are other than Africa? Creole culture has the potential for social integration and forging a new cultural unity, but has the potential been realized fully? Is a postmodernist ideal of egalitarian multiculturalism the Caribbean reality? Globalization, which renders us twentieth-century beings, both local and global social agents, whether ancestrally Chinese, Indian or African, has intensified an opposing tendency in the nation states of the so-called 'Third World'. As these political constructs respond to the economic policies of the dominant global 'partners', the formerly colonized feel compelled to reassert difference and defend their citizenship. Stuart Hall highlights this contradictory tendency of globalization, on the one hand the pull towards borderlessness, assimilation and homogenization; on the other, the reassertion of localism, notably in the form of ethnicity, nationalism and religious fundamentalism.[20] But at the level of the nation there seems to be less possibility of a harmonious integration of cultural difference with national unity; a toleration of that paradigmatic 'code-switching', according to Barry Chevannes, that would allow different sectors to live in Jamaica in all its multilingual and multicultural possibilities.[21] Perhaps this is because, as Carol Narcisse puts it, despite some obvious border crossings since independence, persistent 'border clashes' sparked by endemic elite terms of engagement that rest on the ideology of inequality and cultural hegemony, are still being used as the basis for social integration.[22] Prof Nettleford rightly believes that this ranking will get us nowhere and that in the twentieth century,

> the world's inhabitants, certainly in the Western world to begin with, must stand on sea shores or on mountain tops, look across oceans and sing, [or recite if you cannot sing]: "goodbye motherland" knowing that where one now is, one must call home.

I do not think that this means that we must forget what we call 'roots'. But he insists that 'ethnic and religious spaces must now co-exist with or find form within national polities or established countries, despite the sanctity of flags, anthems and other "national" symbols';[23] that we must exist in creative diversity to carve out a new and viable identity. But he cautions that 'a lop-sided diversity designed to preserve the status quo cannot possibly provide the basis of national unity.'[24] We must interrupt any lingering tendencies to maintain a cultural hierarchy, to uphold cultural enclaves in the name of multiculturalism.

Finally, I wish to go back to the image on the cover, Edna Manley's 'Ancestors'. It occurred to me as I tried to deconstruct it that it could be read alongside the author's call — issued since 1978 — for a working relationship between culture, education and tourism, the rationale being that the development of a sense of history, or ancestral memory, is vital to nation-building.[25] The book highlights six essential tasks critical to nation-building (some of which have already been addressed), the last one being 'the preservation of historical sites and monuments as well as the encouragement of archaeological excavations by the Jamaica National Heritage Trust (JNHT)'. Well, we know all about monuments, especially the one recently erected in Kingston's Emancipation Park, which some Jamaicans have tried to re-title using another Edna Manley sculpture. The JNHT and other bodies continue to seek creative ways to memorialize the ancestors and increase public awareness of them. I know that you support the view, recently reiterated by Jenny Sharpe in *Ghosts of Slavery*, that the enslaved are not just mere shadows of a by-gone past,[26] 'but signposts to the future; clues to how in the postmodern world we can deal with the legacies of slavery and rescue these "Ghosts of Slavery" from an improper burial'. Our ancestors pioneered marronage in all of its creative forms; and their refusal to accept cultural imperialism must be acknowledged as a contribution to the forging of that Caribbean culture of which you speak.

Professor Nettleford, I hope that in time the media, which, from what is said in Part 3, is seen as being critical to the project of preserving and developing Jamaican cultural values, especially in this age of what you label CNNization, will consider it vital to expose more of the contents of this book to a wider audience.

3

'SEX IN THE TROPICS': Women, Gender and Sexuality in the Discourses of Asian Labour Migration to the British-Colonized Caribbean

Plenary Lecture, International Federation for Research in Women's History, August 13, 2003, Queen's University, Belfast, Northern Ireland

After reading in the Jamaican newspapers that a male politician had suggested mandatory virginity testing of underage girls (a medical examination for '*virgo intacta*', according to one reporter),[1] that a female Member of Parliament (MP) had suggested mandatory sterilization of young women as one of the options to control unwanted pregnancies,[2] and that Laura Facey Cooper's sculpture in Kingston's Emancipation Park, 'Redemption Song', with its Marcus Garvey/ Bob Marley inspired line 'none but ourselves can free our mind' had stirred up what one reporter described as 're-nude' controversy over its alleged sexualized images,[3] I could not help thinking that it seems impossible to discuss any aspect of contemporary Caribbean society or of colonial Caribbean history without confronting the issues of gender, power and sexuality. The reaction to these news stories confirmed this view. The politicians were not only labelled 'Crazy',[4] but sexist; with one cartoonist implying that women were in danger of being required to wear chastity panties.[5] Comments about the sculpture ranged from 'Negroes Aroused' (a play on Edna Manley's well-known sculpture) and 'dem shoulda cover dem up wid a loin cloth or something; … why dem coulden free up them mind inna dem clothes!?' to, 'it merely reinforces the stereotypes of black people as sexualized beings' — a representation on which the tourist culture feeds.[6]

Of course, the stereotypical representation of the non-elite in the tropics, in particular women, as sexualized beings, has a long history, pre-dating the age of postmodernity. This is true whether we are relating, revisioning or recasting the history of the conquest of indigenous people, the history of the enslavement of Africans or the history of the post-slavery migration and indentureship of the over half million Indian labourers brought in to replace enslaved Africans after 1838. Indeed, there is no discourse of colonialism in which issues of gender and sexuality do not participate. As Ronald Hyam notes in his *Empire and Sexuality*, historians of empire have to come to terms with sex if only because it is there; that the expansion of Europe was not only a matter of 'Christianity and commerce', but also of 'copulation and concubinage'.[7] Thus there was an intimate connection between, not just power and sexuality in Michel Foucault's sense,[8] but also, in Hyman's and others', sexual power and imperialism. Even the 'protocolonialist discourse of discovery prevalent in early Western Europe' was gendered. Early symbolic representation of the Americas as part of Europe's construction of its collective 'Other' as Louis Montrose and others have observed, was that of a feminized (virgin) space,[9] for the indigenous people did not count (and soon there was hardly any of them to count) ripe for a masculine colonization project. Interracial sex, much of it the result of rape, was intertwined into the imperial project; and as far as the Caribbean was concerned, neither the colonial elite nor those settlers further down on the social ladder exercised sexual restraint in the colonial period, especially during slavery. The revelations in the journals of the enslaver and manager Thomas Thistlewood, who lived in Jamaica from 1750–86, has also forced us to confront the issue of sex, gender and power in the 'colonized tropics' as part of the project of colonization.[10]

Such sexual depravity as was noticed in the Caribbean was the result of the attitude to the enslaved (whose sexuality was constructed as 'animalistic' by people like the planter-historian Edward Long[11]) and later the attitude to indentured women, regarded as easy and sensual. The appropriation of the bodies of women under the legal legitimization of property, a designation that protected men from accountability and censure, legalized rape. Men, and in a few cases, women who were far from home and home conventions, considered this distance conducive to deviant behaviour.

For Thistlewood and others, empire gave them a kind of sexual licence. They used their position as owners or managers of the subaltern to render colonized women sex objects over whom they could exercise power[12] — power and sexuality being inextricably linked.[13] Hyman writes that

in the 18th century, the West Indies do seem to have been a kind

31

of sexual paradise for young European men: it was almost customary for white men of every social rank [but especially of the lower classes] to sleep with black women. Coloured mistresses were kept openly and the practice was integral to West Indian life.[14]

While we may despise Thomas Thistlewood for his behaviour towards enslaved women in the Caribbean, it is undeniable that since the discovery of his journals in the Lincolnshire County Record Office some decades ago, and the publication of Douglas Hall's *In Miserable Slavery*, based on those journals, the issue of sex in the tropics, hitherto considered too private a subject for the attention of Caribbean historians, has been elevated to a position of greater respectability in the academy. The feminist movement, the introduction of gender studies at the University of the West Indies and increasing research on gender issues, helped by the democratizing influence of social history, have also combined to move sex from the private to the public sphere; from the margins to the centre. Caribbean historiography now reflects a growing focus on the issues of gender, power, sexuality, the body, and women's sexploitation in the slavery and post-slavery periods. There is also a serious attempt to show that the Tropics did not accept without resistance, the notion of it being a place that accommodated the sexual energies unleashed on it by men. Beginning with indigenous women's attack on the rapists among Columbus's crew in the fifteenth century, subaltern women acted not as passive victims but resisted 'sexploitation' with as much vigour as they did other exploitative dimensions of the imperial project.

Research on gender, power and sexuality in the Caribbean has been carried out by slavery scholars as well as by those who have focused increasingly on the experiences of Indians subjected to a form of neo-slavery in the post-slavery period. However a look at the various strands of historiography focusing on the Indian experience reveals that those who specialize in the field of migration studies have lagged behind slavery scholars who have, since the 1970s, published numerous works illuminating the ways in which womanhood was targeted and preyed upon by patriarchal authority and interest. Hilary Beckles's essay 'Property Rights in Pleasure' provides a chilling reminder of the fact that under colonialism, systemic violence was sanctioned; that 'New World slavery led to the legal and customary institutionalisation of the slave owner's right to unrestricted sexual access to the enslaved woman as an intrinsic and discrete product.'[15]

Even though enslaved women's sexuality has occupied a more central role in studies on Caribbean women, beginning in the 1980s and expanding in the 1990s, scholars, conscious that the presence of Indian women in the region had to alter the epistemological foundations of Caribbean women's history, began to explore the intersection of colonialism, sex, sexuality and power in the historical experiences of Indian women.

This lecture explores how colonialist writers and modern scholars have treated the intimate connection between power, imperialism and sex in discourses on Asian labour migration, primarily for the British-colonized Caribbean. It seeks to grapple with the question of what combinations of power and ideology legitimized the behaviour of empowered men in charge of the subaltern on emigrant ships and on Caribbean plantations even though there were checks and balances on the abuse of Indian women's sexuality. The emphasis is on women, as writers hardly ever targeted or problematized Indian men's sexuality in their discourses, except where they suggested that there was competition for Indian women (who showed a preference, the argument goes) for the stereotypically constructed 'more virile Black men'. Despite the efforts, sexploitation (especially the traumatic sexual abuse on the voyage as Maharani's rape case illustrates[16]) became a part of that experience that would later contribute to 'Coolitude', a concept recently developed by Marina Carter and Khal Torabully (and explored at length) in their *Anthology of the Indian Labour Diaspora* to capture the essence of the Indian indentureship experience and deconstruct traditional depictions of the status of the coolie in the British Empire.[17] As Torabully elaborates, the conditions of the indentured Indian is part of the first stages of coolitude that must be rediscovered; for 'it is impossible to understand the essence of coolitude without charting the coolies' voyage across the seas. That decisive experience, that coolie odyssey, left an indelible stamp on the imaginary landscape of coolitude.'[18]

Also explored are three areas of the historiography in which women's sexuality played a prominent role: women's reasons for leaving India; the voyage from India in which there were charges of gender-specific exploitation or, more precisely, 'sexploitation' on emigrant ships; and the plantation experience in which there were both sexploitation and resistance to sexual abuse. It is evident that the moral character of the women who were recruited (but not of the men) was placed at the centre of the migration process; issues surrounding their morality, sexual and social behaviour being elevated above their ability to contribute to capital formation.

There is also a fourth or new strand of the historiography — a critique, (increasingly by scholars of Indian ancestry) of historians who, in their view, have misrepresented the Indian/Indian woman in their writings perhaps because of an uncritical acceptance of official sources. Some of this can be seen in *Coolitude* where Torabully and Carter take on, for example, aspects of Brian Moore's representation of the sexual behaviour of Indian women and the resilience of other stereotypes mentioned in Bridget Brereton's work.[19] That strand is however not fully developed in this lecture.

All of these strands reveal the centrality of the issue of power, which is always best explored through the lens of gender. As Joan Scott has already told us, gender is a primary way of signifying relationships of power.[20] Partha Chatterjee confirms this, noting,

> the condition of women's and men's indentured immigrant status, compounded by their colonized position as subjects of an imperial state, the politics of competing patriarchies, and male/female struggles over the construction of the "ideal woman" as "good worker", "moral housewife" and so on, were manifestations of power struggles and constituted politics of gender in the new immigrant spaces.[21]

The Historiography of the Movement from India

There is no consensus among historians, contemporary observers and emigration officials about the reasons for female emigration; and explanations range from the materialist need for alternative means of capital accumulation and the need to escape social oppression at home to the need to provide reproducers and sexual partners for indentured men. The issue of Indian women as reproducers of the labour force has few adherents, however. The idea that emigration would reform women already 'gone astray' and give them a new start has more supporters, especially among emigration officials like Charles Doorly, Protector of Emigrants in the Madras Presidency, Major

D.G. Pitcher, a pro-emigrationist and local government official in the North West Provinces[22] and G.A. Grierson in the Bengal area.[23] In a retrospective look at women's emigration in 1915, Doorly had remarked: 'I am convinced that emigration is a blessing to a large number of the women we send, and opens to them a way of escape from lives of misery, poverty and prostitution.'[24] But Moses Seenarine sees this 'progressive rhetoric'[25] as masking the stereotyping of female indentured labourers; as immoral and a justification for targeting the most vulnerable South Asian women.

Since Indian women were part of what was essentially a scheme of labour reallocation from one part of the British Empire to another relates to the economic potential of female plantation workers; but this is a largely submerged view. Most argue that, even though planters were already familiar with women's productive labour, this did not become as critical a factor as under slavery. Madhavi Kale takes a middle ground, arguing that emigrants probably represented fair shares of both victims and rational maximizers of opportunity.[26]

Once the issue of women's inclusion was settled, questions turned to the type of women to be recruited with much discussion surrounding 'the right kind of women'. This normally rested on the familiar issue of women's sexual history and sexuality. A dominant view was that unaccompanied women were particularly loose, were either already or prone to become prostitutes; would cause trouble on the plantations and therefore the emigration of more virtuous and 'respectable' married women was preferred. The issue of how women were secured for emigration is well-represented in the historiography, with more and more scholars (such as Look Lai and Ken Parmasad) attempting to find support for the view that kidnapping was more of a problem than hitherto believed.[27] The role of kidnapping in the Indian labour relocation scheme has also been captured in literary works such as the recently republished novel *Lutchmee and Dilloo,* in which the author, Edward Jenkins recounts Lutchmee's kidnapping by a rapacious recruiter and forced to embark on the 'Sunda' for Colonial Guyana.[28]

Of course, we lack personal accounts of Indian women that would tell us, unambiguously, why they left India. As Marina Carter has observed in her work on Mauritius, 'the actions and reactions of subordinate social groups in history rarely reach the researcher except through the medium of official reports or observers' accounts'.[29] Nevertheless, people like Carter and Kumar Noor Mahabir have been trying to re-voice the Indian woman offering a counter-discourse to the constructions and representations of the official view. In *The Still Cry*, Mahabir, who is, in Chatterjee's view among those retrieving women's voices 'from the canons of colonial sociological knowledge',[30] relates the story of Maharani, whose reasons for leaving India was her desire to escape abuse by in-laws after her husband died.

Women's sexuality was also at the centre of the opposition to their exportation, opponents arguing that, far from escaping prostitution, they were imported for the purpose of being pressed into prostitution. This became a central argument of many anti-immigration women's groups that campaigned for the ending of emigration in the early twentieth century.

The historiography of migration reflects much attention to the issue of Indian women's sexuality with, as Gail Pool and others note, Victorian, Orientalist and Indian Brahminical notions of sexuality colliding at different moments. Predictably, sexual stereotypes about the women who opted for emigration abounded; and these stereotypes were culture bound, with what was acceptable or moral sexual behaviour being called into question.[31] As Jeffrey Weeks explains, the meanings we give to sexuality are socially organized,[32] so that 'within the wide parameters of general cultural attitudes, each culture labels different practices as appropriate, moral or immoral'.[33] The yardstick by which this was measured was a Western, Christian one, with a limited range of acceptable activities allowed. Not surprisingly, Indian women who migrated were cast in the British Victorian essentialist mould of morally loose. Contemporary Victorian patriarchal notions of what constitutes a good woman critically influenced the gendered ways in which policy toward female labour migration from India was conducted.[34]

The Historiography of the Voyage from India

Sexuality was fundamental to the construction and maintenance of the power relations between men and women on the voyages from India to the Caribbean. All sources testify to the great concern over the sexual abuse of Indian women on the passages from India and the regulations laid down prohibiting 'cohabitation' between the women and the crew, and between single male and female emigrants. It was also obvious from the security measures, restrictive legislation, and the manipulation of both space and human cargo on the ships, that there was concern that such ships should not become spaces of sexploitation, thus giving ammunition to anti-emigrationists.

The distance between regulations and practice was equally evident from nineteenth-century reports that indicated that neither sexual segregation, spatial organization, the maintenance of a hierarchy among sailors and officers, nor the putative separation of the different races on the ships protected Indian women from sexual violence. Indeed, Moses Seenarine recently concluded that, 'the entire "coolie ship" was an unsafe place for single females, as well as married women, as they were frequent targets of sexual attacks.'[35] Look-Lai has also observed that, 'the day-to-day practice of the indenture system, as distinct from the formal laws, was always full of contradictions and technical violations and abuses.'[36] Moreover, class and racial stereotypes and myths about Indian women's sexuality, already developed fully on both sides of the Atlantic by the time of immigration, inevitably collided and were evident in the sexual abuse some were forced to endure on the ships.[37]

Several narratives of this aspect of the emigrants' experience testify to women's exploitation on the voyage from India; and the sexual exploitation of women in this period did not reflect only White, but also Black and Indian masculinity in action. Ships' surgeons commented on the abusive treatment that some emigrant women received from their shipboard spouses, explaining, additionally, that this sometimes stemmed from the contempt with which higher caste men viewed the lower caste women with whom they formed 'alliances'. Some Surgeons-Superintendent complained that Black men were more likely than White men to molest women on board emigrant ships and used this argument to justify their call for a White only or predominantly White crew, though a higher proportion of the complaints about the sexual abuse of emigrant women by officers and rank and file crew on emigrant ships to the Caribbean seemed directed at White men, including the surgeons themselves.

One Woman's Experience

Few men were convicted for their sexual assaults on migrating Indian women. The case of Maharani who embarked on the *Allanshaw* to colonial Guyana in 1885 illustrates. Briefly, during the early morning hours of July 24, 1885, Maharani, along with 660 other contract labourers, embarked at Calcutta on this James Nourse owned sailing ship bound for colonial Guyana. Maharani did not complete her passage to the Southern Caribbean; she was among the 17 who died before the ship reached its destination. Four official enquiries were launched into the voyage of the *Allanshaw*; and at the Commission of Enquiry convened in colonial Guyana, 22 witnesses, including some of the emigrants themselves, gave evidence. While the cause of death of 16 of these was ascertained and recorded without being contested, Maharani's death was the subject of intense controversy, uncertainty and speculation. The Surgeon-Superintendent of the ship vacillated between 'shock to the nervous system', 'inflammation near the womb', 'shock from shame' and 'peritonitis' as the cause of death; a few fellow female emigrants attributed her death to 'criminal assault' based on what Maharani allegedly told them before she died. Inspector Wright of the Guyana Police Force, and Dr Robert Grieve, Acting Medical Officer to the Immigration Department and later Surgeon-General, and a member of the Commission of Enquiry ordered by the Governor of colonial Guyana, at the insistence of the Colonial Office, believed that rape was the cause of her death. Dr Grieve's fellow commissioners disagreed with him, arguing that the evidence presented was contradictory and inconclusive.

Furthermore, at least two of the commissioners believed that Maharani had had consensual sex with the seamen. First, they read something sinister in the fact that Maharani had gone to the water closet by herself, though even the surgeon admitted that this was not an unheard of occurrence; and that she had not complained to the Babu and Sirdar about her ordeal. Second, they ignored the testimony of those who said that Maharani was a quiet, well-behaved girl who hardly fraternized. They preferred to uphold the ideology that non-elite women were 'naturally promiscuous'; that she 'had asked for it'; that she had even attracted the attention of a special man on board. In historical and literary sources the Indian woman has been portrayed as coquettish (and thus responsible, even partially for their sexploitation). In Jenkins's novel mentioned previously, he wrote 'Lutchmee, whose pretty face and coquettish ways had during the voyage won upon the rough English and foreign sailors'.[38]

The Historiography of the Plantation Experience

Stereotypes about the sexuality of Indian women continued into the plantation experience and joined other stereotypes based on the host society's ignorance. Again, first hand accounts by the Indian women in the Caribbean are not abundant, making it hard to gain unprejudiced insights into their plantation experiences. Two conflicting arguments seem to have emerged. One is that the Indian woman's experience of indentureship was one of extreme hardship, exploitation and sexploitation. The other, now closely associated with David Galenson, Pieter Emmer and David Northrup although expressed by Charles Doorly since the early twentieth century, is that emigration was of significant material benefit to those who left India.[39] The first perspective, which reflects aspects of Joseph Beaumont's and Hugh Tinker's neo-slavery thesis, is most clearly articulated in the work of Rhoda Reddock, Jeremy Poynting and Jo Beall.[40] It is also shared at differing levels by other scholars including Brij Lal for Fiji, Rosemarijn Hoefte for Suriname, Verene Shepherd for Jamaica, Marina Carter for Mauritius; Moses Seenarine for Guyana and David Trotman for Trinidad.[41] The work done by some of these latter scholars reveal that even though the majority of Indian women arrived in the Caribbean as single, independent wage workers intent on bettering their lives (and some succeeded in this regard), wages were low and gender-discriminatory and tasks sex-typed, giving an overall advantage to male workers. These facts combined with clear evidence of sexual abuse and other forms of gendered tyranny toward Indian women determined that the overall conclusion of those who fall within the neo-slavery school of thought would differ drastically from Doorly's and Emmer's optimistic 'material benefits' thesis. Indeed, after studying the fraudulent, deceptive, abusive and exploitative elements of the indentureship system, Jo Beall argued strongly that Indian women suffered 'ultraexploitability', Rhoda Reddock that their whole experience was one of 'freedom denied', and Jeremy Poynting that they experienced 'multiple oppression'.[42]

The gender disparity among the emigrants and the indentured

population — which only balanced out by the 1960s — has been used as a rationale for the sexual abuses that occurred.

Table 3.1
Proportion of Women and Children Embarked on Ships from Calcutta to the West Indies, 1850–58, with Per Cent Mortality

Year	Women to Men (proportion)	Child/infants to Adults (proportion)	% Mortality Year On whole no. embarked
1850/51	9.09	5.11	3.61
1851/52	16.93	10.89	4.45
1852/53	23.96	16.53	5.60
1853/54	14.36	7.84	3.30
1854/55	18.34	7.48	2.75
1855/56	35.72	10.82	5.75
1856/57	35.27	14.67	17.26
1857/58*	66.48	29.08	9.10

*figures for Salsette of 1858 excluded

Source: CO 386/91. TWC Murdoch and Frederic Rodgers to Herman Merivale, August 11, 1858.

The Issue of Sexual Freedom and Independence

Indeed, the historiography is replete with references to sexual freedom and women's independence as two dominant results of the male/female imbalance in the population and the predominance of single, unattached females. The dominant view is that abundant in number, and averse to cohabiting with Black women, Indian men competed for scarce Indian women and waged war over them amongst themselves and with Black and Chinese men. It was also used to explain Indian women's behaviour, some writers projecting the view that Indian women found a new-found sexual freedom in the Caribbean. Something sinister was always read into this in the context of the tendency to stereotype all working-class women without partners as morally loose. Tinker went as far as to say that 'the disproportion between men and women was the main factor shaping the life of the coolie lines.'[43]

Several views about Indian women's sexuality surfaced: unfaithful, changing partners at will, practicing polyandry, et cetera. Indeed, if one followed some of the writers, one would believe that all Indian women did in the Caribbean was think about sex and sexual partners: with whom to live; whom to change or exchange. Reddock relates the Presbyterian Sarah Morton's experiences with Indian women and her disapproval of their behaviour, thus:

> The loose actions and prevailing practice in respect of marriage here are quite shocking to the newcomer. I said to an East Indian woman whom I knew to be a widow of a Brahmin, "you have no relations in Trinidad, I believe?" No Madam, she replied, only myself and my two children; when the last immigrant ship came I took a papa. I will keep him as long as he treats me well. If he does not treat me well I shall send him off at once; that's the right way, is it not?[44]

In *The Still Cry*, Mahabir relates Sankar's disapproving view of the new Indian woman in Trinidad, an independent-minded woman who will agree to sexual relations with a man if she is approached correctly; but who did not necessarily wish to convert a sexual relation into a permanent marital relationship.[45] Hoefte writes that, 'The sexual deprivation of so many men resulted in problems ranging from polyandry and prostitution to manslaughter.'[46] And Brian Moore writes, 'the lack of partners of the same ethnic background prompted different sexual solutions among these two categories of immigrants [Chinese and Indians]. Indians adopted flexible mating patterns, including polyandry, to alleviate the problem.'[47]

Indian men reportedly regarded wives as symbols of status, security, prosperity, masculinity and self-esteem and thus they spent their days wondering how to get one (usually an Indian one instead of choosing from among the more numerous Black female population, or from among the Chinese; for the tendency of mixed marriages/relationships, though not entirely absent, was at first infrequent). Reddock argues that while for the Indian man, the ability to possess and control his wife was a requirement of the patriarchal thinking of the day, for large numbers of Indian women, re-subjugation was not the reason they had come to the Caribbean. Their attempts to make a new life for themselves did not include their being re-encapsulated in the patriarchal Indian family.[48]

The historiography also suggests that Indian men saw Indian women's allegedly 'too free' sexual behaviour as challenging traditional values and the belief in the subservience of women. Therefore they murdered, either the woman who shunned them and thus shamed them in a patriarchal society that believed in men's power over women's bodies, or the men who enticed their wives away. Evidence that Indian women's bodies became the site of violent power contestation in a society influenced by moral values that gave men control over and exclusive access to their partner's body abound. Look Lai tells us that so widespread did 'spousal murder' become that the immigration ordinances had to legislate for the physical protection of women from abusive spouses as well as against the practice of seduction of male immigrants' spouses.[49] Others agree that disputes over women formed the main cause of murders, as of suicides, in importing countries. Interestingly enough, the current data indicate that most of the women in jail for murder in Trinidad and Tobago are Indian women accused of murdering their husbands.

A traditional and non-violent way of limiting the freedom and curbing the unbridled sexuality of women was the pre-arranged marriage. Fathers are said to have exploited the scarcity of women and commodified the bodies of their young daughters, practically selling them to the highest bidder (dowry-giver).[50]

Several authors like Hoefte, Look Lai, Reddock, Seecharan and Tinker note the prevalence of sexual abuse of Indian women by white estate managers. Look Lai, for example speaks of 'management exploitation of Indian women' and tells us that the outspoken Bechu, who testified before the West India Royal Commission of 1897 specifically noted that sexual immorality was an integral part of plantation life and the keeping of women by authority figures, created difficulties for Indian men.

Still, it is questionable, however, whether what Poynting euphemistically terms 'immoral relations'[51] between Indian women and White men on the plantations, which had become widespread by the 1880s, could be so easily explained by the sexual disparity and by differences in the social culture of marriages. They were more probably linked to the stereotypical association of working class/lower caste women with promiscuity.[52] Historical and literary sources indicate that the whites on the estates did not respect Indian unions. Jenkins's fictional character, Lutchmee, arrived on the 'Sunda' from India to colonial Guyana hoping to be reunited with her husband Dilloo who had embarked two years previously. Although she located him and the overseers knew of the marital ties and connection, several of them had their eyes on her and dismissed Dilloo's claim. When it was related to one Englishman, called Loseby in the novel, that she cried 'massa no put hand on Coolie woman: Dilloo wife' when one overseer tried to molest her, he reportedly retorted 'Ah, she'll soon get over that! ... Virtue is not an Indian woman's best reward in these regions.'[53]

Women resisted being treated as sexual objects on Caribbean plantations, and at times Indian and Black men supported them. In 1904, there was a strike on a Guyanese estate because the manager and the overseers were having 'immoral relations' with the women.[54] Mahabir relates the case of a woman who got the assistance of five Black men to beat her husband who was cheating on her.[55] Women agitated for the relocation of the men who abused them, they voted with their feet opting to leave the Caribbean as soon as their period of forced residence had expired. They moved out of the rural plantation setting into urban areas where more remunerative non-agricultural jobs could be found and out of abusive relationships when they could.

As Jeffrey Weeks reminds us, the history of sexuality is not just one of control, but also one of opposition and resistance to moral codes. Forms of moral control gave rise to cultures of resistance. Indian women were not voiceless and immobile victims of patriarchal power.

4

The University of the West Indies and
The Decolonization Project

Delivered at the Flag-raising Ceremony and Official Launch of Commemoration Week, February 15, 2002, Assembly Hall, University of the West Indies, Mona

I find it particularly significant that Commemoration Week falls during February, the month in which, following the example of our North American neighbours, we identify and applaud the contributions of our (and their) Black achievers to national, regional and international development. I therefore wish to use the coincidence of Black History Month and Commemoration Week to revisit the mandate issued by two of the better known Black achievers, Marcus Garvey (in 1937) and Bob Marley (later in 'Redemption Song'), for us to 'Emancipate ourselves from mental slavery'. This is a very familiar line and we trot it out frequently, especially when we participate in the 'legacy of slavery debate'. But how many of us have really made a conscious effort to, if you will, 'answer the call'? How many of us have consciously grasped its revolutionary advocacy of self-reliance, indigenization, self-liberation and self-conscious nation building?

I would like to suggest, particularly for the benefit of the ancestors buried on this former plantation, and those who tend to forget the achievers among us, that the University of the West Indies (UWI) has not been among those who have ignored this call but on the contrary, has trained, and accommodated within its walls as Faculty, a long line of scholars, who have in various ways aligned themselves to this project of emancipation.

There are many areas on which I could focus as I seek to highlight UWI's role in the project of emancipation, self-reliance and nation building: Agriculture, Engineering, Cultural Studies, Gender Studies, Law, Literature, Medicine, Pure and Applied and Social Sciences, the promotion of the Nation Language, and Tropical Metabolism Research, to name a few. The focus is on the ways in which the UWI, through its History departments, has made some contribution to this essential project of mental liberation from the shackles of slavery and colonialism.

History, of course, possesses one of the greatest possibilities for anchoring people emerging from a colonial past to a more positive beginning, helping us to deal with the epistemic violence of the imperial project, and providing alternative words for the unbridled indecent colonial bad words (and deeds) of people like Thomas Carlyle, James Anthony Froude, Edward Long, Lady Nugent, Thomas Thistlewood, Elizabeth Fenwick and others.[1] Imagine the potential damage of Fenwick's views that Blacks in Barbados are a 'sluggish, inert, self-willed race of people ... inaccessible to gentle and kindly impulses'![2]

The event that we are commemorating today — the 40th anniversary of the UWI becoming its own degree-granting institution, divorced from the University of London after a 14-year marriage — is not unconnected to my choice of topic — 'the UWI and the Decolonization Project'. This divorce (even if viewed only as a decree *nisi* rather than as a decree absolute), was another necessary step in the long process of decolonization and the search for self-determination for Caribbean people. This decree *nisi* provided the occasion for the first Caribbeanists in the History departments — Roy Augier, Elsa Goveia, Douglas Hall, Keith Hunte, Keith Laurence, Woodville Marshall (who realized early that history has an active cultural and political role because of its perceived relationship to national and regional identity) to march more self-confidently on the road leading to the writing of Caribbean history in the Creole genre if not in the Creole tongue as Barry Higman has observed.[3] This creolization of Caribbean history did not seek to isolate Caribbean people from other historical discourses and viewpoints, but provided an alternative perspective that could be called upon in studying the past.

Building on the examples of the pioneers, historians trained at the UWI in the post-1962 era, many of whom read the History Special with its grueling journey of self-discovery through Africa, Greece, Rome, via France, England, North America and Latin America to the Caribbean, sought to carry out Marcus Garvey's and Bob Marley's charge. Many of us saw the possibility of using history as an emancipatory tool, perhaps believing in Marcus Garvey's concept, that 'History is the landmark by which we are directed into the true course of life.'[4]

After 1962, these Caribbeanists stepped up their efforts to attack the Western intellectual canon or, in Kamau Brathwaite's metaphorical representation, the missile directed at the capsule, with Afrocentric weapons. To invade the terrorist intellectual garrison, all the time destabilizing the donmanship phenomenon started by don Cristóbal Colón that has so resulted in the representation of the Caribbean as 'Other'. They got ample support from Rex Nettleford, Philip Sherlock and Shirley Gordon who believed that there was such a thing as 'West Indian History'.

Some of those trained in the 1970s (myself among them), were a part of that phase of UWI development that saw a broadening of the class base of the student population, helped by Michael Manley's free tertiary education policy. While careers were advanced through writing and publishing scholarly historical works, we continued also the tradition of public education, curriculum development and text book-writing in a long-term effort to ensure the recuperation of Black dignity among future generations. Most refused to be regarded as antiquarians, seeing history as both useful and controversial; useful with lay appeal according to one writer.[5]

Additionally, influenced by the democratizing appeal of social history, many of us sought, in Gayatri Spivak's terms, to develop a strategy of reading that spoke to the historically muted subject;[6] to present 'the vision of the vanquished', with the 'vision of the victors'.[7]

Caribbean historians are not unique in their activist attitude towards history. History is increasingly being used as a form of cultural enquiry in many societies. As Florida University Professor Kevin Yelvington and his colleagues have observed:

> the wider world, currently overrun with the passions of regionalism, ethnicism and nationalism, and in the throes of both modernization and development, has made history the privileged ground of individual and collective identity.[8]

Even Englishman J.H. Parry, first head of the Department of History at the UWI (1949–56), in justifying a greater attention to the history of the region said, that the study of history had three main purposes and two of them were '(1) self-knowledge, and (2) the provision of an intelligible account of the accumulated experience of particular communities, which may help the members of those communities to understand and to deal with the predicaments in which they find themselves'.[9] History as a mere intellectual exercise was placed third. Walter Rodney was, arguably, the best example of a UWI historian who embraced the activist appeal of history, making the link between Africa and the Caribbean, between the halls of academia and the wider society through his groundings with his brothers and I expect also, with his sistren.

The Content of the Historical Research

So how have Caribbean historians continued to intervene in the hegemonic and authoritative discourse that ascribes 'rationality' and 'legitimacy' to its own discursive practice? How have we attempted over the past 40 years to facilitate a more inclusive view of Caribbean history? In order to demonstrate Caribbean historiography, I will highlight a few critical research trends by UWI history graduates and UWI historians in general. These trends include a concerted effort, for example by Alvin Thompson, Helen Seaman and Hilary Beckles, to focus on the self-liberation ethos among indigenous and enslaved peoples;[10] to question the dominant plantation economy model and show, as Barry Higman, Gail Saunders, Kathleen Monteith and I have done, the role of indigenous people and 'new creoles' in challenging the ideologies and institutional arrangements/economic imperatives of the mercantilist system.[11]

Cultural historians like the pioneer Kamau Brathwaite, and later Brian Moore, have stressed the attempt by Africans to preserve their culture even within the constraints of a creolizing trend; and Goveia and Brathwaite have laid the foundations for the still active debate over the nature of Caribbean society in the eighteenth century.[12] Douglas Hall, Beckles, Woodville Marshall and Glen Richards have shown how the enslaved negotiated terms and conditions of work, even wages, and engaged in collective bargaining despite the system of slavery; their personal efforts to defeat the monopolistic tendencies of slave society and promote economic and sociocultural diversification.[13] Enslaved men's resistance to plantation owners' efforts to negate their masculinity and the anti-slavery actions which brought down slavery within an economic environment and as Eric Williams tells us, the declining importance of the Caribbean to Britain, have been other areas of interest.[14]

Some have tried to reclaim marginalized people's voices by unearthing narratives or at best, sources that give voice to the Africans' experience. Lorna Simmonds, Pedro Welch and Beckles have challenged the historical dichotomization of Blacks as powerless and Whites as powerful, showing how even after the end of White indentured servitude, many Whites remained poor and powerless, particularly in urban centres; while there were some fairly well-off freed people.[15] Works by Beckles, Brathwaite, Bridget Brereton, Michelle Johnson, Barry Higman, Lucille Mathurin Mair, Linnette Vassell and others, infused with the new attention to gender discourses that developed in the 1970s, have destabilized the dialectical representation of the so-called 'loose and promiscuous' Black woman and the 'pure and moral' White woman; the cruel White male enslaver and the benevolent White female enslaver; the passive Black woman and the active Black man; the enslaved man as producer and the enslaved woman as reproducer.[16]

African and Indian resistance to exploitative labour regimes and the inequities of the free order so that they could pursue 'perfect personal freedom',[17] is reflected in my own work and that of Veront Satchell, Kusha Haraksingh, and Swithin Wilmot.[18] Indeed, Wilmot's work of counter-discourse opposes the representations of the newly freed people and the Black working class as 'lazy and shiftless'. Douglas Hall's, Satchell's and Wilmot's revisionist work on the search for land, and the political implications of its acquisition and non-acquisition for the peasantry and the plantation sector are now standard reference works in the academy.[19]

Several have explored the factors influencing the social protests of the 1930s, in particular, the ideological foundations and outcomes of those protests. Allister Hinds and Michelle Johnson have been among those looking at the Federal interlude;[20] with others exploring the movement towards independence, even venturing into so-called modern history to assess the results of independence. The role of education in the process of decolonization has been the life work of people like Carl Campbell. Patrick Bryan and Brereton have been among those rewriting the history of individual territories.[21]

UWI historians have not imprisoned themselves within the walls of the university but have made their contributions to local historical societies, international historical associations, examination boards and publishing houses; and all over the region are called upon to play key roles in

Emancipation Day and Independence Day celebrations, and in research arms of the reparations movement. Historians have always been in key administrative positions at the UWI and several like Rodney have been involved in activist politics or, like Brinsley Samaroo, been part of established political parties.

The process of developing and disseminating this body of work has not been smooth of course. Historians have had to contend with limited resources at times and, especially in the watershed 1980s, with the threat of the return of the imperial tradition in historical writing on the Caribbean as some non-Caribbean historians made Caribbean history the subject and object of their attention. But the 1990s saw a virtual explosion of revisionist historical works on the region by both the 'new' and the 'old' generation, helped on by the emergence of local publishing houses; and this new generation has made it quite clear that the empire is writing back. It therefore appears that the future is secure in the hands of the twenty-first-century 'young' historians: John Campbell, Heather Cateau, Michelle Johnson, Kathleen Monteith, Rita Pemberton and Pedro Welch, among others.[22] But this new generation will still have to grapple with the recurring problem of how to ensure that the rich historical research does not remain at the level of theoretical discussion. A way will have to be found to impress upon policy makers and politicians the link between historical works of the postcolonial period and the project of Black mental liberation and economic development; that historical research can inform public discussions surrounding issues of cultural identity, citizenship, inter-ethnic relations and independence. Until present public policy makers and governments realize the practical benefits of the historical research, they will continue to preside over societies torn apart and fragmented by 'border clashes' — a battle for terrain between contending cultures.

SECTION II

ENSLAVEMENT AND RESISTANCE

Introduction

Slavery transformed the Atlantic into a complex trading area, turning it into the centre of the international economy especially during the eighteenth and nineteenth centuries.[1] Indeed, as Barbara Solow has observed, 'firm and enduring trade links between Europe and America [and I daresay Africa], were not forged until the introduction of slavery.'[2] Franklin Knight adds that, 'without African slaves and the transatlantic slave trade, the potential economic value of the Americas could never have been realized.'[3] The Atlantic was the centre of the international economy during slavery and the output of the Caribbean was destined more for external rather than internal markets to the region. However not all commodities produced in the colonies were destined for the extra-regional markets in Europe, though the making of an integrated market culture in the Atlantic has overshadowed the study of intra-Caribbean trading links before and after the conquest. Intra-Caribbean links which pre-date conquest, though not as developed, were not complete casualties of colonization and the monopolistic tendencies of empire. In other words, regional interconnectedness was not lost in the 'making of the Atlantic World'. An understanding of the emergence of the larger Atlantic World needs greater awareness of intra-American labour mobilization and resource exchange that operated within the panoramic context of what Immanuel Wallerstein has described as the world system.[4] Slavery and the plantation system had a catalytic function in the linking of the disparate Caribbean territories.

Despite the dependence of the North Atlantic on the South Atlantic for labour and commodities, the cultural experiences and interaction of Africans and Europeans did not determine the creation of a Creole vision – that ultimately became the symbol of an Atlantic identity. On the contrary, deep division, inequality and instability characterized the 'Atlantic World'. These divisions and lack of egalitarianism, especially in the slave relations of production, which were essentially relations of domination in the orthodox Marxist sense, made the Atlantic World deeply unstable. The indigenous peoples and the enslaved, male and female, were responsible for a great deal of this instability. They were not incorporated into the Atlantic World as citizens with equal rights, but as chattel, enslaved and as the inferior 'Other'. Women, for example, whose contribution to the anti-slavery struggle from the moment of conquest and colonization, have received increasing attention from scholars. They experienced slavery in gender-specific ways resulting in their adopting gender-specific modes of resistance. The enslaved in Haiti successfully overthrew the slave regime and got rid of the French colonizers. Their example not only inspired enslaved people in Jamaica and elsewhere to step up their anti-slavery struggle, but spread fear in the hearts of enslavers in the Americas. As chapter 7 illustrates, Haiti suffered a certain kind of 'demonization' for having taken that bold revolutionary step and is not usually projected as a place that placed freedom and human rights on the Western political agenda.

This section focuses on the socioeconomic aspects of the slave system in Jamaica and the wider Caribbean, in particular the island's trade links with other parts of the Caribbean and the importance of non-sugar plantation activities for the internal trade. It explores the evolution of anti-slavery and the contribution of the enslaved and Maroons to the overthrow of the slave system. These heroes and heroines of the emancipation movement, (as chapter 21 shows in more detail), have yet to be appropriately memorialized.

5

ROOTS OF ROUTES:

Intra-Caribbean Trade Links Since the Fifteenth Century

Delivered at the University of the Netherlands Antilles, Curaçao, July 2003

Slavery's legacies in the Caribbean are manifold and multidimensional and include relics of the commercial relationships devised by the various imperial powers to ensure the transfer of wealth from the 'periphery' to the 'core'. Such relationships ensured that links between the colonies and the various metropoles were cemented, to the detriment of inter-colonial links. For example, according to the tenets of mercantilism laid down by the English for their empire, colonies were primarily sources of supply for the metropole; and they were also expected to import their necessities from the 'Mother Country'.[1] National self-sufficiency was the goal desired by this mutual commerce and, therefore, such valuable possessions required a strict commercial control; one which would effectively exclude foreign trade.

It was the Navigation Acts of the seventeenth century, like the French *le exclusif*, that sought to impose such control. By these acts, the staple produce from England's Caribbean colonies — sugar, rum, molasses, indigo, pimento, ginger and coffee — were to be carried in English ships. Ships were to be manned by a majority of British crewmen and goods consigned solely to English ports.[2] In this scenario, legitimate trade between colonies of the same imperial power (for example, between Barbados and Jamaica), as well as trade between the British and Spanish Caribbean was discouraged. Based on the dictates of mercantilism, each colony developed bilateral economic links with its 'Mother Country'. Trade between the British Caribbean and North America was sanctioned because most Caribbean economies were export-led; and although the major staple had the potential to encourage 'spread effects', the almost full utilization of the land for sugar cane cultivation discouraged a domestic economy that would produce plantation inputs or make colonies self-sufficient in food and livestock. Barbara Solow reinforces the importance of sugar exports by showing that slave-grown sugar provided 60 per cent of British America's commodity exports.[3] The supply of food, work animals and other plantation inputs, therefore, came from external suppliers, mainly the USA and England. Trade with Spanish America remained clandestine for many years, until the opening of the free ports saw its legitimization.

Today, over a century and a half after the full abolition of enslavement in the British-colonized Caribbean, economic and social links between the former British colonies in the Caribbean and Britain (as well as with North America) remain arguably stronger than intra-Caribbean links, despite the existence of the Caribbean Community (CARICOM). For example, Jamaica still buys more of its rice from external rather than internal suppliers, to the disappointment of regional producers. Globalization has also continued the trend whereby the resources of so-called 'Third World' countries continue to find their way to the 'core', whether by way of debt repayment, the out-sourcing of manufacturing industries using cheap labour, or the addiction to fast food, McDonalds and KFC for example, or to brand name clothes such as Tommy Hilfiger.

This presentation seeks to accomplish two tasks: first, it aims to trace the historical roots of the present trend whereby intra-Caribbean economic relations are still weaker than links with the developed countries. Second, it will show that while the dominant trade routes during slavery led from the Caribbean to Europe and North America, intra-Caribbean links, which pre-date conquest, though not as developed, were not complete casualties of colonization and the monopolistic tendencies of empire. In other words, regional interconnectedness was not lost in the 'making of the Atlantic World'; and an understanding of the emergence of the larger Atlantic World calls for a greater awareness of intra-American labour mobilization and resource exchange that operated within the panoramic context of the world system. The main geographic focus here will be Jamaica and the ways in which that island developed trading links with other areas of the Caribbean region, most notably the Spanish islands and (Caribbean) coastal Central and South America.

Pre-Conquest and Immediate Post-Conquest Trends

The study of the birth of the Atlantic World as an integrated and expanding capitalist economy, has engaged the attention of many scholars.[4] The making of an integrated market culture in the Atlantic, associated with international warfare, political tensions, a massive international (forced or voluntary) movement of people and commercial relations involving Africa, Europe and the Americas (including Latin America and the Caribbean), has often overshadowed the study of intra-Caribbean trading links before and after the conquest. Before the establishment of an international commercial system that connected the Americas to Europe, there were trading links among the territories of the 'South Atlantic System', such as indigenous long-distance trade and communication throughout the region.[5] The Incas of Peru, for example, traded in products such as cacao with the Aztecs of Mexico. David Watts notes that: 'inter-community and inter-island contact for trade was encouraged, notably for the purpose of acquiring quality products which were not universally obtainable at a local level.'[6] Among these were stone celts and various cotton products such as hammocks and particular items of clothing. Trade links to South America and, to a much lesser extent, Central America were set up from time to time, though there was none to North America.

Conquest destabilized some of these indigenous lines of trade and exchange and replaced them with new ones. The first post-1492 movement of 'resources' within the region involved the forced relocation of labour, initially indigenous peoples and later enslaved Africans. This was not trade in the true sense of the word but the forced relocation of human resources. However it illustrates the ways in which Spain, through its negative colonizing activities, established contacts among the various Caribbean societies. Watts shows that Barbados, Dominica, Martinique, Saint Lucia, Saint Vincent, Grenada and Tobago had all been targeted for slave raiding by the Spanish by 1512. By 1520, he argues that, it is likely that all native peoples had been removed from the northern Leewards between the Virgin Islands and Barbuda, except for Saint Kitts and Nevis. Further to the south, by this date, Barbados, Tobago and Saint Lucia had been depopulated through slave raiding. Curaçao, Bonaire and Aruba had been raided similarly. Indigenous peoples were raided from as far south as Trinidad for the Pearl islands north of the Venezuelan coast.[7] Nigel Bolland has shown how amidst (and contributing to) the holocaust that devastated Central America the Spaniards hunted, enslaved and exported indigenous peoples from the Yucatán coast and the Bay Islands in the Gulf of Honduras in the sixteenth century to replenish their labour force in Cuba, Hispaniola and Jamaica.[8] The transport of the indigenous Central Americans via the Pacific coast to Panama and Mexico was also part of this imperial system of labour reallocation as the Spaniards increasingly came to regard the indigenous people of Central America as a large reservoir of abundant, available and expendable labour for wider colonial designs.[9] El Salvador, Guatemala, Mexico and Nicaragua were also mined for labourers to Peru.

By the mid- to late sixteenth century, a more recognizable trade developed, as the indigenes were traded for food to sustain emerging Spanish colonial settlements. Bolland estimates that between 1536 and 1540, more than 20 ships sailed regularly from the Pacific coast of Nicaragua, as often as six times a year, to Panama and once or twice a year to Peru. The numbers on each ship varied but at times totalled 400. The 'Indian slave trade', whose quantitative dimensions have not been measured accurately, estimates for the period 1527–1549 for Nicaragua alone ranged from 100,000 to 500,000 and had contradictory results: depopulation and persistent underdevelopment of some areas of the Caribbean, repopulation and development of others.[10] By the early 1550s, according to Bolland, 'the export of enslaved Indians, the first major staple of the colonial economy of Central America, had virtually disappeared.'[11] As will be shown later, this was not the end of intra-regional trade.

From an early period inter-regional trade took place in other commodities; and the large numbers of ships that transported goods from one part of the region to the other led Ruggiero Romano to describe the region as an 'American Mediterranean'. Cocoa from Venezuela to Mexico;

livestock between Cuba and Santo Domingo, and grain from Mexico to Cuba — establishing at an early date a busy network of trading links which continued throughout the entire period of Spanish domination.[12]

Case Study: Jamaica and the Spanish Caribbean During Slavery

A good example of the development and maintenance of intra-Caribbean trading links is that which emerged between Jamaica and the Spanish Caribbean. The trade between Jamaica (English after 1655) and the Spanish Caribbean may seem surprising in an age of mercantilism and during the existence of the English Navigation Acts. The restrictive mercantilist policies under the Restoration so contrasted with the virtual free trade of Cromwell's day during which the Spanish trade to Jamaica had developed, that such laws were virtually ignored. In spite of Britain's efforts to implement the Navigation Acts, the importance of the Spanish trade to Jamaica had been long recognized and moves had been made to legalize it. Spain had consistently refused to sanction any such freedom of trade. Nevertheless, successive governors from the time of Modyford encouraged a clandestine Anglo-Spanish trade, granting licences to traders to sell enslaved Africans and commodities to Spanish America and to import livestock.[13] Spain however did not reciprocate by granting similar licences. On the contrary, the illegal nature of the trade was emphasized in the Anglo-Spanish Treaty of Madrid in 1670. Article 8 of that treaty stated that:

> Subjects of the King of Great Britain shall on no account direct their commerce or undertake navigation to the ports or places which the Catholic King holds in the said Indies, nor trade with them. Reciprocally, the subjects of the King of Spain shall not sail to or trade in the places that are possessed there by the King of Great Britain.[14]

Articles 9, 10, and 11 however, opened up certain loopholes, which were fully exploited and facilitated the continuation of the contraband trade. These provided that, if for any reason — whether pirate attacks, storm, or revictualling ships of either nations found it necessary to enter the other's ports, such ships should be allowed.[15] Furthermore, it was stated that if in the future 'either king shall deem it convenient to grant any general or special licence or any privileges to the subjects of the other for navigating and trading ... the said navigation and commerce shall be practiced and maintained.'[16]

The passing of the Free Port Act of 1766, however, further opened up Spanish trading to Jamaica. This Act sanctioned a branch of colonial trade that had hitherto been conducted in a clandestine manner. It facilitated the importation and exportation of certain types of goods at certain ports in the British West Indies by small vessels from neighbouring 'foreign' colonies. This did not, however, represent a departure from the Navigation Acts, which still attempted to control the trade of staple commodities and English manufactures. The Free Port Act was designed to allow only trade in goods, which did not compete with the products of Britain and her colonies.[17] The trade in African captives, North American supplies and the carrying trade between the Mother Country and her colonies remained firmly in British hands. In Jamaica, Lucea, Savanna-la-mar, Kingston and Montego Bay were declared free ports in 1776 and with the passing of the Act and the opening up of ports other than Kingston, the Spanish trade with Jamaica was revived.

It should, perhaps, be noted at this point that the South Atlantic System was able to maintain trading links with the Caribbean because, while certain sections (like Brazil and coastal Venezuela, like the US 'South') produced staple crops for export to Europe, for the most part, they successfully developed independent subsistence agriculture and a livestock industry and were less dependent on the two-way trade with Europe.[18] Part of this was because, as economic historians have shown, the Iberian powers were never able to fully absorb Latin American products; neither was England able to absorb fully the exports of the Mainland Colonies, especially New England. Regional markets (and trade with 'foreign' powers) played a more crucial role in their economic development. They were forced to view their economic relationships in more regional terms than did the plantation colonies of the Caribbean.

An early item of trade was labour. Though involved also in the direct

59

trade in African captives, the largely British settlements along the Caribbean coast of Central America (between Honduras and Costa Rica) became heavily dependent on West Indian markets, notably Jamaica, for their labour needs — enslaved Africans — from the seventeenth century to 1808. The intra-Caribbean trade in enslaved Africans, was, in fact, a characteristic feature of the regional links that developed during the fifteenth to the nineteenth century. Several ports were notable transshipment points: Curaçao traded enslaved people to the French and Spanish Caribbean, for example; and up to 1663, they also supplied British territories like Barbados. Even when the British managed to dominate the market in enslaved Africans, clandestine trade continued. The Dutch ABC (Aruba, Bonaire, Curaçao) islands continued in the transit trade in Africans to Spanish America and the French Caribbean. Cartagena de Indias was also a notable transshipment port for enslaved Africans, some 135,000 landing there from Africa between 1595 and 1640.[19]

Trade continued even in territories that had passed to Britain and which were recaptured by the Spanish as the case of links between Jamaica and coastal settlements in Central America, San Andrés and Providencia, demonstrates. Nuala Zahedieh has shown that Port Royal became a virtual hub for contraband trade with the Spanish colonists, not to mention a base from which privateering raids were launched on the Spanish Main, even the fortified towns of Portobello, Cartagena de Indias and Havana. The holders of the Spanish *asiento* also obtained enslaved peoples from Port Royal, as opposed to Curaçao, to supply Spanish colonies. Part of the trade was conducted in the island's own sloop fleet, stimulating its growth from 40 in 1670 to 80 in 1679 and about 100 in 1689. Port Royal became the busiest port in the English Caribbean and by the 1680s attracted some 150–200 ships a year.[20]

San Andrés, Providencia, the Corn Islands and Jamaica

San Andrés, along with its sister island of Providencia, and Santa Catalina form the Departamento Archipiélago de San Andrés, Providencia and Santa Catalina of Colombia. However, the relationship between the mainland

and the islands has been complicated by the fact that the archipelago is located 270 km from the coast of Nicaragua and a significant section of the native population, because of its historical legacy, is English-speaking and Protestant.[21] For their inhabitants have largely descended from planters and enslaved people from Jamaica and other western Caribbean territories, several British. Indeed, as Adolfo Meisel shows, well into the twentieth century, there was limited economic and cultural interaction between the islands and Colombia.[22] San Andrés, Providencia and the Miskito Coast were, in fact, so remote from the centres of Spanish settlement that the Crown was only vaguely informed as to what took place there.[23] It was this location and its common and intertwined history that facilitated the development of trading links between the islands and the western Caribbean.

The English Puritans who arrived in the *Seaflower* in 1630 and were captured by the Spanish in 1641 first settled Providencia. The English recaptured it in 1666, but their victory was short-lived as Spain reclaimed it 83 days later. The Spanish were nervous about the military and strategic implications of an 'enemy' settlement so close to the Spanish Main, even though privateering and smuggling activities with Spanish settlers had been going on. Providencia was recaptured and practically plundered and destroyed by Henry Morgan in 1670. There does not appear to have been any sustained settlement on the island until the late eighteenth century when Captain Francis Archbould spearheaded a new settlement initiative under the auspices of Spain. English settlers who wanted to were allowed to stay, once they converted to Catholicism and presumably swore allegiance to the King of Spain. The English settlers from Jamaica who wished to escape English control, along with their enslaved labourers, also settled on Providencia. Other settlers came from the Cayman Islands and other nearby territories, and Curaçao. It appears also that some white (English) settlers from San Andrés and Providencia evacuated to Jamaica after the Convention of 1786 that followed the Spanish take over which called for the evacuation of the Miskito Shore and the offshore islands. In 1822, Providencia, San Andrés and the Corn Islands (Mangle Alto and Mangle Chico) were incorporated to the new Republic of Colombia when Spanish America obtained its independence from Spain.

There has been a long history of contact between the Colombian islands of San Andrés and Providencia, and Jamaica dating back from the seventeenth century, perhaps even earlier. William Dampier on his visit to San Andrés in 1680 noted that several Jamaicans were in the habit of coming to cut ship timbers from the island's fine cedars. Woodcutting and the 'export' of timber to Jamaican customers was also an early activity in Providencia.[24] The Corn Islands (Mangle Alto and Mangle Chico, linked to San Andrés, Providencia and the Miskito Coast) also developed early trading relationships with Jamaica, exporting cotton, cattle, turtles and food supplies. After the abolition of slavery exports of coconuts from the Corn Islands, as in San Andrés, exceeded the export of cotton. In addition to cotton and coconuts, a variety of other goods were produced and exported from San Andrés and Providencia. The variety of goods exported from the Colombian islands reflects the fact that their multiethnic settler populations developed a diversified agriculture, forest, livestock and maritime industry.

One of the most long-standing exports was timber. Indeed, several varieties of wood were exploited for ships' timbers: calabash, mahogany, manchineel, ironwood, and cedar. Other types provided fuel for passing ships. Cotton cultivation was important on Providencia and was cultivated on land holdings, small estates of 30 acres, worked by enslaved Africans. Cotton, along with animal hides, turtles and tortoise shells (described as a white man's job) were the principal trading items on the island into the nineteenth century. Boats from Jamaica called frequently for cotton and timber. Fish, turtle and conch pearls described by one commentator as 'the size of chick peas' were also sold to Jamaican traders.[25] In terms of turtle and tortoise shells, by 1722, several Jamaican vessels were annually visiting the Central American coast to catch and buy turtles, along with tortoise shell, from the Miskito 'Indians'. By the 1830s, around 170 pounds of tortoise shell were being sold annually to Jamaican traders. The much esteemed salted turtle sold in Jamaica at the price of salted beef. Gradually the trade in turtles shifted to the Cayman Islands.

Cotton was an important export product during and immediately after slavery. In 1835, an English visitor to Providencia reported that 30,000 pounds of cotton were traded annually in Jamaica for English goods —

calico, cloths, et cetera.[26] The cotton was re-exported from Jamaica to England, and in English markets was rated better than cotton from Santo Domingo and the mainland. Cotton production and the trade in cotton to Jamaica appeared to have declined with the abolition of slavery in Jamaica (though slavery did not officially end in these islands until 1853, following abolition in Colombia in 1851). Minor quantities of coffee, sugar, indigo, maize, yams, sweet potato, plantains, coconuts, oranges, avocados and tobacco were produced for local consumption. The labourers needed to cultivate cotton and other produce that is, enslaved Africans, were obtained from Jamaica.

Similar to Jamaica, livestock farming was important to the economy of Providencia — especially after slavery was abolished — due to the suitability of the soil for grass (especially after guinea grass was introduced). Some historians indicate that the production and export of animal products seemed to have been as important as cotton during the period of slavery in the British Caribbean. The fine horses traded to Jamaica were cheaper than locally produced ones, selling for £3–£4 a head. While the livestock industry expanded after the abolition of slavery in the British Caribbean, the lines of trade in cattle, hogs and horses shifted to Latin America: to San Andrés, Limón and Costa Rica. During slavery, cattle mills (also drawn by mules and horses) abounded in Jamaica, but declined after 1838 with the decline in the number of sugar plantations and the gradual shift to steam as a source of power.

Trade with Jamaica (more so after the islands became free ports) and Latin America facilitated the development of the maritime industry in Providencia. Individual traders, primarily males, purchased schooners to transport their goods to Jamaica and the port towns of the western Caribbean. They traded along the coastal areas of Honduras, Nicaragua, Costa Rica, Panama, the Cayman Islands and the Colombian Port City of Cartagena.[27] Costa Ricans tended to be better connected to the commercial networks of the Atlantic Coast of Central America and the Caribbean rather than to the international capitalist markets of Europe.[28] Trade led to marital ties, emigration and the permanent settlement of men from Providencia in places such as the Corn Islands, Bluefields, Puerto Limón, Bocas del Toro,

Colón, Grand Cayman, Cayman Brac islands and Jamaica. The massive outmigration developed only after 1900.

The links between San Andrés and Jamaica developed along a similar trajectory as Providencia; trade with Jamaica being highly developed, if not illegal at some points in the history. In theory, San Andrés, like Providencia, traded with Cartagena and Trujillo, however, in reality, it served as an entrepôt and smuggling base for the entire Western Caribbean, Jamaica among them. The main port was at Southwest Cove, although as Parsons notes, some small ships purportedly also used the present anchorage.[29]

The links with Jamaica were long standing. Many Jamaicans, some granted land titles by the Spanish authorities, were noted among the population by the nineteenth century and English was widely spoken due to the Jamaican influence. The early settlers, mainly from Jamaica, were involved in the extraction of wood, the planting of cotton, the use of enslaved labour, and the export of turtles. 'Jamaica pimienta' (allspice) appears to have been produced on San Andrés, perhaps introduced from Jamaica, and formed a part of the trade with Cartagena.

Cotton was the mainstay of the economy from the 1620s to 1853, after which coconut exports, mainly to the USA, took over (1853–1953).[30] But this shift may have occurred earlier as 'US traders' loaded coconut oil and cotton as early as 1841 and transshipped via Jamaica. Exports of coconuts to the USA reached an annual figure in excess of two million nuts by 1873; a decade later it was four million. During its best years, 1900–1906, San Andrés was harvesting 14–16 million nuts annually from an estimated 1½ million trees. By the mid-twentieth century however, because of the decline in coconuts on account of diseases, drought and rat infestation, Jamaica, Trinidad and the San Blas Islands of Panama gradually replaced the Colombian islands as suppliers to the USA. In 1920, the Colombian islands supplied four million nuts as opposed to 33 million nuts from Jamaica and 19 million from Panama.

Goods imported from Jamaica were sold at high prices and for huge profits in the island, everywhere from Cape Gracias á Dios to Chiriquí Lagoon. The position of San Andrés in the trade with Jamaica and the Western Caribbean was, for a while, unique. Parsons notes that it was not only the port from which vessels were licensed for the coastal trade with Colombia, but return cargo was also provided and its prospering population even offered a modest market in its own right.[31] Both San Andrés and Providencia remained free ports until 1871 when a five per cent ad valorem tax on imports was imposed and a customs house established on the islands. They reverted to free port status in the twentieth century.

Jamaicans also became involved as labourers in the exploitation of the phosphate rich guano deposits (used as fertilizer) of the small cays north and east of Providencia. Beginning in 1853, this gave rise to international disputes among the US, Nicaragua and Colombia over claims to the islands. There is a claim that in 1891, 12 Jamaicans taken to Roncador, one of the Guano Islands, to load guano for the Colombian Phosphate and Guano Company were left stranded on the reef with the departure of the first 300-ton shipload; seven eventually escaped in a small boat. Evidence later found by Providencia turtlemen indicates that the rest died of starvation.[32]

More on the Intra-Caribbean–American Trade in Livestock

The impact of long-distance voyages on livestock vital to the productive aspects of the sugar industry and the inability of plantation colonies to maintain significant herds, opened up a market for working stock with North American and other Spanish American suppliers. Within the British Caribbean export-led economies, only Jamaica developed what could be categorized as a 'domestic sector', shaped by the demands of the major staple — sugar. In Barbados, Nevis, Saint Kitts and Antigua, the commitment to sugar prevented lands eminently suitable for livestock to be put into this product, making import vital and giving rise to internal controversies between the livestock and sugar sectors (which were distinct entities).

Jamaica attempted to supply its own livestock needs by maintaining a significant number of livestock farms (pens); but despite their efforts, the pen-keepers and planters or pen-owners were never able to supply the total livestock needs of the island during slavery. In 1820, when 145 pens and 470 estates were returned in the Accounts Produce, only 8,050 head of working stock, or an average of 55.51 per pen, were sold from these livestock farms. On the all-island level, there were 562 estates and c. 400 pens in 1820.[33] Taking 55.51 as the average, and assuming that contemporary writers are correct in their claim that a typical estate needed 100 working steers annually in addition to mules and steers, an estate would need over 56,200 instead of the 22,204 per annum produced by pens. Mules were particularly in great demand on plantations in the eighteenth century. In 1768, it was estimated that a minimum of 3,900 mules were needed for Jamaica's 651 sugar estates. In this year, the estimated number of breeding pens in the island was 200. Even if each pen supplied an average of 12 mules per annum, a shortfall of 1,500 would still remain. At £28 per head, planters needed to spend £109,200 each year to fill their total demand of mules. Next in demand on sugar estates were horned cattle, but this demand like that for mules could not be locally filled. Thus, according to the planter-historian, Edward Long, 'there is likewise a considerable importation of horned cattle from the Spanish coast, for the markets as well as for labour and breeding.'[34] He stressed that such a situation was on account of the lack of sufficient pens in the island.

Long elaborated on two of the reasons which necessitated the importation of mules, asses, horses, and cattle, and emphasized that once these were removed the trade would end. The first obstacle to Jamaican self-sufficiency was a lack of 'a sufficient stock of industrious inhabitants to have been employed in breeding the number of these animals proportioned to the annual consumption'.[35] The second was the absence of:

> the patriotic endeavours and subsidies of the Assembly, as well as for encouraging such breeding farms, as for making good roads in every district, at the public charge, whereby the internal parts of the country must have been settled and improved with greater facility and the waste of cattle in great measure prevented.[36]

Long believed that £10,000 per annum was the sum needed for the latter purpose, a sum that would have been easily recovered by rendering the importation from foreigners inexpedient.

One of the reasons put forward for the failure of more settlers to engage in penkeeping was the fear of overproduction and a consequent price fall. Long records that:

> many persons have been deterred from engaging their time and capitals in this way; imagining that a glut would be the consequence and the price of cattle and mules would be lowered because the Spanish breed are imported and sold at a cheaper rate than they can afford and make a suitable profit.[37]

He disagreed with this reasoning, believing instead that local breeds, by being hardier than imported stock, would be in great demand as plantation working animals. A far more plausible reason in his view was that 'most men have a prejudice in favour of foreign articles, despising their own [despite it being] far superior in value'.[38] As some sugar planters exhibited a preference for imported mules and cattle, this acted as a disincentive for the greater expansion of penkeeping.

The pen-keepers themselves echoed Long's sentiments. In a petition to the Governor in 1790, the pen-keepers in the St. Ann vestry complained of

> the distressing Prospect arising in the Community in general . . . and this Parish . . . in Particular of the trade carried on between the Spaniards of Cuba and a few of the trading or commercial Persons of this country from the vicinity of the coasts which facilitates the impolitic Intercourse.[39]

Like Edward Long, they stressed that the trade posed an obstacle to the expansion of the penkeeping industry,

> which is being partly discontinued by the Introduction of Spanish Horses, mules, mares, and neat cattle, subject to no Impost or Duty whatever, and that at a time when we are paying Taxes towards the support of Government from the time of sale.[40]

The Spaniards were however underselling local producers; for Spanish cattle, horses, and mules were generally about one-third to one-half cheaper than local breeds. A Spanish-American horse for example, could fetch for as low as £10 sterling. Local breeds cost much more. A further request was that livestock be removed as an allowed article of trade under the Free Port Act. This was particularly crucial at a time when, according to them, the local supply of stock exceeded current demand, in their defense planters complained that the form of payment demanded by pen-keepers was at variance with the existing method. Pen-keepers required immediate payment in cash upon delivery of their livestock to sugar or coffee estates whereas importers gave credit, asking for payment at the end of 12 months and charging six per cent interest. However, the scale of operation of importers was far greater than that of pen-keepers who could not afford to wait a year for payment.

The drain of capital occasioned by the import trade from Spanish America was a matter of concern towards the end of the eighteenth century. Planters sold some of their rum internally in order to obtain cash to purchase Spanish stock. Long urged active and immediate steps to end what he termed this 'pernicious trade'. Two solutions were: first, for the Assembly to impose a tax on imported stock, and second, for local pen-keepers to begin to give credit — say six or nine months credit — so as to enable the poorer planter to defray the cost of the purchase out of rent or the succeeding crop. Up to 1816, however, neither solution seems to have been adopted.

Despite these proposed solutions and internal controversies, the lucrative Spanish trade continued well into the nineteenth century, as is indicated by trade statistics contained in the *Blue Books, Votes of the House of Assembly* and information relating to this trade reported in the *Royal Gazette*.

At first the numbers imported were small. Between 1729 and 1739, for example, 124 horned cattle, 1,500 horses, 4,285 mules, 243 asses, 129 hogs and 825 sheep, or an annual average of 826 animals had been imported.[41] A total of 14,456 animals were imported in the following decade and averaged £11,000 per annum. The same level of importation in 1773 was estimated at £16,000. By 1825, the annual number imported increased to 11,836 and the largest share of the total expenditure on imported livestock in the eighteenth century was spent on mules. Between 1729 and 1749, a total of 10,477 mules were imported and in 1774 the cost to the island was £11,175 sterling when 745 mules were brought in.

Unfortunately, few accurate statistics are available for the late eighteenth century at which time it was estimated that the trade was more significant numerically. Later, more estates began using cattle mills and the number of pens established in the eighteenth century became inadequate to meet the estates' demand for livestock. W.J. Gardner indicates that after 1800, trade declined as more estates shifted to wind and waterpower and as the number of pens increased.[42] However, in the absence of complete eighteenth-century trade figures, the *Blue Books* beginning only in 1821, it is impossible to substantiate Gardner's claim that the importation of cattle and mules decreased after 1800. Furthermore, the available statistics for the nineteenth century do not show a declining trend. The level of importation may simply have been determined by demand at a particular time — especially if the local supply was affected by natural disasters such as drought or hurricane. Level of importation could also be affected by wartime conditions as, in times of war, importation would be low and in times of peace, more favourable to trade, importation would increase.

The *Blue Books* and the *Votes* generally do not indicate the specific areas in Spanish America from which livestock were imported. The *Royal Gazette* however supplied this information as it regularly advertised the arrival of imported stock for sale. From these advertisements, closely examined from 1794 to 1845, it becomes clear that the principal areas of origin were Chagres, Rio de la Hacha, Coro and Santo Domingo. Modern authors also indicate that Puerto Rico participated in this trade along with the Spanish Main.[43] Nevertheless the Spaniards were not noted for their economic efficiency. What factors then explained their ability to undersell Jamaican livestock farmers? The answer seems to lie in their unlimited pastureland, large ranches and low labour costs. The plantation system developed late in the Spanish islands and, in Santo Domingo, for example, the most widespread and profitable business prior to 1870 was the raising of livestock. As Scarano points out:

69

the independent cultivators and the ranchers of the Spanish islands fulfilled an important role as suppliers of the sugar islands where specialization in export crops virtually precluded their self-sufficiency in foodstuffs, timber and draft animals. The Spanish islands, prevented by lack of capital and a restrictive imperial trade policy from trading along the plantation course, participated in an intra-Caribbean division of labour which promoted highly sophisticated export economies in some islands.[44]

Blue Books statistics indicate that the greater portion of the money spent on imported stock was paid out to what they referred to as 'foreign states', that is, non-British. In 1832, of £16,383 3s. 0d. expended by Jamaica on livestock imports, Spanish America earned £16,069 11s. 0d. The *Blue Books* do not identify individual 'foreign states', but there is every reason to believe that these were Spanish countries within the tropics. In addition, there was a small trade from British plantations, usually a re-export of animals from free ports in the British Caribbean islands.[45]

From the planters' perspective, so vital to Jamaica's plantation economy was the trade with the Spaniards that any interruption in it was tantamount to an economic crisis. When war with Spain from 1776 to 1783 endangered this trade, there were repeated requests to the English King to suspend the war so that trade with the Spanish islands could continue.[46] A report from a Committee of the House of Assembly appointed to enquire into the state of the island in 1799 and transmitted to the Duke of Portland found that a great cause of Jamaica's distress was the cessation of the livestock trade with Spanish America. According to the committee:

the foreign trade carried on in this island under the authority of the freeport act, in foreign vessels in peaceable times, afforded very considerable advantages, particularly by the importation of cattle and mules; the interruption of which, occasioned chiefly by war with Spain, has been the cause of a very great rise in the prices, by which the article of fresh beef has risen to more than double what it formerly was: the same rise has taken place in the price of mules, which are essentially necessary for the carrying on of the plantations.[47]

The request to the King to suspend his war with Spain was granted and the Spaniards were allowed to trade in their own ships. For the encouragement and protection of this trade, the commander-in-chief, directed by the British government, granted certificates or passports to Spaniards which they used from time to time in the free ports of the island. Unfortunately, in the nineteenth century, Spain confined its trade to bullion, cochineal, indigo and cotton and the exportation of manufactures imported from Great Britain which it then supplied to the Spanish colonies. Though Jamaicans welcomed the inflow of specie from this trade, they lamented the fact that 'since the late protection afforded them, the Spaniards have not imported any considerable number of cattle and mules. This trade has of late been considerably declined as the Spanish government has directed that it be curtailed.'[48]

The Committee recommended that greater efforts be made to settle poorer whites in the interior of the island to establish pens and thereby expand the penkeeping industry to meet the great demand for livestock on the island. Nevertheless, up to 1845, Jamaica's pens had not expanded sufficiently to satisfy this demand. Indeed, in 1845, though the USA and British plantations increased their share of this trade, 'foreign states' continued to dominate it. The only significant change was the shift in the monopoly of trade from the supply of mules to the supply of asses. These were presumably imported to improve breeds of horses in the island.

Conclusion

European colonialism and imperialism sought to fragment and partition the Caribbean into mutually exclusive linguistic zones and political garrisons, and to confine economic relationships to each colony and its respective metropole. The region became a theatre of war from the fifteenth to the nineteenth century as powers battled for terrain and political hegemony, snatching the control of the region from the indigenous peoples in the process. Sugar plantations became the *raison d'être* of the economic life of the majority of captured territories by the eighteenth century, and slavery the dominant mode of production. In an effort to reap maximum economic benefits from the sugar industry and to channel all profits to Europe, England, like France and Spain, formulated legislation to discourage or make illegal, inter-territorial or intra-Caribbean trade. Mercantilism became the ideology of trade and the English used the various Navigation Acts (the French the *le exclusif*), to govern colonial commercial relationships. In this scenario, the Atlantic became the centre of the international economy during slavery and the output of the Caribbean was destined more for external rather than internal markets in the region.

While from the fifteenth to the nineteenth century the constituent sections of the Atlantic World became more and more integrated into an expanding capitalist economy,[49] intra-regional economic and social links were never complete casualties of imperialism but occurred legally through treaties or free ports, or subversively through privateering and smuggling. Interestingly enough, European rivalry and the profitability of the sugar industry both assisted and impeded the maintenance of regional economic relationships. For example, the ideal nature of Antigua and Barbados for sugar cultivation reduced the space for, and interest in, the cultivation of crops other than sugar and necessitated the import of commodities like food and livestock from North America. In territories with a more varied topography and land that could not support cane, estates used up the most arable land for cane and showed a willingness to buy plantation inputs from within the territory. Jamaican planters, for example, maintained a vibrant trade with internal producers of livestock and food; or they sought these products from regional producers who could supply them at a cheaper cost. Therefore, while colonialism threatened regional economic and social links and shifted the lines of communication outside of the Americas, the needs of the sugar industry dictated that such intra-regional links could not be totally destabilized. If anything, the regional links that developed in the Americas, especially that section referred to by Philip Curtin as the South Atlantic System,[50] contributed to the development of the expanding capitalist economy of the larger Atlantic World. Although the colonies had ties to the Atlantic trading system, sending by far the largest volume of the commodities they produced to Europe, they also maintained ties with one another. Those with diversified economies and with goods without a market in Europe, sent supplies to colonies producing sugar for the export market. The colonial powers had tried to curtail the international market of Caribbean demand and supply, but as this paper has shown, their restrictive legislations were constantly contravened.

6

'Groundings' with Tacky (Takyi) on History, Heritage and Activism

Delivered at the Third Tacky (Takyi) Day Lecture, Claude Stuart Park, St. Mary, April 5, 2005

Dear Chief Takyi,[1]

I feel very privileged to have been asked to speak in your honour during a week that marks the 245th anniversary of the war you and your supporters fought in the interest of St. Mary and wider Jamaican freedom.[2] As a daughter of St. Mary, I am also proud to know that I am descended from ancestors who did not willingly accept their enslavement, but 'bawled out for justice' against chattel enslavement from the moment of capture to forced relocation on the island. You were all African soldiers fighting on arrival for your survival, and I join all gathered here in Claude Stuart Park to pay tribute to you.

Chief Tacky (Takyi), you would be pleased to know that your legacy of activism lives on in the many sons and daughters of St. Mary who each day try to make this parish, and by extension this island, a better place for all. The Planning Institute of Jamaica (PIOJ) says that the parish is more economically challenged than the other parishes in the island, but we know that it is unmatched in terms of the talent of its citizens and the potential that resides in its many young people, some gathered here today, looking 'trash and ready' in their school uniforms and costumes. Some of the costumes are African-inspired, an indication that the culture of the West African ancestors lives on. The parish has given birth to a multiethnic range of teachers, nurses, religious and civic leaders, lawyers, doctors, civil and public servants, sportsmen and women, politicians, businessmen and women, farmers, musicians, painters, craftspeople, skilled workers, singers, reggae artistes and deejays like the one Lady Saw. Who can ignore the 'firery' Capleton who always wants to 'bun down de place', figuratively

73

speaking of course, and the cool Beres Hammond. The entrepreneur Audrey Marks who a clean up di place wid Paymaster; the best comedian in the island, Oliver Samuels who has brought down the house with his many plays like 'Ras Noah and the Hawk' and 'Christopher Cum Bukus'; and the revolutionary mayor, self-confident son, Bobby Montaque, are other products of St. Mary. Of course, everyone knows of Antoinette Haughton, the lawyer, advocate, former talk show host and first woman to form a political party in the island — a strong St. Mary woman who is not afraid to tell it like it is.

You would also be pleased to know that the people of St. Mary have never forgotten you and your exemplary life of activism. Not only is there a monument to honour you and an annual ritual of commemoration to celebrate your work, but a school and a waterfall have been named after you. The monument in your honour stands defiant in a location that was once unwelcome to Black people: in front of the court house, the traditional symbol of oppression; beside the Anglican church that was the planters' church; in the churchyard burial site for the elite. In fact, it would amuse you to realize that your monument is located next to the tomb of the white planter, Charles Price. If he could, he would probably get up and run! For imagine being trampled on by a bunch of slave descendants! How times have changed.

But Tacky (Takyi), while the people of St. Mary have done all they can to keep your heroic struggles before the public gaze and to showcase your wonderful life of agency, the wider Jamaican society does not appear to appreciate your place in the island's history. If it did, you would have been declared a National Hero long ago. Look at what you and other Africans in St. Mary endured and accomplished! I will rehearse these for those who do not know or who are suffering from historical amnesia.

Against all odds, you fought for freedom from enslavement, not just for yourself but also for others. You endangered your life in the process, raiding Fort Haldane for weapons, drumming up support from estates like Esher, Ballards Valley, Trinity, Heywood Hall and elsewhere; you had to fight against the British military out in the open because the war escalated so quickly that you and your supporters barely had enough time to conceal yourselves within the tradition of guerilla warfare. Above all, you had to skillfully negotiate with the Maroons so they would not fight against you. Imagine getting the Maroons to pretend only to fight and pursue you and the rebels into the woods! They even returned with a collection of human ears, which they pretended to have cut off from the rebels they had slain in battle, instead of those who were already dead. And they duly collected their reward too![3] It took the declaration of Martial Law (April 10–12) and the cordoning off of the parish by various companies of troops to prevent the war from spreading further and becoming an islandwide revolution.

And while the number of casualties on each side will never be known with any certainty, we know the war took a heavy toll on your people, many of whom were killed in battle. Others chose suicide rather than surrender, some had to face execution by judicial order and still others were deported, some to the Bay of Honduras. But you and your troops also took out quite a few of the oppressors. The Governor is thought to have under reported the number of white casualties, admitting to just 16;[4] but a high of 40–60 were reported by contemporary writers.

Above all, you inspired others to carry on the fight long after you were gone. No sooner had martial law been lifted in St. Mary in mid-1760 than reports began to circulate once more of a rebellion in the parish as well as in St. Thomas-in-the-East. For there were still enslaved people in the area in which your rebellion had been so recently crushed in whom the fire of protest burned fiercely enough to inspire them to another attack. No sooner had the St. Mary and St. Thomas-in-the-East plots been revealed and quelled than a major revolt led by Damon and involving 1,000 rebels broke out in Westmoreland — on 'Whitsun Sunday' to be specific. Twelve whites were killed and martial law had to be proclaimed again on June 3, 1760 and was still in force in July 1760.[5] Troops had to be speedily dispatched to Westmoreland as well as to St. Elizabeth, Hanover and St. James. Joined by French Blacks from Guadeloupe,[6] protest also erupted around this time in St. Dorothy, St. Johns, again in St. Thomas-in-the-East, this time led by Kofi, and in Clarendon. It was around this time that Queen Cubah of Kingston was deported to Cuba for her role in the Kingston protests. She found herself back in Jamaica — in Hanover, where she was caught and hanged. Not until August could the English discontinue martial law; and even then this was later said to have been too optimistic as skirmishes continued down to November.

Undeterred by the brutal punishments of those caught rebelling, and with a plan to court Maroon support, the enslaved from 17 estates in St. Mary, including Whitehall, Frontier, Oxford and Tremolesworth, frightened white society again in 1765 in a war led by Blackwall, a ringleader in your war who had cleverly escaped punishment.[7] As in 1760, the main instigators were Coromantee headmen; and the signal fire started on November 29, on Whitehall estates. The whites from Whitehall were forced to flee, facilitating the enslaved in obtaining arms. Signal fires were lit on other estates and the rebels marched to Ballards Valley. Whites at Ballards Valley had barricaded themselves into the Great House and in an effort to smoke them out, one of the main leaders attempted to set fire to the roof. A white man from inside spotted him doing so and fired at him killing him. He fell on those below who were then thrown into disarray, as he was their leader. Whites took advantage of this confusion and ran out fully armed. This effectively crushed the rebellion involving leaders like Quamin and Blackwall. When it was all over, 13 enslaved had been executed and 33 deported.

Still your fellow enslaved never gave up. Wars of liberation broke out again in Westmoreland in 1766 and 1777 involving 33–45 Coromantees, in which 19 whites were killed and 33 blacks executed. Protest continued into the 1790s, spurred on by news of the revolt of enslaved people in Haiti. In fact, between 1792 and 1796, about 93 enslaved people who were considered dangerous were deported. The Second Maroon war broke out in 1796, followed by other instances of protest: in 1799 after which 1,000 enslaved were deported; 1803 in Kingston during which two enslaved men were executed; 1806 in St. George in which one enslaved was executed and five deported; 1808 and 1809 in Kingston; 1815 in St. Elizabeth led by enslaved Ibos, during which the leader was hanged at Black River.

In 1823, increased anti-slavery campaign in Britain was met in the island and region with even more intense rebellions. In fact, in that same year, a major war erupted in St. Mary. At a trial of enslaved people held near this very spot in December 1823, William, enslaved to Mr. Andrew

Roberts of Port Maria, revealed that his father, James Sterling, who worked on Frontier estate, told him that there had been a plot afoot 'to rise at the fall of Christmas 1823, and desired him to keep out of the way for fear of [him] being hurt, as it was the intention of the Negroes to begin to burn and destroy the houses, trash houses and estates; and when such fires took place, to murder all the inhabitants'. He reported that on two occasions, on going to see his father, he had noticed 'the Negroes assembled in large bodies near a bridge between Frontier estate and Port Maria, where he heard them speak of an intended rising and at that time they were flourishing their cutlasses, declaring that they would destroy all the white people'. Unfortunately, inadvertently, this young boy betrayed the plot. On December 15, in conversation with his master, he told him that he would have a bad Christmas and that if he wished to be safe it would be necessary for him to go on board ship as it would be useless for him to go either to the Fort [Haldane] or to any other house.

> Pressed to give the names of the ringleaders, he said he could only recall the following: James Sterling, Rodney Wellington, Charles Brown, a cooper and former head driver on Frontier, Morrice Henry, William Montgomery and Richard Cosley.

Two other enslaved men, Ned and Douglass belonging to Mr. James Walker, were interrogated on Williams's admitting that he saw them at one of the two meetings described above. Out of their trial came a confirmation of the plot to plan a parish-wide revolt on December 18, 1823. The first part of the plan was to burn Frontier's trash house and sugar works and to murder whites when they came to quench the fire. After that, they were supposed to begin at the top or east of the bay and set fire to the buildings, where a general massacre was to take place.

Williams's warning, plus reports of suspicious goings on among the enslaved at Tremolesworth and Nonsuch, set back the plans and led to the calling out of the troops and the militarization of the parish from December 16. Colonel Cox called out the Grenadiers, the Light Infantry, the Port Maria regiment, the Rio Nova and Bagnalls company, the Leeward Browns, the Oracabessa Company, the Third Batallion or Cross, the Jack's Bay company, the Windward Browns [Coloured regiment]. The captains at Fort Haldane were pressed into giving Marshal Hendricks 'every assistance in their power in making up the ball cartridges', a Troopers Guard was ordered stationed at Frontier and Gayle's estates and the Black Company was ordered to mount guard duty at the court house 'and remain until further order'. A detachment of troops was also requested from Stony Hill to be sent to Fort Haldane, especially after rumours came of a new outbreak on Oxford estate.

This rebellion led to trials and searches of the houses of the enslaved and ultimately to brutal punishment. Henry Cox, Colonel of the St. Mary Regiment admitted in a letter to W. Bullock dated December 20, 1823:[8] 'I have taken up, and issued orders for the capture of every Negro against whom there is the least suspicion and shall proceed to try all or any of them as soon as I think that I have enough evidence to convict them.'[9]

The ringleaders, or alleged ringleaders, were tried and punished brutally:

- James Sterling (hanged)
- Rodney Wellington (hanged)
- Charles Brown (hanged)
- Morrice Henry (hanged)
- William Montgomery (hanged)
- Richard Cosley (hanged)
- Charles Brown (Frontier, hanged)
- Charles Watson (Frontier, hanged)
- Henry Nibbs, enslaved to James Walker (hanged)

All the hangings took place on Christmas Eve 1823. Colonel Cox reported that the hangings had taken place,

with all due solemnity and decorum, attended by the custos and several magistrates, four companies of the St. Mary regiment and a troop of horse. [That] only one of the wretches confessed to the Rev. Mr. Girod that it was their intention to have burnt Frontier

78

Works and Port Maria and killed the whites; but none would
mention any other Negroes concerned with them or show any
symptoms of religion or repentance. They all declared they would
die like men and met their fate with perfect indifference; and one
laughed at the clergyman Mr. Cook when he attempted to exhort
him under the gallows.[10]

In all, 400 enslaved people were executed and 600 deported to the
Bay of Honduras, a much higher casualty rate than in the 1831–32
emancipation war.

Even so, plotting and resistance never stopped. St. James experienced
unrest from October 1823, based on reports coming from Kensington and
other estates. All reports indicated that the enslaved in St. James were
aware of the anti-slavery movement in England, drank to Wilberforce's
health and fully expected to get the news of their freedom soon. Plans were
afoot in St. James in fact to rebel in December 1823 if 'free paper did not
come' before then. The plot was discovered and the ringleaders deported.

But no sooner had that happened than news came from St. George in
January 1824 that plans were afoot — on a larger scale than in St. Mary in
1760, 1765 and 1823 for a rebellion. In that same year came news of the
Argyle war in Hanover in which Richard Hemmings (a free coloured); and
Richard Hanson were believed to have played a significant part.[11] As in
previous wars, Black Haitians were said to have been involved in many of
these 1820s wars; and those suspected of being ringleaders were deported.
Interestingly also — and significant for how we have been taught to view
the Maroons — in the 1824 Hanover war, A. Campbell of the Western
Interior Regiment informed William Bullock that from reports he obtained
'It appears that the Maroons of Accompong Town are the instigators of this
Rebellion and that the slaves of this vicinity are acting only a secondary
part.'[12]

The final battle for freedom erupted in St. James in 1831. The
revolutionary plan laid down by the leaders was that after the Christmas
holidays, when the call for work resumption came, the enslaved were to
demand the rights of free workers — wages — and to strike en masse if the

enslavers refused their demand. But the leader, Sam Sharpe, also had a back-up plan — armed revolt if there was any attempt by the plantocracy to force Blacks back to work as enslaved people after the Christmas holidays. When the rumour came that the Whites were planning to break the strike on the Salt Spring Estate in St. James, the plan to burn the properties was set in motion. Once started, the rebellion continued on its violent path until it was violently suppressed by the British military forces. When it was all over, the cost in lives and property was horrendous; so was the brutality of the suppression. Based on the official estimates some 619 rebels were killed — 307 in open rebellion and some 312 executed by the Slave Courts and the Courts Martial. By contrast, only 14 Whites were killed and 12 wounded. The official records also indicate that three free coloured men were killed and two wounded in the armed struggle. Fourteen free people were also tried and convicted for their role in the revolt (including a white man, a Mr. Ellery, and individuals described as 'brown').[13]

This is what you set in motion; you and others waged a 300-year war for liberation and the people of St. Mary should demand that you be made a National Hero.

We should go even further; our culture of individual heroization at times masks the contribution of the rank and file. Yet one hand cannot clap. How nice it would be to build a war memorial to all the others from the parish who fought for freedom and died for the cause but who are still unrecognized, including: Blackwall, Quamin, Charles Watson, James Sterling, Rodney Wellington, Charles Brown, Morrice Henry, William Montgomery, Richard Cosley, Ned and Douglass. Such a project should become part of a larger process of iconographic decolonization as the descendants of enslaved people attempt to map and re-map the postcolonial landscape, indigenizing it in keeping with a revisioned historical reality.

We know that you and the other ancestors will hold us to this project; otherwise the ghosts of slavery will continue to wander restlessly in search of a proper burial. Maybe we should agitate for such a memorial, at least for the 11 in 2007, the bicentenary year of the passing of the Slave Trade Abolition Act.

7

REVOLUTION AND POST REVOLUTION:
Re-Imaging and Rethinking Haiti

Delivered to staff at the Ministry of Foreign Affairs, Pretoria, South Africa, August 3, 2004

I take this opportunity to congratulate all South Africans on this 10th anniversary year of freedom. Indeed, the bicentenary of Haitian independence and South Africa's 10th anniversary of freedom are wonderful moments for celebration and must be commemorated no matter what other destabilizing forces are at work to defeat the hopes and expectations of old and emerging independent nations. It is fitting that these two events are being celebrated in the year designated by UNESCO the International Year for the Commemoration of the Struggles Against Slavery, and of the Abolition of Slavery, in honour of the Haitian Bicentenary; a year that has seen the intensification of the global vision of the African Union and the ideals of the African renaissance.

Haiti's anti-colonial struggles, its role in the American Freedom Movement; its rich cultural history and the potential of its vast human resources are not in the forefront of public discussions. Indeed, these issues have been submerged beneath the upheavals created by, what Haitian activist Lucie Tondreau tells me has been called, the 'Coup'dknapping' of Jean Bertrand Aristide on February 29, 2004. The events surrounding this event must of course be investigated. But at the same time, students of Haitian history must remind a world suffering from a convenient historical amnesia of the historical context of February 29. This is part of why I have joined my Haitian colleagues on this visit in my capacity as a Caribbean historian able to contextualize and historicize present regional developments. Indeed, one of the challenges that faces Haiti and other Caribbean states is how to correct the barrage of misinformation that circulates about us and that punctuates external discussions about us; how to redress the culture of colonial 'otherization' and revision that misconstrued, imagined history based on what literary scholar Veronica Gregg often describes as the developed world's 'willed ignorance'.[1]

It is no secret that each time Haiti appears on the news or forms the basis of public discussion, it is the negative images of political instability, violent colonial history, poverty, illiteracy, low life-expectancy, HIV/AIDS, thuggery and inadequate social infrastructure that form the illustrative backdrop for the discussion. As a Jamaican, I also know that my country is often associated in the overseas public's imagination as a land of sea, sand, sun, easy sex, reggae and gun violence — not that sea, sand, sun, sex and reggae are negative in and of themselves. It is the meanings assigned to these images that are problematic. Some documentaries on Jamaica shown abroad are full of these images; and I am aware that here in Africa, you are often asked quite silly questions by tourists about the architecture of your houses or the prevalence of dangerous animals in your cities. What I am trying to say is that part of the challenge of postcolonial societies, is how to correct the stereotypical representations laid down in an earlier age by those who prefer to trap us in the images of the past, and project our history through non-imperial lens.

I suggest that one of the best ways in which we can understand Haiti today and make suggestions about the way forward is to immerse ourselves in revisionist history, including cultural history, and address that challenge of public misinformation, 'otherization' and unequal partner in a globalizing world of partners that are not quite partners. This will not only provide us with the intellectual weapons to counter the historical misrepresentations, but will also help those of us who are struggling to understand the present crisis in Haiti with a better understanding of the present. I firmly believe that one cannot understand the present Haitian condition without locating present developments in their historical context. History education — not media representations (except those generated by revolutionary journalists) — is what we need to re-image Haiti in the public imagination and in the current postcolonial discourses.

As part of the project of intellectual preparation and knowledge acquisition, we should ensure, of course, that we understand that comparatively speaking within the Caribbean context, Haiti is not a small dot in the Caribbean sea; for it has a population of 8.3 million and a surface area of 27, 750 square kilometers. To you with your 45.3 million people and 1.2 m sq. km and to countries like France and the US, it is small of course. Nevertheless we should bear in mind that while small on a global scale, Haiti looms large in terms of its contribution to world history, not just Caribbean and African diasporic history. This is part of why all self-consciously patriotic Caribbean people resent the fact that Haiti is not usually glorified or represented in the global imagination as a country that initiated the project of freedom and racial equality in the modern world. The Revolution started by the Jamaican freedom fighter Boukman Dutty and carried on by Cecile Fatiman, Toussaint L'Overture, Christophe, Dessalines and others is not always written about as if it were a central feature of the Age of Revolutions in the eighteenth century; as a significant part of the period that 'shaped Western modernity and placed notions of liberty and equality at the center of political thought' as Sibylle Fischer notes, even admonishes.[2] It is sometimes just regarded as an offshoot of the French Revolution that supposedly gave it its ideological *raison d'être* and not kept sufficiently in the public imagination as the only eighteenth century revolution that centred the issue of racial equality.

On the contrary, the fear of the spread of so-called Haitian-style violence that marked the nineteenth-century discourses, the physical isolation of Haiti that took place after the declaration of its independence in 1804, the literary and historical representations, the centuries old media misrepresentations seem extended to the contemporary period and fixed in the public imagination. The tendency to see Haiti as a violent place without concern for human rights is perpetuated even by those countries that were primarily responsible, under past political regimes, for producing Caribbean societies 'where brutality combined with licentiousness, in ways unknown in Europe'.[3]

We need to remind ourselves, as Hilary Beckles invites us to do, that no other event in the history of the Americas demonstrates in the way the Haitian Revolution does, the tragic and heroic feature of the concomitant struggles against slavery and colonization. Haiti became the first place ever to end slavery through revolution and established itself as only the second independent state in the Americas in 1804. In ideological terms, its magnitude embraced the entire colonized world and its anti-slavery political successes were unprecedented. A generation earlier, revolutionaries in the North American colonies fought and won a war against British colonial rule — and Haitians helped to fight that war — but kept slavery as the socioeconomic basis of their so-called 'independent' dispensation.[4] They were forced to return to the battlefield a century later in order to resolve the problem of slavery with the politics of nation building. Haiti, not the North American colonies, led the anti-colonial struggle in the Americas to its highest level by insisting upon the inseparable unity of political freedom and social liberty.[5] Between 1791 and 1804 as C.L.R. James so brilliantly explains in the *Black Jacobins*, Haitians turned the Atlantic slave-based colonial complex upside down in its search for fundamental human rights. In the process, they broke the wealth and class/caste power of the Whites.[6]

We need to be aware that the present economic crisis in Haiti, and the impoverished state of the peasants and urban proletariat have masked the fact that Haiti was once called 'The Pearl of the Antilles' on account of its economic wealth and its value to France. In 1741–45 of the four larger islands in the Greater Antilles — Jamaica, Puerto Rico, Cuba and Hispaniola — Haiti and Jamaica accounted for 56.2 per cent of their combined sugar output. Indeed, in the latter part of the eighteenth century, Haiti was richer than all other European colonies in the Caribbean. On the eve of the enslaved-led revolution that resulted in the emancipation of the enslaved and the creation of the first black republic in the world, Haiti exceeded all other European colonies in the Caribbean in wealth and prosperity, supplying 30 per cent of the world's sugar needs, with export figures of 71,000 tonnes of sugar, 38,000 tonnes of coffee, and 3,500 tonnes of cotton.[7]

This wealth was created through the labour of thousands of enslaved people moved from Africa in a commercial traffic that was a project of France and other colonial powers. Philip Curtin estimates that just over 830,000 Africans were shipped to Haiti up to 1790.[8] The recent slave trade database by David Eltis and his colleagues indicates a total of 686, 601, with 50 per cent procured from Africa south of the equator. It is worth noting that only in Haiti did Africa south of the equator provide a half of all slave arrivals.

Table 7.1

The Trade in African Captives to Haiti

Number Embarked = 791,085 Number Disembarked = 686,601

Sources in Africa	Number Embarked	% of Total	% Less Unspecified
West Central Africa	333,358	42.10	47.90
Bight of Benin	188,028	23.80	27.00
Africa unspecified	95,117	12.00	--
Senegambia	47,661	6.02	6.85
Bight of Biafra	37,955	4.80	5.45
Gold Coast	30,303	3.83	4.35
SE Africa (Moçam)	26,933	3.40	3.87
Sierra Leone	23,570	2.98	3.39
Windward Coast	7,984	1.01	1.15

Source: David Eltis, et al., Slave Trade Database on CD Rom

1: The figs. in the Eltis CD represent two-thirds of the number of voyages on the transatlantic slave trade from the sixteenth to the nineteenth century

2: The dataset includes 27,233 voyages (of estimated 34,000)

3: Haiti accounted for over 2,000 voyages (in this sample)

4: From this dataset, South East Africa contributed 291,060 captives to the transatlantic slave trade (237,191 actually disembarked)

Table 7.2

Enslaved Africans from South East Africa who Disembarked in the Americas

TOTAL = 237,191 (Sample only in this table)

Where Disembarked	Total No.	% of Total	% Less Unspecified
SE Brazil	158,740	66.90	70.50
St. Domingue	21,640	9.12	9.61
Cuba	16,262	6.86	7.22
Not Specified	11,940	5.03	--
Rio de la Plata	7,599	3.20	3.37
Barbados	5,285	2.23	2.35
SE Africa (incl. Cape of Good Hope)	3,068	1.29	1.36
Pernambuco (Brazil)	2,696	1.14	1.20
Bahia (Brazil)	2,655	1.12	1.18
Virginia	1,098	0.46	0.49
Indian Ocean Islands	741	0.31	0.33
Martinique	641	0.27	0.28
Jamaica	543	0.23	0.24
Guadeloupe	244	0.10	0.11
New York	117	0.05	0.05
NE Brazil	137	0.06	0.06

Source: Slave Trade CD-ROM Database The tables show that Southern Africa and South East Africa were implicated in the slave trade, with large numbers of Yao from SE Africa arriving in the Caribbean.

Where Did This Wealth Go?

Before 1791, most of the wealth generated by enslaved labourers flowed into France, it was not used within Haiti for development. Indeed, the development of the plantation colonies of exploitation was not a part of the colonialist economic plan. In 1775, France received from Haiti 353 ships carrying tropical goods worth approximately four million pounds sterling, goods produced by the effective labour of 249,098 enslaved people who worked on 648 sugar plantations and other properties. C.L.R. James shows that by 1789, two-thirds of French maritime exports went to her colonies in the Caribbean. James attributed the rise of the maritime bourgeosie in Nantes, Marseilles and Bordeaux to the African and Caribbean trades. Dieppe and smaller towns, he argued, sprang up around colonial industries.[9]

This relationship between capitalism and slavery has long been established by Eric Williams who used empirical data from Britain and her Caribbean colonies to make a similar point as James. What has now come to be called the 'Williams thesis' is one of the most controversial theses in Caribbean and world historiography.[10]

The Social Cost of Economic Prosperity

There was of course a social cost to the material wealth of Haiti. Producing exportable quantities of tropical products, whether sugar, coffee, indigo, cotton, cacao or food crops, was an arduous task. Not only was the work arduous, but much brutality was experienced by the enslaved labourers as enslavers tried to extract maximum output from their labour. There was also a racialization of the society as Whites constructed a social hierarchy that placed them at the top, the mixed race in the middle, and enslaved Black people at the bottom. The social fabric of this project took shape after years of moulding; apparently as this was the only way Whites could live in it. They would coerce, using the Code Noir or Black Code of Louis XIV, and Blacks would labour under coercion. There were naturally internal conflicts arising out of the racialization of the society and the refusal of Black people to think of themselves in terms of 'slave', 'criminals', 'rebellious' et cetera. Blacks existed within the Atlantic World and if the White Atlantic would not accept them as Atlantic World citizens, they would claim that right through revolutionary means. In any event, they were not willing collaborators in the establishment of the racial contract or in the construction of the plantation economy model, a model imposed on Taino space using forced labour from Africa, that is, a pre-plantation Africa. Slavery was not the natural state of their existence. This is the context within which the revolution, involving close to two-thirds African (not Creole) enslaved people, broke out in 1791. The ideological basis was the belief that freedom, human rights and racial equality were just causes for which to fight.

The revolutionaries in 1791 struggled for the same rights as the French Jacobins and Jean Casimir notes, 'ignored altogether the tenets of Western philosophical anthropology' used to accord them a position as 'natural slaves'. The Africans could not separate themselves from the body of cultural knowledge and ethnic characteristics that defined them.[11]

The revolutionaries were successful in defeating Napoleon's army and the multinational force that was mobilized against what C.L.R. James calls the 'Black Jacobins'. Even though L'Overture, treacherously removed by France, died in that country eventually, France had to accept defeat. However, France and her allies have never forgotten Haiti who has had to pay dearly for daring to imagine and actualize freedom from racialized bondage. After 200 years of freedom this country with its proud history is still trapped in a cycle of poverty and political instability. Why?

The answer lies in the post-revolutionary history. There is general agreement that when freedom comes through revolutionary transformation, as opposed to gradual transitions, socioeconomic and political development in such a free society will take a radically different form. Coming out of this revolutionary tradition, Haitians inevitably had a radical vision of democracy; one based on the post-slavery ideology of freedom which to many was a peasant political ideology. Thus, as Mimi Sheller points out, 'in addition to the clear demand for full political participation and equal citizenship, it was an ideology that included an explicit critique of white [and even near white] racial domination and of the unbridled market capitalism that built a world system of slavery.'[12] Haiti has had the most developed proto-peasantry (and Maroon culture), perhaps rivaled only by Jamaica; therefore the pursuit of peasantry rather than a plantation-based agricultural economy, or even an industrial economy, was what the Haitians wanted. What scholars label a 'counter-plantation ideology' did not suit those who wanted Haiti incorporated into the international economy; into the international division of labour. Haitians wanted an alternative economic path, a redistribution of economic resources which meant of land, almost as reparation for years of enslavement and a future free of white (external) domination, according to Sheller who explores this 'subaltern political ideology' in her book. This counter-narrative to modernity — manifested in a retreat from accepted (liberal) democratic political systems (into their own peasant style democracy) — was not accepted outside of Haiti initially. Haitians did not wish to be defined as citizens only on paper. The challenge for the leaders was how to meet peasant political demands, maintain military democracy and create the infrastructure necessary to build and sustain a nation. Like Jamaica, Haiti had a strong autonomous peasant culture 'that stressed majority self-determination, popular sovereignty and broad and equal citizenship for all'.[13]

The biggest challenge was finding a way to construct a national order within which to implement the ideals the masses had fought for — liberty and popular freedom. The challenge of how to meet the material needs of the population; to ensure that the sacrifice of the lives of hundreds of thousands of Haitians, not to mention those disabled by war, would not be in vain. We therefore return to the question of what they were up against and how they coped. A few are highlighted below:

- They had to continue the fight in order to cement their independence even after they had secured emancipation in 1793. They realized that it was impossible to accommodate a revolutionary, anti-colonial position within a restructured French colonial authority. Their success was manifested in the fact that the state of Haiti was proclaimed at Gonaives on January 1, 1804 and the Taino name Haiti or Ayite adopted.

- They had to face a real economic fact: the war of independence and the revolution to end slavery had left the country in shambles. Many sections of the country had been destroyed by fire and throughout the country, sugar and coffee plantations, mills, ships, irrigation networks, wharfs and animals had been destroyed. As table 3 shows, compared to the 71,000 tonnes of sugar exported in 1789, only 15,000 were exported in 1959.

Table 7.3
Comparison of Exports from Haiti, 1789 and 1959 (tonnes)

YEAR	WORKERS	SUGAR	COFFEE	COTTON	SISAL	AREA
1789 (400,000 slaves)	400,000 slaves	24,000 (white), 47,000 (brown)	38,000	3,500		500,000 hectares
1959	560,000 peasant families	15,500	25,000	1,000	24,000	600,000– 700,000 hectares

Source: Claire de Bourg, 'Haitian Women at the Backbone of the Informal Economy' (Conference on 'Reinterpreting the Haitian Revolution and its Cultural Aftershocks, 1804–2004', University of the West Indies, St. Augustine, Trinidad, June 15–18, 2004). She mined some of these stats from Moral, Paul L'Economi Haïtienne

- They had to try to build a nation state out of this economic ruin while meeting the socioeconomic and political expectations of the Haitians.
- They had to face world hostility by their perceived anti-white stance. Article 12 of the 1805 constitution which replaced previous ones provided that 'no white person of whatever nationality may set foot on this territory in the role of master or proprietor nor in the future acquire any property here' ([reversed by the USA during their occupation of Haiti). Haitians were trying to construct a society out of their experience of white oppression. They made Black a political rather than a biological category and a category that defined all Haitians.

- They had to address the urgent issue of national security and maintain an army —an expensive enterprise on their resources —to protect their sovereignty and suppress counter-revolution. The French army, though driven from Haiti, remained garrisoned courtesy of Spain in neighbouring Santo Domingo. French loyalists were also still in the island. Many rulers in this period therefore reflected this concern over security.

How Justified Were Their Fears and How Did the Colonial Powers React?

From all accounts, the European fear that the liberation struggles in Haiti would have a ripple effect across the hemisphere and that Haitian revolutionaries would actively promote freedom struggles in other parts of the region, was a real one. Historian David Geggus confirms that rumours of Haitian revolutionary 'agents' circulated in the region, leading to restrictions on immigration from Haiti from 1792.[14] 'Gripped by fear of contagious slave uprising, Europeans articulated their claims to "whiteness" and "civility" in contradistinction to Haitian "barbarism" through a set of stories that can collectively be referred to as the "Haytian Fear".'[15] Certainly, developments in Haiti caused an intensification of the slave versus free state debate in the United States of America, especially after the Louisiana Purchase; and news carried by fleeing refugees to the US of black 'atrocities' against white transformed the fear of a potential increase in slave revolts to a real one. Several enslaved people's revolts in Charleston and North Carolina were attributable to the Haitian influence; and the fear of emancipation struggles led to the imposition of restrictive legislation to control Black mobility and the trade in Africans, especially from the Caribbean.

Additionally, the annexation of Santo Domingo, attempted as early as 1805, and the assistance given to Simón Bolívar under Alexandre Pétion's presidency (on the understanding that the emancipation of the enslaved in Venezuela would occur), all created tension among enslavers in the Americas. To compound the situation for Whites, the 44th article of the new Haitian constitution 'approved the settlement in Haiti of Africans, Indians and their descendants, thereby making Haiti a point of refuge for the enslaved of the Caribbean'.[16] No doubt this constitutional provision was met with alarm by the plantocracy, which stood to lose enslaved labourers through land and maritime marronage.

> French troops stationed in Jamaica were placed on parole in Kingston and Spanish Town and the lower ranks confined to prison ships in the harbour. Their presence, along with the presence of black Haitian labourers brought over with the refugees, served to worsen the security fears in the island. The Assembly reacted by legislating 'to prevent any intercourse or communication, between slaves of this Island and foreign slaves of a certain description and it gave the governor powers to round up all dangerous aliens unto prison ships, in which they could await deportation to New Orleans'.[17]

The journal of a Jamaican governor's wife, Lady Nugent, reflects this terrified consciousness of Whites very vividly. The news from Haiti always seemed to be the topic of discussion at dinner and at breakfast at King's House, and such news kept her in a constant state of agitation. She was at pains to record her moments of shock and terror at the news of violence in St. Domingue. For example, in her entry of November 22, 1801 she admitted that she was 'very much shocked in the evening, by a sad account of the massacre of three hundred and seventy white persons in St. Domingo. How dreadful, and what an example to this island'.[18] She was fearful of the impact that such mealtime conversations about Haiti might have on enslaved domestics who waited table and who were bound to relay the news to other enslaved people. For example, she lamented that

> the splendour of the black chiefs of St. Domingo, their superior strength, their firmness of character, and their living so much longer in these climates, and enjoying so much better health, are the common topics at dinner; and the blackies in attendance seem so much interested, that they hardly change a plate, or do anything but listen. How very imprudent and what must it all lead to![19]

Indeed, Lady Nugent and others became extra suspicious of black people in Jamaica after 1804. They saw impudence and lack of respect in every grin, every face, every failure to bow; every instance in which Blacks looked directly at them instead of looking down or away. On March 4, 1804 she wrote: 'Go to bed with a thousand apprehensions, and in low spirits. People here are so very impudent in their conversation.' On March 10, 1804: 'Drive to the King's House early. Call at several places, and surprise some of the staff, whose secret ménage was unknown to us before; but this is a sad, sad country.'[20] She recorded that in 1805, while taking her two children for a walk in Port Royal,

> we met a horrid looking black man, who passed us several times, without making any bow, although I recollected him as one of the boatmen of the canoe we used to go out in, before we had the Maria. He was then very humble, but tonight he only grinned, and gave us a sort of fierce look, that struck me with terror I could not shake off.

Her maid, Clifford, appeared to have fed her paranoia, thus: 'Clifford tells me that all black people know there is some alarm, but are ignorant of the cause of it, and most of them, it is to be feared, are ready for every sort of mischief.' But, with a marked ignorance of Caribbean history, she expressed faith in her own domestics: 'However, I feel confident in our own servants who all seem as anxious to secure the house, and to be as much afraid of depredators, as I am.'[21] Indeed, in a supreme act of confidence, Lady Nugent employed a black cook from Haiti.

As a result of the destabilizing impact of Haiti — at least in the language of the colonizers — many efforts were made to bring the country to its knees. It is within this context that Haiti understood that it had to have a pan-African policy in the Americas and have slavery eradicated from the Hemisphere. As long as slave colonies existed and fed the wealth of the Europeans, the latter would have a presence in the region and dictate foreign policies.

Although the colonial rulers did not regard Haiti as a good model of emancipation, the early Haitian leaders had to express and implement a clear political ideology and philosophy that centred non-racialized freedom hemispherically.

This did not free Haiti from economic woes. We only have to consider the matter of the debt; the 150 million gold francs debt imposed by France. On order to get France off its back, Haiti in 1825, under President Boyer's regime, agreed to pay France a high price for its freedom. That is, in exchange for recognizing Haitian independence and sovereignty, France demanded an indemnity of 150 million gold francs. The Haitians had to borrow money from a French bank to pay the first instalment. This debt, paid off only in 1947, crippled the Haitian economy. This is the basis of the reparation claim by President Aristide as he feels that this would be worth 21.7 billion dollars today and this would go a far way in helping Haiti's economic and social woes.

Haiti has also had to face political instability and US military invasion. Numerous presidents rose and fell as a result of popular or externally assisted staged revolutions. Few presidents have been allowed to serve out their terms, deposition, exile and murder being their usual fate. The USA occupied Haiti for 19 years between 1915 and 1934. They ended a long period of Black presidents, installing the coloured elite in power between 1915 and 1941. The US occupation deeply wounded the pride of Haitians and challenged their anti-plantation, anti-colonialist, anti-racist, anti-imperialist sentiments and beliefs. It marked the end of Haitian sovereignty, even the independence of the elites and they caused Haiti to become once more dependent on the international division of labour.

Haiti has had to face continued outside interference in its internal affairs, with a tendency to destabilize regimes that are not conservative enough; regimes that are labeled leftist, a carryover from the Cold War years. Economic sanctions have also had wide-ranging effects on the country. There are the continued class conflicts, which are racialized, with the elite and merchant classes reluctant to admit the masses into the political process and share economic resources with them, preferring to see them as units of labour that feed their lifestyles.

It was these characteristic features of the post-revolutionary and modern periods that generated forces that tended towards endemic economic inefficiency, social instability and political disorder — circumstances that did not help development according to the Western model. Internal and external capitalist interests, as my colleagues explain, would try to contort Haiti to fit this model.

Finally, based on my conversations with a few members of the media here and my reading of some of the opinions expressed in your newspapers, sections of the society are seemingly puzzled by the global attention to Haiti — a small, materially challenged country (by your standards), geographically far removed from South Africa. Many South Africans have asked: why should South Africa become involved in Haiti's affairs? Why should President Mbeki have gone thousands of miles across the Atlantic to be in Haiti for the bicentenary, especially when Heads of States closer to Haiti did not even bother to attend? Why should he have tied up so much of South Africa's resources on the trip and on the Haitian bicentenary? 'God knows, we have our own internal problems', many of you have said and I cannot pretend to have all the answers to your concerns, but permit me, by way of recap, to be so bold as to suggest a few. First, Haiti is an integral part of the African diaspora and should be integrated into the global vision of the African Union with its commitment to an African renaissance that includes the diaspora. Second, Haitians should be regarded as African brothers and sisters. On the eve of the enslaved-led revolution in 1791, two-thirds of the Black population in Haiti were born in Africa. Moreover, while West Africa and West Central Africa contributed the majority, close to one million, of African captives to the so-called 'slave trade' to Haiti, southern Africa, especially South East Africa, was also implicated. About 5.1 per cent of the slavers leaving Africa originated in South East Africa. Third, Haiti led the anti-colonial struggle from the eighteenth century, perhaps even from the moment of conquest — and had a developed pan-African ideology. All those who have ever been subjected to imperial exploitation, should feel a sense of solidarity with Haiti. Finally, Haitians, like many other Caribbean nationals, Jamaicans especially, never thought that the anti-apartheid struggle in South African was irrelevant to them; far removed from their interests.

8

'PETTICOAT REBELLION?':

Women in Emancipation in Colonial Jamaica[1]

Churches' Emancipation Lecture, St. Mary the Virgin Church, Molynes Road, Kingston, Sunday July 29, 2001

The presence of so many people here this afternoon to share in the celebration of 163 years of emancipation from enslavement testifies to the fact that our slavery past, and emancipation, are no longer the best-kept secrets in Jamaica. Of course, many still ask: What freedom? What emancipation? — conscious of the enduring legacies of slavery. Nevertheless, we have much to celebrate. For me, the road between Africa and this place has been a long one; and I am humbly aware that in reaching this place, I have benefited from the blood, sweat and tears of countless Black women and men who have paved the way and created a space for women like me. The names of the female ancestors are too numerous to mention; but before going any further, I must identify and salute some of them as a signal that when we speak about women who struggled for freedom from slavery and other forms of domination, we are not talking about mythical figures, but real people whose names and actions have been recorded in historical accounts: Nanny of the Maroons; Congo Sally, the persistent runaway from Breadnut Island Pen; Marcia, the persistent runaway from Cornwall estate; Whaunica, accused by the overseer of Cornwall estate of fomenting 'petticoat rebellions'; Minetta, the 15-year-old girl tried and sentenced for poisoning her enslaver; Phibbah who endured 33 years of sexploitation by Thomas Thistlewood; Mary-Ann Reid who was sentenced to hard labour in the workhouse for helping to plot the 1824 Hanover slave conspiracy; Susan and the other women of the crucial 1831 'Christmas Rebellion'; Caroline Grant, 'Queen of the Morant Bay Rebels'; Amy Jacques Garvey and Amy Bailey who pushed Black pride and supported the move for Universal Adult Suffrage; Aggie Bernard and other women of the 1930s Labour Rebellions; and Iris Collins, a representative of that group of women who pioneered women's participation in electoral politics in the modern period. I also wish to pay a special tribute to one who is still among us — Lucille Mathurin Mair — whose pioneer work on Caribbean women's history contributed so much to the project of educating us and freeing our minds from mental slavery.

This lecture focuses on women's activism and agency. One cannot speak about women in emancipation without detailing their activism and agency, which so subverted and destablized the slavery and colonial systems and eventually led to the granting of emancipation. Activism and agency are, of course, particularly relevant when speaking about ex-colonial societies where issues of freedom, human rights, citizenship and self-determination had to be settled by rebel men and women before the issues of feminism and women's rights could form a part of the national anti-colonial discourse. Indeed, modern-day women's movements and feminism cannot be understood without excavating and locating the prior waves of activism and theorizing on women's conditions dating back centuries. Long before 1857 in New York when female textile workers were fired upon by the army while demonstrating for a shorter work week, and 1977 when UNESCO proclaimed International Women's Day, rebel women in the Caribbean, as in other parts of the Americas, used a variety of strategies to eradicate or at least destabilize and subvert, systems of domination. It was in recognition of the fundamental contribution of women to the anti-slavery movement in Jamaica, for example, that the Maroon rebel woman, Nanny, was elevated to the status of a National Heroine. Today, Nanny does not simply reside in Maroon history; rather, she is the quintessential rebel woman and an embodiment of the spirit of Black women's resistance to systems of domination.

That women, in particular enslaved Black women, were a fundamental part of the struggle for freedom in colonial Jamaica and that resistance to enslavement was not the preserve of male rebels as was argued by the older scholarship, are no longer in doubt. Bernard Senior, a British military officer active in the suppression of the 1831 Christmas Rebellion in Jamaica, in describing instances of malingering, insolence and the attempt to enforce moral economy on several plantations, admitted that 'women as well as

96

men were alike defaulters'.[2] In addition, accounts of Jamaica in the eighteenth and nineteenth centuries testify to enslaved women's rebelliousness, some planters referring to them as female demons who thwarted the overseers in the field and accusing them of fomenting 'petticoat rebellion'. For example, on January 26, 1816, Matthew Gregory Lewis, proprietor of Cornwall estate in western Jamaica, made the following entry in his journal:

> Every morning my agent regales me with some fresh instance of insubordination. It seems this morning, the women, one and all, refused to carry away the trash, . . . and that without the slightest pretence: in consequence, the mill was obliged to be stopped; and when the driver on that station insisted on their doing their duty, a little fierce young devil, a Miss Whaunica, flew at his throat, and endeavoured to strangle him: the agent was obliged to be called in, and at length, this petticoat rebellion was subdued.[3]

What the rather sexist Lewis referred to as 'petticoat rebellion', arguably a metaphor for enslaved women's resistance, was not, of course, confined to Cornwall estate but was a standard feature of the slave system in colonial Jamaica, as indeed it was in the wider British-colonized Caribbean. Furthermore, even though the term 'petticoat rebellion' may have been used by early nineteenth-century planters as a way of peripheralizing women's resistance, later developments proved how wrong they were to do so. Women may not have always been in the vanguard of armed revolts, but their day-to-day strategies clearly bothered enslavers and their supporters and ultimately so undermined the efficiency of the plantation that they played a key role in the abolition of slavery, defying the suggestion of harmless 'petticoat rebels'.

As historian Hilary Beckles asks in his path-breaking book, *Centering Woman*, 'what is the political significance of an argument which says that physical combat in war should be privileged above broad-based ideological preparation?' Why should non-violent day-to-day strategies be marginalized and men's leadership of armed revolts centred as being more important?[4]

In addition to evidence of women's contribution to the freedom project in contemporary historical narratives like Lewis's and Senior's, modern scholars like Lucille Mathurin Mair, Linnette Vassell and Hilary Beckles, who have made women and gender analysis central to the historical discourse, have contributed much to our knowledge and understanding of women's participation in emancipation. They have not only studied emancipation from slavery, but also emancipation from systems of domination in the post-slavery and postcolonial periods.[5] They have provided us with heroines; strong Black women from whom we are descended, whose values and ideals we should continue to emulate.

Despite continued cynicism about the legitimacy of gender-specific history, these and other scholars, attempting to compensate for past discursive shortsightedness, have emphasized that there was no homogeneous slave experience and that analyses of the conditions of enslaved people, and indeed of the society influenced by the slave system, must take gender differentiation into consideration. As part of this project of differentiation, they have embarked on studies of the gender specificity of slave control and the struggles of the enslaved for freedom, showing that while the struggles of the slavery period were inherently collective, in that they were conceived in the consciousness of slave communities, the gender relations of slavery determined actions in many ways. Thus, the ideology of anti-slavery was not gender free.

These scholars, among others, have shown conclusively that Black women were to be found in all aspects of the anti-slavery movement. As non-violent protestors, as strategists in armed revolts, as Maroons, as leaders in areas of social culture, and as mothers, Black women were critical to the forging of resistance strategies; and their diverse freedom strategies functioned at the core of community survivalist culture. Such evidence now provides a counter-discourse to the racist and sexist assumptions of planters and other contemporary writers who argued that enslaved women accommodated themselves more easily than enslaved men to slavery, and often reaped social and economic benefits from the slave system.

Absent Voices, Ventriloquized Voices

The fact that so-called 'petticoat rebellion' was such a central feature of the Jamaican slave system should come as no surprise, given the central features of colonialism. Admittedly, we do not have access to the direct voices and written views of those who tried to liberate themselves. Instead, we have to tap second-hand sources that represent their voices. The problems and pitfalls of ventriloquizing the Black experience and subjecting such experiences to a kind of disfiguring gaze are well-known.[6] But finding enslaved women's written views is a very difficult task. Texts generated by enslaved peoples in the Caribbean do exist; for despite the endemic anti-intellectual culture bred by slavery, many Africans wrote important treatises, dictated autobiographical accounts, presented critical oral testimony to Commissions of Inquiry, and made arrangements for the recording and publication of a wide body of opinions which form an important part of the Caribbean literary tradition. However, unlike other Caribbean territories where letters written by enslaved women and texts based on the narratives of enslaved people have come to light,[7] Jamaica has yet to discover similar detailed letters and texts. In order for us to access for Jamaica the voices of enslaved women, we therefore have no choice but to mine contemporary historical and literary texts, newspapers, reports of Commissions of Enquiries, records of trials of enslaved people and court records generally. Skeptical as we may be about their authenticity and the basis of their authority, we have little choice but to accept these sources as they allow us to make some progress towards discovering how enslaved women participated in the project of emancipation.

These second-hand sources indicate first of all that slavery and colonialism provided enough justification for women's resistance. Caribbean history, like that of other former colonized spaces, has been characterized by imperial domination and by systems of exploitation which have inevitably generated an opposing struggle for liberation. Beginning with Spain in the fifteenth century, six European nations proceeded to impose structural discontinuities upon indigenous Caribbean societies, to import and subjugate White servants from Europe after they had decimated the

Taino and Kalinago peoples, and to kidnap, transport across the Atlantic and enslave millions of Africans. Among these African captives were Igbo, Akan/Aja, Coromantee, Congo, Papaw, Chamba and other peoples from diverse regions of West Africa.[8] Quantitative studies reveal that over the period of the illegal trade to Jamaica, 1655–1807, the dominant sources of captives were (in order of numerical importance), The Bight of Biafra, the Gold Coast, Central Africa, the Bight of Benin, Sierra Leone and Senegambia,[9] reinforcing recent views that the Igbo presence in Jamaica became stronger after the seventeenth century. Indeed, in the years 1792–1807, an estimated 49 per cent of enslaved Africans captured and shipped to Jamaica comprised ethnic groups from the Bight of Biafra, with Central Africa (35 per cent) being the next in significance.[10]

The majority of these enslaved Africans were male. Despite regional variations (with a significantly high proportion of women exported from the Bight of Biafra or, what is today, south-east Nigeria), overall less than 40 per cent of enslaved African captives were female (compared to over 60 per cent in the trade to Muslim areas[11]). In the period 1658–1713, enslaved males made up 78.1 per cent of captives to Jamaica from Senegambia; 58 per cent from the Gold Coast; 61.7 per cent from the Bight of Benin; 51.2 per cent from the Bight of Biafra and 60.9 per cent from West Central Africa.[12]

More Cause for Resistance: The Abuse of Women's Bodies in the Field

Once located in the Caribbean, enslaved women were subjected to various forms of exploitation that led them to launch an opposing struggle for liberation. For example, despite the sexual disparity in the illegal trade in African captives, women outnumbered men in the field gangs where the most arduous work was done. Women weeded, planted, harvested, worked in the sugar factories (where many lost fingers while feeding cane into the mill), and generally contributed to the productive processes on sugar plantations. They laboured in the great houses as domestics and nursed the sick in the hot houses. Men had a wider range of tasks. In the complex and hierarchical division of labour that existed on large plantations, men were valued for craftsmanship or work in the semi-industrial processes of the sugar mill. As field labourers (and as domestics and concubines) their bodies became the site of power contestation. Plantation labour placed great physical strains on enslaved women; and any infraction of the slave codes or the law of the Black slave-driver was followed by severe beatings and other forms of physical abuse of the enslaved female's body.

Sexploitation

In addition to the abuse of their bodies through arduous physical field régime and severe whipping, enslaved women were open to sexploitation — to a far greater degree than enslaved men. Neither colonial statutes nor slave codes invested enslaved women with any rights over their own bodies, but rather, transferred and consolidated such rights within the legal person of the enslavers.[13] Male enslavers claimed violent access to enslaved women's bodies and male and female enslavers to the sale of enslaved women's bodies for money upon the sex market. Not only did laws not allow the enslaved to refuse sexual demands made by their enslavers, but they allowed for the punishment of those who did not acquiesce.

One example of a habitual white rapist was the Englishman, Thomas Thistlewood, who owned and managed properties in Western Jamaica. We know about him because he left detailed journals (over 10,000 pages) that reveal that he sexually abused practically every enslaved female located on Vineyard pen, Breadnut Island pen and Egypt sugar plantation during the years 1751–1786. Betty, Chrissey, Hago, Juba, Marina, Phibbah and Sylvia were among those he raped. He claimed Phibbah as his mistress for 33 years, but never remained faithful to her and she was never freed during his lifetime.[14]

Thistlewood was not alone. In 1824, Robert Wedderburn, a freed man from Jamaica who eventually emigrated to England, underscored the abuse of enslaved domestic women owned by his Scottish father, James Wedderburn:

101

My father's house was full of female slaves, all objects of his lust;
amongst whom he Strutted like Solomon in his grand seraglio or
like a bantam cock upon his own dunghill. . . . By him my mother
[Rossanna] was made the object of his brutal lust.

Robert Wedderburn also confirmed the practice of organized
prostitution, noting that: 'a planter letting out his prettiest female slaves
for purposes of lust, is by no means uncommon.'[15] Organized prostitution
was particularly noted in urban centres where the majority of Black women
were owned by female enslavers who profited from enslaved women's bodies
by using them as domestic labourers and prostitutes.

While some women and their children were freed as a result of their
sexual links with empowered white men, many others continued to exist
within the context of unequal power relations. Cyrus Francis Perkins
captured this historical reality in fictional form. Catherine, ostensibly the
overseer Jackson's slave 'wife', knew that his frequent promises to free her
were empty. Thus,

it not today I hear the story talk of you buying me. S'pose you
goin' buy me like Jack Mowatt buy Sally . . . buy him when him
please an' sell him when he get tired of him. If you caan even buy
me, you can buy de baby? If you get discharge 'spose I am to hand
over to de nex Busha whether I like him or hate him.[16]

The Road to Emancipation: The Body in Resistance

Exploitation in the fields and factories and sexploitation in enslavers'
households provided the context for women's emancipation struggles. There
is overwhelming evidence that enslaved women did not willingly give up
their bodies for reproduction or productive labour; neither did they passively
accept White men using them. They used a variety of strategies to subvert
the slavery system and liberate their bodies from brutal forms of enslavement,
most of these are now common knowledge: malingering, lying, 'stealing',
poisoning, self-purchase and running away. Marronnage was a common
form of removing the body from the site of oppression and the records are

full of examples. Nanny, of course, is now accepted as the quintessential rebel Maroon woman. But there were others. Abigail, Mary and Congo Sally would not be confined to his property despite Thistlewood's attempts and severe punishment. Sally, in particular, in whom Thistlewood had a sexual interest, was a strong, survivalist character who ran away constantly despite the difficulty of the post-1739 Maroon Treaty environment in Western Jamaica.

As a result of the fact that their bodies were targeted in the enslavers' efforts to control them, enslaved women used their bodies, in addition to their voices and minds, in the emancipation project. They did so despite the physical consequences (some gender-specific), of such actions: floggings (such as those administered by Thomas Thistlewood to Mimba, Juba, Cynthia, Jenny and Deborah for theft of supplies on his pen); rape (as manifested in the actions of Thistlewood and James Wedderburn); hanging, transportation out of the island, imprisonment, branding with hot irons, gibbeting and dismemberment.

Women used body language to register their discontent with slavery. Cynric Williams, on his tour of Jamaica in 1823 tells us that among a party of enslaved people who were brought before the magistrate for misdemeanours was 'one damsel in particular who in her defense said she had been harshly used, on one occasion getting 230 lashings at one flogging'. As the magistrate doubted her story, 'the sable nymph without hesitation exposed her behind, whereupon there was no mark whatever; and it appearing that she had so done in derision and contempt, they ordered her a couple dozen'.[17]

The Voice in Resistance

Enslaved women raised their voices in liberation songs and used their voices to curse those who bought them at slave auctions or oppressed them generally. We learn from Mary Gaunt, author of the novel *Harmony*, that Maria, wrongfully enslaved and shipped to Jamaica and bought by a St. Ann enslaver, resisted both the Middle Passage and her sale. Gaunt writes of the way in which Maria used her tongue and body language to abuse her purchaser and his colleague and register her views about the injustice of her capture, shipment and auction. Speaking for her, Gaunt writes that Maria 'faced the two men [Thole and Ridley] and called them every vile name she could lay her tongue to; looked them up and down, noted their weak points [such as baldness] and gave them the benefit of her observation aloud'.[18] Williams also reported that after being lashed by the driver, an unnamed Black woman on an estate he visited, looked over her shoulder and said in a suppressed tone, but loud enough to be heard 'Go to hell' and walked off.[19]

Women petitioned attorneys to get unpopular or particularly harsh overseers dismissed and they also went on strike in order to force compliance with their wishes. Strikes were also resorted to when customary allowances such as time to work provision grounds and go to the markets were reduced or withheld. The enslaved understood that negotiation for some measure of economic autonomy was not only a way of surviving enslavement, but also of asserting their power as workers on whom the productive activities of the sugar plantation and other properties depended. Thus the enslaved practised forms of collective bargaining traditionally associated only with industrial wage workers.[20] Domestic women also found various ways to harass and frustrate their female enslavers. Such activities were not confined to the large estates, but were equally noted on pens and coffee farms.

'Gynaecological Resistance?'

After 1807, when the transatlantic trade in enslaved African captives was abolished, enslaved women's bodies became more crucial to the reproduction of the enslaved population and thus to the perpetuation of slavery. Armed with this knowledge, enslaved women sought to free their previously enchained wombs, refusing to bear children who would themselves be enslaved. Several enslavers attested to the use of abortive agents and the reluctance of enslaved women to bear children. Thistlewood recorded that enslaved females deliberately tried to abort their pregnancies by drinking various herbs. Mountain Lucy, for example, drank 'contrayerva' to abort her pregnancy.[21] Matthew Gregory Lewis confirmed the trend of gynaecological resistance, commenting, 'I really believe that the negresses can produce children at pleasure; and where they are barren, it is just as hens will frequently not lay eggs on ship-board, because they do not like their situation.'[22]

Bodies in Motion: Resisting Sexual Abuse

Women, whether kept by White men as mistresses or not, resisted sexual abuse even though there were no laws to protect them from sexploitation. As Beckles observes, a close reading of Thistlewood's journals reveals that Phibbah was not easily seduced. Even though her 'relationship' with Thistlewood lasted for over three decades, she tried to maintain some autonomy over these years. Thistlewood's diaries contain evidence that Phibbah, even after being his 'wife', disregarded his overtures on occasions. On February 2, 1754, he wrote: 'Phibbah did not speak to me all day.' On Friday of the same week he wrote: 'Phibbah denied me.' As time went on and the 'relationship' matured, she complained of his infidelity and withheld her affection periodically.

In *Busha's Mistress*, (which is not as fictional as it might seem as the author at one time worked on the estate on which the novel is set), Perkins tells us that the overseer of Greenside estate in Trelawny, Jackson, tried to punish Mary-Ann because the latter refused his advances. Mary-Ann complained that 'Busha persecute me all de time', even putting her in the stocks, because she did not encourage him. Catherine upped and left Jackson, 'her' busha when she learnt of his interest in Mary-Ann, making sure to check with the attorney that Jackson could not 'mek I lib wid him against me wishes'. Jackson's entreaties for her to return 'home' were met with a philosophical retort from Catherine:

Home? Home! Has a slave any home? He is here today and there tomorrow. He is sen' to work any property Trustee please, an' praps seld if young Massa owe money. Look at me sister Sarah! Me eber see him since de day Marshall put handcuff on him an' drag him off de estate? An' didn't eberybody Say Mr Hines was a rich man? De grave is de home for such as we.[23]

The Road to Emancipation

Armed Revolt

Armed revolt was more infrequent than day-to-day strategies as a form of resistance, and when it occurred, comparatively few of the enslaved participated in it. When they did, both men and women created the culture of open rebellion that characterized the world of slavery. Despite the tendency to name armed rebellions according to their identifiable male leaders — Sam Sharpe Rebellion, Tacky's Rebellion, and so on — enslaved women, as did rank and file enslaved men, played active, though it would appear gender-specific, roles. Enslaved women in Jamaica were involved in the plots and violent rebellions of 1673, 1690, 1760 and 1824. Mary-Ann Reid is the most important female figure implicated in the 1824 slave conspiracy located in Hanover. She used her house as a regular dance venue; for while overt political meetings of the enslaved were banned, dances were not. Mary-Ann used her dances as political meetings to plan revolts. Whites attended such dances but, as historians have noted, Black and White clearly danced to the beat of different drums. The plot was betrayed by an enslaved man; and the conspirators were all tried and sentenced. Gender differences in the punishments were marked. In 'consideration of her sex', Mary-Ann was imprisoned for four months at hard labour; the men were deported.

In the 1831 'Christmas Rebellion' that has come to be intimately associated with one of its outstanding leaders, Sam Sharpe, women's roles have been recorded by contemporary observers. Enslaved men and women from pens and plantations in the parishes of Trelawny and St. James had apparently agreed that any attempt to force them back to work after the Christmas holidays was to be met by setting fire to the properties (though not their huts or provision grounds). After reports were heard that Whites were attempting to break the strike on Salt Spring Estate, the enslaved man John Dunbar set fire to the proprietor's house on Kensington. This triggered off arguably the most decisive rebellion on the road to emancipation in Jamaica and the British-colonized Caribbean.

Bernard Senior outlined three telling instances of female involvement in this armed struggle. First, at the height of the rebellion in western Jamaica, soldiers from the St. Elizabeth and Westmoreland Regiments on the look-out for rebels, encountered an old, lame, enslaved woman surrounded by numerous iron pots of provisions. Questioned about her activity, she claimed that she and other women were supposed to have been fixing breakfast for the rebels in a nearby camp. However the rebels fled to a location unknown to her as they received news that regiments were close to the camp. As her lame feet would not allow her to descend the steep passes to escape, she had made up her mind to stay put and deliver herself up to the 'bukras for pardon'.[24] The soldiers, however, became suspicious at the way in which, despite her alleged lameness, the old woman moved among the pots, stirring each in turn. It turned out that, as a trap for the military, each pot of food was poisoned; for it was hoped that they would be persuaded to consume it. Neither threats nor promises could induce the old woman to eat any of the food, reinforcing the soldiers' suspicions that the food was indeed poisoned.

Second, although a captain's detachment was posted in the vicinity of the provision grounds on Stracy plantation, an enslaved woman named Susan, who wore an apron with the words 'My heart is fixed/I cannot change/I love my choice/ too well to range,' acted as a guide for a foraging party. Most of the party escaped with provisions, and only Susan and two enslaved men were caught.[25]

Third, a party of soldiers tracking down rebels who had taken 15 White women captive, captured a young Black woman who had, upon hearing the soldiers approach, abandoned her task of filling five gourds with water when she heard them approach. According to Senior, the enslaved woman 'pleaded great penitence, acknowledging that she had long ago left her owner's service, without leave or cause, but (having been out so long) denied any knowledge of the insurrection'. She did admit though that she had heard that as soon as the Baptist parson returned from England, all the enslaved would be free. But she left the plantation because she thought there would be no harm in taking her freedom a little before the time appointed.[26] Asked why one person needed so much water, she explained that she was living in the woods by herself and that she was washing all her clothes that day and wished to carry plenty of water at once for the purpose. One of the soldiers decided that she was lying and commanded her to lead them to where the rebels were keeping the captives. She proceeded to do that — or so the soldiers thought. She was in fact leading them away from the camp. But unfortunately for her this was soon discovered; for one of the soldiers noticed that she carefully avoided every heavily travelled path, and invariably took those newly cut and little used. After going a 100 yards or so past a path with its entrance blocked with newly cut logwood branches (which the woman had passed without so much as a glance), one of the soldiers insisted that he heard voices at a little distance in the wood.

According to Senior, 'she affirmed that it was quite impossible, as she knew every track in the neighbourhood, and the logwood had been cut by herself and placed there to prevent stray cattle from destroying her small provision ground, which they had latterly been in the habit of doing.'[27] The soldiers proceeded further for a short distance, but eventually became suspicious and decided to return and explore the barricaded path they had passed. They also confronted the enslaved woman, accusing her of lying and held a gun to her head to force her to confess. She immediately fell on her knees, acknowledged that she belonged to a strong party of well-armed rebels and that what she had been doing was conducting them to the rebel retreat. She was confident that such a small group of white soldiers would have been easily killed by the slave rebels before they could retreat. At that precise moment of discovery, the soldiers were within a quarter mile of the rebels. She also admitted that the barricaded entrance led to where 15 white women were being held hostage.

What seems clear from these anecdotal accounts is that there was a gender-division of roles during some armed revolts. While enslaved men led the armed, military assaults in 1831–32, women played non-military, supportive roles. Strategic manoeuvring was assigned to the women: supplying water, acting as guides to provision grounds; helping to guard captives; poisoning; acting as lookouts; even as a go-between in the final stage of the rebellion. It was Gardner's wife, for example, who was sent to approach the British lieutenant to inform him that Gardner wanted to give himself up, once he could negotiate terms for his life.[28] On livestock farms involved in the rebellion, women cooked food for the bands of rebels who stopped there for revictualling purposes. There was a division of roles among the men also. 'Daddy Ruler', Sam Sharpe was clearly in charge overall; but, according to Senior, '[Colonel] Gardner took charge of all military movements; and being well acquainted with the characters of his juniors, knew well how to appropriate the squads.' Those in his 'squad' included 'Captain' Dove, M'Cail, M'Lenan, Trail, Largie, Haughton, Hurlock, Peterkin, Simpson, Bernard, and many other unsung, rank and file heroes.[29]

Enslaved men and women thus worked together in this final rebellion before the passage of the Emancipation Act in 1833. By 1832, the writing was on the wall: if emancipation did not come from above, it would come from below from the resistant activities of the subaltern.

Not Two Types of Labour at the Same Time!

In addition to contributing to emancipation through their resistant activities, enslaved women contributed to freedom in two other ways. First, the abolition of the transatlantic trade in enslaved African captives in 1807 placed the British enslavers in a difficult position. They could not import fresh workers, though they could and did move around those they had internally.[30] Their only hope was to get enslaved women to reproduce and we already know that some of the women would not agree to this. Assuming that the women would cooperate and have children, how could enslavers possibly deploy female labour in such a way as to encourage both reproduction and production? How could they ensure that women would perform both forms of 'labour' at the same time? This was a difficult position. Women were the backbone of the field activities, anti-slavery forces were clamouring for emancipation and the enslaved were fighting for freedom. One solution was to improve or ameliorate the conditions of women in the fertile age group. This would mean scaling down the back-breaking gang labour for these women who also were in the most economically productive age group. In the end, it was clear that gender would affect emancipation:

for labour and reproduction, though both needed at the same time, were clearly incompatible. To remove women from the fields would affect production severely and to keep them in the field for production, thus making reproduction difficult, would be to doom slavery anyway. Women's power to hasten emancipation was clear.

Gender in the British Anti-Slavery Campaign: Feminist Sensitivity

Second, as the anti-slavery movement gained momentum after 1807 and promoted its ideas by focusing on the exploitation of Black women, the moral authority of enslavers came under intense scrutiny.[31] Radical White women highlighted the condition of Black women and agitated for their freedom. They presented graphic evidence of women's exploitation that served to align radical women in Britain with the emancipation cause and helped to step up the pressure for complete abolition.

Free at Last?

Black men and women played fundamental roles in their own liberation from slavery and enslaved Black women presented slave society with its principal feminist opposition. Enslaved men and women appropriated and acted on the idea that, as forced colonial subjects, they had a stake in the Enlightenment project of human progress. The slave system made them 'rebel women' and 'natural rebels' and produced among them only one kind of organized radicalism that is recognizable within modern political thought — anti-slavery struggle. Despite the unquestionable importance of economic forces[32] and political reform; despite the claims, in my view mostly exaggerated, of humanitarian (for example, church and missionary) activism as a factor in emancipation, it is now generally accepted by historians that sustained anti-slavery struggle on the ground, not the vigour of the British anti-slavery movement, sealed the issue of abolition. The enslaved gave the British government little choice but to respond with legislative emancipation in 1833.

The passage of the Emancipation Act in 1833 did not end systems of domination. Consequently, women's activism in the cause of unambiguous freedom continued in the period 1834–38. Along with their male counterparts they protested the introduction of the transition period of neo-slavery, euphemistically called the Apprenticeship System, scheduled to last until 1838 for field workers and 1840 for others. Thomas Holt observed that the predominance of women among the leaders and activists during the Apprenticeship years was especially ironic, given that the emancipation law was conceived and written in an unreflectively masculine gender.[33] Yet, as under slavery, women comprised a disproportionate share of apprenticed field workers and it should come as no surprise that women offered the most militant resistance to the Apprenticeship System.[34] Many women refused to work in the non-compulsory hours allowed under the Apprenticeship System even though wages were offered. Some sought to buy themselves out of the Apprenticeship System, while others still participated in violent and non-violent protests (such as strikes),[35] disrupted production as much as they could, brought numerous complaints to the Stipendiary Magistrates who were to act as mediators between former enslavers and apprentices, and used their bodies and voices to register discontent with plantation management.

Holt reports that after some male apprentices on Belvedere Estate were sentenced to prison and were being led away, a 70-year-old woman, 'with the most violent language and impassioned gestures' called upon the other apprentices to prevent the police from taking her three children, who were among the prisoners, to the workhouse. Violence erupted as the workers tried to do just that.[36]

Eventually, the methods used to control women — the treadmills in the houses of correction — created such a furore that once again the plight of women was placed at the centre of anti-slavery activism in England and added to the calls for the immediate end of Apprenticeship. 'Full Free' was finally conceded in 1838.

Women's Activism in the Post-Slavery and Postcolonial Period

Interpretations of freed people's expectations of the new order reveal that the emancipated hoped that the coming of freedom would provide the opportunity for them to take full control of their own lives and lay a new base for the society. They had hoped to realize the revolutionary potential of the legislation to abolish slavery by extending those social, cultural and economic values and institutions which they had cultivated zealously during slavery, particularly those relating to land acquisition and the re-interpretation of African–Christian cosmology.[37] Their revolutionary ideology and programme were clearly anchored in their experience and in their sense of what had become, as Rex Nettleford often terms it, a derided and emasculated ancestral culture. In addition, Black working-class women made it clear that they had no intention of conforming to the Victorian gender order and the gender systems of the new era that sought to confine women to the private sphere of uncompensated labour in the home.

Former enslavers and their imperial support groups had a different perception of post-slavery society and the free order. They had little interest in radically transforming Caribbean society. Thus the authoritarian society of slavery and oligarchic power continued into post-slavery society. Along with their imperial ally, they sought ways to diminish the potential for radical transformation and curb the freedom of Blacks by retaining control of government. Thus, the role of labour as a factor of production within the economics of emancipation and the rights and expectations of labourers as 'citizens' within the politics of freedom proved contradictory and pitched freed people and ex-enslavers in a battle for terrain. In this regard, the legacies of planter mentalities proved the obstacle to Caribbean freedom and continue to do so. The revolutionary potential of land acquisition, for example, was too much for the power holders to contemplate. While they were quite willing to encourage Indian indentured immigrants — initially imported to undermine the bargaining power of freed people — to settle by giving them land in lieu of repatriation (though we should be in no doubt about the conditions of such land for these exploited workers),[38] landholders tried to impede the development of the Black peasantry.

Redistribution of economic resources like land would threaten the social relations of production and the ideological arrangement of post-slavery society.[39]

The inequities of post-slavery Jamaican society ensured that the descendants of enslaved peoples would continue the struggle for complete emancipation; emancipation not just as an event, but as a condition of human progress. Protest action, the most notable being the 1865 Morant Bay Rebellion, was widespread in the post-1838 period and was attributable to the failure of post-slavery regimes to deliver on the promise of freedom by honouring freed people's claims to citizenship, civil rights and political enfranchisement. While the Morant Bay Rebellion has been associated with Paul Bogle and George William Gordon, women also played crucial roles, for example organizing many of Paul Bogle's meetings. Wilmot tells us that Caroline Grant was referred to by a policeman at Morant Bay as 'a queen of the rebels', while Grant and Sarah Johnson ordered fleeing men to return to the scene of action. Elizabeth Taylor even beat Joseph Williams when he tried to run away.[40] Additionally, as Clinton Hutton tells us, women like Caroline Grant, Sarah Johnson and Ann Thompson raided police stations for guns and ammunition; and Elizabeth Taylor, mobilized support for the cause. It also seems that it was a woman who started the violence by throwing the first stone at the constable.[41]

Radical women joined their male colleagues in the decolonization movement that intensified after 1865. After the brutal suppression of the Morant Bay Rebellion, the state reacted by removing the elective principle in government and installing the Crown Colony system of government. The ruling elite believed that the potential for radical transformation would be diminished considerably once measures to curb the freedom of African-Caribbeans by retaining control of the government were effected. But, despite their optimism protest action, far from decreasing, escalated after 1865. Indeed, the decolonization movement intensified by the 1940s, fueled by the radical ideology of the Pan-Africanist, Marcus Garvey.

Despite the association of the Caribbean labour movement of the 1930s, the franchise movement of the 1940s and the independence struggles of the 1960s with men like Alexander Bustamante and Norman Manley, women were very much involved. Amy Jacques Garvey, Amy Bailey and Una Marson lobbied for Universal Adult Suffrage. Catherine McKenzie, Amy Jacques Garvey and Eulalie Domingo lobbied for Black self-determination. Gladys Longbridge (or Lady Bustamante as she is popularly known), Aggie Bernard, Edna Manley and others supported protesters during the 1930s labour protests across the region, with Edna Manley joining Aggie Bernard and Adina Spencer to feed the rebels.

Women supported the movement for the legalization of trade unions and rejoiced when that was achieved after the labour protests. They joined the unions as rank and file members and a few, like Edith Nelson and Gladys Longbridge held important executive positions. The introduction of (restricted) female suffrage in 1919 and Universal Adult Suffrage in 1944 also represented a major victory for Jamaican women, the majority of whom had been denied the vote on the basis of gender before 1919. Women of all classes and ethnicities exercised their franchise in the first elections held after Universal Adult Suffrage was achieved. Women like Mary Morris Knibb, Iris Collins, Edith Dalton James, Rose Leon (1919–1999), Rebecca (Rose) Williams also contested local and general elections before 1962 defying the political culture and gender conventions of the day.[42] When the attempt to create a Federation of the West Indies collapsed in the late 1950s, women were among those who lobbied for independence. The fact that some female politicians did not necessarily lobby for feminist issues should not detract from their pioneering roles. Since the achievement of political independence in August 1962, Jamaican women have continued their political activism as voters, party workers and representatives in Parliament, Cabinet, Senate and Local Government.

Challenges of the Modern Political Order

Today, Jamaican women, as the majority of registered voters possess the potential to influence elections, though as a minority in Parliament their ability to influence legislation in favour of women might be limited. This under-representation of women in government is a global phenomenon. Statistics published in May 2001 reveal that in 178 countries surveyed, women form just 13.7 per cent of members of government in both Upper and Lower Houses. That means that out of 40,819 Members of Parliament and Senators, women members total 5,388. Predictably, their representation is just slightly higher in Lower than in Upper Houses, 13.8 per cent and 13.1 per cent respectively. Among Caribbean States, Cuba leads the way, followed by Grenada, Dominica, Guyana, Suriname, the Dominican Republic, The Bahamas, Jamaica, and St. Kitts and Nevis (which tie at 46th on the world scale along with Israel and San Marino).[43]

Perhaps one of the biggest struggles for women in the postcolonial period was for the true emancipation of women from unequal power relations and gender discrimination at all levels of the society. All of the English-speaking Caribbean territories inherited a common legacy from the colonizers of a gender system that dichotomized public and private, work and family, and sought to confine women to the private sphere of uncompensated labour. Where women struggled against this Victorian gender order and entered the labour force, they were affected by the sex-typing of jobs and the paying of gender-discriminatory wages. The lack of formal education and skills training also handicapped women's economic and social advancement. These and other aspects of postcolonial Jamaican society that adversely affected women were targeted by individual women as well as Women's Organizations. Before 1975 Women's Organizations were mainly concerned with social welfare issues. Women like Nellie Latrielle (of the Women's Social Service Club) and Amy Beckford Bailey were long among those contributing to social welfare issues.[44]

Since 1975 and the declaration of the Decade for Women, the attention has been on the issue of equality. Thus many women and Women's Organizations have become involved in the International Women's Movement and have lobbied employers and governments for the establishment of women-oriented governmental machinery, for the removal of gender-discriminatory practices and legislation; for the introduction of gender-sensitive legislation such as maternity leave with pay; for the increase of minimum wage for domestic workers, the majority of whom are female and for the increase of opportunities and resources to improve the conditions of women. Academic feminists like Lucille Mathurin Mair pioneered research on women's history, paving the way for the acceptance of gender analysis as a central tool of historical investigation at the tertiary level. The Women and Development Unit and later the Centre for Gender and Development Studies represented the initiative and energy of women who wish to ensure that a regional institution of the importance of the University of the West Indies should make a contribution to the promotion of women's development programmes. They aim also to provide research data that will help to promote awareness of women's condition.[45]

Although we can be justly proud of the role that Jamaican women have played in the emancipation and larger liberation struggles of the colonial period which ended in independence in 1962, and in the struggle for rights and true citizenship in the postcolonial period, women of the present era should not feel that activism is a thing of the past. I am conscious of the fact that we are living in an age of individualism; but I believe that we have a collective responsibility to continue to be vigilant about aspects of our social infrastructure, political culture, justice system, crime fighting strategies, tourist culture and economic climate that we find unacceptable to civil society. The high unemployment rate among women (22.9 per cent in October 1999, compared to 10.5 per cent for men),[46] a literacy rate of 79.9 per cent (according to preliminary 1999 figures), the high murder rate and the constant infringement of human rights in our country are four areas of immediate concern. As are the high rate of incarceration of Black men; the violence perpetrated by and against young Black men; the rate at which young males drop out of school and the formal educational system. If men are right that some of these phenomena are the fault of a gender system that places unrealistic expectations on their earning ability and values them only for their economic worth, then we must be concerned as mothers, spouses, friends and sisters.

In addition, not even the most patriotic of us would deny that we have yet to create a postcolonial society in which there is tolerance for differences in religious beliefs, political affiliation and sexual orientation; a society in which there is complete respect for the human rights claims of every citizen; a society in which we have expunged discrimination on the basis of race, class, colour, gender and place of residence; a society in which we have freed ourselves completely from that mental slavery to which Marcus Garvey referred in 1937 and which was later popularized in song by Bob Marley. Indeed, after 163 years of 'Full Free', references to slavery and the ideologies and legacies of slavery are constantly used to frame and contextualize public debates and discussions among Jamaicans, as indeed they are within the wider Atlantic World. And though the descendants of enslaved people now occupy the highest political offices in Caribbean societies radically transformed by the slavery and post-slavery struggles for freedom and justice, the 'up from slavery' concept in public life is strong and indicates that there is a strong opinion that the process of emancipation is not complete. It would, thus, almost seem as if the attempts in the period of modernity to bring about a level of well-being within social formations and to create human rights communities in former slave colonies have failed.

We only have to pay attention to the social commentary in the lyrics of our musical artistes, listen to the concerns of some of those who call in to the radio talk show programmes, read the daily newspapers, watch the nightly newscasts, visit some of our tourist centres and understand the political critique captured in the newspaper cartoons to understand that the legacy of slavery debate lives on over a century and a half after 1838. This 'legacy of slavery' model is used to explain many phenomena in current Jamaican society, from skin bleaching and patriarchal ideologies and practices to the content of educational curricula, policing, the treatment of the poor, and the political culture. It was perhaps the capture and forced transportation to St. Elizabeth of 35 of Montego Bay's street people 'by phantom people in the dead of night' in July 1999 that brought this 'legacy of slavery' debate most sharply into focus in our country. People used various terms to describe the unforgivable action, but all made comparisons with one aspect of slavery or the other. It was characterized as operation 'get tough' by one cartoonist in the *Daily Observer's* official Emancipation Day edition, who, like the Prime Minister, P.J. Patterson, pointed to the irony of this happening so close to the celebration of Emancipation Day.[47] Jamaica Labour Party leader Edward Seaga went even further, invoking the image of the 'Middle Passage', saying that the act was 'reminiscent of the way men and women were captured in Africa, bound in chains and transported 3,000 miles away to lands unknown'.[48] A comparison which also appeared in the cartoons.

There is now the need for women of the present era to join with men and align themselves to a project of true emancipation; emancipation as a condition of human progress and not just as an event of 1838, momentous as that was. Otherwise, the legacy of slavery debate will continue to frame public discussions for some time to come and true emancipation will continue to elude us. I think that aligning ourselves to a project of full and complete emancipation from the negative legacies, mentalities and actions of the slavery and immediate postcolonial periods will be the greatest tribute that we can pay to all the men and women who fought so hard to liberate us from all systems of domination. Finally, let us honour and continue to build on the legacy of these rebel women. Let us continue the emancipation project, fixing what is to be fixed and living as truly emancipated people; so that we can say to one of the phenomenal women — perhaps Nanny — in the not too distant future (perhaps in a language more representative of Nanny's multilingual environment):[49]

Nanny mi dear,

Yuh woulda proud fi know say yuh struggle fi freedom from slavery was not in vain. Neither was de struggle of de odder man and ooman dem wey tek up wey yuh did lef off. Britain was mus an' boun fi pass de Abolition Act in 1833. Yuh is National Heroine now, an' yuh even de pon wi money. Dem try hard fi limit wi freedom after slavery en' wid Apprenticeship, Crown Colony Government an' all kinda tings, but, yuh know Jamaican people, especially de Black ooman dem. Eben afta Morant Bay an' de hanging of Bogle an' Gordon, wi neva tap protes'; till wi get de right fi organize wiself inna trade union, de right fi vote, an' di right fi rule wiself. Wi independent now and all ooman have de rite fi vote fi who dem want. An' dem can run fi election ef dem want. Wi have wi owna flag wid black, green and gold colours. One time de black inna di flag did stand fi hardship but some a wi quarrel bout dat so til dem had wus to change it and mek black stand fi sinting more empowaring fi Black people. De British rule dat yuh fight so hard fi get rid of end now. Yuh woulda pleasen fi know sey nobaddy no haffi pledge allegiance to Queen Elizabeth II and har heirs and successors dem (dat is, Prince Charles, Prince Harry, Prince William an' de res a dem) like firs' time.

Wi mek plenty more progress. Almost ebreybaddy now edicated — 99 per cent literacy! One time more ooman an' gal pickney dan man an bwoy pickney coulda read and write; and plenty more ooman dan man use to go a UWee. But now a nuh suh. An' wi pay de teacha dem good, good money suh till America caan entice dem wid dollas again. Wi nuh need Jamal again and yuh wouldna meet pickney again who sey dem gradiate fram school but caan read wey de cerfiticate sey. We 'tap pay some people indecent salaries and odder people pittance. An' nobaddy nuh lib inna house whey favour slave shacks again.

We have good road (even wey a no tourist area and even when a nuh near election time). You would even fin' Nanny Town easy, easy. We have nice and well-staffed haspitals (not like de hothouses ah fi yu time) and de nurses dem get destant pay. De govament pass laws wey protec' all a de people dem inna de country regardless of colour, creed or race. No more oppressive slave code, chile. An' we can walk any wey inna Kingston wey we waan walk and vote fi anybaddy wi waan vote fah an a no nutten. No more barriers and garrisons. An' decent people nuh haffi lack up inna dem 'ouse like prisoner, for police an' solja have de resources dem need fi fight crime an' voilence and so de criminals dem haffi chill. An' any solja ar police whey pass dem place and brutalize any a wi haffi look out! Nobaddy caan dis wi justice system again an' call it de injustice system.

We have telephone inna ebrey nook and cranny a de country now — C&W, Digicel an' nuff odder CEL! No more conch shell fi tell people a wah a happen!! An nobaddy no depen' pon donkey and mule fe go whey dem a go. Nuff people have caar and de bus system good, good. We nuh look like Middle Passage Charter inna de bus dem again. An plenty taxi dey bout. Not to mention de nice railway service. Wi can pick, choose and refuse how wi waan fi get bout. Wen we reach work now we nuh look like wi jus done fight war.

Tings change fi ooman in plenty ways. One time a man dem did dominate de wider sociecty at de level of palitiks, economic powa, in the traditional 'igh clas' professions, and in public leadership positions.[50] Now, plenty ooman inna de House of Representatives, Senate and Cabinet and occupy tap positions in eberey area of society. Half a de people dem inna govament a ooman now — not de little 15 per cent of 2001; and ooman a head a political party now. De man dem a do alright too an' yuh no hear no more talk 'bout male marginalization.

An' yuh nuh hear people a sing ar talk bout 'mental slavery' and di 'legacy of slavery' as much as one time. Nuff backward attitude to race and colour change too. Yuh memba how de mulatto, mustee and quintroon ooman dem in your time used to get betta treatment over Black ooman like yuh? Well, chile, all Black ooman proud a we colour now and nobady nah bleach again. Yuh wouldna haffi bleach fi enter beauty contest now, Nanny!! We nuh treat browning betta dan odder colour ooman again. An' who waan wear chiny bump and braids free. An' wi have nuff good scholars now wey a write bout ooman; not like de old time one dem who used to say Black ooman caan 'tick to one man at a time, neva tek motherhood seriously and nuh contribute nutten to development. Some a di scholars dem go out inna de schools ar write tex' book so dat de pickney dem will get a better idea of dem 'istory. Nanny, ef yuh eva see wey some a de sexist and racist 'istorians used to write! Dem misedicate di pickney dem yuh see and use edikation as a form of social control! But all dat change now. Wi have we own people dem a write book and mos' a dem (not all) different from de old guard. An pickney learn odder tings than famine and disease 'bout Africa; for we nuh just show whey CNN an' de BBC show bout Africa. We TV station dem du dem own research and show de pickney dem sey Africa ah nuh backward bush. An de more CNN and BBC show violence inna Jamaica, de more we TV station dem show de tribal war inna USA, Englan' and de odder faren places.

People still leaving Jamdown fi go lib abraad; but a nuh becausen sey Jamdown no nice. A odder reason. Dere wus a time when we woulda haffi ask yuh sey ef yuh tink sey yuh, Clash, Cudjoe and Tacky dem did see bullet yuh shoulda tink again. You woulda need more than dat private receptacle fi ketch dem! For we used to kill off wi one anodder like sey life a nuh nutten —espricially de poor. Wi nah kill off wi one a nodder like first time an' you woulda nebba see anodder Braeton 7 case again! An' ef yuh mentally challenged an' escape from de nice hospital dem wey yuh suppose fi inna and go lie dung pan de street corner inna tourist area, nobaddy wouldna scrape yuh up and dash yuh wey. Responsible people woulda come and put yuh back wey yuh can get treatment. Ef anybaddy pass dem place an go trouble de street people dem, Dr Carolyn Gomes and Jamaicans for Justice woulda mek dem go up!

Best of all, all a wi a tek more responsibility fi we action now — even de people dem inna govament an odder 'igh places. Nuh more: me a blak road far de gully full a rubbish an de drain blak up widout tinking about a who did trow de rubbish iina de gully inna di fus place. Nuh more: sacrificing pickney school fee and book fi bashment clothes. Nuh more: 'it wasn't me' as Shaggy used to sey. Nuh more: a globalization, a structural adjustment, a re-engineering, ah de tourist dem whey nah come nuff, nuff again, a de ooman dem, a de man dem, a di indisciplined people — a eberybaddy and eberyting else — but a no me. Bestest of all, emancipation and slavery are no longer the best kept secrets in Jamaica dat dem used to be. Emancipation a Big, Big ting and everybaddy tek part inna big public events. Ah nuh ongle de church dem an' poor JCDC a struggle fi bring de event to people's attention. We have big, big sign fi mark de place inna Spanish town wey de emancipation proclamation did read; an all a de free village dem have sign. An wi nuh fraid fi tell tourist people dem bout slavery — like wi fraid sey it will spoil dem haliday an mek dem feel guilty bout whey odder white people did do. An we show dem more dan Great House — de scene of de crime of slavery. De tourist board put sign on every estate whey tourist visit fi show dem which part de enslaved people dem did lib and wuk. An we now lib like truly emancipated people; free from mental slavery and proud a we colour, heritage and multilingual facility.

Far-fetched? Maybe so. Maybe not. But let us see how, working together, we can come as close as possible to these ideals before it is too late. We need to be mindful of the late Peter Tosh's cautionary lyrics that there can be no peace without justice; equal rights and justice. Justice and peace are both attainable.

*I dedicate this lecture to Lucille Mathurin Mair, scholar and activist who directed much of her energy towards recuperating the voice and experience of enslaved Black women in the Caribbean, and whose work has provided inspiration.

9

'BESIDE EVERY SUCCESSFUL MAN'
The Unsung Activists of the 1831–1832 Emancipation War in Jamaica

Keynote Address, Institute for the Study of Slavery (ISOS) Conference, University of Nottingham, September 8–9, 2003. Also delivered as the Emancipation Lecture, Calvary Baptist Church, Montego Bay, July 2003

This year, 2003, is significant for the history of slavery as it marks the 170th anniversary of the passing of the Emancipation Act in the British-colonized Caribbean. For this reason, I have chosen to focus my lecture on the 1831–32 Emancipation War in Jamaica, arguably the most important anti-slavery war in the British-colonized Caribbean, and a recognized factor triggering the passing of the British Emancipation Act in 1833, barely a year after the brutal suppression of the war. So significant was this war, variously known in Caribbean historiography as the Baptist War, the Christmas Rebellion and the Sam Sharpe Rebellion, that a petition from magistrates and others in the parish of St. George and presented to the Jamaica House of Assembly in 1832 described it as one 'unparalleled in the history of the colony, whether for depth of design or the extent of misery and ruin which it has entailed on the inhabitants'.[1]

Several scholars including Michael Craton, Mary Turner, Barry Gaspar, Sam Reid and Hilary Beckles[2] have already applied their research efforts to the detailed study of the causes, course and consequences of the 1831–32 Emancipation War in Jamaica. While not repeating those ample studies, I will make use of them as I rehearse and summarize the main outlines in an attempt to set the context for the perspective to be discussed. Essentially, this lecture has three objectives. First, it seeks to continue the project of exposing the roles of the unsung male activists who worked alongside Sam Sharpe, the acknowledged hero of the war, in the cause of Caribbean freedom but who have either been ignored or make only fragmentary appearances in the published accounts. Unlike Samuel Sharpe, now one of Jamaica's National Heroes, none of these other men involved in the planning and execution of the revolt have been accorded the status of heroes and their voices remain submerged in the historiography. Turner for example, refers to Sam Sharpe and his aides and names seven of them, (Craton names approximately twice that number) but does not quote from the testimonies. Turner in fact only allows the missionaries who interviewed them to speak. Craton does a little better, using three short extracts from slave testimonies. The naming of the rebellion in the majority of the accounts as the Sam Sharpe Rebellion is in keeping with the historiographical trend to link anti-slavery wars or other social protest movements with an individual hero, giving rise also to the designations 'Bussa's Rebellion' in Barbados, 'Tacky's Rebellion' in Jamaica and 'Kofi's Rebellion' in Berbice. Similarly, in the USA, Gabriel Prosser, Nat Turner and Denmark Vessey have been identified as heroes of three nineteenth-century revolts. The post-slavery historiography continues the trend, associating men like Paul Bogle, Alexander Bustamante, Norman Manley, Grantley Adams, Antonio Soberanis and Arthur Cipriani with the long decolonization struggle. Heroes feature prominently in Caribbean history because of the need for role models, because resistance and revolt are such central characteristics of the Caribbean historical experience and because the ability of Caribbean people to shape their destiny through their agency is a topic highlighted in the various history curricula.

My second objective is to highlight the female activists of 1831–32. That women were involved in the 1831–32 Emancipation War should come as no surprise as evidence abounds that enslaved women did not willingly accept their enslavement; they had an anti-slavery stance and their activism at times took gender-specific forms.[3] Indeed, scholars like Lucille Mathurin Mair, Hilary Beckles, Barbara Bush, Stella Dadzie[4] and others have shown conclusively that Black women were to be found in all aspects of the anti-slavery movement. As non-violent protestors, as strategists in armed revolts, as Maroons, as leaders in areas of social culture, and as mothers, Black women were critical to the forging of resistance strategies. However, while historians like Mair, Beckles, Bush, Brathwaite[5] and others have acknowledged that women were essential to the liberation struggles during slavery, with Craton drawing attention to the numbers of women on the 1832 punishment list, very little detailed analysis has been applied to women's role in this particular Emancipation War; and the published accounts rarely record the names of the female activists. In fact, this absence of names; this tendency to fail to identify and give personality to enslaved women is a perennial problem in Caribbean historiography. Historians have written much about Nanny of the Jamaican Maroons; Queen Cubah of Kingston and Nanny Grigg of the 1816 Emancipation War in Barbados; but very few other names have emerged. Yet there were countless others like Mary-Ann Reid who was sentenced to hard labour in the Workhouse for helping to plot the 1824 revolt in Hanover, Jamaica; Whaunica, accused by Monk Lewis of fomenting 'petticoat rebellions' on his Jamaican plantation; Bina, Charlotte, Eliza Lawrence, Kitty Scarlett, Ann Guy, Becky, Jenny, Susan and many others — all female activists in the 1831–32 Emancipation War.

Additionally, like the unsung male activists these unsung female activists, equally submerged within the historiography, are not accorded the role of heroines of that momentous event. As in the conquest, colonization and decolonization discourses where heroes are all male, in the treatment of resistance and revolts, women appear equally trapped in, and influenced by, a hegemonic gender-power relation of patriarchy.

The third objective of this lecture is to use, more extensively than has been done in the past, the testimonies of those condemned and convicted for their role in the 1831–32 Emancipation War as a way of re-voicing the Black experience; re-voicing because the sources that exist have largely summarized these voices instead of allowing them to speak for themselves. This project of re-voicing slides seamlessly into the objectives of the Text and Testimony Collective (TTC) under whose auspices I have been collecting data on this particular Emancipation War. The aim of the TTC is to find the voices of the 'subaltern' and allow these voices to speak as much as possible. Of course, the confessions, testimonies and trial evidence used are not unaffected by the intervention of scribes — missionary, military or court personnel — who may be said to have ventriloquized the voices of those giving testimony, determining the parts of such testimonies that they wanted to bring to light. The problems and pitfalls of ventriloquizing the Black experience, the speaking subjects who do not speak freely as one writer puts it,[6] have of course been very widely discussed. Nevertheless, skeptical as we may be about their authenticity and the source of their authority, these ventriloquized 'voices' may allow us to make some progress towards discovering the experiences of the enslaved activists in this emancipation war. Indeed the testimonies throw light on issues such as gender roles, organizational structure, successes, failures and the brutality of the suppression. And like historical novels and other literary sources crafted by creative writers who use their imagination to provide data on those who left no memoirs in the conventional sense, they are no less trustworthy than the so-called 'objective archival sources', themselves representations, or if you prefer misrepresentations, by which historians swear. In the end are they not equally sources on which we rely for imagining what transpired in the past? At the very least, they fall into the genre of the neo-slave narrative so aptly discussed by Ashraf Rushdy.[7] For like her novels, they mostly 'assume the form, adopt the conventions and take on the first-person voice of the slave narrative' as we have come to know them.[8]

The confessions, testimonies and trial evidence are even more valuable as finding enslaved men's and women's written views about Caribbean slavery is a very difficult task. Admittedly, we have available to us texts generated by enslaved peoples in the Caribbean. The enslaved not only fought back, but wrote and spoke back as part of an ontological positioning with colonialism that placed slavery under their literary gaze, thus contributing greatly to the broad based Atlantic anti-slavery literature. The enslaved understood and critiqued the dominant European scientific and intellectual dogma on the subject of race and slavery and contributed to a counter-discourse that defeated enslavers' claim that they were beneath and indifferent to the intellectual discourses that surrounded them. Despite the endemic anti-intellectual culture bred by slavery, many Africans wrote important treatises, dictated autobiographical accounts, presented critical oral testimony to Commissions of Inquiry, and made arrangements for the recording and publication of a wide body of opinions, some with overt political intentions, which form an important part of the Caribbean literary tradition. But such conventional slave narratives are rare for Jamaica and so we must use these neo-slave narratives as alternatives. Whether accepted as slave narratives or neo-slave narratives, such narrative sources, uncovered through an ongoing literary archaeology, are not just mere shadows of a bygone past or 'ghosts of slavery' according to Jenny Sharpe's formulation,[9] but signposts to the future. They act as clues to how in the postmodern world we can deal with the legacies of slavery and rescue Sharpe's 'Ghosts of Slavery' from an improper burial.

Historical Context and Background

Before exploring the tripartite objectives in greater detail, I wish to rehearse the main outlines of the 1831–32 Emancipation War. Briefly, this war of enslaved people and their free supporters in Jamaica started on the night of Tuesday December 27, 1831. On that night, an enslaved man, John Dunbar, set fire to Kensington Pen in St. James. The torching of this property, situated at a high elevation, was intended to send a signal to rebels on other properties to join the protest. Indeed, from the data available, it would appear that the chief organizers had numbered these properties in the order in which fires of rebellion were to be lit. Thus Kensington was first, Blue Hole estate second and Leogan third. The proprietor of Kensington, John Henry Morris, also a lieutenant in the troop of the parish of St. James, barely escaped the conflagration.

The objective of the war was quite clear based on the testimonies of the freedom fighters. This extract from the testimony of William Binham demonstrates: 'The Baptists all believe that they are to be freed; they say the Lord and the King have given them free, but the white gentlemen in Jamaica keep it back; they said if they did not fight for freedom they would never get it. I heard them all say this.'[10] John Henry Morris echoed Binham's views when questioned after the suppression:

Q: Can you state any matter or thing relating to, touching, or concerning the cause of the late rebellion among the slaves in this island[?]

A: My opinion of the cause of the rebellion is, that it proceeded from the mistaken idea of the slaves that they were free, and from the proceedings of the British government

The revolutionary plan laid down by the leaders was that after the Christmas holidays when the call for work resumption came, the enslaved were to demand the rights of free workers, that is, wages and to strike en masse if the enslavers refused their demand. This was a legitimate strategy given the declining enslaved population, the end of the trade in Africans and the declining plantation economy. They also had a back-up plan: armed revolt if there was any attempt by the plantocracy to force Blacks back to work as enslaved people after the Christmas holidays. To gain widescale acceptance and support for their impending plan, the inner circle used their positions and relative freedom on the estates as members of the 'slave elite' to influence others among the enslaved population. Political discontent also found expression in religious meetings, dances and leisure activities, and the Sunday marketing network.[11]

When the rumour came that the enslavers were planning to break the strike on the Salt Spring Estate in St. James, the plan to burn the properties was set in motion. The attack was swift and uncompromising. In the end, the torching of the estates prematurely set off the rebellion before the mass strike action could take effect. Once started, however, the war continued on its violent path until its even more violent suppression by the British military forces. The ensuing war, lasting from December 27, 1831 to January 1832, involved close to 60,000 men and women, the majority enslaved, from 300 plantations, pens, rural settlements and urban holdings and engulfed not only the parish of St. James but also spread to Trelawny, Westmoreland, Hanover, Manchester, St. Elizabeth and as far away from the centre of the rebellion as Portland, St. Thomas-in-the-Vale and St. Thomas-in-the-East.[12]

When it was all over, the cost in lives and property was horrendous; so was the brutality of the suppression. Damage to property (which was calculated to include the loss of enslaved people through death, imprisonment or transportation) was estimated at over £1.1 million, most of this in St. James, totaling close to £½ million. The punishment of the activists was savage. The colonial army and the paramilitary forces unleashed a 'reign of terror' on the rebels. The arbitrary hanging of enslaved people, mostly men, and the burning of their property were widescale. There was no mechanism in place to distinguish insurgents from 'law abiding slaves' caught up in the war; and execution was based on phenotype affinity. The local militias shot many of the activists on sight before the authorities could institute the trials.

Based on the official estimates some 619 rebels were killed — 307 in open rebellion and some 312 executed by the Slave Courts and the Courts Martial.[13] Kamau Brathwaite puts the number killed in open rebellion even higher, estimating that over 1,000 enslaved people had been shot or killed by other means during the rebellion.[14] By contrast, only 14 Whites were killed, with 12 having been wounded, a lower White mortality rate than during the 1760 revolt.[15] The official records also indicate that three free coloured men were killed and two wounded in the armed struggle. Fourteen free people were also tried and convicted for their role in the revolt (including a white man, a Mr Ellery, and individuals described as 'brown').[16]

The primary sources that are available to us for the study of the events of 1831–32 include Governor's Dispatches, Assembly Minutes, prison confessions taken down by missionaries, published eyewitness accounts such as Bernard Senior's and trial evidence. The most widely known trial evidence is that of Sam Sharpe; but the prison confessions given to various missionaries by condemned men provide invaluable insight into war planning and tactics and the ways in which Sharpe made use of those men equally committed to the war, or drawn in even if at first reluctant. We do not have complete trial accounts for all of the 1,000 plus activists; but from what we have it is clear that men were in the vanguard of the planning and execution of the revolt and took the brunt of the punishment. Sharpe's chief co-conspirators were George Taylor, John Tharpe, Thomas Dove, Robert Gardner, George Guthrie, Ramsay, Robert Johnston (of Reading Pen), Johnson (of Retrieve Estate), M'Lennan, Plummer and Charles Campbell. Some accounts also list 'Father Robert', M'Lachlan, 'captain' Duhaney and Angus M'Cail among the main leaders. Others who were imprisoned and later punished for their roles were Samuel Cunningham, a Baptist deacon; William Atkins; William Binham; John Morris, Robert Morris, Brooks, David Gibson, David Atkinson, William Atkinson, Linton, (a brown man); William Evans; John Davis; James Fray, Charles Haughton; Richard Lewis and many, many more.

George Taylor seemed to have been particularly important and was described by the condemned prisoner Robert Morris who is said to have been 'a great man among the rebellious Negroes, who the white people should take ... up at once[17] [as] a greater man than Gardner, Dove and M'Cail [and the one who] recommended "the thing", fighting for freedom'. Taylor, says Morris, was 'the head of the whole of this bad business began from Montego Bay ... the head amongst them'.[18] James Gardner also hinted that while at first Sam Sharpe was the only ruler, others became important rulers subsequently, for example Tharp of Hazelymph 'who is a great ruler', George Guthrie and a man called Ramsay.[19] Other prisoners expressed the view that Taylor, not Sharpe, was the principal 'ruler'. Indeed, George Taylor's name crops up time and again in the confessions.

Robert Morrice, who confessed before Rev Thomas Stewart on February 1, 1832 stated:

> As I am now certain that I am going to die I am determined that those who led me to this shall be known. If I die, George Taylor must die also.... The white people must send to the governor, and immediately lay hold of George Taylor. He is a greater man than Gardiner, Dove, and McCail. He recommended "the thing", fighting for freedom, and he saw about the arms at Montego-Bay. The head of the whole of this bad business began from Montego-Bay, and Taylor is the head amongst them.... I declare, as I am going to give up my life this day, that what I have just said is true.

Edward Morrice, a Prisoner in the Savanna-la-Mar Gaol, told Rev Thomas Stewart and Samuel Spence on the same day that:

> I know George Taylor; he lives at Montego-Bay, is a saddler, and a head leader in the Baptist church. Whenever colonel Gardiner is going to do any thing, he goes or sends to consult George Taylor.

Gardiner does not do any thing without consulting George Taylor. I heard colonel Gardiner and my brother Robert Morrice very often say that daddy George Taylor set them on in the rebellion, and told them what they were to do. I consider daddy Taylor the ruler and head man.

James Fray said that:

> I know George Taylor; George Taylor is a head leader; he leads the people at Belvidere, Greenwich, Hermitage and York; colonel Gardiner is under him; Dove is under him. They are all led under George Taylor in the Baptist Church.

Charles Haughton, William Evans and Thomas Dove confirmed these views on Taylor's importance, Dove also reinforced Sharpe's leadership and the involvement of George Guthrie of Barneyside, Robert Gardiner, James Gardiner, Thomas Goodin of Greenwich, William James of Duckett's, and Charles Campbell of York. In his confession on January 5, 1832, Samuel Cunningham, a Baptist deacon, under Sentence of Death, responded to Rev John M'Intyre's questions as follows, reinforcing some of the names above:

> Q: [what are the] [n]ames of their rulers or captains?
> A: Has heard one of them named Johnson, belonging to Retrieve.... Another is named Robert Gardiner, a Baptist leader; can read; belongs to Greenwich. Another is named Robert Johnston; belongs to Reading pen; is a Baptist. These are captains or commanders.

These men were themselves virtually leaders of particular revolutionary zones or 'cells'. William Binham, in his confession explained:

> There are several gangs of rebels. Hazelymph has a gang under command of John Tharp (not daddy ruler Tharp), a doctor man to the property. Greenwich and Belvidere another gang, under colonel Gardiner and captain Dove. Chester castle another under a small

full-faced man, who carries a gun; Copse has one, too; but I do not know the captain.... Charles Campbell, of York, a carpenter, is a captain and leader. Morris, to Ducketts, a yellow man, is a captain and leader. Linton is a brown man, to Mr. Galloway; he is at Hermitage as a kind of busha there. Father Robert, another leader and captain, to Mr. Grignon. M'Lachlan, to Grignon also, and a captain and leader. Robert Morris, to Struie second in command under M'Cail, killed Bellchambers, by cutting off his head.

How did Sam Sharpe utilize the other male activists in his tactics or strategies? I use both, maybe too loosely, based upon Michel de Certeau's distinction between the two, the former as a calculated action determined by the absence of a proper base from which to operate, only able to operate in a 'blow-by-blow' way, seizing opportunities as they come along; the latter as reflecting more planning, having the power of institutions behind them. The tactic of course has more of the element of surprise and is most suitable in conditions of guerilla warfare similar to what takes place today in current warfare. Sam Sharpe used the Baptist slave hierarchy and individual property's slave elite as unifying elements in his plan. Sharpe had no large base of supporters, as Cooper's Hill was a small property of about ten enslaved people, therefore he had to recruit widely and appoint sub-leaders in different 'cells' in western Jamaica. Taylor, for example, is said to have had leadership of the people in — dare we say — 'cell' 12, comprising people at Hermitage, Belvedere and other contiguous properties. Tharpe operated out of Hazelymph; Gardner made Greenwich his operational headquarters, and Dove, Belvidere. The enslaved man called Plummer was head of 'cell' 18.[20] Other groups are said to have operated out of Chestercastle, York and Ducketts and each leader had a particular responsibility and a different area of expertise. Bernard Senior claims that Gardiner took charge of the military side of things while Sharpe focused on morale building and religious encouragement in the camp at Greenwich — Gardiner's hideout. He bound his 'leaders', 'colonels', 'lieutenant colonels' and 'captains' to secrecy and support by having them swear an oath on the Bible.

Those identified as 'leaders', 'rulers' or 'daddies' were assisted by other enslaved men on individual properties — some given the designation of 'captains' to indicate their lesser status — who rallied the masses to rebel by making them swear an oath of allegiance to the war on the Bible. Included among these were Richard Trail and Thomas Haughton (Shettlewood Pen); Andrew Llewellin and John Martin (Silvergrove); Robert Morrice (Struie); Linton, described as a 'brown man', who was said to have been 'a kind of busha' at Hermitage; Angus M'Cail (Woodstock); James Reed (Hermitage); Frederick Gray (Retirement); David Clifton and Daniel Barngum (Clifton).

These were not 'ordinary' enslaved men, but members of what historians have termed the 'slave elite'. The Governor of Jamaica confirmed this when he told the members of the Council and Assembly on Wednesday February 28, 1832 that

> it is a remarkable feature in these transactions, and worthy of particular and attentive consideration, that the leaders and chief promoters of this insurrection appear to have been almost exclusively composed of persons employed in confidential situations on the properties to which they belonged, and ... by their influence and example, the slaves were encouraged to perpetrate the crimes in which they have been so involved.[21]

Membership in this 'elite' and Christianity, learnt and practised in the Baptist churches in St. James, Westmoreland and Hanover, united them ideologically. William Binham told Rev Stewart that 'the reason why Westmoreland did not join the war was because the church of England, Moravian and Wesleyans tell their people not to shed blood; but that the Baptists tell them (the rebels) they might shed blood; any day but Sunday'. The activists also appeared to have been more likely to spare the lives of those activists reluctant to join who were Baptists, rather than, for example, Wesleyans (according to Binham). The Colonial Church Union did not share this view after the rebellion destroyed non-conformist chapels, including those of the Moravians and Wesleyans.

The trial evidence and the punishment list, and the claims for compensation for damage make it clear that Sharpe's helpers were not confined to Western Jamaica, but were as far east as Portland (where 13 men were sentenced to death); and St. Thomas-in-the-East, where Leo [?] Affleck from Haining got the death penalty. St. Thomas-in-the-Vale, now a part of St. Catherine, was also involved. The other parishes did not appear to have joined though unrest was noted in some of them in the months following the suppression. For example reports from St. Mary and Kingston were that all was calm.

Women

Let us now turn to the role of women and pose the following questions: how many women were involved? Were women's roles gendered? What assistance did they give to Sam Sharpe and how successful were they? Our best source for a quantitative assessment is the punishment list, which indicates that on an all-island level, 75 women from estates covering five western parishes were tried in Civil Courts or Courts Martial in 1832 and punished in one way or the other for their activism, including arson, rebellion or rebellious conspiracy in the language of the day, giving false evidence and deliberate absence from work. The records for St. James, one of the main areas of resistance, show that of the women tried, two of them (Kitty and Jenny) received the death penalty. In nearby St. Elizabeth, 26 women were tried by Court Martial, three of whom were punished by deportation ('transportation for life') — exiled from Africa, then exiled from Jamaica![22] Four women were executed, two from St. James, one from Hanover and one from Westmoreland.[23] The rest were either imprisoned or flogged (receiving between 10 and 200 lashes). Few were reprimanded or acquitted; or like Patty from St. Elizabeth, pardoned on account of old age. The majority of the female activists were Creole, as opposed to African (in fact only 18 per cent of the rebels were African-born),[24] and field labourers as opposed to domestics (very few of these were involved). They were not all young; indeed Craton indicates that the average age of the rebels was 37. Charlotte, a Creole field slave from St. James was 60 years old; and

Eliza Wittingham from Westmoreland, an African who was hanged, was 57 years old.

There is anecdotal evidence from Bernard Senior, a British military officer active in the suppression of the war, and other observers, confirming the fact that Samuel Sharpe had female supporters in 1831. He outlined three telling instances of female involvement in this armed struggle.[25]

I now wish to introduce an element of property differentiation into the discussion of women's roles in this Emancipation war. Women on livestock farms, called 'pens' in Jamaica, were instrumental in providing support and sustenance for the rebels. With greater access to food and fresh meat than the sugar estates, pens served as revictualling centres for the enslaved activists who relied on pen women to prepare meals for them. Indeed, it also appears as if the British army commandeered some of the pens to play a similar role.[26]

The 1831–32 Emancipation War provides a very good example of the multidimensionality of slave resistance. It demonstrates the ways in which the enslaved combined violent revolt with non-violent strategies or tactics to achieve the same end. It also illustrates the differences in gender roles during armed revolts, and the relationship between slave occupations, location (rural vs urban, sugar vs non-sugar) and the resistance tactics employed. It forces us to confront the deeply disturbing issue of lack of Black solidarity in these wars, demonstrating from the comparatively small numbers involved (vis-à-vis the total enslaved population of the island), the participation of the Maroons on the side of the enslavers and the confessions that hint at reluctant participation of individual slaves and properties — that we cannot treat the Black population of the Caribbean as an undifferentiated mass with similar political ideology.

Finally, it allows us to see the ways in which the enslaved used armed struggle not just as a way of resisting and overthrowing slavery, but as a self-conscious internal mechanism of accommodation, freedom and social mobility. I would like to illustrate this latter point with evidence from the Assembly Minutes. Although I make no claim to having done a proper quantitative analysis of these April 1832 Minutes, I have already counted 89 (7 women and 82 men) who were either manumitted, promised manumission or paid monetary compensation for helping to protect the lives and property of their enslavers from the activists; guiding the British troops to rebel hideouts or being well behaved during the whole affair. A typical entry read:

> 10 pounds annuity and manumission or 10 extra pounds in lieu of — to James Hair, belonging to the estate of the late Mr. Pierce of St. James for saving the life of Mrs. Pierce and her 3 children[27]

Turner warns against being carried away by absolute numbers, indicating that the numbers rewarded for solidarity with the oppressors were small compared to the total enslaved population — just 1:1,465 in the county of Cornwall.

In conclusion, some historians such as Mary Turner refer to the 1831–32 Emancipation War in Jamaica as 'unsuccessful' and a 'failure',[28] perhaps because it did not achieve the specific and short-term objectives of the rebels. Even if we do not wish to accord primacy to slave agency in this war in the abolition of slavery, we cannot ignore the part it played, especially its economic impact. Those who support the materialist explanation for abolition cannot deny that slave agency as demonstrated by the 1831–32 Emancipation War had an impact on the economics of slavery in Jamaica and hastened emancipation. With a declining labour force (and the Whites help by killing hundreds of what one Presbyterian missionary described as 'able hands it [the island] could ill spare'[29]) along with the threat of more social instability if slavery were not abolished, the rebellion represented a warning to British legislators that failure to act would be at their own peril. Linton, an enslaved man involved in the rebellion, had warned from his prison cell in Savannah-la-mar: 'I tell you again, if the gentlemen do not keep a good look out, the Negroes will begin this business in three or four years, for they think the Lord and the King have given them the gift, and because those who were joined in this business [the rebellion] were all sworn.'[30] The British government responded to this signal in May 1832 by appointing a select committee 'to consider and report upon the measures which it may be expedient to adopt for the purpose of effecting the extinction of slavery throughout the British dominions'. Craton calls the appointment of this Select Committee coincidental — I disagree.[31] The 1831–32 Emancipation War was central, not tangential to the appointment of the Select Committee and the passing of the Emancipation Act in 1833 to be effected August 1, 1834.

I hope that as 2004 approaches, those who either suffered or benefited from slavery will find appropriate mechanisms to memorialize the enslaved ancestors. In several emancipation lectures in Jamaica this year I called for the names of those who fought for Caribbean emancipation from slavery to be inscribed on Walls of Remembrance and I repeat this call. Each year we honour those who have died in the World Wars of 1914–18 and 1939–45. Tangible symbols of red poppies and cenotaphs are used to memorialize the dead. A way should be found to memorialize those who have died in the various anti-slavery wars in the Caribbean. There is no excuse as the terrorist regime provided us with the names of the war heroes. Let us not proceed into the twenty-first century still suffering from historical amnesia with regards to the legacies of slavery; for despite the painful memories unless the proper rites are performed the ghosts of slavery will continue to haunt us. Let us build those Walls of Remembrance in Emancipation Parks all over the Black diaspora, including the various metropoles that benefited from slavery. It is the right thing to do as we seek to reassemble fractured identities. As Jenny Sharpe observed, 'slavery may be a thing of the past, but that does not mean that its legacy is not still with us.'[32]

SECTION III

EMANCIPATION AND MIGRATION:
NEGOTIATING FREE SOCIETY

Introduction

Between 1794 and 1886, the trade in enslaved Africans and the slave systems in all colonized Caribbean territories were legally abolished. Haiti was the first to end slavery which it did through revolutionary means, and Cuba was the last to implement legislative emancipation. With the exception of the French Caribbean territories where slavery was completely abolished by 1848, all other Caribbean territories implemented various transitional systems between the passing of the Emancipation Acts and full freedom – Apprenticeship in the British and Dutch Caribbean territories, Free Birth or Free Womb in the Danish Caribbean territories, *patronato* in Cuba, and *regimen de contratación* in Puerto Rico.

The coming of 'full freedom' in all areas of the Caribbean by 1886 gave freed people unprecedented control over their movement and greater bargaining power over their working conditions. Some, especially females, exercised these rights by moving off the plantation (voting with their feet), and by bargaining. The proprietors tried everything in their power to frustrate the freed people by reducing their bargaining power, re-imposing slave relations of production and recreating the mentalities of the slavery era. Immigration was one such strategy of control and manipulation, used as the 'antidote to emancipation'. The immigration of Africans, Asians and Europeans in the post-slavery period was intimately associated with the new mobility among the African–Caribbean labouring population now freed from the legal obligation to remain in a labour–capital relationship with former enslavers. The result of this mobility was instability and unpredictability in the labour supply, which did not satisfy the landholders' desire for monopoly control of the labour market. The topic of immigration/migration has led to the development of a body and genre of writing on the post-slavery and postcolonial Caribbean as scholars seek to answer questions which have framed their investigations over the years.

The lectures in this section provide an overview of indentured labour migration (intended to replace slavery and prevent the actualization of freedom), and its relationship to emancipation, as well as an assessment of the economic and social impact of immigration on Caribbean societies. In the case of Jamaica – a minor player in the immigration scheme when compared to Guyana and Trinidad – although the Indians never comprised more than 2.1 per cent of the total population in the period under review (and was 1.3 per cent according to the Census done in 1991), this did not mean that they represented an invisible minority. Issues relating to those under indenture and those who had made the transition from transients to settlers attracted national attention and formed the subject of numerous correspondence between the political directorate in Jamaica. The lecture that forms chapter 12, titled 'The Politics of Migration', provides an overview of the Indian-specific issues that preoccupied the political directorate and their implications for the Indian experience in the island. It should be stressed, however, that indentured immigrants had very little knowledge of the politics of migration. They were not to know that they were being used as pawns in the contest over terrain between former enslavers and former enslaved. This should be borne in mind in any attempt to understand inter-ethnic relations, especially conflict-ridden relations, in the modern and postmodern Caribbean.

10

APPRENTICESHIP AND INDENTURESHIP:

Re/Placing Slavery in the British-Colonized Caribbean — Historiographical Trends

Opening Address, Conference on Slavery and Emancipation, Mahatma Gandhi Institute, Mauritius, June 1998

The anniversaries of emancipation have occasioned frequent commemorative conferences. While some of these revisited the process of emancipation itself, with the early ones practically canonizing the humanitarians, others, like this, have focused on post-emancipation developments — a demonstration, according to Seymour Drescher and Frank McGlynn, that scholars are 'less inclined to leave the scene of action at the moment of redemption'[1] and more interested in long-range reflections on post Apprenticeship societies.

In this address entitled: 'Apprenticeship and Indentureship: Re/Placing Slavery in the British-colonized Caribbean' I have chosen not to use 'replacing', but 're/placing'; for what I really wish to review is the way in which new systems of domination, exemplified by, though not exclusive to, 'Apprenticeship' and 'indentureship' were constructed not just as positive and dignified alternatives to slavery — 'replacing' with its implication of 'getting rid of' — but as neo-slavery — 're/placing' — intended to insert and prevent the actualization of freedom and perpetuate the same ideologies and mentalities from the slavery era.

My approach to this topic is essentially historiographical, revisiting the established literature and histories in an effort to chart the development of a body and genre of writing on the post-slavery and postcolonial Caribbean and seeing how scholars have sought to answer questions which have framed their investigations over the years. Questions frequently asked are:

i.   What did the coming of full freedom mean for the metropolitan and colonial legislatures and for the various interest groups in the Caribbean?

ii.   Did the ending of Apprenticeship represent a revolutionary event? Was emancipation just an event or was it a human social condition?

iii. Was the transformation of legal status for thousands of African and African descended people accompanied by real changes in the structure of post-emancipation society, politics and economy?

iv.   Were the ideologies that governed the plantation system transformed, reconfigured or simply cemented; or did new ideologies emerge to shape post-slavery society?

v.   How did race, class and culture shape/reshape post-slavery societies?

vi.   Did emancipation enlarge or constrain opportunities for the various interest groups, particularly the newly freed?

vii. How did emancipation affect the plantations?

viii. What were the radical alternatives to plantation development and to what extent were these adopted?

ix.   How were the interests of capital and labour harmonized? Were labour's interests promoted only insofar as those interests did not endanger capital?[2]

While the empirical data helping to settle some of these issues and questions may be Caribbean-specific, the sameness of colonialism despite the ethnicity of the colonizing power will guarantee that Caribbean historiography has broader implications for comparative, cross-cultural study and relevance to post-emancipation Mauritius. Chronology might differ; but analyses of disparate post-slavery societies have revealed similarities in socioeconomic and political structures evolving from the problem of inequality.

The ending of the Apprenticeship System represented a decisive step in the elimination of what Caribbean historian Woodville Marshall terms 'the legal oddity of property in persons'.[3] The dismantling of one of the most vigorous elements of the capitalist world economy has been the focus of sustained academic curiosity.

The analysis of the Apprenticeship System itself has been a central aspect of the post-slavery discourse in all former colonies, with a dominant interpretation being that it simply continued the racialized imperialist project of domination, which for the Caribbean began in the fifteenth century.

The emergence of Western Europe as the political centre of an Atlantic economy signalled the importance of imperial exploitation to its development. Indeed, development discourse, centring around the discipline of political economy, privileged colonialism as the transformative engine of capitalist growth. European colonial capitalism could see no way to ensure profitable economic activity other than with the mass deployment of servile labour. As the intensity of economic accumulation gripped colonial elites, and the pressures of profits, power and glory fuelled the colonizing enterprise, chattel slavery, rather than white servitude with which Europeans in the Caribbean experimented after the decimation of the indigenous peoples, became the preferred form of servile labour.

From the moment of capture and enslavement, Africans in the Caribbean, as elsewhere, signalled their intention to undermine the European plantations. There were acts of self-liberation, most notably those in French San Domingue (now Haiti), where an enslaved-led revolt in 1791 brought down slavery. Between the Haitian revolution and the last quarter of the nineteenth century, the slave systems in the Caribbean collapsed in a drawn-out programme of legislative emancipation. But Emancipation Acts did not end systems of domination. With the exception of the French Caribbean, Antigua and Bermuda, forms of neo-slavery, whether euphemistically called Apprenticeship, Free Birth/Free Womb, Regimen de Contratación or Patronato, were introduced to the Caribbean as a means of re/placing slavery. Intended to last from 1834 to 1840, the Apprenticeship System in the British-colonized Caribbean collapsed in 1838, one year earlier than in Mauritius, in the face of the anti-slavery activities of humanitarians and apprentices, and the inefficient systems of implementation.[4]

The Apprenticeship System as process and event has engaged the attention of writers since the mid-nineteenth century, with historians debating its necessity and failure. The perspectives have not been unified. As Veronica Gregg has observed, there are important differences in the ordering and emphases on events among European/imperial, settler/creole, and cultural nationalist historians.[5] The writings of such nineteenth-century figures as Thomas Carlyle, and early twentieth-century figures like William Burn, helped to shape the ideological grounds of the debate about the recently freed people and their relationship to labour and the plantocracy.[6] While Carlyle and those of his ilk supported a delayed freedom for 'impetuous and barbaric blacks' and agreed that it was vital to give the planters an added compensation for the loss of their property, the later twentieth-century works, primarily those of Afrocentric Caribbean historians, tended to oppose the hegemonic, imperial discourse. If John Tosh is correct that history is a political battleground,[7] then many Caribbean historians found the ammunition to participate in the war. They sought, in Spivak's terms, to develop a strategy of reading that spoke to the historically muted subject.[8] While there are no post-slavery narratives comparable to slave narratives, a few historians like Woodville Marshall and the late Neville Hall have managed to use sources that facilitate the recovery of the apprentices' voices and experiences — published speeches, petitions, and interviews with missionaries — and have attempted to frame the discourse on Apprenticeship and anti-Apprenticeship within the articulated hopes and expectations of the apprentices.[9] Their investigations reveal the contending views of freedom and the free order held by the former enslaved and the former enslaver.

Their analyses indicate that the apprentices were vigorously opposed to the delayed freedom represented by the Apprenticeship System. They viewed it as the last stage of slavery rather than the first stage of freedom, with the Stipendiary Magistrates the new drivers; and while they had no intention of engaging in the mass murder of former owners and decamping en masse from the plantations, as some had feared, they signalled their intention from very early on to oppose the unjust system. Many refused to apprentice their children, to work in the non-compulsory hours, or gave their labour unwillingly during the period of compulsory labour. Some were reportedly puzzled by Apprenticeship's objectives as explained to them by missionaries and governors. Thomas Holt recounts that an elderly African skeptical of the new law as it was explained to him, reportedly observed that Apprenticeship was for children put out to learn a trade. 'What', he asked, 'was he to learn?' He was too old to become a cooper, carpenter or mason; he knew how to plant the cane, to weed, to hoe — what was he to learn?[10]

This issue of Apprenticeship teaching the labourers industrious habits and fitting them for the wage economy has been picked up in the modern scholarship, historians equally regarding it as ludicrous. During slavery, as Mary Turner and O. Nigel Bolland have shown, some already earned wages;[11] and Eric Williams and C.L.R. James have argued strongly that the productive and industrious labour of the enslaved facilitated capital accumulation and industrialization in the core.[12] Slavery's relationship to the establishment of banking institutions (and lingering anger over this) is captured in Jamaica Kincaid's book *A Small Place*, set in Antigua. She writes: 'Do you ever wonder why some people blow things up? I can imagine that if my life had taken a different turn, there would be the Barclays bank, and there I would be, both of us in ashes.'[13]

The Failure of Apprenticeship

Historians from all sides of the ideological fence agree that the Apprenticeship System was doomed to fail. Almost without exception, the nineteenth-century imperial historians, and a minority of modern historians. Perhaps they should have collaborated in their own exploitation?

There is widespread agreement among revisionist historians that a major factor in the failure of Apprenticeship was the resistance of the apprentices. Indeed, while the British government, Stipendiary Magistrates and local Assemblies have not escaped blame, apprentices' agency — particularly of women, the most oppressed of the class of apprentices — has now emerged as a leading explanation for the end of Apprenticeship. Apprenticed women brought the system into such disrepute by showcasing conditions of punishment in the prisons, especially on the treadmill, that they helped to bring down the system. Diana Paton's work which has injected a welcome bit of gender analysis in the discourse of anti-Apprenticeship, shows that the degradation of women eventually came to bear a large part of the symbolic weight of the condemnation of Apprenticeship by abolitionists, anxious to recreate a proper gender order in the post-slavery Caribbean.[14] As Holt observed in his monumental work *The Problem of Freedom*, it was ironic that the emancipation act was conceived and written in an unreflectively masculine gender; yet the most militant resistance to it came from women.[15] By 1838, it was clear to all interest groups that the apprenticeship system had to end, especially as praedial apprentices had no intention of prolonging their bondage to 1840.

Resistance to Apprenticeship was no less marked in the non-British territories. When the enslaved in the Danish-ruled Caribbean were told in 1847 that adults would serve a 12-year apprenticeship, a violent revolt erupted, forcing almost immediate emancipation. Edward, from Rosenhill plantation articulated the enslaved people's intentions clearly. He told his owner: 'Mr. Van Brackle, here is your hoe and your cutlass. I will no longer work for you and if I work I will buy them myself.'[16] There was no place in their scheme of thinking for re/placing slavery with Apprenticeship. Former owners would of course find other means of re/placing slavery as an overview of the post-Apprenticeship writings will reveal.

From Apprenticeship to Indentureship

The post-Apprenticeship period has, in fact, been subjected to even greater academic scrutiny than the Apprenticeship period. Indeed, an explosion of historical research has expanded and pluralized the historical context of post-slavery Caribbean historiography. The period 1834–1900 saw the proliferation of local histories of specific territories, a few general histories by imperial and ethnocentric professional historians and the appearance of specialist studies by people like Herman Merivale, John Davy, William Sewell, Anthony Trollope and James Anthony Froude. Those that engaged with the issue of emancipation and its socioeconomic impact expressed sympathy for the planter class who were allegedly ruined by emancipation, primarily as a result of the actions of the liberated.[17]

The twentieth century represented the era of burgeoning nationalism when nationalist histories written in what William Green refers to (and opposes) as the 'creole genre'[18] were being written and perhaps were necessary, as Patrick Bryan observes, 'to plant the first seeds of a collective consciousness.'[19] Not surprisingly, much of the scholarship of twentieth-century professional historians, some influenced by Marxist ideology, continued to intervene in the dominative system of knowledge, questioning and replacing the Eurocentric history and master narrative imposed on the Caribbean.

On the whole the historiography has explored the nature of emancipation, seeking to understand what actually transpired at the onset of freedom. Two trends have emerged. One is that the post-slavery period represented continuity, not change; the other is that in the final instance emancipation was a revolutionary measure. Those that hold the latter view argue that, the legislation which ended slavery substituted a wage labour system for unpaid labour, and outlined the basis for the existence of a greatly enlarged community of free people. It achieved this by removing the legal authority which had enabled a small minority to exercise virtually arbitrary power over the lives and activities of the large majority. Interpretations of the expectations of the freed people of the new order reveal that they saw freedom as an opportunity to educate their children, consolidate their family and revitalize African culture. They did not contemplate mass exodus from the estates and would work for just and equitable wages. They had a clear idea of their labour value from wages offered in the non-compulsory hours during Apprenticeship and the value placed on those who contemplated manumission. They wanted no restrictions on their mobility, no contracts and no system of neo-slavery. Women, in particular, wanted flexibility in working days and hours.

Black working-class women had no intention of conforming to the Victorian gender order and the gender systems of the new era, which sought to confine women to the private sphere of uncompensated labour in the home. Above all, they wanted land to consolidate the material base of freedom, independence and upward social mobility. Conscious of the relationship between land and political and social empowerment, the emancipated were determined in their pursuit of the ownership of land.

Access to land had been important even before 1834. What Sidney Mintz calls a 'proto-peasantry' had emerged under slavery. Cultivation of provision grounds and gardens, the marketing of surplus produce and the freedom to dispose of the returns from this transaction had together constituted the enslaved people's main independent activity and their chief adaptation to slavery.[20] The establishment of the peasantry, even in territories like Antigua, Barbados, Nevis and Montserrat where land was expensive and tightly controlled by the planter class, therefore, must be located within the context of the importance of land in consolidating freedom. Land was acquired by various means. The emancipated,

- purchased Crown lands or marginal estate lands
- squatted on Crown lands
- pooled resources to buy land, even whole plantations, and established communal free villages
- rented or purchased plots in missionary-founded free villages
- entered into partnership with planters via the metayage system
- utilized land left by planter benefactors.

Extent of Peasant Development

By the end of the nineteenth century, thousands of Black people in all Caribbean territories had some access to land, no matter how small the acreage and how tenuous the land tenure. By 1858, 15,600 Antiguans lived in independent villages and could at the very least bargain for better wages. In 1897, according to Hilary Beckles, there were about 8,500 independent peasants in Barbados who had legally acquired 10,000 acres, while another 4,500 rented lands.[21] By 1850, 42,000 Guyanese out of a total of 82,000 had acquired land off the estates, and by 1861 Trinidad had about 11,000 small farmers. In Jamaica the number of freeholds of less than ten acres increased from 883 in 1840 to 20,724 in 1845. By

1861, the number of peasant holdings had increased to about 50,000. By this date there were more peasant proprietors in Jamaica than casual estate labourers.[22]

Former enslavers and their respective imperial support groups had a different perception of post-slavery society and the free order. They wished slave-like relations of production to continue and therefore the revolutionary potential of land acquisition, for example, was too much for the power holders to contemplate. It was because of this why that nineteenth-century historian of Saint Lucia, Breen, had opposed the metayage system which had the potential for black economic independence.[23] Land ownership, furthermore, increased freed people's bargaining power with the plantation and provided Black men with the means of enfranchisement and access to political seats. Land ownership threatened to take the initiative of economic development out of the hands of the planter class, and as in Haiti, place it with the peasants and small farmers. Thus the social relations of production and the ideological arrangement of post-slavery society would all be threatened.

Landowners then tried to impede the development of the peasantry by refusing to sell Crown and marginal estate land, taxing land transactions, selling and renting at exorbitant prices, forbidding squatting, refusing to survey lands or grant titles which led to the eviction of at times legitimate landowners. They taxed land on which export crops were not planted and imposed minimum acreage in some territories. In an attempt to maintain the status quo, obstacles in the way of land acquisition were combined with many restrictive class legislation and increases in the property qualification for the franchise, particularly in places where the large plantation made a resurgence towards the end of the nineteenth century with the help of immigration of indentured labourers.[24]

Indentured Labour Migration

Indentured labour migration was used as the antidote to emancipation by many planters in the Caribbean. Most Caribbean territories, as did Mauritius and Fiji, subsidized and encouraged immigration to set up competition for jobs with Blacks, the lower wages reducing their new-found bargaining power and preventing the development of working-class solidarity; though, as Walter Rodney demonstrates for Guyana, the slave-like conditions of Indian indentureship eventually defeated this objective.[25]

The importation of labourers was linked to the unwillingness of freed people to continue in a capital-labour relationship with employers who refused to pay decent wages and improve conditions of work. In seeking support for immigration as a solution to their 'labour problem', pro-planter interests pointed to: the abandonment of a large number of sugar estates, (194 between 1865 and 1900 in Jamaica), the declining sugar economy in places like Jamaica, growing indebtedness, increasing cost of production and the reduction in the numbers of full-time estate labourers. In Jamaica by 1846, for example, the labouring population residing on the estates was only one-third of what it had been in the final years of slavery. By 1847 in Trinidad, the labouring population had decreased by 40 per cent; and by 1851, only 3,116 labourers were said to be working regularly on the estates. In Guyana by the 1860s, only 45 per cent of the labour force as it was in 1834 still worked on the estates. In Mauritius, by 1847 there were just about 189 ex-apprentices on the estates.[26] The reduction in the numbers of estate workers was attributed by some to the alleged 'laziness' and 'idle disposition' of Blacks. This view was reflected in the letters of people like Stephen Harmer. Harmer, overseer of coffee properties in Manchester, Jamaica, wrote to his brother in England in 1840 that:

> I regret to say that this once fine country is going fast to destruction through the want of continuous labour. One half of the negroes have scarcely done anything since they were made free and them that do work demand very high wages from 4/- to 5/- per day and then they will not do even half a day's work for that.[27]

Thomas Carlyle, a leading ideologue of his class and of imperialism during this period, who never visited the Caribbean, a sure indication according to Veronica Gregg that the invention of the Caribbean as a European enterprise required little knowledge of the region and in fact depended upon, as Gregg puts it, 'a willed ignorance'[28] had this to say:

Where a black man by working about half an hour a day can supply himself, by aid of sun and soil, with as much pumpkin as will suffice, he is likely to be a little stiff to raise into labour.... Sunk to the ears in pumpkin, imbibing saccharine juices and as much at ease in the creation, he can listen to the less fortunate white man and "demand" and take his time supplying it.[29]

Anthony Trollope seemed like a reincarnation of Carlyle though he substituted breadfruit for pumpkin, his view being that the blacks' interpretation of emancipation was emancipation from work to eat breadfruit.[30] James Anthony Froude who revived Edward Long's philosophy that slavery had been beneficial[31] also claimed that it was emancipation, and by implication the emancipated, that had now ruined the Caribbean. His perspective influenced J.J. Thomas's late nineteenth-century work of counter-discourse, brilliantly titled *Froudacity.*[32]

Mauritian post-slavery historiography is replete with similar examples. Rev. Patrick Beaton observed in the mid-nineteenth century that 'the Afro-Mauritians are not so industrious or enterprising as the same class in Europe'.[33] As Veronica Gregg, quoting Karl Marx reiterated, the overall picture was that of Blacks observing planters' impending bankruptcy 'with an ironic grin of malicious pleasure'.[34]

Revisionist historians take a different view, attributing the movement to the anti-labour legislations and coercive tactics of planters. As Douglas Hall put it:

the movement of the ex-slaves from the estates was not a flight from the horrors of slavery. It was a protest against the inequities of early freedom. It is possible that, had the ex-slaves been allowed to continue in the free use of gardens, house and grounds, and to choose their employers without reference to that accommodation, there would have been very little movement of agricultural labour at all from the communities apparently established on the estate during slavery.[35]

Immigration and Indentureship

Whatever the reasons for the mobility of freed people, property owners had managed to convince their imperial allies that the import of a fresh labouring population was vital to maintain the plantation system. It was within this context that indentureship re/placed Apprenticeship as the new form of labour exploitation up to the early 1920s. Over half-a-million indentured workers were imported in the post-slavery period, most in the period 1845–1917, beginning with the Gladstone experiment to Guyana in 1838. Though labourers were imported from Europe, North America, Madeira, China, Java and again from Africa, it was India which provided the majority, with Guyana leading the way with 238,909 and Trinidad 143,939. The other territories imported far less than these, with Jamaica for example importing just seven per cent of the total. Mauritius, of course, far outpaced any other importing country.

The adoption of Indian indentureship as the new system of slavery, to use Hugh Tinker's term,[36] illustrates with the greatest clarity how freedom everywhere meant the reproduction of the class struggle within the nexus of a new legal status for the freed. Most scholars of Indian immigration, after studying recruitment, conditions in the holding depots, the voyage from India and conditions aboard the ships, mortality rates on ship and estates, the poor repatriation policies, the transformation of indentured labour migration into a form of settler colonization, economic conditions of migrants, gender discriminatory policies and the abuses of women, have been forced to agree with Hugh Tinker that Indian indentureship was a new form of slavery. They do not ignore the material gains of some settlers, especially those who commuted repatriation for land or money; and they do not deny that the plantation system in Guyana and Trinidad survived and expanded as a result of the large numbers of Indians in their labour force by the late nineteenth century. By 1895, Indian workers comprised 87 per cent and by 1891 80 per cent of the Trinidadian and Guyanese labour force respectively.[37] But the indentureship system has also been exposed for what it really was, that is, a means of re/placing slavery in the British colonies. Its similarity to slavery is still being debated; but it is arguable whether the legal differences between chattel slavery where both labour time and labourer were the property of owners, and indentureship where technically only the labour time belonged to the employer for a contractual period, meant much to the practical experiences of migrant labourers in the Caribbean.

Everywhere the plantocracy, despite the anti-immigration activists and the watchdog role of India, the Protector of Immigrants and Emigrants, and the Colonial Office, tried to recreate the slave relations of production through the indentureship system. What should have been a civil contract between two equal partners turned out to be a system which enshrined the interests of the capitalist class at the expense of the worker. Most experienced exile in bondage and exchanged one form of poverty and servitude for another; many more found only death and disease in the new life. They entered a system in which human values mattered less than the drive for production and for exploitation. The system of indentureship curtailed the mobility of the worker, who was not free to leave his/her employer if better opportunities presented themselves. Moreover, the penal sanction made non-work or transgressions of the disciplinary code a punishable breach of contract. In those cases, the migrants were subjected to fines, hard labour or imprisonment. As Rosemarjin Hoefte's book points out, it was not so much the recruitment as the contract and accompanying laws that constituted the unfree component in indentured labour.[38] Criminal laws reinforced a civil contract.

Revisionists like David Northrup, David Galenson and Pieter Emmer have challenged the neo-slavery thesis, focusing instead on the economic rationale of emigrants and their material gains in the colonies.[39] Pieter Emmer for example, has argued that for women, emigration and indentureship was a route to emancipation and upward social mobility. Though revisionists have sought to modify the idea that indentured migration was based on fraud, they largely ignore the very foundation of the indenture system — the legal mechanism to control the contract labourers. While pointing to the regulatory aspects of indentureship, they fail to acknowledge sufficiently the lack of compliance of planters. The indentured themselves, by their resistance activities, expressed their views on indentureship in no uncertain terms; for despite the planters' hope of importing 'controllable workers', a factor which caused those in Jamaica to discourage Muslims and Tamils from south India, Indians did not passively accept their bondage.

In the end, however, for planters in Trinidad and Guyana; and for the large sugar and banana estates in Jamaica, indentured workers fulfilled the objective of reducing the reliance on local labourers and, if not reducing wages, kept them from going up considerably. Historians like Michael Craton, Gad Heuman and Kusha Haraksingh have shown that protest action, including the Morant Bay Rebellion of 1865 in Jamaica, which Governor Eyre had so brutally suppressed, was widespread in the post-slavery period and was attributable to the failure of post-emancipation regimes to deliver on the promise of freedom.[40] As sociologist Don Robotham observes, in elevating land hunger as a primary cause of the rebellion, the people were freed in 1838, but the material basis of real freedom was denied them.[41] After 1865, the state reacted to increasing black claims for political enfranchisement by removing the flawed Old Representative System and introducing in most colonies, the Crown Colony system of government. For the ruling elite, the potential for radical transformation was considerably diminished once measures to curb the freedom of blacks by retaining control of the government proved effective.

Experiences varied across the Caribbean but there is general consensus among historians that, on the whole, the class continuities of hegemony and subordination of enslaved by enslavers were reproduced in a new regime. If I am reading Jamaica Kincaid correctly, emancipation as a process is still 'in action'. In *A Small Place* she observed that 'they [Antiguans] speak of emancipation itself as if it happened just the other day, not over 150 years ago. The word "emancipation" is used so frequently, it is as if it, emancipation, were a contemporary occurrence, something everybody is familiar with.' However she hastens to suggest that it has not really materialized in all its dimensions: in Antigua, people cannot see a relationship between their obsession with slavery and emancipation and their celebration of the hotel training school — a school that teaches Antiguans to be good servants.[42]

Conclusion

In conclusion, a review of the scholarship of the post-emancipation era in the British Caribbean reveals that the emancipated hoped that the coming of freedom would provide the opportunity for them to take full control of their own lives and lay a completely new base for the society. They hoped to realize the revolutionary potential of the legislation to abolish slavery by extending those social, cultural and economic values and institutions which they had cultivated zealously during slavery, particularly those relating to land acquisition and the reinterpretation of African/Christian cosmology. The planter/state counter-revolution was vicious and one manifestation was the importation of labour in many Caribbean territories. It was not a simple case of expanding the labour market; for the importation of labour was combined with anti-labour legislation and denial of land for economic independence. This is not to suggest that indentured workers — themselves subjected to the arbitrary power of the planter class, leading many scholars to view their experiences as one of neo-slavery — deliberately contributed to the erosion of black independence, though their rapid economic power in Guyana, Suriname and Trinidad vis-à-vis the African–Caribbean population and the increased inter-ethnic conflicts in the post-indentureship years, requires explanation.

I do not, of course, have time to provide that explanation now; but I will say that part of the answer lies in the post-migrant years when the state power deliberately tried to co-opt Indians in their project of black disempowerment, manifested in the pro-commutation and anti-repatriation policies which facilitated Indian settlement at a time when blacks were being disenfranchised and denied the material basis of freedom. Whether Blacks were indigenous as in Fiji, Natal and East Africa, or claimed native status because of prior settlement as in Mauritius and the Caribbean, they strove to protect the socioeconomic and political status which they perceived were threatened; thus leading to inter-ethnic conflict and racial stereotyping.

Unfortunately, the preoccupation with inter-ethnic conflict has tended to overshadow the history of class solidarity against the ruling elite, which, as Walter Rodney's Marxist analysis has shown, was consolidated from the late nineteenth century and early twentieth century.[43] This period saw people's protests in Trinidad and Guyana in which workers and unemployed from across the racial groups demanded economic justice within the market economy, racial equality within social life, and political freedom within a democratic ethos as well as an end to the legacies of slavery and indentureship, abuses of empire, and colonial domination. Armed with the radical ideology of Marcus Garvey, labour rebellions spread across the entire British-colonized Caribbean in the 1930s and continued into the era of decolonization and black power struggles of the 1960s and 1970s. Though many territories are now independent and the colour and ethnicity of the rulers have changed, with the 1990s witnessing the coming to power of Prime Ministers of Indian ancestry in Guyana, and Trinidad and Tobago, people still see the need to struggle for West Indian nationhood, true independence, freedom and social justice.

One only has to listen to the revolutionary reggae rhythm and lyrics of Bob Marley, Peter Tosh, Jimmy Cliff and Buju Banton and the social commentary in Trinidad calypso; feel the passion in Kamau Brathwaite's call for respect for the nation language; listen to Rastafarians talk about Babylon captivity, 'sufferation' and the 'shitstem'; read the poetry of Brathwaite and the late Mickey White and the literature of Jamaica Kincaid; view and interpret the graffiti on the walls of Caribbean cities to understand the cry of the Caribbean masses or 'massive' in the nation language, for justice and equal rights. The walls of academia have not been untouched. On a visit from Queen Elizabeth II someone sprayed a fundamental anti-imperial statement — 'a nanny a fi wi queen' — on the newly painted university entrance. This was a reference to that Maroon woman warrior, Nanny, who helped to secure freedom for escaped slaves from the English in the eighteenth century.

During April 19–21 of this year (1998), the people of Jamaica took to the streets to protest, through roadblocks, burning of tyres and arson, the excessive taxation on petrol. The protests were less about the micro-issue of the tax hike in petrol and more about what they perceive as continued injustices in a so-called democratic and free society of the post-independence era. The reports of these events in the local and international press were instructive, some couched in language very similar to the racist and classist language of the nineteenth century, indicating that there still is limited understanding of the meaning of freedom.

11

'MY FEET IS [SIC] MY ONLY CARRIAGE':
Gender and Labour Mobility in the Post-Slavery Caribbean

Lecture to Undergraduates, Sarah Lawrence College, New York: November 8, 2000

I was listening to a Bob Marley album as I prepared this talk and was attracted to the line, 'My Feet is my Only Carriage, So I've Got to Push on Through', taken from his 'No Woman Nuh Cry' track. 'My Feet is My Only Carriage', (and let us not argue about the lack of agreement of verb and subject here; Bob used the Jamaican nation language) seemed to capture precisely low income women's agency expressed through their mobility in the post-slavery and post-independence Anglophone Caribbean. 'Feet', then, — especially feet used as carriage, transportation, choice of employment location — thus seemed like an apt metaphor for the mobility of women labourers.

My particular focus, of course, is on the Black working-class woman's mobility in all its dimensions:

i. Internal relocation
ii. Intra-Caribbean migration
iii. Out-migration from the Caribbean
iv. Circulation (the migration cycle of exile and return)
v. Asian immigration in so far as it affected African Caribbean women's experiences.

Theoretical Framework

My discussion will not be located within the old institutional tradition established by labour historians who studied labour movements, collective bargaining and trade unionism, but more within the tradition of social history and what is now being called 'subaltern studies' — that genre of historical writing that incorporates a focus on working-class people as historical agents.

The Post-Slavery Caribbean: Overview

The pioneer historian of Caribbean women's history, Lucille Mathurin Mair, once posed the rhetorical question in respect of enslaved women's agency: where on earth did women, the subordinate sex, get the nerve [to confront their enslavers?][1] The answer of course, lies in an understanding of the brutal assaults that slavery inflicted on their minds and bodies. The same question could be posed for the post-slavery period as we seek to understand women's rationale for the decisions they made as they sought to adjust to changing post-slavery conditions. My view is that the choices they made, especially the choice to move in search of better conditions of work, were influenced by the prevailing ideological and socioeconomic circumstances. Let us consider the ideological terrain that acted as a push factor in labour mobility.

The ideological terrain

1. *Colonial Gender Ideology* Although there is no evidence that the political directorate in practice ever stated an explicit colonial policy of women's labour, a clear policy could be identified. Gendered subjectivity was evident in the actions of the political directorate and other agencies, including missionary agencies. Gendered subjectivity is produced and hierarchically organized by state discourses and practices (for example, in education, wage rates and employment practices). Gender constructions are constituted within and by the official discourse, by administration practices, within social spaces defined and delineated by state policy. Unlike during slavery, in the post-slavery period gender categories of women were constructed more as wives and mothers and less as workers. Feminist historians and other scholars point out that it was this

active ideology of the male as breadwinner that so served to radicalize women. By designating men as breadwinners, the colonial state maintained male control over female labour, largely confining women to household chores and childcare while minimizing male contributions to the household. As several scholars have observed, these practices contradicted the crude profit and loss strategies of the planter class; for women's labour was cheaper than men's. However they also bought into society's view of the place of women and paid them lower wages, leading women to protest by leaving traditional workplaces.[2]

2. ***Racism and Gender*** Of relevance too was the racism (of Whites and the coloured middle class) that informed attitudes towards the working class. Racism has traditionally been one of the central elements in the ideology used to justify exploitation in the Caribbean and thus justifies and reinforces relations of class and gender domination or exploitation.

3. ***Class Discrimination*** A race and class hierarchy remained which determined access to resources.

4. ***Colonial and Slavery Mentalities*** Despite the abolition of that brutal slave system that had tyrannized Africans and their descendants in the Caribbean for centuries, post-slavery regimes, which continued to be administered by a White minority (and later by the mixed race male middle class), failed to deliver on the promise of freedom by honouring freed people's claims to citizenship, civil rights and political enfranchisement. On the contrary, the mentalities of the slavery period survived in the period after 1838 and naturally fostered protest action, one of which was expressed through migration out of the plantation environment where attempts were being made to recreate slave relations of production. Employers, for example, imposed rents per head of household; began to charge rent for provision grounds; rented working tools; evicted those who could not pay rent; and tried to link estate residence to continued full-time labour, thus attempting to curtail freedom of movement and choice of employment.

The Socioeconomic State: Overview

This environment of social domination was accompanied by economic developments that created economic hardships for the working class and acted as push factors for the movement of labourers. What were these economic developments? First there was a decline in the sugar industry, traditionally the largest employer of labour. Second, there was a lack of expansion in the productive sectors to compensate for the decline in agriculture. Interestingly, these changes should have reduced the overall need for labour; but the need to maintain control over the labour force by creating a labour surplus, by depressing wages and by reducing the cost of production led planters to import labourers rather than restructure. Women were more affected than men by labour importation; for gender ideology dictated a change in attitude towards female agricultural labour. More men than women were imported, thereby displacing more African women. Where women did opt to remain on the plantations, they were affected by the manifestations of the post-slavery gender ideology; gender division of labour; gender discriminatory wages; the 'sex-typing' of jobs into light and heavy, with light work being given to women and remunerated at a lower rate.

Third, the period was characterized by a strengthening of capitalist relations of production in agriculture in what has been termed the modernization process. Within this process, Western European ideals of femininity and the place of women were transferred to the Caribbean. Both modernization and the gender ideology served to increasingly alienate women from agricultural activity. Modernization has usually viewed women as marginal to the process of national development. Fourth, while the coloured middle class, agents of the White minority, experienced upward mobility through access to education, economic resources and entrance into the professions, the Black majority remained free but a disenfranchised — the franchise was the privilege of propertied males — largely illiterate rural proletariat. Some eked out a living in urban centres. Given this socioeconomic and political environment where that triple alliance of merchants, colonialists and sugar planters adopted anti-worker policies to protect its economic interests, it should not be a surprise that it was in this context that women's 'feet became their only carriage'. This is not to imply that all women discontinued as plantation workers. A significant number continued, especially in territories like Barbados where planter control over land was extreme. However, they were not all full-time workers as they combined plantation work with other occupations. In fact, in colonial Guyana in the 1840s, 43 per cent of the workforce at emancipation was still on the sugar estates, a significant proportion female.[3] Afro-Guyanese women continued to be cane cutters well into the nineteenth century until Asian indentured workers displaced many. A significant number also shunned the plantations for peasant holdings. Thus after the abolition of slavery, two African–Caribbean classes developed simultaneously: a proletariat consisting largely of itinerant and plantation-based farm workers, and a landholding peasantry.

Where did Afro-Caribbean Women's Feet Take Them?

After the abolition of slavery some women withdrew their labour entirely from the estates, despite coercive or conciliatory efforts by the planters to keep them on the plantations. They became full-time housewives; combined home-making with peasant farming; moved to free villages; shifted from one plantation to another depending on labour conditions; or shifted from sugar plantations to non-sugar properties where the work regime was less regimented. The result was a reduction in the labour force in most territories, especially in those where land was available for free village and peasant development. By 1860 in Jamaica, for example, there were just 20,000 workers on the sugar estates, most of whom were male. Between 1921 and 1943, almost 80,000 Jamaican women were displaced from the agricultural sector whereas the number of men increased.[4] The historiography shows that women moved off the estates in greater numbers than men in the immediate post-slavery period. Research on Jamaica shows that in the Plantain Garden River district in St. Thomas-in-the-East where the sugar industry was dominant, women withdrew their labour. For example on Golden Grove estate, one of the largest sugar estates in Jamaica with 279

161

workers, 137 were female and worked before 1838. Up to October 12, 1838, only 19 had returned. Only five of the 142 men had absented themselves.[5] The men had responded to more attractive offers of job or task work. The sex-typing of jobs and gender-discriminatory wages made provision grounds and marketing more attractive prospects for women.

Similarly, on Green Park estate in Hanover parish where there were 404 workers before August 1, 1838, of which 204 were female, the vast majority refused to return to work unless slavery practices such as shell-blowing and the driver system were abolished or replaced. Up to October 1838, only 35 freed people had returned to fieldwork.[6]

Continued involvement in agriculture

Despite the choices made by rural women to relocate in search of better wages, women's participation in agriculture remained strong. In Jamaica in 1891, 49 per cent of those in agriculture were women. In Guyana, the figure was 31 per cent and 39 per cent in 1881 and 1891 respectively. In Barbados in the 1880s there were 21,000 males and 24,000 females in the agricultural sector.[7] These figures must be taken with caution as they do not reflect women's flexibility. Many moved in and out of agriculture depending on the economic climate; or combined plantation work with other occupations.

Migration to Towns

Pushed out of the rural wage-earning force for one reason or another, many Black women migrated to urban centres of Kingston, Port of Spain, Bridgetown, et cetera. The movement to urban spaces was definitely female dominated, a reflection of the employment opportunities in the urban centres. The following table reinforces this female dominated trend of rural to urban migration in Trinidadian towns in 1931.

Table 11.1
Migration Trends of Men and Women to Urban Areas in Trinidad, 1931

	Males	Females	% Females
Port of Spain	30, 469	39,865	56.67
San Fernando	6,699	7,654	53.32
Arima	2,354	2,731	53.70
Tobago	12,280	13,078	51.57

What did Women do in the Urban Areas?

In the urban centres, women found work mainly as domestic servants, laundresses; street and market vendors and seamstresses. Domestic service was one of the highest employers of urban Black women. By the late nineteenth century, one-quarter of the urban workers in Guyana were domestics. The 1891 census for that country shows that of a population of 28,355 women, 7,432 were domestics. In Jamaica in the same year, there were 26,686 domestics, 5,254 men and 21,432 women. As the century progressed, women found jobs in other service industries, for example in offices and hotels. The service sector in fact has superseded agriculture as the major employer in the region. In Barbados, 15,200 women were in this industry in 1946, declining to 13,200 by 1960. By 1970 the number had again moved upward to 15,000. The Jamaica censuses of 1946, 1960, and 1970 show that the service industry was consistently the largest employer of female labour — absorbing over 50. Domestic work was essentially 'woman's work'. Each year from 1891–1931, male domestics in Trinidad numbered less than 4,000, but for the same years ranged between 14,849 and 25,348 for females. In 1921, 90 per cent of the 28, 213 domestic workers in Trinidad and Tobago were female.

With urbanization and industrialization from the 1940s, work in garment factories became an outlet for urban women. During the late 1960s and 1970s, many governments invited foreign companies to set up offshore manufacturing operations in Caribbean countries in an attempt to stimulate economic growth in the region. Promises of tax concessions, a steady supply of cheap unskilled and semi-skilled labour, low wages and the absence of strict legislation to control operations have resulted in the establishment of a significant number of export-oriented industries — many electronics and textiles — in several countries in the region. The garment industry showed a preference for women workers; with the growth of this manufacturing sector many young women moving from the rural communities into the urban areas to seek employment found jobs in these new industries.

Emigration

Emigration was, from the mid-nineteenth century, an outlet for Caribbean women. The economic rationale has always been the principal push and pull factor. By the mid-twentieth century the possibilities for greater educational opportunities, and ultimately self-improvement, factored into Caribbean people's motives for emigration. Caribbean governments, dominated as they were by the landholding class, tried to legislate against outmigration, but this did not deter people. Intra-Caribbean migration was popular from the mid-nineteenth century, usually from countries like Barbados and the Leeward and Windward islands of the Eastern Caribbean to larger territories with a low population density and land for peasant development like Guyana and Trinidad. Though upward social mobility could not be achieved without working on the plantations in those colonies, the higher wages made the effort worthwhile.

In the 1880s, intercolonial migration gave way to emigration to Central and South America and farther afield. Central America and Cuba attracted thousands of workers. The largest waves of emigrants (1880–1914) went to Panama to help build the Panama Canal. Construction work itself was male dominated but women were used in many ancillary services. During the 1890s emigrants (British Windward islanders) went to Guatemala, Colombia, Ecuador, Costa Rica, Cuba, Venezuela and Santo Domingo, mainly for railroad construction and work in the sugar, coffee and banana industries, which drew their labour once the railways were completed. Between 1915 and 1919, 43,909 Jamaicans left for Cuba and Central America mainly, the majority male.

Emigrants from all Caribbean territories also headed for the USA. Indeed, the UK and the USA were the major destinations of emigrants after the 1930s. Karen Fog Olwig's research indicates that approximately 270,916 people from the British-colonized Caribbean left for the UK during the period 1948–61.[8] The first period of massive emigration ended shortly after World War I. After World War II, another wave of large-scale emigration began, this time to the UK, reaching its peak in the 1950s. The *SS Empire Windrush* carried Jamaicans to Britain in 1948 for work. Half of the population of Montserrat emigrated to the UK in the 1950s. The impact of volcanic activity in Montserrat in 1995 and 1996 also created a new wave of migration from that island to the UK and elsewhere. A census in the UK in 1966 showed that immigrants from the English-speaking Caribbean comprised 273,700 Jamaicans and 180,300 from the rest of the region. Canada has also been a recipient of immigrants from the British-colonized Caribbean. Between 1974 and 1976, net emigration from Jamaica to Canada was estimated at 26,779; the emigration of seasonal contract workers was estimated at 8,755 during the period 1975–77.

Some of this migration was temporary; but people increasingly settled, establishing a Caribbean flavour to many communities, such as Brixton in South London. Other people circulated, participating in a constant cycle of leaving and returning — exile and return.

Gender Profile in Caribbean Emigration

Out-migration before the mid-twentieth century was male dominated, a reflection of the needs of construction (railway, canal, et cetera) and plantation work in host countries. Around 56 per cent of all those who left Nevis for Trinidad in the post-slavery period were women. By the 1970s women dominated emigration from some territories. During this decade, 56 per cent of emigrants from Trinidad, 54 per cent from Jamaica and 51 per cent from Grenada, were female. Female participation fluctuated according to their opportunities for employment. Up to the 1920s, for example, emigration to Panama was male dominated. After the completion of the canal, male emigration declined and female emigration rose as the growth of the tourist industry in the Caribbean, notably in the US Virgin Islands (especially St. John), and Dutch St. Maarten, created a demand for female workers. While some professional women emigrated, up to the 1950s most went as domestic workers. Paule Marshall, in her semiautobiographical novel, *Brown Girl, Brownstones*, described how her mother and several other Barbadian women worked as domestic servants in New York just after World War II:

> Each morning they took the train to Flatbush and Sheepshead bay to scrub floors. The lucky ones had their steady madams while the others wandered those neat blocks or waited on corners each with her apron and working shoes in a bag under her arm until someone offered her a day's work.[9]

Implications for Sending and Receiving Countries

The main benefit for the countries of origin was in the form of remittances, which still remain important to Caribbean economies today. The proliferation of Western Union outlets right across the Caribbean testifies to this. Emigration boosted the economic, social and political development of the countries to which Caribbean people emigrated. It is well known that Caribbean labour was crucial, for example female emigrants helped in the transformation of the Virgin Islands and The Bahamas into successful tourist resorts. In both places, while the men assisted in the building of hotels such as the colonial hotel in The Bahamas (1922), women served as maids in these hotels.

Caribbean women also assisted in the war effort in the twentieth century. While men were wanted as soldiers in World War I (1914–17) and World War II (1938–45), women participated in the war effort despite the sexist ideas which tried to keep women out of such 'dangerous activities' or to give them 'women's work'. Ben Bosquet and Colin Douglas record that in 1943 a group of 30 West Indian women arrived in England. They were the first of 100 recruits who would serve in the British Air Transport Auxiliary (ATA), a racially mixed group.[10] After World War II, Caribbean people continued to flock to the UK where they helped to develop the postal service, the transport sector and steel mills in London, Liverpool, Birmingham and Nottinghill.

Caribbean migrants and their children also made important contributions to political activity in the USA and the UK. Men and women of Caribbean descent have played leading roles in local and national politics overseas. Between 1900 and 1930, some of the Caribbean people who settled in Harlem and Brooklyn quickly came to dominate neighbourhood politics. Many of New York's Black elected officials, judges and civil servants are of Caribbean background. Former congresswoman Shirley Chisolm, for example, is of Barbadian and Guyanese parentage. The parents of outstanding personalities such as Colin Powell, Louis Farrakhan and Malcolm X, are from the Caribbean. Colin Powell, who rose to fame in the USA as head of the joint chiefs of staff of the military, had hardworking Jamaican parents; Louis Farrakhan's father was Jamaican and his mother from St. Kitts; Malcolm X's mother was Grenadian.

Women from the Caribbean who moved to the USA, permanently or temporarily, also became active in political movements in their own right. Some examples are Louise Little, Malcolm X's mother; Amy Ashwood Garvey, Marcus Garvey's first wife who helped to organize the Universal Negro Improvement Association (UNIA) in the USA in the early twentieth century, becoming secretary of the New York branch; Amy Jacques Garvey, Marcus Garvey's second wife, who was also crucial to the Garvey movement; and Claudia Jones, freedom fighter, communist, writer, publisher, public speaker and a convenor of Afro, Asian and Caribbean organizations, from Trinidad. This tradition of political activism by Caribbean men and women in the USA, Canada, the UK and elsewhere has continued into the late twentieth century, with well-known figures like Diane Abbott and the late Bernie Grant being part of representational politics in the UK.

For the Afro-Caribbean Women

Emigration had both a negative and positive impact on Caribbean women. One positive effect was that many of those who eventually returned home

167

brought back new skills learnt in the new countries. These skills helped them to create new businesses, or enter new and better paid areas of employment in the Caribbean. Employment opportunities for women left behind often expanded as they occupied employment gaps left behind by others; and women often improved socioeconomically in the new environment and some became activists in political life.

Problems and Obstacles

I wish to stress that women's movement for betterment was hardly an uncomplicated matter. Many countries imposed immigration restrictions; they had to make huge adjustments to the host (inhospitable) countries, not least of which was in the weather; and we are all aware of the racism with which many had to deal. Women dealt with these problems as best as they could. Some solutions were easier than others. It is easy to buy or beg a warm coat but not as easy to deal with racism. Nevertheless where possible, women joined civil rights and other movements to press for improvement. The Black Power Movement, fired by the radical ideology of that Jamaican pan-Africanist, Marcus Garvey, was a powerful influence on some Black women outside of the region. Those who did not wish to be permanent migrants chose to become what we now call transnational workers: living in the Caribbean but working in many locations. They take seriously the concept of the global village.

Conclusion

The Caribbean has had a long experience with labour migration. Indigenous women were internally relocated to perform labour in households, mines and plantations; White indentured women voluntarily or forcefully worked as domestics and field labourers under exploitative conditions in the seventeenth and eighteenth centuries and enslaved African women were forcefully transported to the region to contribute to European capitalistic enterprises. In the post-slavery period, this experience with migration continued as African and African-Caribbean women explored various routes to socioeconomic betterment. The Caribbean was also the recipient of thousands of Asian women, relocated largely from India, as Britain sought to maintain slave relations of production in her colonized territories. Throughout, I have mentioned this Asian migration and perhaps given the impression that Asian women caused the economic destabilization of African-Caribbean women. Let me hasten to say that it is a historical fact that Asians were brought to the region to satisfy the capitalistic enterprises of Europeans who saw the plantation system as the best means of maintaining their socioeconomic and political dominance over the region.

With Asian immigration, the landholders, particularly in Guyana and Trinidad, were able to expand agricultural production, lower wages or at least keep them constant, and retain the upper hand in labour bargaining. I however do not wish to convey that the Asians were willing collaborators in this project of exploitation. Indeed, many argue that Asian women's experiences were of neo-slavery. The adoption of Indian indentureship as the new system of slavery, to use Hugh Tinker's term, illustrates with the greatest clarity how everywhere, freedom meant the reproduction of the class struggle within the nexus of a new legal status for the freed.[11] Some revisionists have challenged the neo-slavery thesis, focusing instead on the economic rationale of emigrants and their material gains in the colonies. For example, Pieter Emmer has argued that for Indian women emigrating to Suriname, emigration was a route to female emancipation 'from an illiberal, inhibiting and hierarchical social system in India'.[12] Most of us who do research into Indian labour migration argue oppositely, that emigration for women exposed them to multiple oppression and gendered tyranny. Many were kidnapped from India, sexually abused on the ships to the Caribbean, and exposed to brutality on the plantations.

Above all it must be noted that everything about indentured laws sought to tie women's feet and imprison them within the walls of first, the estate and second the Caribbean receiving territory! They had to get passes before they could leave the estates; they had to contribute to return passages before their feet could carry them to the ship of repatriation; there were penalties for leaving the estate without a pass; if they infringed laws their feet were tied in prison; and there were high penalties for desertion. These restrictive conditions led Indian women to carry on the radical tradition of protest in the Caribbean, often through migration (in their case off the estates, out of the Caribbean and back to India).

Chandra Kumari, for example, took one look at the conditions of indentureship in Jamaica, flatly refused to work, and demanded to be released from her contract and returned to India. Furthermore, she claimed that she was Indian royalty — the daughter of the King of Nepal — and had come to Jamaica just to look at the place. Long after the officials had released her news came from India that she had lied about being royalty; that the person she claimed as her father was no more the King of Nepal than Gladstone was King of England. Of course, by this time, Chandra was long gone.

Maharani's Misery

Others refused to accept what we now know to have been the uncontrolled sexploitation on the ships bound for the Caribbean. Women's complaint of rape and the death is manifested in the case of a young Indian woman on the ship *Allanshaw* en route to colonial Guyana in 1884 which led to an elaborate nine-day commission of enquiry in which 22 witnesses were called to give evidence. This is the first case of its kind ever to come to light and helps to explain the attractiveness of the neo-slavery thesis to analyse indentureship and the use of the term 'the other middle passage' to describe the nineteenth-century voyages from India.[13] There is debate about whether we can really equate nineteenth-century Asian migration with the brutal middle passage of enslaved African captives and I wish to point to the fact that the migration discourses have been pluralized to include other ethnicities as we seek for a more inclusive Caribbean history and Caribbean women's history.

12

THE POLITICS OF MIGRATION
OFFICIAL POLICY TOWARDS INDIANS IN
JAMAICA, 1845–1945

Annual Richardson Lecture, Beloit College, Wisconsin, October 30, 1998

I will attempt to discuss the political implications of migration within the context of a multi-ethnic Caribbean society where ethnic groups competed for social and cultural space, political power and economic resources. My examples will be located primarily within the context of Jamaica, an island where post-slavery migration, especially of Indians, was not that numerically significant, but where minority status did not necessarily imply complete political invisibility.

Jamaica imported around 38,000 Indians between 1845 and 1916 as the plantocracy attempted to curtail the bargaining power of African-Jamaican labourers and save the declining plantation economy.[1] Like other Caribbean importing countries, except Guyana, Trinidad and Guadeloupe, the number of Indians shipped to Jamaica was small;[2] and Indians never represented more than 2.2 per cent of the total Jamaican population up to 1943.[3] Minority status did not signify complete marginalization within the larger Jamaican society. Issues relating to the Indian community attracted national attention and the attention of the colonial government in Jamaica, the colonial office in England, the India office in London, and the government in India for close to a century after their importation. Between 1845 and 1945, the 'Indian question' generated copious correspondence between the Colonial Governors, the Colonial Secretary, the Secretary of State for the Colonies, the various Protectors of Immigrants and Emigrants and the government in India. The colonial government was forced to formulate special legislation for Indians and to modify legislation in response to various local or external pressure groups.

Indians arrived in Jamaica during the operation of the Old Representative System with its planter-dominated House of Assembly. By 1866 in the aftermath of the Morant Bay Rebellion, the House of Assembly had surrendered its powers and the limited elective principle in operation under the Old Representative System, in favour of Crown Colony government. Between 1866 and 1944 several constitutional changes took place which eventually restored the elective principle and eventually popular government when universal adult suffrage was granted. Whatever the type of government and constitution, Indian immigration operated at a time when the planting interest formed the politically influential elite and when overall control of the island was vested in the metropole.[4] Up to the end of indenture, government policies toward the Indians generally reflected planter interests rather than the interests of the Indian labourers. However, they could not totally ignore the liberal humanitarian pressure of the still active Anti-Slavery Society, elements in the colonial office and the government in India which insisted on certain beneficent clauses in the Immigration Laws so as to avoid the charge of the introduction of neo-slavery. In the twentieth century, as the Indians made the transition from sojourners to permanent settlers, policies towards them reflected the colonial government's view that a small and economically uninfluential minority should integrate and not seek special, ethnically discriminatory privileges which had the potential to anger the black majority.

The rest of this lecture will examine how the political directorate demonstrated its attitude towards the Indian immigrants and settlers through legislation affecting the terms of the financing of their importation; indentureship and mobility, seeking to restrict rural to urban migration, outmigration, and repatriation. As settlers, government policy affected the Indians' social customs and institutions, and their call supported by the government in India for special ethnic representation in the legislature.

Immigration Policy

The decision to import labourers into Jamaica in the aftermath of the abolition of slavery cannot be divorced from the tremendous influence which the 'sugarocracy' and later the banana barons exerted on the political directorate. It was these large planters rather than the non-sugar agricultural elements, the merchant class and the coloured elite which clamoured for immigration as the antidote to emancipation. The planter class, anxious to maintain its traditional control over labour implemented coercive tactics which, rather than keeping labourers on the estates, served to hasten the trek from the plantations. It was within this context of a diminishing resident labour force that planters exerted pressure on the government to import labourers. Planter evidence before the Select Committee of the House of Commons in 1842 influenced the decision of the committee that: 'one obvious and most desirable mode of endeavouring to compensate for this diminished supply of labour is to promote the immigration of a fresh labouring population to such an extent as to create competition for employment.'[5]

The political directorate in Jamaica, acting on the recommendations of the House of Commons, facilitated the importation of Indians despite the existence of an anti-immigration lobby. The lobby consisted of the Anti-Slavery Society which feared the appearance of neo-slavery, the African–Jamaican masses who feared economic competition from imported labour, the non-sugar producers who could command an adequate local labour supply, and some churches (for example, the Baptist Union) which feared the social and economic impact of non-Christian immigrants on the larger (especially Black) population.[6] Additionally, the Jamaican Legislature sanctioned the contribution of general revenue to the costs of immigration — though after 1884 as the Legislature became less planter dominated, the percentage contribution declined significantly. Up to the 1860s, planters paid less than 50 per cent of the cost of immigration of Indians, leaving general revenue to pay the bulk. Thereafter, a ratio of one-third (general revenue) and two-thirds (planter contribution) was proposed. Increasing opposition from the non-sugar sectors in Jamaica led to a reduction of general revenue's contribution to only the local costs of immigration, such as medical care. By 1910 continued opposition caused planters to bear all costs. The point though is that from the 1850s to 1910, general revenue bore from 25 to 50 per cent of the cost of immigration, satisfying planter interest at the expense of the larger society.[7]

Indentureship

When Indians were first imported into Jamaica in the 1840s, they were indentured on (optionally) renewable one-year contracts. The reluctance of Indians to reindenture and the high mortality rate associated with their departure from the estates influenced the call for longer employment contracts — a call which the government heeded. The government not only allowed three-year contracts in 1850 and five-year contracts in 1862 under Section 30 of Jamaica Law 23 of 1879, but Sections 41 and 43 of the Law provided that on the expiration of the first 5-year contract immigrants could enter into fresh contracts. Reindentured Indians were subjected to the terms of the immigration law as if they were fresh importees. Reindentureship was abolished in 1891.[8] The government was only willing to reduce the contract period for female immigrants as an incentive to get more of them to emigrate to the island and satisfy the 40:100 female–male ratio laid down by the colonial office.[9]

The call for longer contracts was allegedly based on humanitarian concerns for the Indians; but it should also be recognized that it was influenced by the ill-effects of the Sugar Duties Act on the sugar economy and the need to have a nucleus of resident labourers available to the planter class for a much longer period. Contracts would anchor the labourers to the estates and make them, hopefully, 'more controllable'. To satisfy the wishes of the influential plantocracy, the political directorate also participated in the criminalization of the indentureship system, imposing penalties ranging from flogging and fines to imprisonment for breaches of what the state deemed 'crimes' and 'infringement of the law'.[10]

Repatriation, Settlement and Land Acquisition

The provision of a return passage to India for all contracting immigrants had been obligatory on the part of the importing colonies, and was, in fact, an essential ingredient of the contract signed by each emigrant. Rather than requiring the importers to fund the total cost of repatriation, the Jamaican Assembly came under pressure to fund it. There was, initially, some reluctance tied to the opposition of the non-planter elements in the legislature; but the government soon relented and the new Immigration Act of 1853 made provisions for general revenue to contribute to the cost of return passages through the Immigrants' Colonization and Return Passage Fund.[11] Increasing opposition to this decision caused the government to modify its repatriation policy; and between 1861 and 1897, the importers were required to bear the cost of repatriation which averaged £6.10s. per statute adult. The plantocracy was never supportive of the compulsory return passage particularly when it was required to bear the full cost of repatriation. Not surprisingly, it pressured the government to remove this obligation, reduce it, or discourage immigrants from taking it up through the offer of bounties or compulsory contribution towards their own passages. The Jamaican Assembly assisted the plantocracy at the expense of the indentured worker. At first the government sanctioned the offer of colonization bounties in cash (£12) or land (ten acres of Crown land) to each immigrant, male and female, who agreed to exchange repatriation for settlement. Nearly 1,500 Indians accepted the colonization bounty between 1845 and 1848, the majority opting for cash over land especially as the lands offered were in mountainous and inaccessible parts of the island.[12] Up to 1877, close to £32,000 had been spent on bounties.[13] The increasing expense of the colonization bounty caused cash grants to be discontinued in 1879 and land grants to be abolished by the government in 1906.

For Indians who settled after the abolition of land grants, access to land had to be on their own initiative, just as it was for the majority black population. Some of them tried to get land under the Government Land Settlement Scheme introduced on the recommendation of the Moyne Commission in 1939; but most could not afford the downpayment. To solve this problem, the East Indian Progressive Society (EIPS) petitioned the government to waive the ten per cent downpayment for poor Indians. The request was refused on the basis that 'there can be no justification for extending special privileges to the Indian community beyond those which they at present enjoy under the legislation regulating their marriage, divorce and succession';[14] and that the facilities for settling people on the land:

are the same as those open to all persons in Jamaica who wish to take up land under the island-wide Land Settlement Scheme as it is not considered necessary or desirable to differentiate between East Indians and the rest of the community in regard to terms of settlement.[15]

Indians who were imported after 1897 and who wished to return to India were thereafter required to pay a portion of their passages. Despite the cost, there were some Indians who still continued to request that the government provide ships and send them back to India at the expiration of their period of compulsory residence. Government arranged repatriation from Jamaica ceased altogether in 1930 partly because of pressure from India to discontinue this process, the high mortality rate on return ships and the high cost of repatriation after World War I. The requests for repatriation continued into the 1940s but the government never reopened this provision, angering the Indians and the East Indian Associations.

The Mobility of Ex-Indentured Labourers

The government in Jamaica consistently assisted the planter class in curtailing the mobility of ex-indentured Indians. Not only did they try to discourage rural to urban migration on the basis that that movement would draw away Indians from agriculture, but they prohibited the emigration of Indians to third countries, including Cuba (lifted in 1905), Ecuador, Mexico and Guatemala. The Immigration Law provided that Indians could not leave the island until they had remained in the island for five years of contract and five additional years of continuous residence after indentureship. Indians who wished to emigrate from Jamaica thereafter had to apply for permission, get clearance from the Immigration department, secure a passport on pain of a fine of £10 and fund the entire trip. The law stipulated that once Indians left the island, they forfeited any claims to repatriation or colonization bounties.[16] The colonial government's attitude towards the re-emigration of Indians got some support from the government in India which argued that Indians should not be allowed to leave Jamaica unless it was to return to India — unless it could be ascertained that they had adequate means of subsistence.[17]

By 1912, despite the obstacles placed in their way, 2,649 Indians had left the island for Cuba, Panama, Mexico and Ecuador. Between 1913 and 1930 another 2,011 left, the majority for Cuba.[18] Wartime conditions led to the cessation of outmigration from 1930 to 1940.

Education

Prior to 1879, there was no official government policy towards the education of the Indian immigrant population in Jamaica, perhaps because (i) between 1875 and 1916, Indian children made up no more than 9.4 per cent of the total Indian population in the island;[19] (ii) Indians were regarded as transients who would shortly return to their homeland; and (iii) both parents and employers showed more interest in the labour power and economic contribution of children than in their educational needs. Initially, missionaries, traditionally associated with educational efforts in the post-slavery Caribbean, were more concerned about their mission to the newly emancipated than with the plight of people they regarded as 'pagans', from whom the African-Caribbean people had to be 'protected'.[20] The increased settlement of ex-indentured immigrants in Jamaica from 1879 caused missionaries, education officials and the Protectors of Immigrants to pay more attention to the educational needs of Indian children. In 1879, the government ruled that the Protector of Immigrants had the power to 'order the child of any immigrant, with the consent of such immigrant, to attend the nearest suitable and most convenient day school'.[21] This law had no noticeable impact on school attendance among Indian children, partly on account of parental objection to the Eurochristian content of the school curriculum, the use of the English language — as opposed to Hindi — as the language of instruction, the lack of Indian teachers, and the extent of ethnic mixing in the schools.[22]

The continued non-attendance of Indian children in the elementary schools became the concern of various groups and individuals in the Jamaican society who increasingly thought that the government should make special provisions for them. In 1880, the Inspector of Immigrants for St. Catherine called on the government to establish special schools for Indian children on strictly non-sectarian principles as 'it is a matter of pain to me . . . to see no active steps yet taken to educate the children of a class of persons who are doing so much by their steady labour for the capitalists of the country'.[23] The Education Commission appointed in 1897 also recommended the opening of special (Indian) Government Elementary Schools in areas where 30 or more Indian children resided.[24]

Initially, the colonial government in Jamaica opposed the establishment of ethnically segregated schools. Its policy was that all children in Jamaica, regardless of ethnic origin, should attend the same schools. Lord Chamberlain, Secretary of State, wrote to the Governor of Jamaica in 1899 in response to this issue, 'the aim of education should be to assimilate the different elements of the population, not to accentuate racial distinctions.'[25]

The authorities also took the view that it did not make good economic sense to provide special educational institutions for so few children and it was left up to the missionaries to respond to these calls for special schools for Indian children. The Quakers and Scottish Presbyterians opened day schools for Indian children in their mission stations. In 1898, the Quakers opened a school for Indian girls at Seaside (called Happy Grove). The missionaries opened other schools at Albany, Amity Hall, Spicy Grove and Cascade; but not all of these catered to Indians exclusively.[26] The Quakers, Scottish Presbyterians and Anglicans also established Industrial Schools, Homes and Orphanages to cater to Indian children. In response to the appeals of the church groups, some planters made estate buildings available to be used as school rooms.

Despite these efforts to educate Indian children, registration in the schools — especially in those admitting children of other ethnic groups — remained low. Calls intensified by 1910 for the government to step in and establish government schools catering exclusively for Indian children as an incentive to increase their attendance. Following the repeated representations made, the government decided in 1910 to accede to the pressure for two Special Indian Schools at Orange Hill in St. Mary and Fellowship in Portland, both areas with large populations of Indians. The government made it clear that these two schools would be experimental, and based on an assessment after two years it would make a decision whether to open more schools or abandon the experiment. The Legislative Council voted for money for funding the two experimental Indian schools. Other special Indian schools were established following the visit of Messrs. Chimman Lal and James McNeil in 1913.[27] Acting upon these suggestions, the Legislative Council voted for funds for the opening of an additional school, run by the Presbyterians, at Smith Village in (Denham Town), Kingston.[28] A Government Morning School was established in Alley, Vere in 1916 under an Indian teacher.[29] Two other special Indian schools were opened in 1916 — at Trinity (Quaker Hill) in St. Mary and at Constant Spring in St. Andrew.

Coincidentally, with the end of government-sponsored repatriation in 1930, the government overturned its decision to operate ethnically segregated schools and withdrew funding, forcing some to close and others to shift their focus and admit non-Indian children. One rationale for government's decision, as expressed by the Acting Director of Education, Tucker, was that, 'there is no distinction made in elementary education. For the separation of East Indians or Chinese children from the remainder, the desire being that if these children remain in Jamaica, they should become its citizens.'[30]

The Indian community protested against the government's closure of the Special Indian Schools,[31] but the government did not overturn its decision. It was sensitive to the heightened ethnic economic competition in the war years and wanted to diffuse the hostility of African-Jamaicans to the special treatment of minority groups. The Moyne Commission supported the governments' position, pointing out that in 1939, 90 per cent of the Indians were born in Jamaica; so that, 'any measures which cause the East Indians to look upon them or to be looked upon, as a people apart, will at once pave the way for inter-racial rivalries and jealousies.'[32]

Social Customs and Institutions

The period 1930–1945 not only witnessed the end of repatriation schemes and the increased permanent settlement of Indians in the island, but marked a change in government policy towards Indians. Such change was manifested in its 'civic assimilationist policy', involving the homogenization of the island's institutions: the judicial system, marriage, divorce and burial practices and form of access to political positions. After indenture, there were no official governmental attempts to force Indians to abandon their cultural practices in such areas as food, dress, music, dance, language and family system; though creolization was inevitable given the small and scattered nature of their communities. However, the policy was different on questions of Indian traditional customs, specifically marriage, divorce and the disposal of the dead — all areas in which a small but vocal section of the Indian community lobbied for special, ethnic-specific legislation.

Beginning in 1896 with the passing of the 'Immigrants' Marriage, Divorce and Succession Law', an official policy regarding marriage practices was laid down. The law addressed the very early age at which Indian couples were married (girls even from age ten), considered much too early by Jamaican and British standards. A minimum age of 13 for females and 15 for males was stipulated.[33] The law was revised in 1929 by the 'Age at Marriage Act' (chapter 36), which made it illegal for a marriage to be contracted between parties under age 16. Law 22 of 1896 also prohibited Muslim polygynous marriages and stipulated that while Hindus and Muslims could marry according to their traditional customs, the marriage had to be registered. Christian ministers could not perform marriages of Hindus or Muslims who had not converted to Christianity; and Indians who had converted could not marry according to their traditional rites. Christianized Indians were to become subjected to all the laws of Jamaica and to any special laws relating to the Indian community. The Indian community objected to several aspects of the Marriage, Divorce and Succession Law. The main objection was to the requirement that marriages be registered as this was considered an insult to Hindu and Muslim religious customs and the authority of their priests. In India, once they were married according to the prescribed rites of their own religion, such marriages were legal and did not require registration to be valid.[34] As such many Hindu and Muslim priests refused to register marriages and as a result the children of unregistered marriages were deemed bastards and unable to inherit property.[35] The government did not change its stance despite the Moyne

Commission's support of the Indians' position.[36] The Government of India and the Sanatan Dharma Sabha, which passed a resolution after its public meeting in India on April 10, 1939 stated that:

> the registration of marriages performed by Hindu rites in Trinidad, British Guiana, Dutch Guiana and other similar colonies being obligatory for the purposes of making their offspring legitimate is to nullify the Hindu religious tenets and amount to interference in their religion.[37]

The suggestion by the EIPS — which took its case to the Colonial Secretary and even to the British Privy Council[38] — that Indian Marriage Officers should be appointed as a solution to the whole problem was rejected by the government in Jamaica. One basis of objection was that marriage officers had to have a place of public worship, which Hindu priests and Muslim *Moulvies* did not have (an argument which the government only dropped in 1960); another was that the number of priests and *Moulvies* were too few (19 pandits and 4 *Moulvies* in 1943) to serve the total Indian population (21,396 in 1943). In any case, many Hindu and Muslim priests viewed such appointment as capitulation to Christian laws and did not wholeheartedly support the campaigns of the EIPS.[39]

The Jamaican government also met some opposition with a section of the Indian population over the matter of divorce. Though Muslims permitted divorce, the Hindu law did not contemplate it. In Jamaica, the law provided for two alternate means of divorce, as it did for marriage. Indians who were married in either of these two methods could legally receive the corresponding method of divorce. Indians married according to their own personal rites and customs could only be divorced according to their personal law on the grounds of adultery. Those married by a Christian minister could be granted divorce according to English law. Even though Hindu law did not contemplate divorce, the Protector of Immigrants reported that Hindus applied for divorce; but up to 1927, all Hindus applying for divorce did so according to English law. In 1928, the law which said that those married according to their personal law could get a corresponding form of divorce was put to the test for the first time when Sukeya of Charlottenburgh Estate in St. Mary filed for divorce against her husband, Parag. Both had been married under the provisions of Law 22 of 1896 on November 23, 1926. Sukeya accused Parag of infidelity[40] and the government had no idea how to proceed. Firstly, Hindu law did not permit divorce and secondly, the couple had been married according to their own religious rites and therefore divorce had to be according to such rites. The Attorney General wrote to India for advice but did not like the response, which included information that divorce for Hindus and Muslims need not involve the courts. The Hindu priests in consultation with the parties involved could handle the matter.[41] This custom was unacceptable to the government who thereafter insisted that all Indians had to use the courts and English law in all divorce cases.[42]

The final cultural issue that pitted (Hindu) Indians against the Eurocentric colonial government related to the issue of cremation. Whereas traditionally, Muslims buried their dead, Hindus traditionally used the method of cremation by the pyre system, immersing the ashes in the sea or river. Up to 1950, cremation facilities were unavailable in Jamaica; and the laws relating to Indians contained no provisions for allowing cremation.[43] After the 1930s, the Hindu community, supported by their communal organizations, increasingly pressed for cremation facilities. The East Indian Association of Jamaica pointed to the Indian official on the Moyne Commission that: 'to quite a number of Indians here cremation of the dead is a religious injunction. The law is not clear on the matter so the Indians who want to cremate their dead are afraid of doing so. The law should be made clear, permitting those who want to cremate to do so.'[44]

The Moyne Commission, while not supporting Indian separatism, expressing the view that Indians who settled should not be accorded any special treatment over the native population, urged the Jamaican Legislature not to put any obstacle in the way of Hindus who wished to cremate their dead. Support came from India. At a public meeting of citizens of Krishna Nagar Lahore, a resolution was passed urging colonial governments to 'redress this grievance without any further delay'.[45] The response of the government was that there was no law in the island relating to cremation but that a bill on the subject would be introduced 'at a suitable opportunity'.[46] Up to 1946, the Government had not passed any legislation to deal with cremation. Governor Huggins eventually ruled that (i) the introduction of legislation to deal with the practice of cremation in accordance with Hindu rites would require a great deal of detailed work; (ii) the safeguards which it would be necessary to apply would render the system impracticable, and (iii) the use of modern crematoria would not meet the wishes of the Indian government or of the local Hindu community (who wanted cremation using the pyre system) and as there was little general public demand for their introduction, his government would not proceed with the legislation which former Governor Richards had contemplated.[47]

Political Representation

In general, the political life of the Indians did not preoccupy the colonial government beyond nullifying the judicial and political role of the Indian village council, the *Panchayat*, and refusing to remove (until years later) the literacy in English (not in Hindi) qualification attached to the franchise introduced in 1884. After they made the transition from sojourners to settlers, more and more of the adult males became registered voters. On the eve of the granting of universal adult suffrage, 1,043 adult male Indians (5.2 per cent of the total Indian adult male population) were registered voters.[48] From the 1890s, a few individuals also sought to be elected to political positions. The Protector of Immigrants, P.C. Cork reported in 1895–96 that a high caste ex-indentured Indian, who owned 2,600 acres had been elected to the Trelawny Parochial Board. Deosoran Tewari, a large landowner in Clarendon, was also a member of the Clarendon Parochial Board and he was the only Indian to offer himself as a candidate in the elections of 1944.[49] While some voted in the limited elections before 1944 and also in the 1944 elections; and while there were a few large landowners in parochial government, up to 1944, none were in the Legislature. By contrast, by 1941 there were two nominated and four elected Indians in the Guyanese Legislature. The Acting Chief Justice in Guyana was also an

Indian and in Trinidad, four Indians had been elected to the Legislative Council by 1940.[50]

In Jamaica, however, the Indian community was too small to return its own members to the Legislative Council; and up to 1943, none had been nominated. Rather than accepting that this was a function of numbers and integrating themselves in the political life of the island, voting for non-Indian candidates, the Indian organizations decided to lobby for ethnic representation in the Legislature. J.D. Tyson represented this concern to the Moyne Commission pointing out that, 'at present there is no one whose special care it is to see that the Indian community is not prejudiced when Legislative or Executive action is in contemplation, and the community itself is quite unable to take any steps for its own protection.'[51]

The Moyne Commission recommended that the post of Protector of Immigrants, abolished in 1933, be revived to meet the gap identified by Tyson; but the local Indian community and the government in India, which had taken an increasing interest in the Indian diaspora, opposed this. They wanted seats to be reserved in the two Houses of the Legislature — in the new constitutional changes suggested by the Moyne Commission — for Indian representatives. Specifically, the Government of India wanted an Indian to be nominated to fill one of the seats in the House of Representatives and one seat in the Legislative Council to be reserved for an Indian who 'would feel himself pledged to the interest of his community'.[52] Part of the rationale for this support of ethnic representation was that, 'the East Indian population was not numerous enough or sufficiently organised in any electoral area to succeed in returning its own representative to either Houses under a system of universal adult suffrage.'[53] The lone Indian who later contested the 1944 elections polled only 6.5 per cent of the total of 13,362 votes polled, losing to his opponent H.C. Cork.[54]

The Secretary of State for the Colonies, Oliver Stanley, informed the government in India that since the proposed House of Representatives was to be an entirely elected House, the Government of Jamaica could not reserve a seat specially for Indians;[55] for the government could not single out any ethnic group for special favours.

Conclusion

It seemed clear, then, that in the period 1845–1916, the political directorate appeared more inclined to formulate policies to appease the landholding classes; thereafter government policies were influenced by the need to avoid the charge that they were pandering to an ethnic minority at the expense of the larger, Black-dominated population.

SECTION IV

SLAVERY'S LEGACIES IN POSTCOLONIAL
JAMAICA

Introduction

Despite the abolition of slavery in the British-colonized Caribbean over 160 years ago, references to slavery and the ideologies/legacies of slavery are constantly used to frame and contextualize public debates among people in the region, as, indeed, they are within the wider Atlantic world. And although the descendants of enslaved people now occupy the highest political offices in societies radically transformed by the slavery and post-slavery struggles for freedom and justice, the 'up from slavery' concept in public life is strong and indicates that there is an equally strong opinion that the process of emancipation is not complete; that, in Swithin Wilmot's terms, emancipation is still 'in action'.[1] Even the annual rhetoric that accompanies Emancipation Day commemorative activities is located more within the discourse of slavery than within the discourse of anti-slavery and freedom, giving the impression that the attempts in the period of modernity to bring about a level of well-being within social formations and to create human rights communities in former slave colonies have failed.

My letter to Mary Seacole reflects on how racism, during and after the period of enslavement, 'coloured' her experiences, especially as she negotiated the sometimes perilous social worlds and warfronts of the Americas and Europe. The inaugural professorial lecture at York, required as part of my appointment in 2000 as one of the Network Professors there, identifies the areas in which slavery's legacies are manifested and engages with the reasons so many of the problems of the Caribbean are framed within the discourse of slavery.

One of the obvious legacies of slavery and colonialism is what I refer to as 'the ranking game' or social hierarchizing, and this framed my second inaugural lecture on the occasion of my appointment to a personal chair as professor of Social History at the Mona campus of the University of the West Indies (UWI). In its simplest definition, 'ranking' is a metaphor for social ordering, social and cultural hierarchizing. Within the Jamaican context 'ranking' represents the linguistic, oral and literary aspects of social culture that is the ritualized and politicized codes and consciousness of difference. If we view its iconography and consider its lyrical content, then we will understand that 'ranking' is the engine that drives Jamaica's political sociology. For some, situating difference establishes the boundaries of belonging; for others, situating difference is a way of signifying the opposite tendency of 'unbelonging'. This tension between 'belonging' and 'unbelonging' is a fundamental characteristic of the 'ranking game', a ritual that is invested with all the social and political capital available to the society. Ranking is understood historically within the colonial formation in terms of access to restricted status, as manifested primarily in signs and symbols that along with social consensus offer respect and respectability. The 'ranking game', of course, was intensely practised in the age of modernity. My research into the complex interaction of sugar planters and livestock farmers (pen-keepers) during slavery, Indian indentureship and inter-ethnic relations in an increasingly multicultural post-slavery society, afforded me an opportunity to explore the evolution of this historic phenomenon.

13

'DEAR MRS SEACOLE':

'Groundings' with Mary Seacole on Slavery, Gender and Citizenship

Speech Delivered at the Institute of Jamaica's Function to Honour Mary Seacole, November 21, 2005

I am pleased to share in honouring a phenomenal woman, Mary Seacole — born Mary Jane Grant in 1805 in Kingston, Jamaica, but self-identifying as Mrs Seacole after her marriage to Edwin Horatio Nelson Seacole, godson of the British Naval Hero Lord Nelson of the Battle of Trafalgar fame who ironically died the year she was born.[1]

With your permission, I will read a letter to her. As many of you know, since 2001, and following in the footsteps of my colleague Professor Rupert Lewis who wrote a letter to Garvey a few years back,[2] I have developed this habit of writing and reading aloud, letters to dead ancestors (sometimes in English, sometimes in Creole to remind them of their roots), starting with Nanny (2001) and continuing with Walter Rodney (2004), Tacky (2005) and Sir Alexander Bustamante (2006). Before I begin, let me say that the tone and content of my letter were informed by the sassiness and independent-mindedness of this woman, as reflected in her bestselling autobiography. So, here goes.

Dear Mrs Seacole,

Please accept best wishes from all Jamaicans on the occasion of the bicentenary of your birth. We realize that others have tried to 're-nationalize' you; but more on that later. Thank you for leaving us with your bestselling autobiography, *Wonderful Adventures of Mrs. Seacole in Many Lands*[3] and allowing us to understand your world through your own eyes, rather than having to rely on the sometimes ventriloquized, sometimes empowered bad words of people like Edward Long,[4] who had such negative words to cast on Black women in the eighteenth century. Of course, with all your traipsing around the world and battling with wars and diseases, I doubt that you ever found time to read Edward Long — which is just as well.

You certainly picked a momentous and turbulent year in which to be born, judging by events that occurred in 1805: New Jersey's policy of gradual emancipation; the issuing of the first British Order-in-Council announcing the phased abolition of the Transatlantic Trade in enslaved Africans;[5] the drawing up of Haiti's emancipatory constitution;[6] Britain's victory at the Battle of Trafalgar; Nelson's death; Thomas Jefferson's second term as President of the USA and Lady Nugent's departure from Jamaica, so terrified was she that a Haitian-style revolution would erupt in the island.[7]

On the local scene, the war of slavery raged — both the war to maintain it and the wars to end it. The tyranny of the pigmentocracy created the ranking game and led to the process of 'desmadification' and ethnic upgrading from free coloureds to honorary white. Restrictions on free-coloured occupations such as law and medicine forced you to become an informal commercial herbalist! No wonder you travelled 'very regular'. Who would not wish to escape from that nineteenth-century environment, which, even after emancipation, was organized along a neo-slavery trajectory? So, even though you practised your trade in Jamaica, following in the footsteps of your mother, your most able teacher, alien lands would become your stage, especially after the death of those you held dear: your husband, mother and patroness.

I was surprised that you had only your little maid for a travelling companion; but admired you for defying the gender conventions of the time. Still, you were lucky it was then: now a single Black woman roaming all over the world like Digicel and Cable & Wireless and carrying herbs would certainly have attracted attention including a body scan! As an attractive Jamaican woman, brown or not, you would perhaps, have been mistaken for a drug mule, sniffed by colour-prejudiced dogs and have your ample body 'feel-feel' up by strange men and women.

Like the Informal Commercial Importers (ICIs) of the modern age, you did not allow language to be a barrier to the places you visited. So what if you could not 'habla español' at first? That did not stop you from charging into Panama and other parts of Central America; and when your little maid shouted out 'Hombro-landro!' on one occasion, you recognized that as 'A man thief in the house!' and took appropriate defensive action.[8]

Although you were a 'browning' and free, you did not 'diss' your Black ancestors. This has earned you respect. You loved your mother and verbally terrorized all who would seek to cast aspersions on blackness or would suggest that you were less a person because you were not White; and the US citizen in Panama who offered to bleach you got the full verbal treatment. As you tell it, his offer was entangled in a tortuous toast he invited his fellow Americans to drink to your health at your brother's hotel in Cruces at a party to celebrate the anniversary of American independence. I can imagine how annoyed he made you with his:

> So, I say, God bless the best yaller woman he ever made ——, from Jamaica, gentlemen. Well, gentlemen, I expect there are only 2 things we are vexed for — and the first is that she ain't one of us — a citizen of the great United States; and the other gentlemen — that Providence made her a yaller woman. I calculate gentlemen you are all as vexed as I am that she is not wholly white — but I do reckon on your rejoicing with me that she is so many shades removed from being entirely black — and I guess if we could bleach her by any means we would.[9]

I was not surprised at these words in your autobiography:

> It may be supposed that I did not need much persuasion to return thanks, burning as I was to tell them my mind on the subject of colour. Indeed, if my brother had not checked me, I should have given them my thoughts somewhat too freely. As it was I said
>
> > But I must say that I don't altogether appreciate your friend's kind wishes with respect to my complexion. If it had been as dark as any

nigger's, I should have been just as happy and as useful ...; and as to his offer of bleaching me, I should, even if it were practicable, decline it without any thanks. As to the society into which this process might gain me admission, all I can say is that judging by the specimens I have met here and elsewhere, I don't think that I shall lose much by being excluded from it.[10]

You adjusted to so many different situations and your resilience is now legendary; nothing phased you. Your self-confidence was amazing! And you outwitted those who thought they could outwit you! I was struck by the fact that you hardly had space or time for despair; ever the eternal optimist.

You were a snob though. You turned your British nose down at the US gold prospectors and their ladies and did not mince words when describing them; though I am sure your mother and your patroness taught you better manners. How do you mean that it was no use giving some of the American travellers carving knives and forks? That 'expectoration' was a great American national habit?[11]

Anyway, your activities in Central America brought you fame and respect; just as your helping hand with the cholera and yellow fever epidemics in Jamaica in the 1850s has done. I see you could not keep still after returning to Jamaica from Panama. You had to seek out another war front. But why the Crimea?[12] Was it really because you had heard that soldiers you knew in Jamaica were serving there and you were concerned about them? Of course, you know that some said that you had a nose for hustling at the battlefront and saw the possibility of making a buck in the Crimea. But did you really think that the people at the War Office in England would embrace you wholeheartedly and send you to help Florence Nightingale? Or were you fooled by your acceptance as a nurse in Jamaica and Central America?

Anyway, no one who followed your life up to 1854 would have been surprised at the fact that even though, on account of your colour and ethnicity, you were not granted an interview with the War Office — were in fact refused an interview four times — you used your own meagre resources and funds raised with the help of others, and funded the trip and found yourself in the Crimea. Not only did you go there, you established the British Hotel near Balaclava to provide a mess-table and quarters for the sick and convalescent officers. On the battlefield, and known as 'Mother Seacole' [here in Jamaica the men would call you 'Mummy'] you attended to the wounded. You saw 'mother' as a term of endearment and one that reminded you of the warmth of home — not for you some Jamaican women's response, especially to some of the 'hardback' man dem a call dem 'mummy': *Go whey! Mi couldna be your mumma.*

Your exemplary life indicates that women are not necessarily ambivalent to warfare. Not for you any female squeamishness about disease, illness and death. You experienced first hand the death, disease and grueling work of being in the battlefield. Your testimony constitutes a challenge to the gender inequalities inextricably linked with war and militarism. You used your maternal narrator to challenge the conventional dichotomies associated with respectable Victorian womanhood and with war. When you insisted that the battlefield is your rightful place, you demolished the boundaries between the home front and the battlefield.[13]

I notice that you did not return to Jamaica to live after returning from war but stayed in England. I guess you did not see much prospect in nineteenth-century Jamaica, a society emerging out of a slavery past and trying to come to grips with freedom; an island that did not immediately recognize your importance; an island where women did not have many rights. Well, in any case you were broke, so broke that in 1856 you were declared officially bankrupt in a London court, an order rescinded by the court in 1857. When I read this I could not help thinking: poor thing! Anyway, people in England, including British royalty rallied around you and hosted fundraising activities to help you out. I doubt that anyone in Jamaica would have held a fundraising bashment for you; so it is just as well you did not return. I was amused by some of the lyrics the soldiers heaped on you at the 'bashment' in 1856:

And now the good soul is "in the hole,"
What red-coat in all the land, But to set her upon her legs again
Will not lend a willing hand?[14]

At the time you died (at age 76 on May 14, 1881), Jamaica was a more hopeful place for melanin abundant people. It is true that the Morant Bay Rebellion had led to the introduction of direct Crown rule, taking away Black people's hope of representative government. The 1880s however ushered in a period of agitation for the return of democratic government. But the 1880s also saw the intensification of the emigration movement, as Jamaicans sought a way out of economic hardships.[15] You were thus not alone in your trek away from the island to seek a better life. You must have felt so happy when you were recognized for your life of work: the Crimean Medal, the French Legion of Honour and a Turkish Medal — even if Sister Florence was not thrilled by your celebrity status and wrote that you were not deserving of the praise because you kept a house of ill repute in the Crimea (hinting that it was little more than a brothel) and you were primarily a business woman rather than a nurse. She never heard about multi-tasking?

The land of your birth also honoured you — naturally after you died. By the way, the *Daily Gleaner* carried your death notice almost a month after the event — on June 9, 1881. Only in 1954 did Jamaica officially decide to find various ways to honour you. At the initiative of the nurses, a ward at Kingston Public Hospital (KPH) was named after you in 1956. In 1957, a hall of residence at the University of the West Indies (UWI) was named after you and the first warden was Lucille Mair, herself a phenomenal woman who pioneered the field of Caribbean women's history.[16] Mary Seacole House was opened in 1960. A plaque to honour you now has pride of place at the entrance of the place you once lived but which is now the Institute of Jamaica. This should please you. The place still nourishes people; but their minds rather than their bodies. In 1990, Jamaica awarded you the Order of Merit.

But I wonder how you would have reacted to the news that people in England call you British? In 2004, you came first in an online poll to name the top 100 Greatest Black Britons. This matter of citizenship is really interesting. Were you not born in Jamaica? So, if you were born in Jamaica and if in your days children took the status of their mother and your mother was Jamaican, how you come to be a Black British? William Andrews calls you an Afro-American woman in one of the many introductions to your fantastic autobiography.[17] Indeed, what are Caribbean and African diaspora icons such as Mary Prince, Henry Sylvester Williams, Olaudah Equiano, Claudia Jones and Robert Wedderburn doing on the list?[18] If all who were born in the British Empire before independence are entitled to be called British, then would Sam Sharpe, for example, qualify?[19] Or would he have had to live in Britain for a little while? I wonder if those rebels deported to England after major rebellions were regarded as British? As to Black: I wonder if you would have objected, preferring to project your status as a 'browning'? But being named the greatest Black British has still not given you as much honour as Florence Nightingale. Indeed, while a statue of Florence Nightingale was erected as part of the Crimean war memorial in 1915, you were left out. You would be pleased to know that since November 24 2003, there has been a statue appeal campaign in Britain to right this wrong. Also, recently your lost portrait was found and it now hangs in the National Portrait gallery facing Florence Nightingale. You should get a kick out of that.

Anyway, I want to tell you that being called a Black British is not necessarily a permanent state. Other countries only claim Jamaicans who are very good and squeaky clean. When Ben Johnson won the 100 metres in Seoul in 1988, he was hailed as a Canadian. A few minutes later, when his drug test came back positive, he had reverted to being Jamaican-born Ben Johnson; and even more so after his life ban in 1993. I hope that you revealed everything in your autobiography because woe be unto you and your canonization by the British if any scandal should come to light — even 200 years after!! I hope you did not lie, cheat, or murder anyone. I hope you did not practise any mercy killing in your herbal life. If anything negative about you ever comes to light, they would deport your memory back to Jamaica faster than you could say Crimea! You might even then begin to hear appeals for the Government of Jamaica to dig up your remains from St. Mary's Catholic Cemetery at 679–681 Harrow Road, in Kensal Green in NW London and haul it back to Jamaica.

Anyway, so far, so good. Everyone making a fuss about you this year, with your recovered painting displayed and documentaries made about you. Students in Britain now must and bound fi study your life as a part of

196

a new curriculum. I do not know if that reach Jamaican children yet. But dem not even studying the foremost pan-Africanist Marcus Mosiah Garvey to dat, much less you. In closing, like others have done, I salute your courage and indomitable spirit; your urbanity and cosmopolitan wit; your acceptance of your foibles, but also your pride in yourself and your race.

Rest in Peace. Until next year.

Your admirer,

Verene A. Shepherd

14

'UP FROM SLAVERY': The Legacy of Slavery
and the Project of Emancipation in the
Commonwealth Caribbean[1]

*Inaugural Network Professorial Lecture, UNESCO Nigerian Hinterland
Project, March 28, 2001, Founders College, York University, Toronto*

This lecture, a part of the lecture series initiated by the York–
UNESCO Nigerian Hinterland Project, is a fitting tribute to
Harriet Tubman, a woman who because she 'grew up like a
neglected weed — ignorant of liberty and having no experience of it',[2] as
she said, dedicated her life to leading other enslaved people out of bondage,
in defiance of the US fugitive slave law. My choice of topic was, therefore,
not un-influenced by Harriet Tubman's life and work. As she, like other
'rebel women' such as Nanny of the Jamaican Maroons and Nanny Grigg
of the 1816 enslaved-led rebellion in Barbados, worked so hard to
destabilize that brutal slavery system that for four centuries tyrannized
generations of Africans and their descendants in the Americas, I thought
that I should not only focus on slavery and its legacies, but also address the
project of emancipation that was so important to this woman of underground
railroad fame who claimed that, 'I nebber run my train off the track and I
nebber lost a passenger'; that: 'I was free, and they [her enslaved kin]
should be free also.'[3]

The Legacy of Slavery

I begin with issues relevant to the legacy of slavery debate in Jamaica and
the wider Caribbean. Discourses surrounding the 'legacy of slavery' have
engaged my attention since I was six years old — and I know that you are
thinking: 'that was a long, long time ago before she even know the meaning
of "discourses"'; and, of course, you are correct. But that was the age at
which I became aware that a lingering legacy of slavery in the African

diaspora colonized by Europeans, was the negative representation of Africa as backward; of the fact that blackness was viewed as a disability by those (not necessarily all Caucasian), who adhere to Caucasian standards of beauty. You see, a section of the district in which I grew up in rural Jamaica was called 'Africa' — not for any celebratory reasons — because it was (how shall I put this?) infrastructurally challenged and was inhabited by phenotypically Black people in contrast to the other part of the district, Hopewell, with an ethnically mixed population, many of them Asians.

Happily, that was then. The denigration of Africa and Africans in the Caribbean segment of the African diaspora that lingered on in the colonial and immediate postcolonial period is now hardly apparent. On the contrary, the activism of cultural nationalists and pan-Africanists influenced by the radical philosophy of Marcus Garvey, the legacies of the Black Power Movement of the 1970s, the ever-increasing contact with Africa; and the introduction of African history in primary, secondary and tertiary educational institutions in the Caribbean have all combined to ensure that the 'othering' of Africa is no longer a dominant tendency in the region.

The existence of a more empowering image of Africa in the Caribbean does not, of course, mean that the legacy of slavery debate does not continue to inform discussions at several levels in contemporary Caribbean society. There are many issues that fuel the legacy of slavery debate, particularly among those who maintain that Africans in the diaspora have not fully emancipated themselves from that 'mental slavery' to which Marcus Garvey referred in 1937[4] and Bob Marley later popularized in song.

Some of the issues that very often invoke the legacy of slavery explanation for their persistence are inter-ethnic and class relations, skin bleaching and beauty contests. The latter two are still hotly debated as it is said that they perpetuate the colour hierarchy, the pigmentocracy of the slavery era. Jamaican singer Buju Banton's 1992 song, 'browning' did not help. He offended countless Black Jamaican women when he sang: 'mi luv mi car, mi luv mi bike, mi luv mi money and ting; but most of all mi luv mi browning.' The translation of this will sound utterly ridiculous to those of us who understand Creole poetics and will do violence to Buju's lyrics; but I will translate anyway: *'I love my car, I love my bike, I love my money and other material things. But above all, I love my brown-skinned woman.'* Buju later wrote another song to appease black-skinned women, while, at the same time (I am told) explaining that he was only singing for his 'browning', not brown women universally.

There are numerous other phenomena that invoke the 'legacy of slavery' explanation, not only among those of us who live in the Caribbean, but also among diasporic communities: racial profiling at Caribbean and international airports, the policing of the poor, Black male marginalization, African-Caribbean family structure, the commodification of the bodies of Black men and women, negative aspects of the tourist culture; the lingering colonial system of education, domestic violence, and the list goes on.

For Antiguan novelist Jamaica Kincaid, it is the hotel training school in Antigua that 'teaches Antiguans how to be good servants, how to be a good nobody', which is reminiscent of the mentality of slavery; for in Antigua, 'people cannot see a relationship between their obsession with slavery and emancipation and their celebration of the Hotel Training School'.[5]

In Jamaica, it was the capture and forced transportation to St. Elizabeth in July 1999 of 35 of Montego Bay's street people (who presumably were not fit sights for tourists) which brought this 'legacy of slavery' debate most sharply into focus. People used various terms to describe the unforgivable action, but all made comparisons with one aspect of slavery or the other. It was characterized as operation 'get tough' by one cartoonist in the Jamaica *Daily Observer's* official emancipation day edition, who, like the Prime Minister, the Most Hon P.J. Patterson, pointed to the irony of this happening so close to the celebration of emancipation day.[6] The Jamaica Labour Party leader, the Hon Edward Seaga, went even further, invoking the image of the 'Middle Passage', saying that the act was 'reminiscent of the way men and women were captured in Africa, bound in chains and transported 3,000 miles away to lands unknown'.[7]

So, despite the abolition of slavery in the British-colonized Caribbean 163 years ago, references to slavery and the ideologies/legacies of slavery are constantly used to frame and contextualize public debates among people in the region, as, indeed, they are within the wider Atlantic world. In a recent Black History Month lecture at the University of the West Indies, fellow Network Professor, Elisée Soumonni reminded us about the ways in which the transatlantic trade in captured Africans still affects inter-ethnic relations in contemporary West Africa. And though the descendants of enslaved people now occupy the highest political offices in societies radically transformed by the slavery and post-slavery struggles for freedom and justice, the 'up from slavery' concept in public life is strong and indicates that there is an equally strong opinion that the process of emancipation is not complete. This feeling remains despite the fact that, I am proud to say, Emancipation Day is celebrated in most parts of the Commonwealth Caribbean as an official public holiday, with Trinidad and Tobago embarking in 1999 on plans to build an appropriate memorial to mark the end of slavery.[8]

Still, like Independence Day, Emancipation Day is just another holiday for some who do not necessarily participate in the official activities designed to mark the day. Sometimes, too, the annual rhetoric that accompanies Emancipation Day commemorations is located within the discourse of slavery rather than within the discourse of anti-slavery and freedom. This gives the impression that the attempts in the period of modernity to bring about a level of well-being within social formations and to create human rights communities in former slave colonies have failed.

Why are the problems of the Caribbean so often framed within the discourse of slavery even when many of the ills of the region have more to do with the impact of structural adjustment and globalization? Some scholars also seem to attribute some of Jamaica's problems to the collapse of the 1970s experiment with democratic socialism, garrison communities, the marginalization of the middle class, the abandonment of radical politics, the decline in influence of the trade unions and elitism in the conduct of the process of governing and policing. University of the West Indies (UWI) scholar, Anthony Harriot's recent book, *Police and Crime Control in Jamaica* pointed to differential treatment of citizens on the principle of status congruence rather than equality before the law. A result of the larger issue of an exclusionary social structure and gross social inequalities which postcolonial societies emerging out of colonialism have not managed to solve completely.[9] Racial politics and tensions in plural societies like Trinidad and Tobago, and Guyana have also been blamed.

However, my concern is with why the legacy of slavery debate is still so strong and why it has to be addressed, even as we in the Caribbean try to solve post-independence problems. I suppose we should not really be surprised that slavery survives in the collective consciousness of people in the Caribbean, given the long history of this brutal system of human exploitation in the region, dating back to the Columbus dispensation. The emergence of Western Europe as the political centre of an Atlantic economy signalled the importance of imperial exploitation to its development. Indeed, development discourse centring around the discipline of political economy privileged colonialism as the transformative engine of capitalist growth. It was within this context that six European powers targeted the Caribbean segment of the Atlantic world for their imperial designs and colonization enterprises. Having conquered the land resources of the indigenous Caribbean, European colonizers turned to coerced labour to extract returns from this captured land. Indeed, European colonial capitalism could see no way to ensure profitable economic activity other than with the mass deployment of servile labour. As the intensity of economic accumulation gripped colonial elites, and the pressures of profits, power and glory fuelled the colonizing enterprise, chattel slavery became the preferred form of servile labour. Other labour institutions like indigenous and White servitude (mainly of the Irish), and White slavery were tried for varying periods in most places. With the development of productive activities in all colonies, the incompatibility between continued white labour exploitation and the colonial ideological project caused the enslavement of Africans to become centred as critical to economic accumulation and cultural imperatives. By the mid-eighteenth century, slavery had become an integral part of North Atlantic capitalist accumulation and defined the economy and society of all Caribbean societies regardless of the ethnicity or religious affiliation of the imperial power.

Conquest and colonization were not only accompanied by the decimation of the indigenous population, the introduction of a brutal system of exploitation, denigration and 'othering' of 'natives' and enslaved Blacks comparable within the region only to Apprenticeship and post-slavery indentureship, but also by the textual invention of the Caribbean. As we all know, many of the early narratives focused on the Caribbean were written without reference to the historical Caribbean and its inhabitants, and fall into the realm of historical (even fictional) literature, a sure indication, according to literary critic Veronica Gregg, that the invention of the Caribbean as a European enterprise required little knowledge of the region and in fact depended upon 'a willed ignorance'.[10]

Among the contributors to this genre of writing were Edward Long who wrote when the pro-slavery ideology had reached its zenith;[11] and Maria Nugent, a nineteenth-century Jamaican governor's wife, who despite her typically elite benevolence to the 'underclass', manifested during slavery in her habit of forever 'teaching the blackies their catechism', endorsed the stereotype of the African, on two occasions describing them as savages and cannibal-like. Yet somehow contented with slavery of the new African recruits in the West India Regiment, she wrote: 'they made a most savage appearance, having just arrived from Africa'; and on another occasion:

> in returning home from our drive this morning, we met a gang of Eboe negroes, just landed and marching up the country. I ordered the postilion to stop, that I might observe their countenances . . . and see if they looked unhappy; but they appeared perfectly the reverse . . . the women in particular seemed pleased . . . one man attempted to shew more pleasure than the rest by opening his mouth as wide as possible to laugh, which was a rather horrible grin. He showed such truly cannibal teeth, all filed as they had them, that I could not help shuddering.[12]

In similar vein, according to historian Bridget Brereton, Elizabeth Fenwick described Blacks in Barbados as 'a sluggish, inert, self-willed race of people, apparently inaccessible to gentle and kindly impulses'.[13]

Legislative emancipation in 1834 did not signal the complete end of this textual invention of the Caribbean, especially the African–Caribbean, judging by the writings of such nineteenth-century figures as Thomas Carlyle, Stephen Harmer, Lafcadio Hearn, James Anthony Froude, William Sewell, Charles Augustus Stoddard and Anthony Trollope, and early twentieth-century figures like William Burn.[14] The nineteenth century was a period in which freed people in the Caribbean sought to actualize their hard-won freedom through refusal to continue in a capital–labour relationship with former enslavers; when work was equated with plantation labour; when 'idle' and 'lazy' were terms applied to those who tried to carve out a life which did not involve full-time estate labour. Such representations of course ignored the entire economic reality of an industrious, though coerced African population who, as historian and late Prime Minister of Trinidad and Tobago, Eric Williams has shown, helped to industrialize England.[15] The nineteenth century was also a period when the English, influenced by developments in Haiti where Blacks were in power by 1804, feared what they termed the threat of the 'Haitianization' of the region (a sentiment resurrected in some parts of the Caribbean in the 1980s). The so-called 'negatives' of the peasant mode of production and the 'civilizing' possibilities of the plantation system were influential ideologies. It was within this context that proprietors actively sought to import additional White immigrants, and north Asians who were themselves socialized into a caste/colour hierarchy, to 're/place' Black labourers and bolster white ideologies in the Caribbean.

Ironically, the importation of indentured labourers, particularly Indians, so conjured up images of the Middle Passage and plantation slavery itself, that it ensured that the legacy of slavery debate would continue up to and beyond 1917 when indentured labour immigration was discontinued. Historians like Hugh Tinker, Pieter Emmer, Marina Carter and Rosemarjin Hoefte revived the debate over indentureship and slavery in the 1970s, 1980s and 1990s, with some supporting and some opposing the slavery model applied to Indian indentureship and emigration.[16] For the Dutch historian, Pieter Emmer, Indian women in particular benefited from emigration and indentureship, using them as routes to emancipation[17] — a view opposed by the 'legacy of slavery' adherents who point to the fraudulent aspects of recruiting emigrants, the high incidence of kidnapping of women, the sexploitation on the voyage from India, the punitive aspects of the immigration codes and the exploitation and resistance on the plantations. While I sympathize with the legacy of slavery model to describe Indian emigration and indentureship, I however support David Eltis's view that the transatlantic trade in Africans was unique in its severity even when compared with the shipping of White and Asian indentured labourers.[18]

There were only a few nineteenth-century writers who opposed the dominant representation of the newly freed pushed by Carlyle, Trollope and those of their ilk — of lazy, inferior Blacks observing planters' impending economic ruin 'with an ironic grin of malicious pleasure'.[19] An outstanding example of the beginning of Caribbean counter-discourse was the Trinidadian J.J. Thomas's *Froudacity*[20] in which he opposed James Froude's misrepresentation of the Caribbean and Caribbeans.

The twentieth century has also seen the emergence of texts that continue to reflect the influence of Eurocentric and plantercentric views grounded in the 'official' voice of the colonizers. Some of my students include as an example William Green's text which is quite popular among sixth form history students across the Caribbean, some of them styling it the 'A' Level Bible'.[21] Philip Sherlock's and Hazel Bennett's, *The Story of the Jamaican People,* while to be lauded for the bold, Afrocentric objectives, has not managed to rid itself totally of remnants of the colonialist ideology, presenting in many aspects the same old story — the 'official' view of Caribbean history.[22] Interestingly, as various other non-White groups entered post-slavery Caribbean society to further the capitalistic enterprises of the British, racialized representations were broadened to include the Asian population. Many people in Britain and the Asian diaspora expressed shock at the Duke of Edinburgh's remark that messy electrical wiring in parts of the UK looked 'as though it was put in by an Indian'.[23]

There is a widespread view that it is these images and representations which still circulate in the educational material, which are transmitted via the various media, and which, locally and globally, still inform the attitude to and treatment of Black people as 'other', which are largely responsible for the current feeling among some elements that emancipation is not complete. We only have to listen to the lyrics of our musical ambassadors and read our novelists to understand the popular feeling that emancipation is, somehow, a continuing process.

The question of how to construct a Caribbean identity that will negate the images and representations of the colonial and present eras and challenge the epistemic violence of the imperial project remains an important and pressing one. Debates over solutions ebb and flow particularly during the annual observance of emancipation day, independence day, Black History Month, Marcus Garvey's and Bob Marley's birthdays. The celebration of Black History Month this February was particularly high profile, thanks to the showing of the PBS documentary on Garvey, 'Look for me in the whirlwind' which angered some Jamaicans, masses and scholars alike.

Before closing, I would like to suggest how those of us who have the interest of the Caribbean at heart can align ourselves to a project of true emancipation — emancipation as process rather than as event, momentous as that was. The project of emancipation is crucial for self-evident reasons; but especially because many of us who live in postcolonial societies or who write (or mis-write) the Caribbean have failed to make the positive images, achievements, representations and lessons from the slavery and post-slavery eras left by our ancestors part of a more sustained public debate. What is being projected about the 'legacy of slavery' is really only part of the total legacy, ignoring the ways in which our ancestors survived centuries of exploitation, marginalization and 'othering'.

There are several possible emancipatory strategies, however I shall elaborate only on two: recovering and publicizing that lost legacy of slavery which is often not taught and transmitted, and re-imaging Caribbean people through public education, using the media (especially television) as fundamental tools. All of us can play a role in these strategies.

The Media Media representations are powerful cultural forces through which audiences receive cues about themselves. As several cultural historians like Stuart Hall have noted, the media produce and transmit ideologies because the rituals and myths they produce for public consumption justify practices and institutions.[24] They can thus be transformative or they can serve to oppress. In the Caribbean, as elsewhere in the Black diaspora affected by colonialism, media messages do not do enough to challenge dominant ideologies about racial hierarchies, Black inferiority and White superiority. What UWI Vice Chancellor Rex Nettleford has often described as the 'CNNization of the region', has not helped. Thus, there are insufficient television programmes that contest and oppose, by their visual imagery, the stereotypical representations of Black characters. In Europe and North America, representations of the Caribbean also continue to perpetuate negative images. Even where the Caribbean is depicted as paradise, it is often as a paradise where unbridled sex and ganja smoking abound and where tourists can do things they would, perhaps, never dream of doing in their own country — such as getting married in the nude.

History Education I should also like to suggest that the project of emancipation of the mind requires a greater knowledge of, and engagement with history and modern historiography and that history education must continue to be expanded at all levels locally and in diasporic Caribbean societies. Diasporic Caribbean communities, I think, need to have some exposure to revisionist Caribbean history in order to provide ammunition against the racist forces with which they are often confronted. We can no longer say that there are no history books that provide counter-discourse to the Eurocentric texts on which earlier generations grew up. A few of those early texts do survive, but there are enough newer writings that challenge them.

I should like to explain why I have singled out history as an emancipatory tool. One overarching reason is that history and historical evidence are crucial to a people's sense of identity. Second, only the project of history has the ability to elucidate the future through an understanding of the past. Indeed, as some scholars point out, 'what historians do best is to make connections with the past in order to illuminate the problems of the present and the potential of the future.'[25] Third, history is increasingly being used as a form of cultural enquiry in many societies. The view is that history and historical consciousness belong to culture, and culture, of which historiography is a part, is the background against which we can form opinion about the usefulness of, say, certain scientific research or political objectives.[26] As Florida University Professor Kevin Yelvington and his colleagues observed:

the wider world, currently overrun with the passions of regionalism, ethnicism and nationalism, and in the throes of both modernization and development, has made history the privileged ground of individual and collective identity.[27]

History education should be grounded in the alternative discourse of the new generation of historians. There is a view, particularly in postcolonial societies that are multiethnic and which are emerging from modernism into postmodernism, that there are contested versions of history. The twentieth century represented the era of burgeoning nationalism when nationalist histories written in what historian William Green refers to as the 'creole genre' were being written[28] and perhaps were needed, as UWI Professor Patrick Bryan observes, 'to plant the first seeds of a collective consciousness.'[29] The end of World War II, the escalation of decolonization, the globalization of Western culture and the re-empowerment of non-Western states, all signalled a new age. Not surprisingly, much of the scholarship of twentieth-century professional (and cultural–nationalist) historians, some influenced by Marxist ideology, continued to intervene in the hegemonic and authoritative discourse which ascribes 'rationality' and 'legitimacy' to its own discursive practice. They questioned the essentialism of traditional historiography and replaced the Eurocentric history which had as part of its mandate the imposition of a kind of 'master narrative' on formerly colonized people, with writings that opposed the epistemic violence of the imperial project. In the postmodernist era, they support the realization that Europe is no longer the unquestioned and dominant centre of the world. Additionally, influenced by the democratizing appeal of social history, many sought, in Spivak's terms, to develop a strategy of reading that spoke to the historically muted subject;[30] to present 'the vision of the vanquished' rather than the 'vision of the victors'.[31]

Of course, not everyone is happy with the postcolonial writings of cultural nationalist professional historians, and many find the fact that the empire is writing back extremely destabilizing, as is evidenced by caution about history written in the 'creole genre'. Similarly, Canadian historian

208

Donald Akenson, while observing in *If the Irish Ran the World* that 'how Montserratians of the twenty-first century should invent their own history is no business of professional historians such as myself', nevertheless could not resist the swipe at nationalist perspectives, saying that 'the Montserratians have the right to create whatever fiction makes it easier for them to get through the day'.[32] Nevertheless, the reality is that in the post 1970s period, the old intellectual absolutisms have been dethroned and the post-independence generation in the Caribbean has constructed what Joyce Appleby and others describe as 'sociologies of knowledge, records of diverse peoples, and histories based upon groups and gender identities'. The question 'whose history and for what purpose?' is now heard frequently by students and that generation of scholars who became historians after the 1970s and who have now 'made skepticism and relativism common currency in intellectual life'.[33]

Despite Akenson, Green and others who share their perspective, 'the present', 'should never be opposed to history, because the contemporary is a special case of history'.[34] Whether we like it or not, as many societies, influenced by the postcolonial discourse, become increasingly historicized, struggles over history and its representation are implicated. Some years ago when sections of Britian contemplated honouring John Hawkins,[35] the slave trader, there was an angry outcry from sections of the Black British population at the insensitivity of Whites to the slavery experience that affected African people. As Yelvington and others reveal, when, as part of a strategy of urban redevelopment, White elites in Tampa, Florida in the 1990s attempted to attract a museum with a piracy theme based on artifacts recovered from the *Whydah Galley* — an eighteenth-century pirate ship (which, as it turned out, was originally used in the slave trade) — there was an outcry from local African-Americans. The protesters used a counter-discourse that challenged interpretations of 'history' by addressing issues of identity, partially through references to slavery. Exposure to the newer historical works will facilitate a more inclusive view of Caribbean history and, above all, will recover that part of the historical legacy which hardly features in public debates but which is vital if Caribbean people are to be anchored firmly to a more positive beginning. The newer works show that

Caribbean history began neither with slavery nor with Columbus. Indigenous Caribbean society had its own internal logic, dynamism and culture. The early Caribbeans had an economic system, a developed cosmology, a political system, family structure, gender system, ways of settling disputes and communication system. The presence of descendants of the indigenous Caribbean should remind us that despite the effort to exterminate them, they never collaborated with colonialism, fighting wars of resistance and engaging in Maroon activities as survival strategies.[36]

Those who engage in the debates over slavery and its legacies should also familiarize themselves with the revisionist works that are more focused on people's agency, while not, of course, negating the brutality of the slavery experience.

In aligning ourselves with the project of true emancipation, we must also advance the view, as Ivan van Sertima has done, that Blacks did not begin their lives in the Caribbean as enslaved peoples.[37] Equally, the historical dichotomization of all Blacks as powerless and all Whites as powerful during the colonial era must be corrected. Many Whites started their lives in the Caribbean as slaves or indentured labourers; and even after the end of White indentured servitude, many remained poor and powerless, particularly in urban centres, relying on enslaved people for economic assistance.

Finally, those keen to invoke the 'legacy of slavery' model should embark on a serious research project to reclaim marginalized people's voices which would provide them with much to counter the hegemonic discourse and master narrative; for it was not only through violent rebellions and day-to-day acts of non-cooperation that Blacks demonstrated their opposition to slavery and racism. In other words, Blacks did not only fight back; despite the endemic anti-intellectual culture bred by slavery, they wrote and spoke back as part of an ontological positioning with colonialism that brought slavery under their literary gaze. The literary output, written or narrated, of people like Olaudah Equiano, Mary Prince, Juan Francisco Manzano and Esteban Montejo, serves to situate anti-slavery ideology at the core of enlightenment modernity.[38]

Statements like:

'I am a prince . . . I was much greater in guinea.'; 'I am a prince . . . for the time being, I am in your power, but nothing will ever persuade me to serve you; I would rather end my life by voluntary death.'; 'I was much greater in Guinea than you are here . . . now you expect me to be your slave?' are powerful reflections of positive self-identification by Africans captured for enslavement in the Caribbean.[39] It is the need for the recuperation of the voices and ideas of subaltern peoples, enslaved and free, that informed the Text and Testimony Collective (TTC) and the Caribbean Historical Database Project, collaborative efforts between the York–UNESCO Nigerian Hinterland Project and individuals at the University of the West Indies. Although the TTC to date has no budget, it has managed to form alliances with individuals and institutions that feel that these initiatives are important. For example, the York–UNESCO Nigerian Hinterland Project, the Institute of Caribbean Studies in the Faculty of Arts and Education at the UWI, and the Jamaican office of UNESCO contributed to the first TTC lecture by Network Professor Elisée Soumonni at the UWI during Black History Month and the public launch of the TTC. With the assistance of Professor Judi Byfield, Dartmouth College in association with the York–UNESCO Nigerian Hinterland Project will host the first TTC workshop on women's voices in May 2001. The TTC however has much more to do.

Conlusion

The strategies that I have outlined should go some way towards educating Caribbean people about their rich and diverse historical legacy with a view to broadening the 'legacy of slavery' debate and anchoring us to a more positive past. I enjoin those of you who have an interest in Caribbean affairs to align yourselves to this exciting project of emancipation and respond to Marcus Garvey's and Bob Marley's appeal to 'emancipate ourselves from mental slavery; none but ourselves can free our minds'.

15

THE RANKING GAME

Discourses of Belonging in Jamaican History

Inaugural Professorial lecture, University of the West Indies (UWI), Mona, April 12, 2002

et me begin by admitting that it was Dr Betty Wood who was assigned the onerous task of focusing my academic challenges in a way that facilitated my completion of the doctoral programme at Cambridge. She successfully redefined the role of an academic supervisor and played a fundamental role in my journey here; a journey that was 'a multi-layered, contradictory, chaotic, cantankerous and unruly journey to self-discovery', to borrow a line from Vice Chancellor Rex Nettleford's address at the January 2002 launch of the book *Questioning Creole.*[1]

While the journey (which took me to the University of the West Indies (UWI) through the opening created by Michael Manley's tertiary education policy, and later to the University of Cambridge courtesy of a Cambridge Commonwealth Trust Scholarship) may have been long, complex, and at times reckless, it was by no means lonely and directionless. Critically, there were ideological signposts erected along the way that guided my intellectual trajectory. These markers, men and women who represent the ontological expressions of our oppressed ancestors, are now claimed as icons of our collective consciousness, foremost among them being Nanny of the Maroons, Boukman Dutty, Mahatma Gandhi, Marcus Mosiah Garvey, Elsa Goveia, C.L.R. James, Walter Rodney, Eric Williams, and rebel woman Susan who impressed me with her courage and unambiguous anti-slavery stance during the 1831–32 anti-slavery war. A stance perhaps reflected in the words sewn into the apron she was wearing when she was captured: 'my heart is fixed/I cannot change/I love my choice/too well to range.'[2]

In addition, there were teachers, mentors and comrade spirits whose commitment to Caribbean and wider African diasporic issues and subaltern studies (not to mention their irreverent attitude towards 'the canon'), provided courage and self-confidence for the journey: Hilary Beckles, Kamau Brathwaite, Carolyn Cooper, Rupert Lewis, Rex Nettleford, Maureen Warner-Lewis, (who were forever turning the canon inside out and upside down with their Afrocentric weapons and in Carolyn's case, also with 'Ooman tongue'.)

There were other guides, among them Patrick Bryan, the late Douglas Hall, Barry Higman, Woodville Marshall and Lucille Mathurin Mair — who encouraged me as I made what may appear to some to have been a rather promiscuous journey into the study of Asian labour migration, inter-ethnic and gender relations, slavery, economic diversification, women, especially the so-called 'petticoat rebels', and the legacies of slavery. All the time intervening in the hegemonic and authoritative discourse that ascribes 'rationality' and 'legitimacy' to its own discursive practice and irritating those who oppose the Creole genre (and tongue) of post-independence Caribbean historical writing.[3]

Nevertheless there was method in this apparent madness, the connecting thread being an abiding interest in the history of traditionally marginalized groups: Indian immigrants, women, enslaved Africans, and livestock farmers operating within the context of a society where top ranking went to those who owned sugar plantations.

Above all, this multilayered journey introduced me to the creative ways in which Caribbean scholars have constructed indigenous interpretations of Caribbean history, fashioned by explicit formulations and theoretical constructs which have had important implications for my own work and for scholarly debates in the international academy. By offering the antithesis to the imperialist view of the Caribbean world, some of these 'Creole interpreters' of Caribbean history presented the counter-discourse to the empowered 'bad words' of racist narrators such as Edward Long, James Anthony Froude and Thomas Carlyle.[4] Carlyle, we know, in his proslavery essay entitled 'The Nigger Question' gave political imagery to the concept of 'Quashie' as 'Black mind and body that was unprepared for freedom'. A century and a half later, Jamaican poet Lorna Goodison, armed with a battery of metaphorical representations, reacted to the epistemic violence of the imperial project by calling for a renegotiation of such 'bad words' to create an internal liberating narrative of self.[5]

These creative representations of Caribbean history also provided direction as I confronted in the historiography and society the legacies of colonialism, slavery and indentureship: the 'otherization' of the Caribbean, as indeed of Africa and India; the Western intellectual tradition (or some would say, the terrorist intellectual canon); the donmanship phenomenon evident in academic discourse — legacy of the dispensation of don Cristóbal Colón and the era of rule Britannia — and the cult of 'ranking' on which I wish to focus.

In its simplest definition, 'ranking' is a metaphor for social ordering, social and cultural hierarchizing. But 'ranking' should not be seen simply as a euphemism for the static social stratification model of sociologist M.G. Smith in which the racial, cultural and class categories are conflated into a simple social hierarchy.[6] It is more about the ideological and cultural aspects of why Jamaican folk say 'Jackass seh world no level' than the social and economic structure, which as Gramsci has shown us, do not align nicely in well-worn models of social structure and stratification.[7]

Within the Jamaican context 'ranking' represents the linguistic, oral and literary aspects of social culture that is the ritualized and politicized codes and consciousness of difference. I am less concerned with ritual in Michel Foucault's sense of 'signs taken as wonders',[8] and more with the phenomena associated with the wonder of how signs have been taken. If we view its iconography and consider its lyrical content, then we will understand that 'ranking' is the engine that drives Jamaica's political sociology. For some, situating difference establishes the boundaries of belonging; for others, situating difference is a way of signifying the opposite tendency of 'unbelonging'. This tension between 'belonging' and 'unbelonging' is a fundamental characteristic of the 'ranking game', a ritual that is invested with all the social and political capital available to the society.

Stuart Hall is correct to assert that the persistence of such colonial creations as ranking contradicts the cultural desire of postmodern mentalities for the celebration of difference in an egalitarian fashion rather than hierarchically.[9] The effects come in strange and curious ways, and as he reminded us, postcolonial structures such as our nation states have sought to downplay rather than 'downpress' that ranking game that dollarizes difference. 'I too love my browning', for example, has resurfaced as a view from the ghettos with the same vigour as it was a vision from Great Houses at an earlier time.

Indeed, all of us will agree that even in the postmodern age, boundary-maintaining mechanisms have not disappeared in a society we call 'Creole'; that ranking signs, codes, conventions and other rituals are active as meanings by which we understand and live our political and social culture. The 1970s' engagement with social democracy for some fell not on a hard reality of hunger but on the sword of signs that were empty supermarket shelves and USA visa lines.

Ranking is understood historically within the colonial formation in terms of access to restricted status as manifested primarily in signs and symbols that, with social consensus, offer respect and respectability. In this regard, neither emancipation in 1838 nor Independence in 1962 constitutes reliable markers of change; for we still adhere to boundary-maintaining mechanisms, elevating English over Jamaican English or Nation Language, uptown residence over downtown residence, Brown over Black and both under White, urban culture over rural living; and among some sectors, wine over white rum, Bach over Buju Banton, the style of Luciano Pavarotti over Jamaican Luciano (and vice versa) — and I could go on.

The ranking game, of course, was intensely practised in the age of modernity. My research into the complex interaction of sugar planters and livestock farmers (hereafter pen-keepers) during slavery, Indian indentureship and inter-ethnic relations in an increasingly multicultural post-slavery society, afforded me an opportunity to explore the evolution of this historic phenomenon. I cannot go into all the minute details of this research at this time,[10] but I will share some snapshots with you, particularly in relation to how the contested category of 'Creole' (used here in the Brathwaitian sense of being born in Jamaica and evolving a local, indigenous culture and identity[11]), featured in the deeply historically embedded 'ranking game' in a society in which the players were colonials and Creoles,

Africans and English, Euro-Creoles and Afro-Creoles and (from 1845) also Indians, Chinese, Indo-Creoles and Sino-Creoles.

I will begin with the intensely charged racial atmosphere of mid-twentieth-century Jamaica. On February 3, 1950, the *Jamaica Times* published a letter from the Organizer-General of the Afro-West Indian League (AWIL) in which he stated that 'simply being born in Jamaica does not make one a Jamaican, ... in the same way that a chicken hatched in an oven cannot be called a bread.'[12] This was a complexly constructed metaphor for the claims and rights of citizenship, to be read as a distinctive production of antagonistic cultural designs in mid-twentieth-century Jamaica. It spoke to who had the right to appropriate social space and to benefit from the material resources of that space; who had cultural legitimacy in a multicultural society that rested on the ideology of racial and ethnic inequality. It also showed clearly that while 'Creole' in the sense of being 'Jamaican' could imply unity and solidarity, 'Creole', as Percy Hintzen has observed, could also be inserted into a discourse of exclusion.[13]

The socioeconomic context of this declaration by the Organizer-General of the AWIL was the charged racial environment of the mid-twentieth century, the result of the 1930s labour protests and the economic and social dislocations caused by the two World Wars and the resultant world depression. Locally this was manifested in massive unemployment, a problem that escalated as workers who had sought outlets for jobs in Cuba and Central America were subjected to forced repatriation. This was so as sugar estates were reorganized to increase labour productivity and reduce the estate labour force, and as the market for peasant output contracted. The situation that resulted was favourable for employers. They now had a competitive labour market, a reserve army of labourers, with, according to Ken Post, as many as three people competing for the same job.[14] They could not only lower wages as a consequence, but they could pick and choose labourers, and they did. Their preference in the post-slavery period had always been for male African-Jamaicans and they reorganized the labour force to reflect this preference, thereby alienating women, and Indians[15] imported since 1845 to replace or supplement the African-Jamaican labourers from the wage labour force. Many of the Indian and Indian-

Jamaican plantation workers had not even taken any active part in the labour rebellion of 1938, believing that non-involvement would guarantee them continued employment after the protests ended.

During the 1940s, the colonial government created a system of 'Relief Work', administered through the Public Works Department of rural parishes and the Kingston Employment Bureau, to help to solve the problems of rising unemployment and impoverishment of workers. Soon, the unemployed from all ethnicities were joining long queues at the Kingston Bureau in search of jobs. As only about 20 per cent of those who registered at the Bureau ever managed to secure jobs,[16] African-Jamaicans in Kingston and St. Andrew reportedly resorted to 'elbowing' Indians and Indian-Jamaicans out of the queues to increase their own chances of securing jobs. African-Jamaicans decided that on the basis of Indians' and Indian-Jamaicans' tendency to display ethnic exclusiveness, their explicit expression of Indian diasporic consciousness and the failure of many of them to participate in the 1938 labour rebellions,[17] 'Indians' were not entitled to scarce benefits in Jamaica. Above all, they regarded both Indians *and* Indian-Jamaicans as 'aliens' (albeit 'resident aliens'), who did not truly 'belong' to Jamaica and used the term 'Indian' (as did the state) to refer to even those who were Creole (biologically, if not ideologically). Ticket distributors also allegedly discriminated against Indians *and* Indian-Jamaicans, facilitating very few of them who managed to stay in the lines and register for relief work. By the end of 1940, 95 per cent of the Indians and Indian-Jamaicans in Kingston and St. Andrew seeking jobs were still unemployed, including most of the 247 who had registered for jobs at the Bureau.[18]

This intensely charged episode between Indians and Indian-Jamaicans, and African-Jamaicans that gave rise to debates in the period 1930–50 over the definition of 'Jamaican',[19] emblematizes the post-slavery and twentieth-century disputes over 'belonging', 'citizenship', and the contested category of 'Jamaican'. It spoke to the criteria for 'belonging', 'unbelonging' and ranking in a multiethnic society where some cultures were deemed superior and others inferior. Where those African-Jamaicans (even those calling for a return to Africa) were struggling to re-assemble the fragments of African identity, reassert Africanness as part of Jamaican citizenship and exclude 'aliens' from assuming the designation of 'Jamaican' — a designation that they appropriated, especially based on their demographic dominance.

My research did not reveal widespread consensus among the island's several classes and ethnicities on all the criteria that could transform an 'immigrant' from 'alien' to 'citizen' (I will speculate on those later on); but it was clear that local birth alone could not render all Creoles 'Jamaican'. Dr Douglas, the Organizer-General of the Afro-West Indian League, was, therefore, sending a not so cleverly telegraphed message to those Indians born in Jamaica who were under the mistaken impression that they were Jamaicans, that being Jamaican was more than just 'I man born ya'.

Some obvious questions at this juncture for all who have some idea of the social structure of the colonial period as well as current tendencies to flaunt foreign birth and passports in the face of those of us whose anatomies are firmly Creole, are: when did Jamaica become a preferred place for residence? How deeply embedded in our historical past was this attempt to construct citizenship within the discursive space of Creole? And of related interest is the question of how early did an articulated Black consciousness (as displayed, for example by the Afro-West Indian League) emerge that would attach itself to an anti-alien 'native' consciousness? The answers must be sought by historicizing the political struggles for identity and status ordering.

During the seventeenth century, there were discourses over the rights of Englishmen in Jamaica; but those discourses revolved around the claim for the same constitutional rights as England's citizens — rights that were no different from those accorded to English citizens residing in England. It was related more to the opposition by White male elites in the colonial government to political interference from England and was not a reflection of a self-conscious commitment to Creole society. On the contrary, my research into the slavery period of the eighteenth and nineteenth centuries indicates that being born in Jamaica was sufficient reason for low ranking within the context of a society where top ranking went to those who were White, metropolitan born, the owners of large sugar plantations, able to live as absentee proprietors, or, if in the island, as members of the elite class of Whites who controlled the socioeconomic and political life of the island

and lived grandly in Great Houses staffed by a large army of enslaved domestics. This elite was usually Anglican, married, and an adherent of the Western European culture which it elevated above African, Euro-Creole and Afro-Creole culture. The only exception to this rule of devaluing local, Creole birth applied to those of African descent who were born in the island and placed in a dialectical relationship with the devalorized African culture. As a consequence, Black and coloured Creoles were ranked above their African kin and, by the nineteenth century when planters had a choice, given tasks suited to their alleged 'superior Creole status' — for example, domestic, supervisory and artisan work. Not all of the enslaved accepted the negative attitudes towards Africa and many wanted to return 'home'. While resistance to enslavement was therefore endemic, the liberation struggles were not necessarily all linked to a desire on the part of Africans and Afro-Creoles to live as free people in Jamaica.

The complex relationship between the sugar sector and the penkeeping sector in Jamaica during slavery can usefully illustrate the ways in which status mobility was attached to factors that did not include being 'native' or 'belonging' to Jamaica. Even those Creoles, such as locally born pen-keepers whose livelihood depended on 'native' enterprises, maintained a colonial mentality that devalued their Creole origins, rendering such pen-keepers 'Creole colonials'. Part of this social attitude was linked to the fact that during slavery, land use was an important factor that ascribed social position; and status mobility was, therefore, fundamentally related to the type of economic activities in which settlers and colonizers engaged. It was within this context that sugar planters were ranked above those involved in other economic enterprises and, on the basis of the higher status of sugar planters, the primarily Creole pen-keepers struggled to acquire the trappings to enable them to become a part of the English elite. Although Jamaican society of the slavery period was described by Kamau Brathwaite as a Creole society — a society in which a certain 'Jamaicanness' developed at the interstices between the cultures of Europe and Africa[20] and where the creolization process (a process of cultural interaction and synthesis, with its twin components of acculturation and inter-culturation) defined the process of cultural change and resulted in a tentative cultural norm[21] —

such localization or 'indigenization' as occurred did not have unanimous support from the various classes and ethnic groups in the island's social structure. Even though Jamaican, like wider Caribbean identity, currently occurs within the discursive space of the Creole, during slavery (and perhaps even now) 'Creole' was associated with 'inferior', 'local', and was always 'alternative' to the so-called 'pure' culture of the European elite or aspiring Euro-Creole elite. In other words, 'Creole' during slavery was placed in an antagonistic relationship with the symbolic capital of Whiteness.

I should perhaps explain the pen-keepers' origins at this point. A penkeeping sector was able to emerge in Jamaica because, as Barry Higman and others have shown, the island's physical environment was not ideal for the support of cane growing in every 'nook and cranny'.[22] In the competition for good agricultural land, sugar planters eventually came to control the most arable areas, confining the pens and coffee plantations to interior parts of the island and mountainous locations respectively.[23] The establishment of pens contributed to Jamaica's diversification and partially explains the inapplicability of the classic plantation economy model advanced by scholars such as George Beckford, Lloyd Best and J.R. Mandle.[24] Indeed, no Caribbean economy conformed rigidly to the 'classic plantation economy' which was supposed to display among its distinguishing features: mono-crop/sugar production for export, the importation of all inputs, the export of all outputs, the maintenance of exclusive trading relationships between each plantation and the imperial country, the absence of a domestic economic sector and the lack of backward and forward linkages.[25] Despite the large-scale cultivation of sugar cane in Jamaica in the period after 1740, there emerged a vibrant group of small settlers who were occupied in the local production of goods and services for the internal market and in creating a 'domestic economy'.

The sugar plantation acted as a dynamic factor in the expansion of the penkeeping sector, representing its principal market for work animals and food. In contrast to the plantation economy school's conceptualization of each plantation developing as a 'total institution', relatively isolated as a social unit and interrelated through its connections with the political economy of the metropolis, Jamaica's agricultural units maintained vibrant internal trading links.[26] In other words, the island was not characterized by the existence of autonomous plantations whose links were only with the imperial country, as Orlando Patterson has suggested.[27] By 1782, according to W.J. Gardner's estimate, the island had 300 cattle farms or 'pens' to which sugar planters could turn for a variety of goods and services.[28] By the time of emancipation, this number had increased to around 400.[29] Some of these pens were owned by sugar planters as 'satellite units' to serve their own sugar plantations; but a significant number belonged to individuals with no direct investment in the sugar economy.

In an attempt to understand the role of the pen-keepers in Jamaica's socioeconomic and political history several questions have to be answered. As Barry Higman has argued, did they contribute to the development of Creole society 'in every way'?[30] In contrast to the sugar plantation that has been associated with Caribbean underdevelopment, did the pens represent a contribution to Jamaican development through their generation of internal linkages and their contribution to the growth of something recognizable even during slavery as a domestic economy? Did pen-keepers represent simply an economic interest group, uniting around narrow economic self-interests or did their participation in the 'Jamaican'/Creole economy imply a Creole consciousness and a commitment to the development of Creole society? Was their greater local resident status due to choice or economic circumstances? Finally, were they clearly ideologically differentiated from the sugar planter-class?

The economic rationale for the establishment of pens by small settlers is clear. Pens required a lower capital investment than sugar plantations, and, based on correspondence generated by pen-keepers such as George Forbes and comments on the economic state of pen-keepers by Edward Long and Gardner, a profit could be made to enable pen-keepers to live fairly comfortably.[31] Furthermore, there was a ready market; for sugar estates needed pen outputs including working steers and mules, horses, fresh beef, and services such as pasturage and cartage. Small pen-keepers could also combine working on estates as bookkeepers and overseers with owning their own pens.

Participation in the local economy as a signal of a commitment to Creole society is, perhaps, more doubtful. Admittedly, in their various petitions to the House of Assembly in the 1770s, pen-keepers claimed that they had employed much time, labour and money in establishing pens and that their efforts had contributed to the development of the interior of the island and the opening up of new roads and lines of communication;[32] but such pronouncements were really designed to help their cause in getting preferential tax laws passed in the Legislature to protect the local cattle industry from external competitors. Those who patronized them equally seemed to have reacted to materialist concerns. It is true that penkeeping was encouraged by the colonial government during and after the American War of Independence as a strategy to offset the shortfall in the import trade of plantation supplies with North America. In anticipation of a disruption in trade with North America, members of the House of Assembly had established a sub-committee in 1775 to investigate the possibility of producing local supplies of grain, staves, lumber and food. Several Resolutions and Acts of the Assembly passed between 1775 and the early 1800s provided for the encouragement of local production of plantation supplies, the expansion of the coffee industry, the removal of the restrictions on new (White) settlement in the interior, the encouragement of immigration and settlement of loyalists from North America, the Bay of Honduras and the Mosquito Shore, and for new experiments in sugar and other industries.

But these were short-term measures. As soon as the crisis was over, it was business as usual, with trade resuming with external suppliers (including Spanish America under the 1766 British Free Port Act); and sugar planters refused to support any effort on the part of the pen-keepers to protect the local industry from external competition, leading planter-historian Edward Long (himself only a pragmatic supporter of Creole economy), to accuse them of a lack of Creole consciousness and of being prejudiced against local goods.[33] Disputes over the cattle taxes and to a lesser extent the price and quality of local beef (described by one subscriber to the *Royal Gazette* as sometimes so tough that it seemed designed 'to wear out [consumers'] teeth, and fret their guts with their tough, rigid and indigestible carcass'[34]) attest to the lack of planter support for the local economy. The issue of taxes caused prolonged debates in the island's legislature. In 1816, for example, the pen keepers of St. Elizabeth and Manchester petitioned the House of Assembly to impose a tax on imported stock on account of 'the hardships they suffered from the allowance of foreign imports.'[35] The St. Elizabeth grazers, supported by those in Manchester, complained that, 'from late large importation of horned or neat cattle, mules and horses, the stock of the native breeder and grazier has become almost unsaleable, more particularly in respect of mules, there having been scarcely a spell of mules disposed of this season in the whole pen district.'[36]

This was particularly crucial at a time when, according to the petitioners, the local supply of stock exceeded current demand.[37] Most sugar planters refused to support the increase of the import tax to give local producers a chance to compete, or agree to the removal of animals as articles allowed under the Free Port Act; and no prohibitive tax was ever imposed, though around 1843 — by which time the influence of the 'sugarocracy' in the House of Assembly had declined — a higher tax level was imposed.

However, during slavery, the pen-keepers were not sufficiently numerous in the House of Assembly to be able to operate as a solid political bloc within the colonial government and protect their economic interests directly. Admittedly, as early as 1757, 50 per cent of pen-keepers had the property qualification to vote; and many held lower-level parochial and military positions. But the House of Assembly was the bastion of elite, sugar–planter power and remained so even as some pen-keepers became materially well off to become members of the Assembly at various periods in the eighteenth and nineteenth centuries. Sugar barons protected their own interests and marginalized those of the pen-keepers. This led to Brathwaite's conclusion that, 'at every step …, the creatively Creole elements of the society were being rendered ineffective by the more reactionary colonial.'[38]

Of course, this suggestion of a dichotomous relationship between colonial and Creole is problematic, one reason being that it masks the heterogeneity of non-sugar producers. Class, colour, gender, educational level, place of birth and ideology, for example, differentiated the pen-keepers, internally. The majority were White males, but there were also a significant number of women (like the Englishwoman Catherine Buckeridge who owned pens in St. Catherine), and freed people of colour (like Anna Woodart, Benjamin Scott-Moncrieffe and John and Robert Anguin) among their ranks. White pen-keepers, by virtue of their status as property owners, may not have fitted into the categories of 'petit blanc' and 'poor whites' used by M.G. Smith, Elsa Goveia and others to differentiate the various classes of Whites.[39] But as economic activity and land use were used along with colour, class, gender, origin, residence and ethnicity as ranking tools in Caribbean slave systems, all pen-keepers were ascribed a social position below that of the 'sugarocracy'. Indeed, in the eighteenth century, the term 'pen' was used derogatively to apply to small farms. John Moreton also noted in the late eighteenth century that:

> grass-pens were considered as despicable objects for enterprising adventurers to hunt after; nor would any man accept the management of one who had any hopes of preferment on sugar plantations, because the salary and accommodations were equally indifferent; so that managers of ... pens were considered as friendless; nor would those of sugar plantations, or even the overseers, associate with them.[40]

It was also clear that because of the high percentage of pen-keepers who were born — and continued to reside in Jamaica, with inferior social status accorded those who could not afford to live abroad[41] — relations of super-ordination and subordination defined the relations between colonials and Creoles.[42] The absentee sugar planters had global ranking. They sat in the British parliament, they had knighthoods and London offices and they lived in grandeur among the British elite. Pen-keepers, not surprisingly, aspired to re-ranking through the medium of absenteeism. In a letter to his brother Peter in 1811, George Forbes of Thatchfield Pen in St. Elizabeth stated that as soon as his financial circumstances permitted, he would return to live in Britain.[43] Even Free-Coloured pen-keepers shared this preference for metropolitan residence, Robert Hilton Anguin expressed a similar desire to live in Britain.[44]

Despite their lower social ranking and general lack of political power, the pen-keepers maintained an ideology that closely paralleled that of the sugar planters. The Free-Coloured Creole pen-keepers were as colonial in their mentality as the Whites. While the Whites tried to transform the enslaved Africans into Creole, therefore ascribing a higher social status to Blacks born in Jamaica or to Africans who showed evidence of 'creolization', Free-Coloureds themselves looked down on those of their ethnicity who were born in Jamaica and affirmed a Euro-Creole worldview. There was thus a class and ethnic difference in how Creole was constructed and assigned meaning in the Jamaican slave system. Distance from the idealized European phenotype and from Europe's cultural practices determined and defined the Creole's position in the social hierarchy.

I have come across only very few exceptions to this general rule of Creole pen-keepers exhibiting an articulated colonial mentality and valuing an English identity. One such appeared to be the St. Ann pen-keeper, simply referred to as 'Mr Matthews' in Cynric Williams's published account of his 1823 tour of Jamaica. Matthews was represented as a White Creole who articulated an unambiguously Creole sentiment and orientation. Matthews professed that he was totally anti-aristocracy and that he loathed the economic links that bound Jamaica to England. Wherever he could avoid it, he deliberately snubbed British goods including soap, candles, oil and salted provisions. Cynric Williams reported that Matthews 'had neither tea, cider, porter, wines, fish, sauces, nor hams from England'.[45] His intention was supposedly to be as self-sufficient as possible in food and manufactured goods from England. He manufactured his own plates on the pen and his clothes were locally made.[46] His enslaved male carpenters made all his furniture, his carriage was locally built and his mattress was stuffed with local silk cotton. His blacksmiths even made tools such as machetes. In addition, for the defense of his pen, 'his own blacksmiths [were said] to have been known to make bows and arrows of the most diabolical invention that can be conceived'.[47]

But Matthews was not typical; and even his so-called 'Creole consciousness' and his articulation of sentiments that reflected a feeling of 'belonging to Jamaica' were manifested in his economic decisions rather than in his social actions. Despite the fact that he prided himself on his benevolence and 'Jamaicanness', he was one with the majority of planters and fellow pen-keepers with respect to slavery and abolition. He abhorred the anti-slavery saints and particularly the humanitarian politician William Wilberforce. He was opposed completely to the abolition fervour of the nineteenth century and though he was in other respects a 'paternalistic despot', he believed that enslaved peoples were totally unfit for freedom, 'and the entire disposal of their own time', and so should be 'kept in a state of pupilage under constant, though humane, restraint'.[48] Indeed, apart from isolated cases like that of the Barclay brothers from Walthamstow, Essex, owners of Unity Valley Pen in St. Ann who freed the 32 people enslaved on their pen in 1795 and relocated them to Philadelphia in light of opposition to their continued residence in Jamaica,[49] the majority of pen-keepers (even the coloured Creoles), like the sugar planters, were unsupportive of Blacks' claims for rights and citizenship. Even the Barclays did not advocate the immediate abolition of slavery, instead supporting gradual emancipation and amelioration. Some like Mr Matthews, David Finley and John Blagrove who left each of his slaves the sterling equivalent of US$1.00 in his will,[50] may have been described as 'benevolent' enslavers by virtue of the fact that non-sugar economic activities afforded the enslaved a less frenetic work regime; but this did not make them anti-slavery. Irishman Hamilton Brown, (Browns Town's 'benefactor'), like John Blagrove and other pen-keepers, opposed the perceived anti-slavery stance of the Baptists. He accused them of inciting the 1831–32 rebellion of enslaved people or 'Baptist War', and joined other members of the Colonial Church Union in burning the chapels of this denomination.[51] At one stage, the governor had to send the military to subdue him. This was no easy task as Brown reportedly had armed retainers. Eventually, the military caught him at one of his properties, Minard Pen, and entreated him to give up his sword. Instead of doing this, he broke it across his knee and threw it at the lieutenant, wounding him badly in his face.[52]

As a result of their socioeconomic and political marginalization, the pen-keepers sought to negate themselves as a class and to pursue 'acceptable' routes to top-ranking, utilizing a variety of ways to enter the world of the 'sugarocracy': for example, affiliation with the Established [Anglican] Church, emigration to Britain as soon as they could afford it, marrying into elite sugar planter families, seeking ethnic reclassification in the case of the Free-Coloureds, and the education of their children in Britain. Some were successful. Irishman Hamilton Brown sent his Jamaican-born son, Alexander Hamilton Brown, to be educated abroad. So did Francis Smyth, whose son William was educated at Eton and Christchurch College, Oxford. Free-Coloured Benjamin Scott-Moncrieffe, owner of Thatchfield Pen in St. Ann (among other properties), sent his son Peter to England to be trained as a lawyer.[53]

The legal provision that Free-Coloureds could apply to be reclassified as White — honorary Whites — to use a more current term, was a strategy to reinforce the ideology of White supremacy in the Caribbean and to reinforce further the denigration of Afro-Creole. Free-Coloureds, some of whom shared the prevailing White racial view of Blacks, tried various strategies to win acceptance into White society. As class and relation to Black ethnicity blocked their social aspiration to enter White society,[54] they sought the loophole of ethnic reclassification allowed by the colonial laws in operation in Jamaica. Free-Coloured pen-keepers, including John Anguin and Benjamin Scott-Moncrieffe of St. Ann, legally gained White privileges for themselves and their sons in 1827. As was customary, Anguin supported his petition to the Jamaican House of Assembly on the basis of his 'White blood', economic status and the fact that he had 'obtained the good opinion of the most respectable inhabitants of the . . . parish of St. Ann'.[55] Those who successfully applied for these privileges were required by law to marry into White society so that property could be passed to their 'White' offspring.

Some of the routes to re-ranking were easier than others. Pen-keepers, for example, who married into the sugar elite were few. It was not only that single White women were scarce; but many of those in the colonies were non-elites who were themselves looking to improve their 'ranking' through marriage into elite society. Pen-keepers themselves aspired to marry upper-class White women. Creole White women had also taken on the manners of Creole society, manners that were looked down upon by Europeans and those who aspired after European ways. The influence of African social culture upon European and Creole White women did not meet with elite planter Edward Long's approval. He was saddened by the 'cultural deterioration' he thought White women experienced on account of their interaction with Black people, rendering their dress, speech and manners below the standard expected of people who were White.[56] Similarly, Maria Nugent, wife of George Nugent, Governor of Jamaica between 1801 and 1806, implied that Creole White women were culturally inferior to their European counterparts, using language as a case in point. According to her, 'The Creole language is not confined to the Negroes. Many of the ladies, who have not been educated in England, speak a sort of broken English . . . that is very tiresome if not disgusting.'[57]

In the meantime, as was the culture of the day, pen-keepers lived in open concubinage with Black and Coloured women over whom they could exercise social power. John Anguin, for example, had lived with an enslaved woman, Sarah Tracey Williamson. She had three children for him and was catered for in his will with the usual proviso that she would forfeit this money if she left him before he died.[58] Similarly, pen-keepers James Kelly, Francis Graham, John Moncrieffe, Charles Stirling and Thomas Thistlewood all had 'permanent' coloured 'housekeepers' who were provided for in their wills. Like Anguin, Charles Stirling stipulated that his 'housekeeper', Rebecca Ash, would get £1,300 sterling and a £112 annuity 'as long as she remains single and does not begin to live with any man as housekeeper or mistress'.[59] This was one way of embedding and intertwining the creolization process deeply into the Jamaican sociocultural context, through the medium of interracial sex. Pen-keepers contributed to the rise of a Creole group with local origins, but rejected Creole values and culture.

Social mobility through the ultimate ideal of ownership of sugar estates was harder. Sugar was an expensive business. The capital needed to establish a pen of 300–500 acres in the late eighteenth century was estimated at approximately £10,000 — just one-third of the estimated cost of developing a sugar estate in the same period.[60] In addition, according to J.B. Moreton, 'a pen [was] a better property, and [was] attended with less trouble and expense than a sugar plantation.'[61] Still, pen-keepers hankered after the more prestigious sugar plantation and bought at least one when they could. Hamilton Brown, owner of Minard Pen, Retreat Pen, the whole of the Browns Town and Buxton area, Antrim and Hilton Hill estates[62] provides a good example of a pen-keeper who later invested in sugar.

The foregoing analysis thus brings into question Brathwaite's suggestion that there was a dialectical relationship between Creole and colonial, since pen-keepers, even Creoles and Free-Coloureds, were as colonial in their ideological orientation as the sugar planters. There was no necessary dichotomy. Jamaican slave systems encouraged the coexistence, though not always peaceful, of colonial Creoles and Creole colonials. The ideal among Whites and Free-Coloureds of all classes was not to belong to Jamaica. Those who were forced by economic circumstances to remain as small-farmers, involved primarily in the Creole economy, developed a symbiotic economic relationship with the sugar economy; and they did their best to lobby for the protection of their economic enterprise. However, their conflicts with the dominant sugar sector over laws and taxes must be interpreted more as necessary strategies to protect their economic activities rather than a demonstration of a commitment to Creole society. They may have contributed to the development of a Creole economy, but their attitude to living in Jamaica, to colour, class, slavery and abolition made them colonial reactionary elements rather than a group interested in the development of a true Creole society.

And what of enslaved peoples, whom enslavers over time tried to discipline and transform into New World Creoles and place in a dialectical relationship to African by rendering invisible the African ingredients of the cultural mix that became Creole or Jamaican? How successful was the enslavers' attempt to decentre 'nation' or African ethnic identification and shift the enslaved's allegiance from Akan, Igbo, Yoruba, et cetera to 'Creole' or Jamaican, assigning cultural meaning to Creole that went beyond a linguistic term meaning born in the Americas?[63] Certain social characteristics were attached to Creole which constructed the African as 'savage' and 'barbaric' and the Creole as more sensible and able to assume positions of responsibility in the slave hierarchy. A related question is, were the enslaved born in Jamaica self-consciously Creole in the sense of being amalgamated into a new identity? We know that they contributed to Creole economy by their participation in the internal marketing system and that they helped to shape the devalorized, hybrid Creole language and culture; but did they recognize 'Jamaica' as a place to which they could belong and of which they could become its citizens, or was it simply a colonized space where the English placed themselves in an antagonistic power relationship with the enslaved? How should we interpret, for example, the reluctance of the newly freed Blacks from Unity Valley Pen to embark for Philadelphia in 1795 on the grounds that they had changed their minds?

Given the paucity of first-hand sources, it is difficult to study the products of the mind of the enslaved. We know that they had an anti-slavery stance and we even know that those on pens were regarded by sugar planters as having a heightened sense of anti-slavery consciousness when compared to those enslaved on sugar plantations. We know, too, something about their spirituality and their views about how they could be metaphysically transported back to Africa, even when the physical body died or was killed in the Caribbean. But while resistance is important, as it is an aspect of the power relationship through which the subaltern expressed its distinct and autonomous identity (though Monica Schuler and Douglas Chambers suggest that this identity was ethnic, not 'African', Akan and Igbo respectively representing an obvious paradigmatic form of signifying identity and difference)[64] and because its study is a methodological procedure by which one can obtain access into the consciousness of the subaltern, as Ranajit Guha has noted,[65] our grasp of the slavery period is still not informed by sources that would help us to know unambiguously what the enslaved thought about living in Jamaica or about becoming Creole. The coloured heroine in Cyrus Francis Perkins's unpublished 1855 novel, 'Busha's Mistress or Catherine the Fugitive' did say, in response to the overseer's request that she return 'home' to live with him after she had left in a huff in reaction to his advances to a rival:

Home? Home! Has a slave any home? He is here today and there tomorrow. He is sen' to work any property Trustee [the attorney] please, an' praps seld if Massa or young Massa owe money. Look at me sister Sarah! Me eber see him since de day marshall put handcuff on him an' drag him off de estate? An' didn't eberybody say Mr. Hines was a rich man? De grave is de home for such as we.[66]

But can we read this as a reflection of a sense of loss, of exile or rootlessness that would give support to Maureen Warner-Lewis's authoritative discourse that ascribes a Kikongo as opposed to the usual Portuguese origin to the word Creole?[67] That being born in Jamaica would indicate exile from Africa in a profound way and would explain why African diasporic consciousness would not be a necessary casualty of creolization? The post-slavery period, with more developed discourses of 'belonging' and 'unbelonging' in which African-descended peoples participated overtly, would provide greater clues to this polemic; for it is then that we get clear articulation from Rastafarians (as well as from Indians and Indian-Jamaicans) about exile and repatriation.

Research into the post-slavery period did, indeed, reveal the intensification of discourses over 'belonging', 'citizenship', and the meaning of 'Creole' as opposed to colonial; over what it meant to be a Jamaican in an increasingly segmented, multiethnic and culturally plural context where each ethnic group sought to create definitive ethnocentric enclaves.[68] These discourses were not confined to elite Creoles and the Black Intelligentsia and the focus was not all on the kind of Creole nationalism that was, in Partha Chatterjee's formulation, 'built upon the ambitions of classes whose economic interests were ranged against the metropole; that drew upon the liberal and enlightened ideas from Europe, which provided ideological criticisms of imperialism and *anciens regimes*'.[69] While the main participants in the ranking game and in the Creole discourses of the slavery period were the White and Free-Coloured property owners, Asians and African-Jamaicans became central players in the post-slavery period; but wherever the debates were located, they demonstrated, in a way observed by postmodernists, that the collective identity of homeland and nation was a constantly changing set of cultural interactions that fundamentally questioned the idea of 'home'.

The elite Coloureds, the result of interracial sex mostly in Creole space, used local birth to claim priority over metropolitan, even Creole Whites, who could legally claim to be English. Their struggles with the colonial White elite were mainly over constitutional and political rights — the right of those born in the colonies to chart their own political future. The Black Intelligentsia fought its own separate war for identity and social space within the context of a society where material and intellectual progress did not confer equality with the White and Coloured elite; but, like the Coloureds, their intervention into the discourses of belonging was often framed within the context of distancing themselves from Africa and African. Rather than claim the designation of African, they claimed 'Jamaican', though in its Euro-Creole cultural manifestation. Several letters to the editor in the first half of the twentieth century attest to this tendency. One citizen who wrote to the editor to oppose any ethnic identification with Africa was certain that 'the only race we belong to is the Human Race and our nationality is Jamaican, not African'.[70] Another, as Colin Palmer notes, looked skeptically on any attempt to de-emphasize links with England and strengthen those with Africa.[71]

The Black masses, struggling against the efforts to achieve cultural homogeneity that implied a removal of Africanism and the African worldview from the Jamaican culture, also intervened into these discourses. They too were preoccupied with the question of who mapped the terrain of citizenship or the criteria for belonging in a society emerging out of slavery. This preoccupation was demonstrated in several ways, but I will review only their relationship with 'equal subordinates', in particular with the Indians and Indian-Jamaicans. In their conflicts with this ethnic group, which they viewed as 'newcomers' to the island, they used cultural difference (as opposed to cultural diversity in Homi K. Bhabha's terms[72]) to authorize and construct their own meaning of cultural identification.

Blacks and Indians were able to observe each other's culture and to form opinions because there was no ethnic, residential separation in Jamaica. Inevitably the juxtaposition of the two groups led to some social contact and perceptions about the ethnic 'other'. These perceptions, which took on a racially stereotyped form, itself played a part in the formation of an

Indian ethnic identity. This identity came about both in terms of how Indians felt they were perceived by others and sometimes in an enlarged sense of difference from their Afro-Creole neighbours.

As cultural difference was viewed hierarchically in post-slavery Jamaica, it was not surprising that African-Jamaicans, after observing the Eastern culture of the Indians, considered themselves superior to Indians and their descendants. This was despite the fact that fair-skinned Indians and Indian-Jamaicans whose origins were North Indian and who claimed affinity with the Aryan race, looked down on black-skinned African-Jamaicans. This racism, expressed through the medium of skin colour did not seem to have had much impact on African-Jamaicans however. They still ranked Indians and their descendants unfavourably on the social scale. The criteria by which African-Jamaicans ranked Indians and Indian-Jamaicans and deemed them 'alien' were not Afrocentric norms, but those that had some degree of consensus among most social groups in Creole society. In other words, Indians and Indian-Jamaicans were not considered socially inferior because they could not speak African languages or because they did not dress African and practice Myal and Kumina. The descendants of enslaved peoples had increasingly become creolized, participating in the locally evolved habits, language, customs, cuisine and popular culture of the Caribbean,[73] while Indians and Indian-Jamaicans (whose anatomy was firmly Creole, according to George Lamming),[74] still viewed Creole as something negative (especially where it occurred as a result of interracial sex)[75] and tried to resist the acculturative forces of Creole society. Consequently, like the colonial government, the imperial government, the churches and missionary societies, and other sections of Afro- and Euro-Creole society, African-Jamaicans ranked Indians and Indian-Jamaicans lower down on the social scale because they did not practise Christianity, spoke supposedly 'bad English', dressed 'indecently'[76] and had 'strange' habits and customs. In addition, unlike the practice during slavery, 'foreign' birth was used as a basis for exclusion.

The Presbyterian perhaps best reflected the host society's attitude towards the languages spoken by the Hindu and Muslim Indians when they said that Indians spoke in 'different tongues'. The implication was that this was due to backwardness, Indian society failing to achieve the supposed linguistic uniformity of a country like England. Even when by the 1890s many Indians and Indian-Jamaicans spoke the 'accepted language', the Presbyterians described this as 'bad English', 'the badness of which is a different badness from that spoken by Jamaicans of the same class'.[77] Also, even before Indians had arrived in Jamaica, the Baptists had built up suspicion about their culture in the minds of their African-Jamaican flock. Fearful of the impact that Indians might have on the African-Jamaican population, they opposed the import of so-called 'pagan' Indians, noting in 1845 that

> The importation of a number of heathen and pagan foreigners with their religious superstitions, idolatory and wickedness, will act most injuriously on the morals of the [Black] population and hinder . . . the efforts that are now in operation for their moral and religious improvement.[78]

Continuing in a similar vein two years later, a letter appearing under the name of 'Publicola', in a letter to the editor of the *Morning Journal* (a newspaper that openly supported White and African immigration but opposed Indian immigration) lamented: '[B]etter for Jamaica if her soil had never been pressed by the foot of a Coolie — it appears to be of little advantage to them — [for] they show little disposition to imitate us and will never make a material progress in our customs.'[79]

But the Scottish Presbyterians and Quakers, in particular, tried to ensure that such 'imitation' would eventually take place by setting out to convert Indians to Christianity and socialize them along Euro-Creole lines. They shared Alfred Caldecott's view that the Indian presence was a 'serious addition to the responsibilities of the Church',[80] and their culture was another challenge to a society where 'English Law was but striving with African-rooted habits among Jamaicans'.[81] They considered religious customs such as the Shiite Muslim Hussay, as 'strange'; and were appalled at the Indian marriage custom that involved young children, considered minors in the Jamaican society. Their special mission to the Indians was therefore designed to achieve cultural assimilation. Their success was measured by the fact that whereas in 1912, only 29 per cent of the Indian population was categorized as Christians, by 1943, only 20 per cent of the Indian population identified openly with religions apart from Christianity. In addition, by 1950, very few parishes in which the Quakers and Presbyterians were active, including Westmoreland which had a large Indian and Indian-Jamaican population, still observed the Hussay festival.

Indians and Indo-Creoles responded in different ways to the low ranking of their culture by Afro- and Euro-Creole society. Like the pen-keepers almost a century earlier, many tried to seek re-ranking and acceptance through a process of selective creolization. Many inter-married with other ethnic groups (though not with the elite as in the case of the pen-keepers), converted to Christianity, adopted Western dress and language and discontinued certain social practices like ethnic-specific marriage customs. While some changes would have come about through the natural process of inter-culturation, this deliberate effort to conform to the norms of Afro- and Euro-Creole society caused a creolized Indian and Indian-Jamaican society to emerge by the 1950s.

Some Indians and the Indo-Creole elite sought a different route, pressing for the recognition of their distinctive culture. They had quickly realized that 'Jamaicans' made little class or caste distinction, referring to all Indians and Indian-Jamaicans as 'coolies'. They therefore set out to win recognition for their ancient and 'superior' customs and to change the low evaluation of their culture. They established communal organizations such as the East Indian Association of Jamaica (1930), the East Indian National Union (1937), and the East Indian Progressive Society (1940) and sought to promote the Indian culture. They also began to press for ethnic-specific rights and benefits such as, special schools, special consideration for land and poor relief benefits, cremation of the dead by the pyre system, customary marriage and divorce practices, ethnic representation in the legislature and repatriation. The larger society protested against the claims for ethnic-specific rights and benefits, interpreting the action of the Indian organizations as an attempt on the part of people of Indian descent to maintain ethnic exclusivism by rejecting Jamaica and Jamaican culture. This interpretation was strengthened by the ways in which some Indians and Indo-Creoles articulated their views about belonging. For example, even though the East Indian Progressive Society had stated that one of its aims was to instruct Indian-Jamaicans on their rights as citizens of Jamaica, it and other communal associations made statements that indicated a contrary tendency. Mr Coy, the East Indian National Union's Solicitor-General, is reported to have said to the Royal Commission: 'the majority of Indians regard themselves as a separate community. . . . Only a very minor proportion . . . feel that they are Jamaicans.'[82]

This feeling that India was home was reflected in the calls for repatriation despite the imposition of the requirement in 1909 that returnees should contribute a portion of the passage money. Poiri who came to Jamaica on the ship *Dahomey* in 1903, summed up the views of many Indians and Indian-Jamaicans towards continued residence in Jamaica when he wrote as follows to the Protector of Immigrants in the 1920s:

> I am very much desirous to go home and I shall be very gratitude [sic] if you kindly send me away to India. . . by the next ship. . . .
> I feel very sad in Jamaica. . . . I am willing to pay passage and clear off from this island.[83]

In 1930, the year in which the colonial government's legal obligation to repatriate ex-indentured Indians and their family ended unilaterally, 1,300 Indians and Indian-Jamaicans requested repatriation.[84] Calls for repatriation continued into the 1940s; these calls were not limited only to Indian nationals. Fifty per cent of the calls for repatriation in 1941 came from Jamaican-born Indians, many of whom harboured the view that the colonial government was responsible for their relocation to Jamaica and continued to hold them responsible for their 'entrapment' in the island.

Those that returned did not always have smooth re-entry into Indian society. Mahatma Gandhi is reported to have said in an article in *The Young Indian* that most of the repatriates had in fact jumped out of the frying pan, into the fire; and after returning, their constant cry soon became 'anywhere out of India'.[85] He urged the colonial governments in the Caribbean to use the money that they would otherwise spend on repatriation on programmes to settle the Indians in the Caribbean. Part of his justification was that many of the returnees were colonial-born, 'descendants from uncultured, half-disindianized parents . . . social lepers not even knowing the language of the [Indian] people'.[86] Gandhi's views were not irrelevant to the discontinuation of repatriation at the colonial government's expense in 1930. Thereafter, the Indians and Indian-Jamaicans were encouraged by the colonial and imperial governments to 'creolize' and become 'Jamaicans'.

As part of the project of forcing settlement and creolization on Indians and Indo-Creoles, the colonial government reversed or refused to entertain ethnic-specific benefits and claims. The colonial government pushed for civic assimilation in non-articulating sectors of subordinate minority cultures as a way of achieving 'social order'. It sought to outlaw ethnic-specific marriage, divorce and practices for the disposal of the dead, and except for the 20-year period between 1910 and 1930, ruled against ethnic-specific schools and curricula. In justifying the closure of these schools in 1930, Mr. Tucker, Acting Director of Education stressed: 'there is no distinction made in elementary education . . . for the separation of East Indian or Chinese children from the remainder, the desire being that if these children remain in Jamaica, they should become its citizens.'[87]

The lobby for ethnic representation in the Legislature by the Indian organizations and the colonial government in India was also not entertained. The colonial government in India had requested that seats be reserved for Indians in both Houses of the Legislature after 1944 on the basis that the Indian population was not 'numerous enough or sufficiently organized in any electoral area to succeed in returning its own representatives to either Houses under a system of universal adult suffrage'.[88] Oliver Stanley, Secretary of State for the Colonies, however, dismissed the request, arguing that the colonial government could not possibly single out any ethnic group for special favours.[89]

The colonial and imperial government's injunction to 'creolize' was reinforced by the Moyne Commission whose view was that, with 90 per cent of Indians born in the island by 1939, 'there are grave objections to treating the Indian Community separately from all others'. The Moyne Commission Report had gone on to stress that any measures which cause the East Indians to look upon themselves or to be looked upon as a people apart will at once pave the way for inter-racial rivalries and jealousies, and at the same time prejudice the handling of the many problems involving all the peoples of the West Indies.[90]

But colonial policy was one thing; the reactions and perceptions of the larger society, another. Given the socioeconomic climate, the 1930s and 1940s were not the right years for an all-embracing attitude to people African-Jamaicans insisted on categorizing as 'aliens'. Their attitude to these 'aliens' was translated into violent conflicts in the early to mid-twentieth century. It would seem though, that it was economic competition rather than social ranking specifically that explains the conflicts that developed. According to Pierre van den Berghe's typology of competitive race relations, economic competition determines race relations in capitalist societies where equal subordinates compete for scarce resources. Such competition usually manifested itself in racial prejudice, expressed in such ways as aggression and the treatment of the newcomers as 'alien'.[91]

Why were these conflicts delayed until the mid-twentieth century when Indians had been imported since 1845? The answer is that it was only then that 'Indians' were perceived as posing a real economic threat to African-Jamaicans. This late development of economic competition between African-Jamaicans and Asians might seem surprising in light of the reasons Indian labourers were relocated to the colonial Caribbean. Emancipation had resulted in a contraction of the plantation labour force as the newly freed sought alternatives to estate wage labour or were forced to leave because of the poor labour relations and planters' coercive strategies. The planter-class had responded by importing additional labourers to flood the labour market, depress wages and defeat the attempt by the newly freed to actualize their freedom in meaningful economic ways. The importation of additional labourers, mostly from Asia, was perceived by the African-Jamaican working class as a deliberate strategy to defeat emancipation. Swithin Wilmot's research indicates that Samuel Clarke, an African-Jamaican carpenter and outspoken Vestryman from the parish of St. David bordering St. Thomas-in-the-East, who was executed in 1865 in the repression following the Morant Bay Rebellion, captured Blacks' views on such a coercive strategy at one of his public meetings in St. David between 1853 and 1865. He reminded his audience that it was the newly freed people's assertion of their freedom from estate labour that had caused the planters to tax the labouring population 'for the purpose of bringing out competitors [Indians]'.[92] In addition, Indians received certain benefits within the context of African-Jamaicans' struggle for improved conditions in the post-slavery period: free or assisted repatriation up to 1930, £12 cash or ten acres of Crown land in lieu of repatriation up to 1910; free medical care and housing; guaranteed agricultural wage labour and a Protector of Immigrants to watch over their welfare.

However, only 38,000 Indians were ever imported to Jamaica, representing a mere seven per cent of the 500,000 relocated to the post-slavery Caribbean; and at no time did Indians form more than two to three per cent of the total Jamaican population. Unlike territories like Trinidad, Indians were not imported when the economy was depressed; and repatriation kept their numbers in the island small. The fact that they formed a significant portion of the agricultural labour force by the early twentieth century was also not an indication that Indians and Indian-Jamaicans were displacing African-Jamaicans, many of whom emigrated or sought non-plantation avenues to upward social mobility. The landholders' expectation that Indians and their descendants would contribute to the building up of a large pool of reserve labourers and create intense economic competition with the local labouring population was, therefore, not achieved in the nineteenth century.

The situation changed in the 1930s and 1940s. By then, the end of government-assisted Indian repatriation and the (mostly forced) return of African-Jamaican migrants from Cuba, Honduras and Panama, caused the build up of a pool of reserve labour; and for the first time, there was real competition for scarce agricultural jobs between Indians — Indian-Jamaicans and African-Jamaicans. Conflicts were inevitable within this economic context. The events of the 1940s and 1950s must be seen, then, as delayed effects of the coercive post-slavery labour strategy when Indians were imported into Jamaica as indentured labourers to compete with the newly-freed for plantation labour. The statement of the Afro-West Indian League (AWIL) and the various manifestations of inter-ethnic rivalries and hostility were deeply embedded episodes in colonial strategies to control African-Jamaican labour in the post-slavery period, using Asian relocation to the island as a punitive and coercive strategy. It was economic competition that reinscribed this discourse of 'alienism'.

The Chinese were even more affected than the Indians and Indian-Jamaicans in the early to mid-twentieth century. Patrick Bryan reminds us that the Chinese, emigrating to Jamaica since the 1850s and even earlier to Cuba, colonial Guyana and Trinidad, were also objects of the mid-twentieth-century nativist assertion and the articulated anti-Asian views of groups such as the AWIL, and the anti-alien Native Defenders Committee (NDC). The NDC was established in 1930, years before the AWIL, ostensibly to protect the interests of 'natives' (that is, African-Jamaicans) against foreigners (Indians and Chinese in particular but also Whites), manifested in their slogan 'Jamaica for Jamaicans'.[93] As in the case of the AWIL, many of the NDC's leaders and activists, like Benjamin Wilson and one Mr Ricketts, were returnees from Cuba, Honduras and Panama where they had experienced racial discrimination and forced repatriation to Jamaica and had returned home to a situation where 'foreigners' seemed favoured.[94] NDC members, like the Rastafarians and the Ethiopian Salvation Society among other groups in the 1930s[95] were unambiguously Black conscious; and while not all supported Garvey's and the Rastafarians' back-to-Africa ideology, were committed to Black empowerment in an increasingly anti-Black masses environment.

The strong economic position of the Chinese, who had, by the mid-twentieth century largely displaced other ethnic groups in the retail trade, caused them to be increasingly viewed by Black Jamaicans as 'economic oppressors'.[96] They maintained a strong sense of group cohesiveness based on a distinct racial and cultural identity and though, by the 1950s many had been born in Jamaica, they were still identified as 'Chinese', much as Indian-Jamaicans were perceived as 'Indians'. In the strained economic climate of the mid to late twentieth century, the Chinese, not surprisingly, became the targets of 'xenophobic racism' that was clearly linked to competitive racism in Pierre van den Berghe's terms. It was within this context that the NDC established a Native Co-operative Traders and Consumers Society to further the cause of native support for native small business people against the Chinese.

The 'Indians' probably escaped equal attention by the NDC because they were not as dominant in the retail trade by the 1930s and 1940s. It is true that Indians and Indian-Jamaicans had entered the shopkeeping trade in the late nineteenth and early twentieth centuries, and that the majority of those engaged in non-agricultural pursuits were shopkeepers in the period 1891–1921. But the numbers had declined gradually, for example from 415 (264 men and 151 women) in 1891 to 204 by 1921, with a corresponding reduction in the number of trade and spirit licences held by the Indians — from 416 in 1903 to 290 by 1933. These reductions were attributed by the Protector of Immigrants to 'the invasion of the Chinese who control practically all the small retail trade of the country'.[97]

Conclusion

The debates over 'alienism', 'nativism' and Jamaican identity and the inter-ethnic conflicts that intensified in the twentieth century reveal that up to the mid- twentieth century, Creole society, a distinctive common culture as a basis for national unity, remained an unrealized ideal. If anything, while not as pronounced as in Trinidad, Guyana and Suriname, the society displayed tendencies of a plural society. The desire to embrace and promote the culture of the Euro-Creole minority had become the yardstick for social and political behaviour, thus making folk culture, an officially submerged minority culture with low prestige for the socially mobile or for the elite hegemonic society.

Unhappily, these tendencies are not confined to the historical past. The 'ranking game' has survived despite attempts at social integration and national unity in the postcolonial era. On the first anniversary of independence, someone using the name 'disappointed investor', wrote to the editor of the *Jamaica Times* suggesting that at least one basis of ranking, the politicized colour-coding of people in the island, had ended. The view was 'that we are a coloured [that is, Black] people and we are proud of ourselves as Jamaicans irrespective of what tint'.[98] 'Ranking' on the basis of colour, ethnicity, gender, et cetera has perhaps simply taken new, subversive forms within the social and political culture, ensuring that Jamaicans make the transition from colonials to Creoles to citizens in a milieu of turbulence and violent changes. The tendency to lessen the claim on citizenship by those whose ancestral homes are other than Africa is also still present. If Creole culture has the potential for social integration and forging a new cultural unity, then that potential has not been realized fully. The motto adopted at independence in 1962, 'Out of many one people', has masked the ranking of ethnic groups, cultures and spiritual well-being that is our social reality. Nevertheless this strategy has not been successful; and a postmodernist ideal of egalitarian multiculturalism is not the Caribbean reality. Globalization, which renders us twenty-first-century beings, both local and global social agents whether ancestrally Chinese, Indian or African, has intensified an opposing tendency in the nation states of the so-called 'Third World'.

As these political constructs respond to the economic policies of the dominant global 'partners', who themselves engage in an international ranking game, the formerly colonized feel compelled to reassert difference and defend their citizenship. Stuart Hall highlights this contradictory tendency of globalization, on the one hand the pull towards borderlessness, assimilation and homogenization; on the other, the reassertion of localism, notably in the form of ethnicity, nationalism and religious fundamentalism.[99] But at the level of the nation there seems to be less possibility of a harmonious integration of cultural difference with national unity; a toleration of that paradigmatic 'code-switching', according to Barry Chevannes, that would allow different sectors to live in Jamaica in all its multilingual and multicultural possibilities.[100] Perhaps this is because, as Carol Narcisse points out, despite some obvious border crossings since independence, persistent 'border clashes' which speak to endemic elite terms of engagement that rest on the ideology of inequality and cultural hegemony, are still being used as the basis for social integration.[101] There needs to be a concerted effort to redress the inequalities, based on class, gender, colour, ethnicity and culture. Critically, the inequality based on existential awareness, feelings of social worth and spiritual value, the contemporary core of the ranking game that has derailed our journey towards social integration, nationhood and human development, must be fought and defeated.

SECTION V

'I WANT TO DISTURB MY NEIGHBOUR':
ACTIVISM IN AN AGE OF INDIVIDUALISM

Introduction

With the exception of certain minor irritants, unavoidable as long as one is part of an academy that has become increasingly competitive, I enjoy immensely my occupation as a historian at the University of the West Indies and my core responsibilities of teaching, advising, evaluating students' work, researching, writing and publishing. I also enjoy the variety provided by teaching and lecturing to students and faculty at universities outside of the Caribbean. But I do not believe that those aspects of my professional life are as rewarding to me as those which afford me the opportunity of engaging with the off-campus, preferably non-academic publics, conscious of history's important role in public education.

Postcolonial revisionist history is a fundamental emancipatory tool that needs to be shared, especially with the Caribbean public; for history and historical evidence are crucial to a people's sense of identity. Indeed, as some scholars point out, 'what historians do best is to make connections with the past in order to illuminate the problems of the present and the potential of the future.'[1] History is increasingly being used as a form of cultural enquiry in many societies. The view is that history and historical consciousness belong to culture, and culture, of which historiography is a part, is the background against which we can form opinion about the usefulness of, say, certain scientific research or political objectives.[2] As Florida University Professor, Kevin Yelvington and his colleagues observed some years ago:

> the wider world, currently overrun with the passions of regionalism, ethnicism and nationalism, and in the throes of both modernization and development, has made history the privileged ground of individual and collective identity.[3]

Since the 1990s, I have increasingly and eagerly accepted the invitations extended from local and international organizations, associations and institutions and wholeheartedly embraced the opportunities to travel and share my ideas with a wider audience. The lectures in this section represent this more activist phase of my career as I sought to expose history's relevance to national development, especially as I deepened my interest in slavery and gender studies.

The first speech, delivered at the plaque unveiling ceremony at the Old King's House in Spanish Town, appealed for Jamaicans to endeavour to honour the memory of the ancestors who fought for freedom by aligning themselves to a project of true Emancipation. Emancipation not just as an event of 1838, momentous as that was; but Emancipation as a condition of human progress. The rationale was that our ancestors did not fight so hard to dismantle the authoritarian society of slavery and the oligarchic power that continued into the post-slavery society, only to have us turn around and enchain ourselves with violence against one another and with unprogressive ideologies and social attitudes. One way of honouring them, I suggested, was to expand what I called the 'mark the spot' project already started by the Institute of Jamaica (IOJ), the Jamaica Cultural Development Commission (JCDC), and the Jamaica National Heritage Trust (JNHT). Despite the fear in some quarters that 'slavery' and 'sadness' are not among the several S's for which tourists flock to the island, I feel that we must mark all the historical spots; and not just Great Houses, the symbols of oppression that some still glamourize today, but of the enslaveds' burial grounds, huts, dungeons, the canefields and factories on those very plantations that are tourist attractions. In celebration, we should also mark the spot of the first free villages in every parish. Similarly, we should seek to replace events such as the euphemistic 'Encounter Day' with 'Indigenous Peoples' Day' which would represent a more liberating narrative of self.

On the occasion of the unveiling of the Emancipation Proclamation plaque in Spanish Town, as well as at the graduation speech delivered at Brown's Town Community College, I challenged the audience to internalize and appreciate the transforming power of education and use this power to help to heal some of the wounds in contemporary Jamaican society. I argued that many of these wounds were legacies of the island's slavery and colonial past; though others were more recently postcolonial, inflicted upon us by the descendants of enslaved people who have inherited the reigns of power from our colonial oppressors, making these wounds not only harder to endure, but harder to heal.

Emancipation and independence ought to have paved the way for the creation of a society that was more just and equitable than the colonial period; a society that ensured and protected the rights of citizens without regard to colour, gender, ethnicity or class. We have undoubtedly made great strides towards that end, but despite the obvious gains in education and literacy; in the building of the social and physical infrastructure; in the creation of a democratic system of government; in the security and justice systems – we still have a long way to go. I challenged the students to help to complete the democratic revolution started at the moment of independence; to forgive those that have trespassed against them and their ancestors; to put behind them, while not forgetting the lessons of, such moments in our recent history as the attempted hiding of some of Montego Bay's mentally challenged people, deemed an eye sore to tourists, and the case of Ivan Nettleford who, because of inefficient record-keeping, was renamed Burrowes and therefore became lost to his relatives in the prison system for 29 years. I issued a call for activism; for us to adopt as our motto, as Bob Marley and others have done, 'I want to disturb my neighbour.' 'I want to disturb my neighbour' can be a metaphor for adopting an activist stance in an age of 'me-ism', 'myself-ism' and 'I-ism'. This age of individualism threatens to destabilize the spirit of activism, philanthropy and neighbourliness that has traditionally been a part of the Jamaican social landscape.

'After the Exhibition is Gone' was delivered at the official opening of the travelling exhibition, 'Lest We Forget', organized by UNESCO, Jamaica office, in April 2005. I found it ironic that while influential elements in the Jamaican society were attempting to steer our attention away from slavery discourses, UNESCO was trying to refocus our attention on all aspects of the slavery past. I raised the issue of what would happen after the exhibition had closed. Would Jamaicans then return to their comfort zone, confining slavery to a distant memory, or would we find creative ways to cement the slavery past into our collective consciousness? I argued that if we were never to forget either the pains or triumphs over slavery, then we would have to put post-exhibition plans in place; but that we needed to invest the keepers of our historical memory with the vital, enabling resources. Perhaps 2007 will provide the opportunity to implement some of my proposals.

I was particularly keen in this section to revive the public debates around such issues as reparation, male marginalization and hegemonic masculinity (promoted by home, media and schools' curricula), and embraced the opportunity provided by the History Department's public forum on reparation, the one-day symposium of the Jamaica Reparation Movement and the invitation to deliver the Planning Institute of Jamaica's (PIOJ) public lecture on education, to re-ignite such debates.

All of these issues continue to be prominent in public discussions, with the issue of reparation for slavery, arguably, causing the most heated debates (even among historians, some supporting, some opposing the idea), especially in the wake of the 2001 Durban Conference. Since then, several lawsuits have been filed against banks (such as, Lloyds) and companies that benefited financially from the transatlantic trade in Africans and slavery. There have also been renewed efforts to calculate Britain's financial liability to the Caribbean. A recent documentary initiated by Robert Beckford of Birmingham University in the UK puts this figure at 7.5 trillion pounds sterling, perhaps an underestimation. No doubt the bicentenary of the passing of the British Act to abolish the trade will see renewed interest in these issues. My hope though is that 2006–2008 – the dates when various countries in the Commonwealth Caribbean will commemorate the bicentenary of the phased abolition of the transatlantic trade in Africans by Britain – will be used as the occasion for the UWI and Caribbean governments to (i) educate the region's people about the history and consequences of slavery and the trade in Africans, (ii) establish a Centre for Slavery Research at an appropriate location, and (iii) construct War Memorials (including on the Mona campus, which is built on the site of two former sugar plantations), to the anti-slavery patriots. The Caribbean needs a wider range of tangible and national sites of memory to memorialize the period of enslavement and the Black anti-slavery activists. In the process of mapping and re-mapping the postcolonial cultural landscape, singling out 'leaders' and sculpting and mounting them in parks and museums; or constructing artistic impressions and representations of the African experience, the rank and file in the liberation struggles have been forgotten. War Memorials would pluralize the objects and subjects that we either select for historic preservation or erect for honour and commemoration and I will continue to seek funds and agitate for their construction on and off the Mona campus.

16

THE EMANCIPATION PROCLAMATION
and August 1, 1838 Text and Context

Speech Delivered at the Plaque-Unveiling Ceremony to Commemorate
Emancipation, Emancipation Square, Spanish Town October 19, 2001

This is a fitting tribute to the men and women who ensured that the system of neo-slavery, introduced on August 1, 1834 as part of the Emancipation Act, and euphemistically called the 'Apprenticeship System', ended in 1838, two years ahead of the stipulated time.

Governor Sligo, himself a property owner with 286 formerly enslaved peoples,[1] had told the newly-designated apprentices in August 1834 that 'the first of August [1834] has passed over you, and you are no longer slaves. You have been raised by the generosity and humanity of the British nation and of those who had power over you from a state of slavery to that of apprentices';[2] but Africans and African-Jamaicans wanted immediate and unambiguous freedom. As one elderly African, skeptical of Apprenticeship as it was explained to him in 1834, reportedly observed, and here I quote from Thomas Holt, 'Apprenticeship was a term used for children put out to learn a trade [so,] what, [he asked,] was he to learn?' He was too old to become a cooper, carpenter or mason; he knew how to plant the cane, to weed, to hoe — what was he to learn?[3]

Mounting protest to continued bondage and the unfair practices of the former enslavers by those who shared his views, reinforced the fact that the more coercive power is applied to deny freedom, the central political value in Western political theory, as Anthony Bogues has observed, the more the struggle for individual freedom escalates.[4] The so-called 'apprenticed' men and women appropriated and acted on the ideology that as forced colonial subjects, they had a stake in the enlightenment project of human progress. Apprenticeship, like slavery, produced among them only one kind of organized radicalism that is recognizable within modern political thought — anti-slavery struggle.[5] Despite several amendments to the Jamaican Abolition Act to get proprietors to adopt a more conciliatory approach to apprentices and give the Apprenticeship System a chance to work well, the British government was in the end driven to advise the Colonial Legislatures, in their own interests, to terminate the Apprenticeship System on August 1, 1838.[6] Even before that, however, as early as 1835, the Speaker of the House of Assembly, fed up with constant British intervention in the affairs of the island, had spoken publicly in favour of ending Apprenticeship; and in 1837, Edward Jordon, leader of the Black legislators, introduced a Bill in the Assembly designed to end Jamaica's Apprenticeship System. No action was taken until June 16, 1838 when Governor Lionel Smith duly presented the draft Emancipation Proclamation to the Council, to be effected on the first of August.[7] It read:

Whereas an Act has been passed by the legislator of this our island of Jamaica for terminating the present system of Apprenticeship on the first day of August next, and thereby granting the blessing and privileges of unrestricted freedom to all classes of its inhabitants, and whereas it is incumbent on all the inhabitants of this our island to testify their grateful sense of this divine favour. We do therefore by and with the advice of our Privy Council of this our said island, direct and appoint that Wednesday the said first day of August next be observed in all churches and chapels as a day of general thanksgiving to Almighty God for these his mercies, and of humble intercession for his continued blessing a protection on this most important occasion and we do hereby call upon persons of all classes within this our island to observe this said first day of August next with the same reverence and respect which is observed and due to the sabbath.[8]

Of course, this proclamation gave the impression that emancipation was the result of divine benevolence and humanitarianism, but we know better. The planting elite greeted the news of impending freedom with noisy opposition; but it could not stop the march of freedom. This is the context within which Governor Lionel Smith, standing on the portico of the Old King's House, told the thousands of newly freed who gathered in this square, on the first of August 1838, as they did in town squares across the island, that an Act had been passed granting unrestricted freedom to all classes of the island's inhabitants and congratulating them on their freedom. Smith anticipated violence on the part of apprentices and former enslavers (although his proclamation urged both groups to pass the day in church), and so took the precaution ahead of August 1, 1838 to ask the British government to dispatch a naval vessel to the island. Smith's letter to the Secretary of State in the Colonial Office in May 1838 declared the Assemblymen 'ignorant, violent, mad and likely to provoke an insurrection for the pleasure of destroying the freed-people and the missionaries'.[9] Of course, the day passed mostly in worship and jubilation on the part of the freed, unmarked by the anticipated violence.

But even as we celebrate those who made full freedom possible in 1838, let us not forget those who paved the way; those who participated in numerous violent and non-violent protests in the long struggle for freedom — a struggle that began with the indigenous peoples and continued throughout the period of African enslavement. I want us to focus especially on those who participated in the 1831–32 rebellion; for it was this rebellion more than the vigour of the British anti-slavery movement that sealed the issue of abolition.

Our insistence on isolating individual heroes and heroines has caused us to focus almost exclusively on Daddy Ruler Sam Sharpe; but let us remember the others, among them:

- Col. Robert Gardiner, Sharpe's military commander
- George Taylor, recognized by many of those who confessed at the trials as a principal leader of the rebellion
- members of Gardiner's squad: 'Captains' Thomas Dove, M'Cail, George M'Lenan, William McKinley, John Wilson, Trail, Linton, Dehany, Largie, Haughton, Hurlock, Peterkin, Simpson, Bernard

- Susan who helped to feed the Black rebels
- the old woman who tried to poison soldiers from the St. Elizabeth and Westmoreland regiments
- the young enslaved woman who helped to guard hostages taken during the rebellion and to lead the soldiers away from the rebel camps.
- John Davis, Robert and Edward Morrice, George Guthrie, William Spence, Eliza Mason, William Binham, and Alexander Benlos.

These men and women were among the hundreds who suffered for the cause of freedom. Compared to the low casualty among Whites and Free-Coloureds, over 200 enslaved Africans and Creoles died during the violence, among them Amelia Pinnock of George's Valley estate and Sophy, a 22-year-old pregnant woman from a Manchester estate who were shot during the rebellion. Accounts differ; but some sources indicate that when it was all over, 406 people were tried before civil slave courts and another 427 by court martial.

The account of the punishment makes chilling reading: 580 were executed, most from Hanover and St. James, among them Sam Sharpe, George McLennan, John Wilson, Robert Walker, James Bennett, Linton, George Taylor, Robert Morrice, William Binham, William Evans, M'Kinley, Samuel Cunningham, Robert Gallimore, Robert Hall, and William Merrick. Some were deported, others flogged with lashes varying from 50 to 500. Some of those who received the worst flogging also got life imprisonment. Some got prison terms varying from one month to life. Few were acquitted.[10] Of particular interest was that at their confession, more than one of these heroes said, as Linton did, that 'in about 3–4 years the [enslaved] will break out again [if freedom is not granted'.[11]

The timing of the August 28, 1833 Emancipation Act that came into effect on August 1, 1834 was testimony that this warning was heeded. If Emancipation would not come from above, it would come from below. I hope that in the not too distant future we will place the list of names and attendant punishment of the 1831–32 heroes and heroines in a place appropriate for public viewing. And here we are, with a plaque to commemorate the end of the long anti-slavery struggle. What an appropriate spot. The spot is appropriate not because this was where Sir Lionel Smith addressed the newly emancipated who gathered in this square 163 years ago; but because this square stands as a reminder of the triumph of people's activism over oppressive state power. All around us we see the scene of the greatest crime against humanity: a monument to a war hero, a reminder of the European battle over terrain on which they could impose further structural discontinuites; a courthouse that reminds us of the way in which the justice (or the injustice) system was stacked against the enslaved; a governor's house, the symbol of racism and colonial rule; a House of Assembly that passed so many repressive anti-people legislation and which caused Governor Sligo to once remark that humanity and justice would require the displacement of the Jamaican Assembly.

As this plaque is unveiled today and we reflect on these tremendous odds faced by our ancestors on the long road to freedom, let us endeavour to honour their memory by aligning ourselves to a project of true Emancipation. Emancipation not just as an event of 1838, momentous as that was; but Emancipation as a condition of human progress. Surely our ancestors did not fight so hard to dismantle the authoritarian society of slavery and the oligarchic power that continued into the post-slavery society only to have us turn around and enchain ourselves with violence against one another and with unprogressive ideologies and social attitudes. We can honour the memory of our freedom-fighting heroes and heroines during this year's heroes' week, by pledging to create a truly free society. We can start by:

- dismantling the last vestiges of the oppressive plantation system
- creating a society in which the human rights claims of all citizens are respected
- educating our people, especially anchoring them to their rich past with a sense of their history
- expanding what I am going to call the 'mark the spot' project started here this morning by the Institute of Jamaica (IOJ) and the Jamaica Cultural Development Commission (JCDC)

Despite the fear in some quarters that 'slavery' and 'sadness' are not among the several S's for which tourists flock our island, let us mark the spot, not just of Great Houses, the symbols of oppression that some still glamourize today, but of the enslaveds' burial grounds, huts and dungeons. Let us mark the spot of the canefields and factories on those very plantations that are tourist attractions. And in celebration, let us mark the spot of the first free villages in every parish.

Finally, let us honour our ancestors by adding our voices to the international call for redress for the crime of slavery. We know that there is still resistance to the call for an apology from countries that participated in the transatlantic trade in enslaved African captives; to the call for the declaration of slavery as a crime against humanity; to the idea of reparation. But we should make it clear that we find it unacceptable that: the enslavers in Jamaica received just over £6.6 million of the £20,000,000 million compensation money (at least £1 billion in today's money) paid by Britain and the enslaved received nothing but freedom, crucial as that freedom was.

The claims for compensation and the financial settlements made make interesting reading. For example, William Beckford received £20,000 in today's money for the freedom of those he had enslaved and George Cunningham, owner of Maxfield and Greenside estates in Trelawny put in a claim for £18,880 on 383 Africans and Creoles. Imagine the circumstances under which: the children of Esther Mendes Álvares claimed a financial compensation on three Black people; Margaret Austin of Strawberry Hill on 35; James Hunt on 138; the Reverend Robert Morgan on 215; Benjamin Scott-Moncrieffe on 240.

It is true that no amount of money could ever repair the damage done by slavery; but a start can be made to redress the wrongs and we as a nation must continue to lobby for such a redress. At the same time, however, let us at home stop squandering our ancestors' legacy and instead create a society of which they would be justly proud. After 163 years, freedom remains a contested notion. Unless we can agree on the basic requirements of freedom in the modern political order, the institutional framework of rebellion will remain.

17

'I WANT TO DISTURB MY NEIGHBOUR' AND 'THE MAN AT THE DOOR'

In an Age of Individualism

Graduation Address, Browns Town Community College, St. Ann, June 26, 2002

I know that some of you will remain in Jamaica and help to develop further the island's economy and society. But I also know that others will seek a larger regional or international stage; for unfortunately, Jamaica cannot absorb all the talent that it produces. If you do choose to leave, be good ambassadors for Jamaica from your new geographical spaces; and of course, return as often as you can.

However, whether you remain in Jamaica or choose to live abroad, I hope that you will continue your education. Neither a school-leaving certificate nor a College Diploma is considered sufficient insurance in this competitive environment. So, in about five to ten years' time, when I ask your teachers about you, I hope to hear that each of you has progressed to the highest ranks in your chosen field or career, be it teaching, nursing, engineering science or the fields of art and music. If you pursue higher education in countries such as the UK or the USA, do not be deterred by the racism that you will inevitably meet. Just march forward as self-confident Jamaicans and bear in mind that racism is a by-product of ignorance and that ignorance is a feature even of this postmodern age in which we live. We confront it at international airports, in shops and even hear it in the commentaries of sports events such as cricket and football matches. Journalist Tony Robinson, in critiquing the commentary at World Cup Football matches, reminded us that as far as some commentators are concerned

> the African players have natural ability, skill and flair, while the Europeans play with intelligence, strategy and creativity.... If a European is fouled by anyone else, [he continues], it is a brutal

254

tackle and FIFA should clamp down. While the South Americans and Africans are nameless brutes with no personas, some of the European lads who love tea and crumpets, have their mothers worrying over them.[1]

Above all, I hope that you will internalize and appreciate the transforming power of education and, when and where you can, use this knowledge to help others; to be the 'man at the door' so powerfully illustrated in the following episodes in the life of the Jamaican, Godfrey Henry Oliver Palmer. You should also take inspiration from the way in which he overcame racism to rise to the top of his field. As the *Times Higher Educational Supplement* tells it, Palmer arrived in England from Jamaica barely literate, but with help overcame racism to become a world-renowned professor of brewing.

Professor Palmer has reportedly said repeatedly that he would have achieved nothing 'had it not been for the man at the door'.[2] Briefly, in March 1955 when he was 14 years, 11 months old, Palmer arrived in England from Jamaica to join his mother who had been working in London since 1948, saving her dressmaking wages until she had the 86 pounds sterling for his passage. The next morning, after his arrival, his mother woke him up at 6:00 a.m. to get him ready for a job as a grocery boy as the family needed to earn extra cash. But they stepped out of their single room only to find a man wearing a three-piece pinstripe suit and a bowler hat, carrying a briefcase standing outside the front door. This man, obviously from Immigration, said to Palmer: 'here you don't leave school till you are 15.' Despite his mother's pleas, the man reiterated that Palmer, even though being just one month shy of 15 years, had to go to school, reminding them also that he did not make the rules. Palmer duly went to school where the principal insisted that he should stay not one month but 6 months as to do otherwise would be to ruin his orderly register! At his new school he was assessed as 'academically sub-normal', a not unusual categorization of Caribbean children in some English schools. But he was a star on the cricket field and was soon playing in fixtures against sides like Eton, Winchester and Harrow.

His cricketing prowess led to a grammar school offering him a grant to stay on. Despite his poor early education, he earned an O' level in biology and at 17 applied for a job as a junior lab assistant at Queen Elizabeth College, now part of King's College, London. On arrival, Zoology professor, Garth Chapman, asked his name. On being told 'Godfrey Henry Oliver Palmer', Chapman reportedly retorted: 'you can have the job if I can call you Geoff';[3] so Geoff he became in the interest of a job. You may well disagree; but Palmer did not find it politically incorrect. To him, Chapman was finding a reason to provide him with a job for which he was probably not qualified. Chapman proved as significant as 'the man at the door' in helping Palmer carve out his future. The professor sent his new lab assistant to the Polytechnic for one day a week and by the time Palmer was 20, he had acquired three A' levels and seven O' levels. But even with such qualification, the Jamaican was unable to secure a place at a university. Chapman was appalled at this apparent racism. He one day said to Palmer, 'stay outside my door and do not move.' When he emerged, it was to tell Palmer that he would be going to the University of Leicester, an institution that had already turned him down.

After gaining an Upper Second Class degree in Biology at Leicester, Palmer applied for a sponsored MSc. However, one of the interviewers, a Keith Josephs, turned him down and with a complete disregard for Caribbean geography told him to go back to Trinidad and plant bananas. He went on to get his PhD largely because of a female professor, Anna MacLeaod, and others at Heriot-Watt University who he says 'weighed my achievements against my difficulties ...; [they] had the ability to make decisions on my potential, giving me the benefit of the doubt'. The rest is now history, as his achievements are now world-renowned. According to Palmer now:

> everybody always said you've got to work hard, but if you belong to certain sectors of society, hard work without the good Samaritan doesn't work, because you cannot access the system [without them. He warns] the most dangerous thing in society is people who are in a position to make a difference [but] prevent other people from achieving.[4]

So, the importance of being 'the man or woman at the door' for someone else, is evident from this real life story.

Finally, I wish to urge you to become activists in the Jamaican society and adopt as your motto, as Bob Marley and others have done, 'I Want to Disturb My Neighbour.' This is not a licence for you to crank up the decibel level of your sound system. There are still penalties for this, let me hasten to remind you. A report in the *Daily Gleaner* of Friday, April 3, 2002 indicated that Worrell King, a Westmoreland entertainment promoter was fined a total of $65,000 for breaching the Noise Abatement Act; and Clive Pringle, a promoter from Negril, was fined $15,000 under the same Act for the same offence of playing music too loudly, that is playing music so that it can be heard beyond the prescribed 100-metre limit.[5]

'I Want to Disturb My Neighbour' can simply be a metaphor for adopting an activist stance in an age of individualism. This age of individualism threatens to destabilize the spirit of philanthropy and neigbourliness that has traditionally been a part of the Jamaican social landscape. So go out and 'disturb your neighbour'. You already have some preparation for an activist orientation through your Social Outreach Programme. Indeed, I congratulate this college for not only training students in the straight academic disciplines, but for encouraging co-curricular activities and fostering a cooperative spirit of goodwill on the campus and within the community. Armed with this college preparation, go out as goodwill ambassadors and start community literacy classes, and shake people out of their ignorance, the rationale being that illiteracy is one of the problems that creates ignorance about people's rights as citizens. In 1999, according to preliminary figures, Jamaica had a literacy rate of 79.9 per cent; with just over half of that percentage being functionally literate.[6] We need to do better, especially within a context where education represents the route to material advancement for those without family financial legacies. Use education to destabilize the existing social order and claim your right to material betterment in this postcolonial society.

Join Jamaicans for Justice and help to shake this island out of its complacency and acceptance of injustices. Write letters to the editors of the major newspapers and call in to the talk shows to register your annoyance and disgust with human rights abuses. And do not be deterred when you are cut off because your views do not accord with those of the host. Read and educate yourself on matters that many of the Cable TV stations that you watch will not address, issues such as the true reasons for the Israeli/

Palestinian conflicts and the present state of Cuba–US relations. Become familiar with the debates over reparation for slavery and the economic impact of globalization on weaker trading partners. You will not be popular for supporting certain causes, for example, the reparation movement. Some people take the position that chattel slavery, genocide against indigenous Caribbeans and the transatlantic trade in Africans are of too remote a historical nature to attract reparation; that is, making amends for or repairing the damage done by the trade and enslavement. Do not be deterred by negative public opinion. Align yourself with a cause and remember the motto 'I Want to Disturb My Neighbour'.

18

AFTER THE EXHIBITION IS GONE:

Public Memory in an Age of Historical Amnesia

*Delivered at the Official Opening of the Exhibition, 'Lest We Forget',
Institute of Jamaica Auditorium, April 14, 2005*

I must admit that when I first saw the 'Lest We Forget' part of the title
of the exhibition, my first thought was: how could anyone possibly
forget such a fundamental episode in Caribbean and world history? I,
for one, to borrow the title of an anthology I saw a few years back, 'am a
long remembered woman'. But then, just as swiftly, I recalled a criticism
in a February 2004 issue of the *Daily Gleaner* that: 'given the paucity of
resources to finance the university and the urgent need to generate wealth
in and across Caribbean societies, the [University of the West Indies] UWI
cannot continue to afford expenditure on subject matters such as slavery'
— a sure route to forgetting the past.[1] I recalled that a Stone Poll result in
the *Sunday Observer* of July 21, 2002 had revealed that 53 per cent of
Jamaica's adults believed that the country would have been better off if it
had remained a colony of Britain. I recalled too that there has been
opposition in some quarters to my public appeal that rather than continue
to build an endless number of busts and statues to individual heroes and
heroines, Jamaica should build parish war memorials to honour those who
fought to liberate us from slavery. War memorials not only with the names
of the well-known heroes and heroines, like Nanny, Tacky, Sharpe, Dove,
Gardner and Taylor, but also with the names of lesser known leaders like
Damon of the 1760 Westmoreland revolt, Blackwall of the 1765 St. Mary
revolt; James Sterling and the other ringleaders of the 1823 St. Mary plot;
Bina, Becky, Joseph Brown, William Barnett, George Brissett, Elizabeth
Ball of the 1831–32 war; Fidelle [alias Dundo] and Goodluck, who were
tried for

forming a rebellious conspiracy of which being found guilty after a long trial, and on the clearest evidence, they were sentenced to be hanged by the neck on the Parade of Kingston, their heads severed from their bodies and placed on poles — one on the Slipe Pen Road, the other on that [road] adjoining the City, leading to Windward.[2]

I recalled too that the mark the spot campaign — that project of iconographic decolonization — that should have been completed in order that we would stamp a postcolonial ideology on the landscape, still has a far way to go. As a result, we still do not know the names of the enslaved people who worked on the various plantations, pens and estates; the site of every rebellion of enslaved people; every slave village; every slave burial site on the plantations, every provision ground that provided the possibility of economic autonomy; every free village — or as many of them that can be identified.

And so I began to doubt the boldness of my initial reaction and to support the title: LEST WE FORGET: THE TRIUMPH OVER SLAVERY, conscious of the fact that, while the title is a reminder that we did overcome, it does not hide the brutalizing experience suffered by our ancestors. We get a good dose of data to enable us to answer the question: over what did we triumph and how did we mange to triumph? These data might cause some of us pain as we read the narratives on the storyboards and view the photographs. However, we should take comfort in the fact that all the suffering was not in vain. Our ancestors stood up and fought, following the self-liberation tradition of the indigenous people. They ensured that instability, largely as a result of slave resistance, made the Atlantic World an unstable place for the colonizers. The reason that deep division, inequality and instability characterized the 'Atlantic World' was that not all of the people who inhabited this 'world' were equally committed to its ideals. The exploited regions in this world of partners that were not really partners as Walter Rodney has long reminded us, subverted the ideals of the Atlantic World.

I thought then that I would use the title: 'After the Exhibition is Gone:

Public Memory in an Age of Historical Amnesia', for if we are never to forget either the pains or triumphs over slavery, we will have to put post-exhibition plans in place. This general title will be explored under the following headings:

- How will we remember slavery after the exhibition is closed and gone?
- Who will ensure that we never forget the pains and triumphs over slavery?
- Who will be the keepers of the historical memory and make it part of public memory? Who will support the keepers of our history? For it takes cash to remember!

How Will We Remember Slavery After the Exhibition is Gone?

There are several avenues that we can pursue, especially through our educational institutions, libraries, museums and institutes, media and publishing houses and appropriate ministries. Some of these include the need to,

- intensify the project of mapping and remapping the postcolonial landscape with a mark-the-spot project that will identify the slave route and the sites of slavery and emancipation. *Why? Lest we forget!*
- establish heritage markers in areas visited by tourists. Let us stop hiding the so-called darker side of our history from visitors; as if we do not wish to spoil their appetites. *Why? Lest we forget!*
- intensify public education through lectures and documentaries. A monthly lecture on slavery in Emancipation Park and the various parish town halls every month from August 2005 right up to August 2007 would be a good idea. Even better if such lectures are taped by TV and radio stations and aired frequently so that our people can be educated outside of the walls of academia. *Why? Lest we forget!*

- mount a permanent exhibition on slavery in the Institute of Jamaica and in various museums around the island. In this regard, I would urge us to support the local UNESCO committee that is planning a local version of the 'Lest We Forget' exhibition — a Jamaicanized exhibition, hopefully to be opened in 2007, the year that will mark the 200th anniversary of the abolition of the trade in Africans. *Why? Lest we forget!*

- agitate for the war memorials that will form permanent markers on our landscape. Have a public ritual of wreathlaying and remembrance each first of August — *Why? Lest we forget!*

- develop Heritage Tourism, even if it is to be labelled 'dark tourism'. *Why? Lest we forget!*

- establish a cross campus, inter-disciplinary Centre for Slavery Research at the UWI by 2007 similar to the Wilberforce Institute for the study of Slavery and Emancipation (WISE) at Hull and the International Centre for the History of Slavery (ICHOS) at Nottingham. *Why? Lest we forget!*

- build monuments in your communities where you can identify historical events. On the Mona campus we have our own Heritage and Museums Committees, both with plans to declare the entire Mona campus a heritage site; establish heritage markers; house our artifacts; tell our story; and build monuments to those enslaved and indentured ancestors who trod the earth there ahead of us. *Why? Lest we forget!*

- publish books on slavery and launch one book on slavery each month in 2007. *Why? Lest we forget!*

- develop appropriate entrepreneurship so that come 2007, emancipation memorabilia will be on sale at world cup cricket venues. *Why? Lest we forget!*

Who Will Ensure that We Never Forget?

There are several people and entities that must be charged with this responsibility:

- Authors, poets, historians and history teachers; the museums division; our folklorists; our librarians, artists and artistes, musicians, DJs, archaeologists, the state through the Ministry of Education, the Jamaica National Heritage Trust (JNHT); the Parish Councils; our publishers;
- Hotels and owners of private homes on properties that were former plantations; community workers and activists and others.

If the Centre for Slavery Research is to become a reality however, the people we need most at this time are our historians in alliance with our publishing houses. Pioneers and present historians alike embrace the philosophy that history prepares us for activism; that history is a way of ordering knowledge, which could become an active part of the consciousness of the uncertified (not the uneducated) mass of ordinary people and could be used by all as an instrument of social change.[3] In the tradition of Walter Rodney, they have embraced the role of the public intellectual. As Rodney stressed so often, the Caribbean was the site of the formation of European ideas of modernity and their construction of notions of hegemony and all of us who live in Caribbean space have been deeply offended by the actualization of such notions of hegemony and feel the need to preach against it constantly. We have shunned the path of the classic intellectual, associated traditionally with 'ivory tower' and 'snobbishness',[4] despite the persistence of this meaning of the intellectual in the popular perception. We share the views articulated so well by Edward Said that:

> the intellectual is an individual in society that confronts orthodoxy and dogma; who cannot be reduced simply to being a faceless professional, a competent member of a class going about his/her business [but] an individual endowed with a faculty for representing, embodying, articulating a message, a view, an attitude, philosophy or opinion to, as well as for, a public.

I know only too well, sometimes the public intellectual must be prepared to be an exile and marginal.[5]

Who Will Support the Keepers of Our History?

It takes cash to engage in a project of mental and iconographic decolonization and so I appeal to governments and, private and financial institutions to provide the financial backing to support slavery research. Fund those who are preparing Exhibitions for 2007 and beyond; pour financial resources into the history departments of all schools and tertiary institutions, adopt a History department in a school or any other educational institution.

   –   Protect heritage sites in your village, community or town centre. Tell those who are guilty to stop using Sam Sharpe Square as a rubbish heap. Do not pee on Sam Sharpe and the brothers dem! Chase the goats away from the Tacky monument. Prevent arson if you can so that our historic buildings will be left standing for a long time and cut the bush away from our monuments.

In closing, let me pose the question: So what if we forget? What would be the consequence of such historical amnesia? Put simply, this would to quote Professor Rex Nettleford, condemn us to driving without a rearview mirror. Those who do not learn from history are bound to repeat it. I leave this thought with you just as I do with my students before they prepare for final exams.

19

THE CASE FOR REPARATION: Historical Basis

National Reparation Symposium, University of the West Indies, Mona, February 22, 2003

The subject of reparation for slavery as well as for genocide against indigenous peoples has been elevated to a more prominent position in the public discourse since the Durban Conference of 2001. During that conference, despite the fact that disagreement over the issues of apology for participation in the slave trade, compensation and reparation for slavery, the slave trade, and genocide against indigenous peoples had threatened to derail the proceedings, the final declaration dropped the call for reparation and the call for apologies (no doubt because of the litigious implications). While the European and African delegations agreed to acknowledge slavery as a crime against humanity as a way of getting some result from the conference, it is a well-known fact that there is nothing to enjoin countries to do much more. In the case of our own Jamaican media, exposure continued in the aftermath of the panel discussion on this subject held in November 2001, the submission of a petition to Queen Elizabeth II by some Rastafarian leaders in February 2002, and the Queen's so-called response to that petition in January 2003. In between, many of us watched in disbelief as White people, some from our very own region, were expelled from the African and African-descendants World Conference Against Racism held in Barbados in October 2002 — which had on its agenda the issue of reparation. Since then, the topics of governance, repatriation and reparation have continued to form a significant part of national debate, with opinions ranging from either side of the ideological fence.

My task is not to settle any of these debates, but to outline what I understand to be the basis for the support for reparation by some individuals and groups in the Caribbean. My presentation will, of necessity, reflect a historical perspective; for as several Rastafari leaders noted in their recent petition to the Queen: 'to understand the necessity and moral issues for repatriation and reparation, one must understand how and why Africans were brought to the West *en masse*.' And, I might add, what contributions they made to the development of the West.

The first basis is that the Caribbean was a primordial site of slavery. The region accounted for 42 per cent, of the estimated 15–20 million Africans forcefully removed from Africa from the fifteenth to the nineteenth century. The British-colonized Caribbean accounted for between two and four of the estimated 15–20 million. Colonizing activities imposed structural discontinuities upon the Caribbean. The colonizers practically wiped out the indigenous Caribbeans and reorganized Caribbean economy to discourage a domestic economic sector in favour of the export production of agricultural staples. The labour of enslaved Africans, to a greater extent than the labour of indigenous peoples and White indentured servants, contributed to the export production of commodities, especially sugar. Quantitative data produced by Barry W. Higman demonstrate that the majority of those enslaved worked on the sugar estates. For example, around 1820, 77 per cent of the enslaved in Antigua, 77 per cent in Barbados, 52 per cent in Jamaica, 87 per cent in St. Kitts and 90 per cent in Nevis worked on the sugar estates.[1] In the specific case of Jamaica, once the English had turned the island's economy into one dominated by the production of sugar for export, they increased their importation of enslaved Africans, placing a large percentage (49.5 per cent in 1832), of them on the sugar plantations. Higman tells us that by 1832, sugar, rum and molasses earned about close to three million pounds and accounted for 76 per cent of the total receipts of 960 properties he sampled.[2] The only other significant commodity was coffee which accounted for six per cent, and an estimated 80 per cent of the output on sugar estates was exported; 70 per cent on coffee. Even accounting for the obvious bias in the Accounts Produce, it is clear that while there was a domestic economy, far fewer resources were put into its development. After all, the development of the local economy was not compatible with the economic imperatives of colonialism. By 1700, Jamaica had received three times as many Africans as the Leeward Islands, yet was exporting less than two-thirds of the produce of these islands.

A second basis is that slavery in Jamaica took its toll on the enslaved population. The brutality of the slave system combined with other factors led to a demographic disaster. The USA imported less than one million enslaved Africans over the entire period of the trade; yet just before abolition, had four million enslaved people.[3] The British-colonized Caribbean imported just over two million, with Jamaica accounting for about one million. So bad was population decline in the Caribbean that those anti-slavery activists in England who opposed slavery on moral grounds believed that the failure of the enslaved population to maintain itself by natural means put the seal of confirmation on all other charges against the system. Thomas Fowell Buxton, influenced by Malthusian population theory, believed that it was only misery that prevented what is a law of nature, that is, the increase of populations, to occur; that only the luxurious rich tended to be barren. The enslaved population in Jamaica was 345,252 in 1817, by which time the trade was abolished, and 309,167 in 1834. Therefore conquest, slavery and colonialism had a negative demographic impact on the Caribbean.

A third rationale for support for reparation in the region is that the trade in captives, and slavery were crimes against humanity (as defined by the Charter of the Nuremberg Tribunal) as recognized a century earlier by anti-slavery activists. William Pitt's anti-slavery appeal in the English parliament referred to slavery as the 'greatest practical evil that has ever been inflicted on the human race'; 'the severest and most extensive calamity recorded in the history of the world'.[4] A case can be made for reparation according to the dictates of international law. According to Lord Gifford, 'international law recognises that those who commit crimes against humanity must make reparation'; that 'there is no legal barrier to prevent those who still suffer the consequencies of such crimes from claiming reparations even though the crimes were committed against their ancestors'; and that 'there can be no statute of limitation on such moral injustice.'[5]

Additionally, those who benefited most from slavery have not adequately compensated the descendants of enslaved peoples in the Caribbean for past wrongs and they should make amends — if only out of a sense of moral obligation. England, for example, must bear a large portion of the responsibility for the enslavement of Africans in the Americas. The British and Portuguese together accounted for seven out of every ten transatlantic slaving voyages and transported nearly 75 per cent of all captives taken from Africa. Joseph Inikori has argued that the phenomenal expansion of world trade between 1451 and 1870 depended largely on the employment of enslaved Africans in the exploitation of American resources. The development and growth of West European and North American economies during this period were greatly influenced by the expanded world trade.[6] Even Britain's major eighteenth-century economic spokesmen, Joshua Gee and Malachy Postlethwayt, both placed the importance of enslaved Africans in the Americas at the core of their visions of the requirements for national expansion. They believed that British participation in the slave trade and in the maintenance of plantations in the Caribbean was key to their industrial development.[7] Eric Williams and others have since refined and reinforced the argument.[8] In the same vein, Rastafarian leaders recently reminded the Queen of England that 'It is an undisputed fact that the toils, blood and sweat of the African captives throughout the Caribbean and the Americas built the sound economic bases that now allow the West to live in leisure and wealth.'[9]

Another basis for the support for reparation is the view that full freedom in August 1838 was not accompanied by adequate state aid to help the newly freed to cope with the new demands of a free society or to adjust to the disabling structure of post-abolition society. The newly emancipated Blacks did not get a new start, unlike their enslavers who were compensated to the tune of 20 million pounds sterling to enable some of them to recover from the loss of 'property'. Also, the consequences of slavery and colonialism are still evident in the postcolonial world — racism, the tyranny of skin colour or the pigmentocracy.

I am well aware that the anti-reparation and anti-compensation voices locally and globally are loud and many. You might be familiar with David Horowitz's 'Ten Reasons Why Reparations is a Bad Idea for Blacks — and Racist Too'. Among them are that, 'the historical precedents used to justify the reparations claim do not apply, and the claim itself is based on race not injury'; 'the reparations claim is based on the unfounded claim that all African-American descendants of slaves suffer from the economic consequencies of slavery and discrimination.'[10] In an unscientific internet poll created by CNN on September 7, 2001, just about the time of the World Conference Against Racism in Durban, 78 per cent voted 'NO' and 22 per cent 'YES' to the question: 'Should European countries pay compensation for the slave trade?'[11]

Some people take the position that chattel slavery, genocide against indigenous Caribbeans and the transatlantic trade in Africans are of too remote a historical nature to attract reparation. Thus, there can be no present day liability for a historical situation. Indeed, in the now infamous Queen's Reply of January 2003 (which some people have said reminds them of the so-called Queen's Advice of 1865 — a response to the petition signed by 108 people of St. Ann in April 1865 just before the outbreak of the Morant Bay Rebellion)[12] she reportedly stated: 'Governments today cannot take responsibility for what happened over 150 years ago. We regret and condemn the inequities of the . . . slave trade, but those shameful activities belong to the past.'[13]

The anti-reparation faction dismisses the fact that African-descended people are not the only ones in the world who are seeking, or who have sought, reparation. In fact, as Professor Chinweizu noted in his plenary address at the First Pan-African Conference on Reparation held in Nigeria in 1993, by only now pressing a claim for reparation, Africans and African-descended peoples are latecomers to a varied company of peoples in the Americas, in Asia, and in Europe. He reminded us that perhaps the most famous case of reparation was that paid by Germany to the Jews. These were paid by West Germany to Israel for crimes against Jews in territories controlled by Hitler's Germany, and to individuals to indemnify them for persecution. In the initial phase, these included US\$2 billion to make amends to victims of Nazi persecution; US\$952 million in personal indemnities; US\$35.70 per month per inmate of concentration camps; pensions for the survivors of victims; US\$820 million on to Israel to resettle 50,000 Jewish emigrants from lands formerly controlled by Hitler.[14] All that was just the beginning. Other largely undisclosed payments followed; and even in 1992, the World Jewish Congress in New York announced that the newly unified Germany would pay compensation, totaling US\$63 million for 1993, to 50,000 Jews who suffered Nazi persecution but had not been paid reparation because they lived in East Germany.[15] Reparation has also been paid to First Nation People in the USA and Canada; Japanese-Americans, Koreans and Japanese-Canadians. But these settlements have been dismissed as being incomparable to the Caribbean situation. So clear difficulties remain for those who promote the idea of reparation. There are many questions that have been posed:

- Does an apology imply financial liability?
- Was slavery a crime against humanity when it was committed?
- Can there be present day liability for a historical situation?
- Can a financial settlement be put on the experiences of the enslaved? In other words can any sum really be enough?
- How would one begin to calculate a financial cost?
- Is there a statute of limitation on claims for wrongs committed over 300 years ago?
- Is the claim for reparation and compensation valid in international law?
- Are the victims and perpetrators of this crime against humanity clearly identifiable? (Enslavers were a diverse group, including Blacks themselves).
- Do compensation and reparation have to be monetary? [A CNN report stated that Nkosazana Dlamini-Zuma, the South African foreign minister who chaired the Conference, said reparation and apology 'do not mean money, but dignity'].
- Can a settlement be in the form of a commitment to tackle racism and discrimination in contemporary societies?
- Will reparation be in the form of debt relief and other economic and developmental assistance?
- Should Africans who sold others into slavery also be held responsible?

- Should Africa pay compensation to the descendants of Africans in the Caribbean?
- Is this call for reparation, if financial, going to encourage black people to line up waiting for their share?
- Is this call for compensation going to transfer responsibility for injustices in colonial societies that have nothing to do with slavery and its legacies from current political directorates, many the descendants of enslaved people, who have squandered the legacy of the ancestors, continue to maintain the worst legacies of the hated plantation system and to deny the human rights claims of all its citizens?
- Will the financial settlement solve all the problems of globalization?
- Will reparation solve the problem of mental slavery? Will it help our people, some of whom are still trapped within the cycle of shame and guilt?

My own view is that despite the difficulties, those who participated in the slave system in the Americas, especially long after the institution was declared illegal in their own countries (and long reminded of its inhumanity by philosophers), should acknowledge a moral duty to Blacks in the Americas. They must adopt reparation if only as an act of reconciliation. It must be evident to such countries that slavery's legacy is felt in the social conflict and tension attributable to racism that is affecting their own countries, that military might will be inadequate to control the tensions. Nevertheless the dialogue will continue for some time.

A version of this speech was also presented at the History Department's Public Panel Discussion on Reparation, November 2001.

20

CHALLENGING MASCULINE MYTHS: Gender, History Education and Development in Jamaica

The Planning Institute of Jamaica's Dialogue for Development Lecture, Jamaica Pegasus Hotel, Tuesday, November 19, 2002[1]

I do not suppose that when the Planning Institute of Jamaica (PIOJ) selected the theme of education for its development series it could have known that education would have been the flavour of 2002. As it turns out, education was made a prominent part of public discussions and campaign speeches in Jamaica this year, particularly in the months leading up to the general elections, giving rise to much public cynicism as well as to newspaper articles and cartoons suggesting that education was being used as a political football.

Nevertheless, the attention was no doubt welcomed by all the stakeholders in educational development in the island, not least, the students and parents who anxiously await the fulfillment of campaign promises. As one politician observed, and we all endorse the view, 'education is a key component of development, a needed investment in nation-building, and a means of empowering a nation's people by developing their minds.'[2]

This is not a novel perspective, of course. Ever since 'international development' became an area of intellectual enquiry in the post World War II period there has been an ongoing global debate about the role of education in development. The inclusion of education in discussions of development is quite in keeping with the United Nations Development Programme's (UNDP) definition of human development, now viewed as a much broader concept than macroeconomic growth.

In addition, and thanks to major United Nations (UN) initiatives, especially between 1990 and 1995, and despite the competing development paradigms, such development discourses are no longer gender neutral. This is not surprising. Discourses surrounding gender are familiar phenomena of the age of postmodernity. It is now quite widely accepted that gender as a category of analysis must be incorporated into the development paradigm and that development planning must take gender issues into account to maximize the impact of measures and policies.

Within Jamaica, as is indicated by public discussions, it is the education of males that is of concern to policy makers, educators and those interested in gender, education and development. Indeed, the educational standard reached by males was the subject of discussion even in the age of modernity. In their histories of Jamaica, Charles Leslie (in 1740) and Edward Long (in 1774) remarked on the lack of education, particularly among men in eighteenth-century Jamaica, and the impact that the presence of large numbers of ignorant men had on women. Leslie noted that this lack of education was an impediment to the development of colonial society and that the women found the planters to whom they were married 'barbarous, ignorant and dictatorial'.[3] Long remarked that the majority of men in Jamaica remained semi-literate and the common butt of every conversation.[4]

The conversation has continued. Even the most cursory review of the literature on gender and education will reveal that, first of all, there is a current preoccupation with what several researchers and observers have labelled an apathy on the part of males towards formal education. This is manifested in the lower numbers, compared to females, participating in the educational process at both secondary and tertiary levels. Successive Caribbean Examinations Council (CXC) and General Certificate in Education (GCE) A' Level results have been subjected to microscopic, gender-specific analysis; and the lament heard in several fora and media is that girls continue to outperform boys, even in subjects traditionally labelled as 'male subjects'. Here I introduce the first of my 'masculine myths', which is that males are better at subjects that require 'cognitive skills'. In 1997, results for the CXC examinations in Jamaica showed that the only subjects in which the performance of boys was much better than that of girls were mathematics and integrated science, with girls outperforming boys in the science subject of physics.[5] Admittedly, the last three years have shown a reversal of that position with more boys than girls registering for CXC physics and with results in 1999, 2000 and 2001 showing that boys outperformed girls in that subject. Nevertheless, the numbers of girls sitting and passing physics has increased.

The results for the years 1999, 2000 and 2001 also show that girls are outperforming boys in Information Technology (IT), previously considered by some as a 'male subject'. The Common Entrance Examination and Grade Six Achievement Test (G-SAT) results have not escaped analytical attention in the debates over gender and examination results.[6] In terms of the G-SAT, the 2002 results reflect better female performance in all five subjects; and this has been a continuation of the trend set at the inception of the G-SAT.

The concern with the gender gap in education and with the performance of males is not confined to the primary and secondary levels. The 1999 edition of *You We* put out by the Board for Undergraduate Studies at the University of the West Indies (UWI) focused on the gender gap in education at the Mona campus, an institution that is now really and truly 'La Universidad'. The inventors of the Spanish language had great foresight! If the word 'Mona' ever meant 'Isle of Man' as some sources hold, that meaning is clearly inappropriate now — at least when applied to the composition of the student population.[7] Reverting to the previous name, 'Yeaman', would not help. Recent figures indicate that females make up over 70 per cent of the student population at the UWI (and 75 per cent of the 2002 graduating class).

The under-performance of many males in the formal educational system however, as demonstrated by examination results and enrollment figures at educational institutions (which has given rise to the 'male underachievement thesis'), the high illiteracy rate and marginal economic and political position of many working-class Black men do not seem to have affected males' self-confidence. Neither does it affect the ways in which, regardless of class, educational level, ethnicity and age group, they display the tendencies of hegemonic masculinity. In fact, there seems to be a clear disjuncture between the general perception of male marginalization and underachievement and the persistence of male hegemonic masculinity and power in Jamaican society. This has led scholars like Mark Figueroa to argue, that the phenomenon of male underachievement in education is not symbolic of male marginalization but is an ironic outcome of historic male privileging. His premise is that the male gender has occupied a wider social space, controlled more resources, maintained a higher social position and exercised greater power, a view shared by feminists like Barbara Bailey.[8] The report on the status of Caribbean women prepared by the CARICOM Secretariat for the 4th World Conference on Women as well as the data generated for Jamaica also indicate that, 'strong and persistent income disparities exist between males and females in spite of the fact that the female population is being better educated.'[9]

There are many factors that contribute to hegemonic masculinity, a term that refers to the culturally dominant form of masculinity that is constructed in relation to femininity as well as various subordinated masculinities. Hegemonic masculinity emerges as the configuration of gender practice that legitimizes patriarchy and guarantees a dominant position for men alongside the subordination of women.[10] Hegemonic masculinity, of course, borrows from Antonio Gramsci's use of hegemony in his analysis of class relations and has come to mean a cultural dynamic by which a group claims and sustains a leading position in social relationships.[11] Although it is now generally accepted that there are different and often conflicting images of men and masculinity, certain masculinities are clearly favoured. For example, within Jamaican popular culture and, within the local media in particular, one sees traditional 'macho' images of men. In Jamaica, a general standard seems to exist for the 'typical' male, a standard constructed by both males and females. In other words, there seems to be a peculiar ideal for Jamaican hegemonic masculinity: leadership, political power, dominance in gender relations, provider, head of family, lack of fear, self-confidence, physical strength, aggressiveness, et cetera. It is these social roles and ideals that boys are taught to adopt.

Obviously, the mass media must share a large part of the responsibility for how young men see themselves; how they construct their self-identity and masculinity. But the home, peer pressure and school curricula also play a part in sending out clues about the preferred masculinity that young males should adopt. My concern is with the curriculum, specifically the ways in which history education contributes to the perpetuation of hegemonic masculinity and the implications of such hegemonic masculinity for development in the age of postmodernity. My rationale is that if education is going to provide the tools for development; and if boys are to be educated and socialized so that they can make useful contributions to the development of Jamaica, then they need to be anchored to a more accurate history that will have a positive impact on the kinds of gender policies they adopt when they become policy makers — as many eventually do in Jamaican society.

So, while increasing budgetary allocation to the education sector — paying teachers a respectable wage and increasing access, especially the access of boys and males in general — remain pressing concerns, the content of the education taught and received must return to a position of importance in our debates on educational issues. I do not mean to trivialize the issue of gender-specific access, for we still have a way to go based on the recent human development index (HDI) of the UNDP Report which ranked Jamaica 86 out of 173 countries and placed it in the 'medium development' category.[12] For a developing country like Jamaica, the issue cannot only be related to that of the provision of hardware and software but also of inputs. More specifically, the provision of quality inputs in terms of the books used must be related to the overall objective of education as articulated by the government, which is 'to improve quality, equity, relevance and access.'[13] Alongside with its socializing function, postcolonial education has a major responsibility for identity formation; and this identity should incorporate gender identity.

The question then is: What kind of gender identity does history education provide? My contention is that several of the books used to teach history to Caribbean children reinforce hegemonic masculinity and therefore the images about masculinity already perpetuated by the larger society, the home and the media. The school curriculum, like the media and other external forces, gives boys a role-identity, an imaginative view of themselves; the basis on which they continue to aspire to hegemonic models of masculinity. As Kay Deaux and Brenda Major observe, external cues can invoke gender identity, moving it into the working self-concept.[14]

The relationship between history and hegemonic masculinity will be explored by interrogating the content of history education and exposing the gender inequalities in the historiography itself as well as in the texts used to teach the subject. The simple point I wish to make in the process is that what boys learn in history class matters and has implications beyond the examination results they achieve.

The ability of the classroom environment in the specific area of curriculum followed, to influence students, has been well-established by leading scholars. For example Elsa Leo-Rhynie, while acknowledging the role played by popular music and the advertising media in subtly conditioning girls and boys in the roles to which they are expected to aspire, has also observed that,

> Another area which exerts substantial influence, but which is often overlooked, is the actual content of the curriculum. This frequently portrays gender stereotypes and so insidiously conveys to boys and girls in the educational system the roles to which they ought to aspire.[15]

Joyce Cole has also observed that education is an important institution in the formation of social attitudes and values. Formal schooling not only socializes children into the prevailing values and norms of society, but also has a major responsibility for identity formation and the preparation of individuals for their future adult roles.[16] Thus while the forces of production are reproduced through the capitalist economic system, ideological state apparatuses reproduce the social relations of production.[17] Similarly Odette Parry shows that the classroom functions as an arena for the construction or maintenance of gender identities and notions of masculinity/femininity.[18]

In the specific case of history education, despite great strides since the 1970s, the texts do not all provide boys with the kind of information they need to overturn their views of women as the subordinated sex; and gender stereotypes abound. Indeed, since the end of slavery, male attitudes towards females have cemented. Traits related to instrumentality, dominance and, assertiveness and aggressiveness, 'macho-ness', for example are believed to be more characteristic of men than women; while such traits as warmth, expressiveness, and concern for others are thought more characteristic of women. As Mark Figueroa has argued, 'The historic privileging of the male gender has constructed maleness as dominant, appropriate to the public sphere, technologically capable, strong and hard. Femaleness has been constructed as submissive, appropriate to the private sphere, sensitive, caring and in need of protection.'[19] Many still believe that the woman's place is in the house (and they do not mean the House of Representatives); that women are more suited to inside work and that females have certain inherently physical and psychological characteristics which predispose them to non-marketable roles such as childrearing and home maintenance. Masculinity is presented as essentialist; that is, intrinsically different natures are attributed to men and women. These attitudes find legitimacy in the larger society and are reinforced through education. When adult men internalize these ideas and values, they pass them on to their children who then use them to structure their worlds of home, school and community, and later on life and work.

CXC, Gender and the History Syllabi

An examination of the content of history education and the ways in which it contributes to young males' views about masculinity shows that far from learning that they were marginalized, even under slavery, boys learn from history that power was invested in men at all levels of society historically and that women were assigned a less important role in development.

First, judging by sections of the syllabi, the awareness that education needs to address gender issues has been shown by the CXC at the Caribbean Secondary Education Certificate (C-SEC) and Caribbean Advanced Proficiency Examination (CAPE) levels. While their larger objectives are astonishingly gender-free, some of the objectives under specific themes are gender-specific, signalling to students and teachers that they must not complete the syllabus without having a sense of the differential historical experiences of males and females.

However, up to now, the Caribbean Examinations Council does not commission textbooks nor do they adhere to the interventionist model of development, preferring instead to leave the field open to market forces. Unfortunately, many of the books used to teach the syllabus do not support CXC's gender-specific aims and do not go far enough to challenge the many masculine myths about masculinity that shape contemporary gender relations. As these books are mostly male-authored (as even a cursory look at the booklists of the C-SEC and CAPE will show), male historians have to, rightly or wrongly, bear the brunt of the accusation that they are the ones who perpetuate 'masculine myths about masculinity'. We know of course, that women authors — though comparatively few — are also transgressors.

More girls than boys take Caribbean history, but an increasing number of boys are also taking history at the secondary school level; so that more and more of them are being exposed to the gaps in gender education that are, unfortunately, enshrined in some of these texts.[20]

The Content of the Textbooks

The sample selected was drawn primarily from the books on the CXC (specifically the C-SEC) bibliography that cover the themes of conquest, colonization, slavery, emancipation and modern Caribbean–Jamaican society. The CAPE texts are not discussed as even fewer boys proceed to the study of advanced level history. The sample is therefore confined to where the history is having the most impact, the C-SEC level.

There are just over 40 relevant books under these headings and themes that cover these issues for Jamaica. The ones that students seem to use widely (and some of these are not on the published bibliography) are:

1. Bridget Brereton. *Social Life in the Caribbean*. London: Heinemann, 1985.
2. Patrick Bryan. *The Haitian Revolution*. Kingston: Heinemann, 1984.
3. W. Claypole and J. Robottom. *Caribbean Story*, Book 1. 3rd edition. London: Longman Caribbean, 2002.

4. W. Claypole and J. Robottom. *Caribbean Story*. Book 2. 3rd edition. London: Longman Caribbean, 2002.

5. Isaac Dookhan. *A Pre-Emancipation History of the West Indies*. London: Collins, 1971.

6. Isaac Dookhan. *A Post-Emancipation History of the West Indies*. London: Collins, 1975.

7. Douglas Hall. *The Caribbean Experience*. Kingston: Heinemann, 1982.

8. Shirley Gordon. *Caribbean Generations: A CXC History Source Book*. Jamaica: Longman Caribbean, 1983.

9. Philip Sherlock and Hazel Bennett. *The Story of the Jamaican People*. Kingston: Ian Randle Publishers, 1998.

Of the books listed above, the two volumes by Claypole and Robottom, now in their 3rd revision, are the most popular among students and the most widely used in the schools. The simplicity of Dookhan's volumes makes his books student favourites; but all are deficient in their representations of gender issues. Yet, all of the books were published after the 1970s. I am pointing this out because it was in the 1970s that, influenced by the feminist movement, issues concerning gender began to be highlighted in historical research globally, with pioneering works done by Lucille Mathurin Mair, Kamau Brathwaite and Barry Higman serving to transform and 'engender' the discipline of [Caribbean] history. The lack of adequate gender-differentiated data in the history texts written for schools after the 1970s was thus not a function of lack of material or of a consciousness in the academy about the need for gender analysis. Those books that were revised after 1999 should also have had access to *Women in Caribbean History*, a volume put out by the Department of History's Social History Project in 1999. It is not quite clear to me that recent texts have made adequate use of that book or that students use it widely, especially as the C-SEC history syllabus no longer carries a specific theme on women. Indeed, hardly any of the popular texts articulate any specific gender objectives in their preface or introduction; and none set out to explore gender relations.

What do boys learn about females and males and about masculinity from these texts? I elaborate on the treatment of a few of the themes in the major books.

Colonization, Indigenous Societies and Political Power

In general, in all the texts, conquest and colonization are represented as male endeavours, characterized by violence, aggressive and deceitful male behaviour and intra-European rivalry. The 'macho' image of men predominates, with indigenous Kalinago men defined by their tendency to capture and carry off Taino women, caveman-style. Indigenous women functioned in the private sphere as homemakers and as agricultural labourers providing drudge labour. Only Shirley Gordon's text implies that indigenous women were more than marginal to indigenous society.

Most of the books suggest that 'politics' was a male preserve as political activities were narrowly defined and interpreted. That women were a fundamental part of the political struggles, from conquest to decolonization, remains undeveloped in all the texts.

While the African background to the Caribbean experience receives very good treatment from Claypole and Robottom, and from Sherlock and Bennett, the accounts of African society serve to empower boys rather than girls; for the impression they give is that Africa was a place where women hardly played any significant roles.

Labour, Slavery and the Plantation System

Most of the texts hardly differentiate indentured labourers by gender (except for the Irish women forcefully rounded up at Oliver Cromwell's instructions and deported to Jamaica in 1656). Indeed, students are left to assume from Claypole and Robottom that the indentured 'bondservants' were male. This has implications for the foundation of a perception that work was a male domain from the beginnings of large-scale agriculture.

Isaac Dookhan's *Pre-Emancipation History* is completely gender-blind in the discussion of the plantation system, the *raison d'être* of slavery in the Caribbean. Of course, as in most accounts of Caribbean economy, and as is shown in Claypole and Robottom, the staple is masculinized, being described, as is the case in most other books, as 'King Sugar'. The students are not introduced sufficiently to women's role in agriculture and, as in Claypole and Robottom, the gender division of labour is marginalized. That men were not more physically able to do manual labour and that at the height of slavery and the plantation system, enslaved women formed the majority of workers in the field as there was an absence of gender division of labour in field tasks are facts that remain buried in most of the texts. Gordon does concede that women were the burden bearers in the society, however. Overall, in the absence of gender-differentiated data and based on their socialization, students would feel that enslaved domestics were female and agricultural labourers male.

The landholding elite and the propertied 'planter-class' are also presented as male. Slavery is said to have undermined men's role as fathers, husbands, heads of households, protectors and providers. In Claypole and Robottom we read that, 'On islands where slaves grew their own food, the man might still have a place as the provider of food but on most plantations even this position was taken away from him.'[21] That women also had provision grounds and provided for their family needs is not mentioned, thus reinforcing this male-as-provider characteristic so associated with masculinity.

Slavery, Resistance and Heroes

Heroes feature prominently in Caribbean history because resistance and revolt are such central characteristics of our historical experience and because the ability of Caribbean people to shape their destiny through their agency is a topic highlighted in the syllabus. The majority of the texts present the heroes as males who remain idolized, even if some of them like Touissant, Christophe and Dessalines are not identified with policies that empower women. As in the colonization discourses where heroes are all male, in the treatment of slavery, resistance and Maroon society, we seem equally trapped in, and influenced by, a hegemonic gender-power relation of patriarchy that needs to be destabilized.

Slavery, Family and Fatherhood

The popular perception in the Caribbean about males and slavery is that men had no opportunity to develop fatherly attributes or paternal feelings under slavery as slavery defeated Black people's attempts to reconstruct or construct family. The views that Black men were 'naturally promiscuous', were unable to be good lovers and husbands and that they were studs also persist. That White men in colonial societies were more promiscuous than Black men remains undeveloped. Evidence of Black men who were good husbands and fathers; and evidence of the existence of stable black families with women playing a central role are missing from most of the texts.[22] One of the most brutal White rapists in Jamaican slave society of the eighteenth century, Thomas Thistlewood, escapes detailed srutiny in the texts.

Access to Freedom

The view that women, more than men, had the opportunity to achieve gratuitous manumission is predominant in the texts. Ignored is the fact that this female dominance is only seen if enslaved domestics are being discussed alone. The data on manumission as a result of 'heroic acts' during enslaved led revolts reveal that men were more frequently the traitors — not women.

Emancipation, Free Village and Peasantry

The representations of male dominance are carried over into discussions of free society when men of all ethnicities became much more involved in political questions, although White men lost ground to Black men in the realm of political dominance. The books all portray men of all racial or ethnic origin as dominant authority figures in the economy, society and political life of the modern Caribbean. After emancipation, women appear to go back to the private sphere and cement roles in the family. There is ample coverage of issues such as the rise of the peasantry, diversification, labour protests of the 1930s, trade union development, education and decolonization. However, the gender-specific roles of ordinary men and women are hardly treated. Sherlock and Bennett treat the free village and peasant movements as male enterprises, whether the subject is the Black peasant or White (facilitating) missionary.

The treatment of the post-slavery issues as far as gender is concerned is particularly disappointing in the 3rd edition of Book 2 of Claypole and Robottom. I expected much of the revisions especially because of the availability of *Women in Caribbean History* and other data on Caribbean women that would have been unavailable to the previous editions. But revisions in the 3rd edition that appeared seemed more focused on bringing the book up to date with the revised CXC (C-SEC) syllabus in terms of the extension of data beyond 1962. Details on women are added here and there but the revisions do not challenge common perceptions of femininity or masculinity. The book still reflects some of the sexism noted in earlier editions. On the first page of the 3rd edition, terms like 'masters', and 'freemen' are used although the data clearly also apply to women, as in: 'the British government believed the main aim of the new schools should be to train freemen to be obedient to their masters.' The book uses the word 'skilled' to apply to men who were carpenters et cetera, but 'semi-skilled' to apply to women who were seamstresses and cooks. This again supports the kind of hierarchy that is fundamental to masculinity. Sharecroppers under the metayage system are presented as male; plantation owners and benevolent people who facilitated land acquisition are presented as male; and the voices quoted are those of empowered males. The actors in the Morant Bay Rebellion of 1865 are also male. Morant Bay in fact is represented as a violent contest among Black, Coloured and White men. Brereton admits but does not problematize the gender division of labour and the gender discriminatory wages in the 1838–1938 period. We do, however, get a clear sense from her about women's contribution to post-slavery society: as emigrants who sent back remittances (a topic that is masculinized by Claypole and Robottom); as rural and urban workers; as wives, caregivers and mothers; and generally as strong, independent women who were not confined to the private sphere. She is the exception to those who portray the man as the only head of the household in a nuclear setting, though she does admit that the father had great authority in the home among rich and poor. She provides data that reinforce common beliefs about 'barren women' being pitied. Only those who study the theme, 'Social Life'— an optional theme — would read these more empowering images of women in Brereton's text.

The Black challenge to colonialism is a male enterprise as far as Claypole and Robottom are concerned. The students are introduced to names like Edward Blyden, J.J. Thomas and Sylvester Williams, but they learn very little about individual women. Claypole and Robottom reinforce the domestic role of women and male dominance in the arena of work and politics.

Decolonization, Trade Unionism, Independence and Integration

In all texts, the discourse of decolonization, federation and independence is a male discourse. Indeed, the view seems to be that men had a natural right to political leadership in post-independence regimes.

Outcomes and Implications

What are the implications and social outcomes of the gender representations? With few exceptions, the books most widely used by students to prepare for the CXC examinations in Caribbean history contain precious little gender-differentiated data. This means that there are still sources that serve to reinforce certain 'masculine myths'. Many boys will leave school having done Caribbean history without knowing that in some cases, as in the case of Aracaona of Hispaniola, indigenous women became caciques. They will not understand that military roles and the aggressiveness many associate with male masculinity were not confined to males. Kalinago women, for example, were a part of the indigenous society's defence system. When Columbus arrived in Guadeloupe on his second voyage, he was met by indigenous women 'armed to the teeth', who greeted him and his crew with a shower of arrows.[23] Indigenous men were also not solely confined to the public sphere, but were engaged in what society has stereotyped as 'feminine occupations', helping their women in agriculture and so-called domestic roles like child socialization. Even the pirates and buccaneers, so associated with brutality, rape, 'machismo' and a lack of honour, maintained a certain code of respect towards captured White women. It is also clear that some pirates married and had emotional ties with women. A few were female. The most famous were Ann Bonny and Mary Read born in Ireland and London respectively. Read at first enlisted in the army and fought in Flanders and Holland and later sailed to the West Indies to seek her fortune in a Dutch vessel. The ship was captured by pirates, whom Read joined. Both Read and Bonny eventually sailed together in the crew of the experienced pirate, John Rackman, alias 'Calico Jack'.

European men were not the only ones associated with the conquest and colonization of the region; White women were crucial to the colonization project as labourers, soldiers, 'encomenderas', spouses and exploiters of subaltern peoples. In the Spanish Caribbean, women were recognized as crucial to the creation and maintenance of a stable, healthy society.[24] Thus the image of the Spanish 'Don Juan' and of 'Don Juanism' (an obsessive exaltation of virility and a Faustian conviction of the boundless nature of the male ego)[25] needs to be tempered by accounts that suggest that many men in the Spanish Caribbean led orderly lives as family men.

Although slavery had brutal effects on enslaved people of both sexes, it did not totally emasculate Black men. While those who argue that Black masculinity was submerged beneath White masculinity during slavery are basically correct, as what mostly defined men's masculinity in Africa (political dominance, economic power, domestic dominance) was severely affected by slavery, it is also true that slavery afforded some Black men privileges denied to most Black women. Thus Black men did not emerge from slavery as the more disadvantaged gender; and there was no single, unified masculinity under slavery. Some masculinities were marginalized but equally some were hegemonic.[26] Those Black men co-opted into the White patriarchal order as slave drivers, managers, artisans and military personnel, displayed hegemonic masculinity. Such social space enabled them to assert their own ideas of masculinity, which were in fact similar to White men's.

Of course, while Black men did dominate the slave management hierarchy, there were also females in positions of authority. These women operated primarily, but not exclusively in the domestic sphere. Indeed, it was not only women who functioned in the private space of domestic work. Men worked in or around the Great House as cooks, valets, grooms and gardeners.

Hidden from several of the history texts is the fact that Black masculinity under slavery was not always linked to anti-social behaviour, violence and perceived 'macho' characteristics. Indeed, it was not Black men who were the main perpetrators of violence and so there was nothing essentially violent and aggressive about them.

Resistance was not the preserve of men, not even in the areas of military strategizing and leadership as the 1831–32 'Christmas Rebellion' (called the 'Sam Sharpe Rebelion' by most historians) demonstrates. Gardner's wife, not Gardner himself, tried to negotiate the terms under which he would give himself up. So there is no basis for the male appropriation of power on the basis that leadership roles are natural to men.

The impression conveyed in the texts that slave ownership was a male enterprise is false. Kathleen Mary Butler and others have shown that White and Coloured women bought and sold property and that such property was not necessarily acquired through their association with property-owning men.[27]

Finally, while Black 'male marginalization' in the specific sense advanced by Errol Miller was indeed a deliberate characteristic of the post-slavery period, at the same time, the prevailing gender ideology reinforced male power and privileged men. A Victorian gender ideology that promoted the sex-typing of jobs, the masculinization of the labour force, the male-as-provider ideology and the payment of gender-discriminatory wages was promoted by missionaries, employers and state officials. Such an ideology helped Black men to recover their submerged masculinity under slavery and to assume a dominant position in gender relations that was never seriously challenged until the late twentieth century.

Conclusions and Recommendations

Since boys, as we have established quantitatively, are exposed, albeit in smaller numbers than girls, to historical accounts that do not sufficiently provide them with a balanced view of men's and women's historical experiences; and since the elimination of gender inequality in educational material is a necessary task of human development, all the stakeholders in educational development in the country should take certain corrective measures. The Ministry of Education, the CXC, and the History Teachers' Association (HTA) should keep a closer watch on the texts used for history education in the schools. The texts have responded to those CXC goals that go beyond simple certification to embrace the larger objective of empowering Caribbean students as an explicit developmental goal, getting rid, for the most part, of the colonial, Eurocentric biases. However, despite the fact that the CXC has embraced a gendered approach to history teaching since 1993, many of the texts on the market have failed to respond to this aspect of the syllabus needs. While not banning any books, the Ministry of Education, the HTA and the CXC should strongly recommend to teachers and parents those that present a more balanced account of gender in Caribbean history. They should act as watchdogs on the texts used to teach Jamaican and wider Caribbean history, ensuring that the content and ideological perspectives are suitable for the educational needs of our developing region.

As Olwen Hufton has observed, both inside and outside academe, and whether or not feminism has suffered the demise of the 'grand narratives' that have been part of the Western intellectual tradition, women and gender in the past will have some part in the historiography of the twenty-first century. The historical assumption regarding the two sexes should be incorporated in some way into the school curriculum so that the emergent 18 year old has as part of their intellectual package, a cognizance of exclusions and arbitrary categorization attendant upon sexual identity in the past and consequently the significance and value of some hard-won victories.[28] We have to bear in mind that development is not static; the notion of development assumes the human ability to influence and control the social environment.

Public education should also be intensified. The reality is that many boys do not progress beyond the primary school level and proceed to secondary schools where they can be exposed to a more gendered and anti-Eurocentric history, however imperfectly researched and taught. In addition, many males remain totally outside of the formal educational system. Therefore, they do not get access to the type of 'citizen education' that history can provide. They are largely unexposed to the philosophical ideas and intellectual tradition of our ancestors and are often unmoved by the 'hoopla' that is made during August each year. Yet, developing countries cannot afford to have their citizens ignorant of vital historical information. Historical research can inform public discussions surrounding issues of cultural identity, gender relations, nationalism and citizenship. Governments, therefore, need to embark on a radical plan to ensure that history education, but one that incorporates issues of gender relations, reaches young males outside of the context of the classroom. This can be done by systematic public history education led by a committee of committed experts. In this regard, I wish to reiterate the call I made in August 2002 when the Emancipation Park on Knutsford Boulevard was opened officially, that the Park should be used as a venue for public history education — consistently — not as a public spectacle three times a year, that is, February, during the USA's Black History Month; August, during emancipation and independence celebrations; and October, during Heritage Week.

The call for greater attention to public history education is not irrelevant to Jamaica's developmental needs, though my interventionist development model might be opposed. History has an active cultural and political role because of its relationship to national and regional identity. We are seeing in Jamaica and the wider Caribbean a growing significance of historical issues in public discourses. It is quite obvious to those of us who are professional historians that much of what passes for historical facts constitute popular myths. We have learned from the 'Stone Poll' that 53 per cent of Jamaica's adults believe that the country would have been better off today if it had remained a colony of Britain rather than gaining its independence

40 years ago.[29] More recently, we have heard from a prominent Jamaican figure that UWI academics are focusing too much on slavery and colonialism.[30]

I submit that these attitudes show that we are not focusing enough on slavery and colonialism. Today, the debate over history, truth and objectivity unleashed by postmodernism has become, according to Richard Evans, 'too widespread for all but the most obscurantist to ignore'.[31] Many history 'texts', the critique goes, exist in a dialectical relationship with their social and historical context, failing to take on 'contemporaneity'.[32] Among the questions being posed by the postmodernists are, whose history gets told? In whose name? For what purpose? Whatever the answers might be, it is clear that most agree that to become proficient in and understand history is the key to understanding the present. Despite the postmodernist challenge to History as a discipline, what we need is more, not less, history; though of course, as a historian observed some time ago, history with 'lay appeal'.[33]

21

FROM REDEMPTION SONG TO REMEMBRANCE WALLS: Establishing War Memorials for Anti-Slavery Heroes

Lecture Delivered at the UNESCO Steering Committee Meeting, University of the West Indies, Cave Hill, Barbados, December 2, 2003

In August 2003, during the annual emancipation celebration, the Laura Facey-Cooper designed monument titled 'Redemption Song' erected in Kingston's Emancipation Park, was unveiled. At the base of the monument are the Marley inspired words, 'none but ourselves can free our mind." The monument stirred up what one newspaper report described as 're-nude' controversy over its alleged over-sexualized symbolic images of emancipation. Comments ranged from 'Negroes Aroused' (a play on Edna Manley's well-known sculpture) and 'dem shoulda cover dem up wid a loin cloth or something; . . . why dem coulden free up them mind inna dem clothes!?'[1] to, 'it merely reinforces the stereotypes of black people as sexualized beings' — a representation on which the tourist culture feeds.[2]

Such negative reactions to the monument itself must, however, be differentiated from the overwhelmingly positive response to the idea of symbolic monuments to slavery and emancipation. Most Jamaicans agree that all postcolonial societies should build sites of memory in honour of those who died in the cause of emancipation. Indeed, the tradition of building commemorative monuments to both victims and liberators is already well established in Jamaica, the wider Caribbean and Africa. It even extends to those European countries that were primarily responsible for the trade in African captives but who have been forced to acknowledge the slave trade, slavery and their legacies. In Jamaica, a Sam Sharpe Square has been created in recognition of the role of the acknowledged leader of the 1831–32 Emancipation War. Jamaica also has a more inclusive National

Heroes Park in Kingston, which boasts statues of slavery and post-slavery heroes like Garvey. Other Caribbean states as well as non-Caribbean countries like Mauritius and the USA have constructed monuments to anti-slavery heroes and heroines. Savannah and Mauritius have also built commemorative emancipation monuments.

Even former colonial powers are yielding to pressures from the African diaspora citizens within their borders and are erecting monuments to commemorate emancipation. This has been done in Amsterdam, Norway and the UK. A group of concerned citizens in Lancaster in the UK, the fourth largest slave port in Britain in the eighteenth century, conscious of that city's involvement in the transatlantic slave trade (TST), recently launched a project called the STAMP project — the Slave Trade Arts Memorial Project. Philadelphia plans to build a slavery memorial on its Independence Mall; and there is a monument in Kentucky called Broken Silence, Broken Chains.

The designs of these monuments represent a change from earlier ones. As Laurence Brown has pointed out, 'in the wake of emancipation, representations of freedom across the nineteenth century focused on the image of the Liberator through monuments to leading abolitionists like Schoelcher, constructed from the Caribbean to Edinburgh, from Edinburgh to New York, from Strasbourg to London.'[3] Such monuments often depicted the enslaved as passive recipients rather than active initiators of his or her freedom.[4]

Still, the tendency has been to build monuments to heroic figures, to individuals who have been singled out as leaders of emancipation movements. In the process, the African disapora has failed to memorialize the unsung heroes and heroines of Emancipation Wars. As far as I know, no Caribbean state has a Wall of Honour on which the names of enslaved heroes and heroines of wars of emancipation are inscribed. There is no cenotaph to the Glorious Dead in Maroon and other anti-slavery wars. This is why in Jamaica, recently, support has begun for the treatment of the anti-slavery heroes and heroines who died in action to be commemorated in a different way. It is not a mass movement by any means — but some individals, drawn from among Caribbean history students, the Jamaica

National Heritage Trust, the Jamaica Historical Society and members of the Haiti 2000 National Planning Committee, have looked at the tradition of monuments to the fallen soldiers in wars around the world and have called for the establishment of War Memorials to the anti-slavery rebels. Supporters of this idea believe that the statues of leaders like Bussa, Sharpe, Kwakoe, Alida, Tula, Cudjoe, Cuffee and others will not serve the same purpose as War Memorials.

There is a long tradition of war memorials in the Western Hemisphere of course. In the United States, war memorials have been constructed in various states to honour those who died in the 1860's Civil War. Some states have even dedicated monuments to the Black soldiers and the coloured regiments. Some of these Civil War Memorials are in the form of plaques with the names of the soldiers inscribed. In Washington, there is an African-American Civil War memorial called 'Spirit of Freedom' which honours more than 200,000 Black soldiers and sailors who fought for the union. I have read that the names of the (209,145) coloured troops and the 7,000 white officers who led them, are inscribed on the 'Wall of Honor' nearby.[5]

The most familiar twentieth-century memorials are perhaps the war memorials to the soldiers who died in World Wars I and II, or as George Lamming prefers, the First and Second European Civil Wars. The period of memorialization after WWI has been described as the largest public arts project the UK, maybe even the world, has ever seen. There are cenotaphs to the Glorious dead in these wars in the UK, Australia and in different parts of Canada, for example, the Westchester Station War Memorial.

One at Chester is particularly significant as it lists the names of the soldiers. On the east side of the memorial is a bronze plaque with the names of those lost in WWI; on the west side, those lost in WWII. Washington also plans to build a new National World War II Memorial to be opened in May 2004.[6]

The experiences of the six million Jewish victims of the Holocaust during the years 1933–1945 have been preserved in sites of memory and monuments, for example some concentration camps, and monuments as is found in California. Behind the bench where people 'sit Shivah' (mourning) for relatives or friends lost in the horror, is a wall where the names of family members lost in the Holocaust can be memorialized.

We in the Caribbean have never failed to do our part to honour those who died in the 1914–1918 and 1938–45 conflicts. Jamaica, for example, has its Cenotaph in Heroes Park and most Caribbean states hold Remembrance Day services during the month of November.

I wish to suggest that people in Africa and the African diaspora should also hold special Remembrance Day services to honour the 'The Glorious Dead' — men and women killed during anti-slavery wars.

The Case for Calling Rebels War Victims and for the Construction of War Memorials

Let me now rehearse the case for constructing war memorials to anti-slavery heroes and heroines. My examples will be drawn from the Caribbean, specifically Jamaica; but they have broader application for the African diaspora. The first rationale is that war memorials are now familiar sites in the landscape of many countries. These provide insight into the changing face of commemoration, as well as to military, social and political history. Second, there has been a change from the construction of war memorials for elite and high-ranking soldiers only; the commemoration of the war dead of all ranks is no longer an unusual occurrence as was the case in the years before WWI. Before that, as data from the British Imperial War Museum indicate, 'the rank and file were viewed by many as the sweepings of society, only one stage removed from criminals, and often the two groups were seen as interchangeable.' It was not until the late nineteenth century that this perception began to change.

Third, it is now generally recognized that slave resistance, especially armed revolt, played a fundamental role in achieving Caribbean freedom. I do not wish to detail the history of armed revolt in this lecture; but I believe that it is important to reinforce the point that instability, largely as a result of slave resistance, made the Atlantic World an unstable place from the period of colonization. This aspect of Atlantic World history has not escaped the attention of those involved in the study of the birth of the Atlantic World as an integrated and expanding capitalist economy.[7] They have shown, first of all, the centrality of Africans in creating this Atlantic World. Slavery transformed the Atlantic into a complex trading area, turning it into the centre of the international economy especially during the eighteenth and nineteenth centuries.[8] Indeed, as Barbara Solow has observed, 'firm and enduring trade links between Europe and America [and I daresay Africa], were not forged until the introduction of slavery.'[9] Franklin Knight adds somewhat prophetically, that, 'without African slaves and the transatlantic slave trade, the potential economic value of the Americas could never have been realized.'[10] Since the emergence of the concept, scholars have engaged in a rigorous and vigorous theorizing of the Atlantic World. However the ideological perspectives from which they have approached the study of the Atlantic World have not been unified. Debates have ebbed and flowed, for example, around the issue of identity, essential questions posed being: Was there a discrete Atlantic or Creole identity that was distinguishable from a burgeoning imperialist mentality? Was there a 'Black Atlantic' that was dichotomously opposed to a 'White Atlantic' or was there an inevitable 'double-consciousness'? to quote Paul Gilroy.[11] Did the cultural experiences of Africans and Europeans determine the creation of a Creole vision that ultimately became the symbol of an Atlantic identity? Was there really a sense of community in this world or was it unavoidably unstable?

Obviously those who coined the term Atlantic World did so because they discerned common threads that seemed to have given a recognizable pattern and sense of community to the civilizations that developed and maintained intercontinental interconnections. As City University of New York (CUNY) Professor of History, Michael Kraus, observed in, arguably, one of the earliest works to conceptualize what he termed at the time the 'Atlantic Civilization', 'out of the play of influences crossing the sea westward and eastward emerged a sense of community sufficiently distinctive to be called the Atlantic Civilization.' This 'civilization', he said, embraced 'the whole Western Hemisphere and much of Europe (and even African Negro culture)',[12] which he added almost as an afterthought. The linkages facilitated by colonialism, imperialism, trade, slavery and migration also facilitated the transfer and exchange of political systems, ideologies, religions, mentalities and social culture. Despite differences of location, imperial economic and political zone, origin, class, gender, ethnicity, colour and status, the argument goes, common ideologies, loyalties and institutions developed in various parts of the Atlantic World.

Critics maintain that very little apart from transnational trade and finance and perhaps common imperial relationships and experiences held this world together — albeit loosely. There was no such designation as an Atlantic world citizen. On the contrary, deep division, inequality and instability characterized the 'Atlantic World' as not all of the people who inhabited this 'world' were equally committed to its ideals. The exploited regions in this world of partners that were not really partners as Walter Rodney has long reminded us, subverted the ideals of the Atlantic World: the export production of staples; the import of inputs, bilateral trading relationships; and what Charles Mills has described as the 'racial contract' founded on white supremacy, and Eurocentrism — the political philosophy or *raison d'être* of the Atlantic World. As this contract was one between the socially dominant Whites of the North Atlantic, it was predictably contested by those who were not 'signatories' but were nevertheless deeply affected — mostly negatively.[13]

One of the most rebellious parts of the Atlantic World was the Caribbean. In this part of the world, the practice of marronage was honed, used here in René Depestre's broader sense of a historical process resulting from 'Maroon activity' outside of the plantation system that 'engendered new modes of thinking, of acting, of feeling, of imagining'.[14] As Rex Nettleford pointed out in *Caribbean Cultural Identity*, while

> The Caribbean shares in the great drama of the Americas of which it is an integral part, in this part of the world people engaged in a "process of shaping an indigenous Caribbean lifestyle and a new, viable, worldview born out of the collective experience of a long-dominated but rebellious people — now enslaved, now brutalized . . . now pressured into cultural submission, now colonized, but never defeated".[15]

The divisions and lack of egalitarianism, especially in the slave relations of production, or in the orthodox Marxist sense, relations of domination, made the Atlantic World deeply unstable. Scholars of slave resistance have shown that the indigenous peoples and the enslaved were probably responsible for most of the instability that characterized the Atlantic World; for they were not incorporated into the Atlantic World as citizens with equal rights, but as chattel enslaved and the inferior 'Other'. The anti-slavery struggles (and later decolonization movements) would illustrate the lack of consensus even within discrete economic zones like the British Empire.

Many wars were staged in the Caribbean from the moment of conquest and colonization. Indeed, Hilary Beckles has long argued that the many slave revolts and plots between 1638 and 1838 in the British Caribbean alone could be conceived of as the 200 years war — one protracted struggle launched by Africans and their Afro-West Indian progeny (at times with minimal participation from free people), against their enslavers.[16] Liberation wars continued after 1832 in the case of the Danish, Dutch, French and Spanish Caribbean and the 1848 war led by General Buddhoe in the Virgin Islands led to emancipation in the Danish Caribbean. La Escalera and the Ten Years War in Cuba are also considered significant to slave emancipation.

Michael Craton has provided us with an overview of the chronology, frequency and intensity of the wars in the British Caribbean. He has tracked the geography of some of these, like the 1760 war in Jamaica; the 1816 war in Barbados and the 1823 war in Demerara. He has also provided us with contemporary visual images, representations by the English militia that suggest that these were no mere skirmishes but outright wars; organized, armed revolts. The images of enslaved people, free Blacks and White militiamen with rifles and in military gear and formation abound, starting from visual representations of Maroon wars and continuing through to nineteenth-century liberation struggles.[17]

I am aware that many of us are not convinced that what many historians refer to as slave rebellions, were really organized, armed struggles reflective of sophisticated and intellectually conscious action. But John K. Thornton reminds us that we should not be reluctant to acknowledge that revolts of enslaved people in the Caribbean were planned and executed primarily by enslaved men with military skills and experience; it was not only the so-called heroic leaders who possessed such skills. Using the example of Haiti, he stresses that the enslaved had remarkable capacities for war; and that they did not fight desperate wars. The love of liberty and enthusiasm alone could not win wars; it could not defeat cold steel.[18] So, on the contrary, the enslaved did not suddenly rise from agricultural labourers to military prowess as many arrived from Africa with military skills. Indeed, African military service had been the route through which many had entered the transatlantic trade in Africans as war captives or Prisoners of War. Several had served in African armies prior to arrival in the Caribbean. Thorton uses this issue of military prowess among new African arrivals to help to explain the success of the Haitian Revolution. Later revolts in other territories would demonstrate, however, as Craton reinforces, that 'the lack of a military tradition did not prevent [New World Creole Blacks] from seizing, sometimes spontaneously, the weapons that came to hand.'[19] During the war led by Tacky in Jamaica, the Akans from several estates seized 40 muskets and 4 barrels of gunpowder from a Port Maria storekeeper and obviously knew how to use them.

The accounts of the 1831–32 Emancipation War in Jamaica, especially that narrated by Bernard Senior, one of the English military officers active in the suppression, reinforce the military aspects of the war. In fact, Senior used military terms to describe the male rebels — Captain, Colonel and General being the most common. The reports of that war indicate that Sam Sharpe himself had no military skills; he appointed Colonel Gardner to be the military tactician and strategist. The principal enslaved leaders also organized western Jamaica into revolutionary cells, called units; and the leader of each was given a military designation. Hilary Beckles[20] also indicates that the leaders of 1816 laid down precise military plans involving the use of small contingents drawn from most estates to attack the militia. Their plans did not include attacking non-militia targets.[21]

The questions I wish to pose, therefore, are: where are our war dead? What were their names? Where are the explicit sites of memory to them? There are statues to commemorate the revolutionary heroes all over the region. But where are the unsung rebels? Our culture of heroization has relegated the rank and file participants to a historical backwater. Nevertheless they can be rescued. Let me illustrate using the 1831–32 Emancipation War in Jamaica. There are available sources on this war that can allow us to recover many of the names for the proposed Walls of Remembrance. The main geographical area of the war was western Jamaica and there is access to a map which details the estates involved; so that we have many choices for the location of the Walls. This 1831–32 Emancipation War has been credited with hastening emancipation in the British Caribbean. Variously known in Caribbean history as the 'Christmas Rebellion', the 'Baptist War' or the 'Sam Sharpe Rebellion', it was said to have been 'unparalleled in the history of the colony, whether for depth of design or the extent of misery and ruin which it has entailed on the inhabitants'.[22]

It is widely acknowledged that Samuel Sharpe was the 'hero' of the rebellion; but we also have the names of the other key leaders and those tried and executed for their participation. There are several sources that have helped to identity and list the names:

- Secondary sources[23]
- CO 137/185: trials, testimonies and punishment lists
- Jamaica House of Assembly records with the trial testimonies

Below is an extract from one of these many confessions. It shows the number of people involved in the actual planning as well as the justification for the designation, 'war'. The extract is derived from Thomas Dove, Prisoner in the Savanna-la-Mar Gaol:

Samuel Sharp was leader of the whole of the negroes at the commencement of the rebellion. George Taylor was the last of the Baptist leaders who came up to Belvidere. George Guthrie, of Barneyside, was the second in advice. After service at the Baptist chapel on Christmas day, George Guthrie, Robert Gardiner, James Gardiner, Thomas Goodin, of Greenwich, William James, of Duckett's, and Charles Campbell, of York, met together at Guthrie's house to dine. Before dinner they took some wine, when Guthrie said "I hope we shall overcome Little Breeches" [meaning colonel Grignon] "for he has said that before Jamaica shall be free, he [colonel Grignon] will lose every drop of his blood." John Tharp, of Hazelymph, told Thomas Dove, the prisoner, that he got his gun and pistol from a white man at Lethe, who had shewed them how to make ball-cartridges. The prisoner was at the fight at Montpelier, but at no other; he had then a macheat. Johnson, the captain, belonging to Retrieve, was killed on the spot; Charles Campbell, of York, next in command, died of his wounds next day, three others were wounded.[24]

The Punishment List

The punishment list provides further evidence of the fallen in this Emancipation War and is a chilling testimony of the brutality of the suppression.[25] The punishment of the rebels was savage. The colonial army and the paramilitary forces unleashed a 'reign of terror' on the revolutionaries. The arbitrary hanging of enslaved people, mostly men, and the burning of their property were widescale. There was no mechanism in place to distinguish insurgents from those who were 'law abiding'. The local militia shot many of the rebels on sight before the authorities could even institute the trials.

Based on the official estimates some 619 rebels were killed — 307 in open rebellion and some 312 executed by the Slave Courts and the Courts Martial.[26] Kamau Brathwaite puts the figure killed in open rebellion even higher, estimating that over 1,000 enslaved people had been shot or killed by other means during the rebellion.[27] According to Craton's account, of those executed, 28 per cent were shot and 72 per cent hanged.[28]

Jamaica is not unique in having access to the names of such war heroes. While not a complete list, we have some clues from slave revolts in Barbados, for example, the list of those executed for their role in rebellions during 1685–88; and the main leaders of the 1816 emancipation war. Some reports put the casualty list in the 1816 war at over 144 executed, 70 sentenced to death and 123 sentenced to transportation. Others maintain that the figure is more likely 1,000 killed in battle and executed at law — which would put this war on par with the 1831–32 war in Jamaica.[29]

Conclusion

I wish to restate the need for war memorials to the men and women who died in the cause of Caribbean freedom. Indeed, the Caribbean needs a wider range of tangible and national sites of memory to memorialize slavery and the trade in Africans and to honour those who were soldiers in the people's army. Some support the construction of cenotaphs, as a cenotaph means a monument erected in honour of a person or persons who are buried elsewhere. While the cenotaph has been the most common war memorial, different types have surfaced in the post WWII years, with a growing trend towards inscribing names on Walls of Honour as some of the examples I have mentioned have demonstrated.

I realize that there is much more global attention to issues such as reparation, restitution, the legacies of slavery and contemporary forms of slavery. But while we call on those who trespassed against our ancestors to help to redress the legacies of slavery, we must also look into our backyards and show that we too feel that it is important to rescue the ghosts of slavery from an improper burial, to use the literary critic Jenny Sharpe's characterization.[30] As one young Bristol filmmaker said, 'we [the descendants of enslaved peoples] want somewhere to leave a flower'; to lay a wreath — just like those who lost loved ones in World Wars I and II, do each November.[31]

If not, the pain and loss captured in Toni Morrison's 1989 poem will continue to haunt us:

No place you or I can go
To think about or not to think about
To summon the presence of
Or recollect the baseness of slaves
Nothing that reminds us of the ones who made the journey
And of those who did not make it.[32]

301

Notes

Preface

1. See Raymond Williams, *Keywords: A Vocabulary of Culture and Society* (1976; reprint, New York: Oxford University Press, 1985), 170 for views on this classic and negative interpretation of the intellectual.
2. Antonio Gramsci, *Selections from the Prison Notebooks*, trans. Quintin Hoare and Geoffrey Nowell-Smith (New York: International Publishers, 1971), 9.
3. Julien Benda, *The Treason of the Intellectuals*, trans. Richard Aldington (1928; reprint, New York: Norton, 1969, 43), quoted in Edward Said, *Representations of the Intellectual: The 1993 Reith Lectures* (New York: Vintage Books, 1996), 5–7.
4. Said, *Representations of the Intellectual*, xii–xvi, 11.

SECTION I
HISTORIOGRAPHY AND KNOWLEDGE PRODUCTION IN JAMAICA AND THE WIDER CARIBBEAN

Introduction

1. See for instance Christopher Columbus, *The Voyage of Christopher Columbus: Columbus's Own Journal of Discovery*, trans. John Cummins (New York: St. Martin's Press, 1992); Edward Long, *The History of Jamaica; or, General Survey of the Ancient and Modern State of that Island: With Reflections on its Situations, Settlements, Inhabitants, Climate, Products, Commerce, Laws, and Government* (London: T. Lowndes, 1774; reprint, Kingston: Ian Randle Publishers, 2003); Lowell J Ragatz, *The Fall of the Planter Class in the British Caribbean, 1763–1833* (New York: American Historical Association, 1928).

Knowledge Production in the Caribbean

1. An expanded version has been submitted for publication in the *Journal of the Centre for African Renaissance Studies* at the University of South Africa.
2. This was discussed in Dani Nabudere, 'Development Theories, Knowledge Production and Emancipatory Practices' (50th Anniversary Conference Reviewing the First Decade of Development and Democracy in South Africa, Durban, October

2004). See also, Edward Said, *Orientalism* (London: Penguin, 1992).

3. Ibid.

4. Richard Ligon, *A True and Exact History of the Island of Barbados 1647–1650* (1657; London: Frank Cass & Co, Ltd, 1970); Charles Leslie, *A New and Exact History of Jamaica* (London: printed for J. Hodges, 1739, 1740); Jean Baptiste du Tertre, *Histoire Général des Antilles Habitées par les Francais 1667–1971* (Forte de France: Edition des Horizons Caraibes, 1973); Edward Long, *The History of Jamaica; or, General Survey of the Ancient and Modern State of that Island: With Reflections on its Situations, Settlements, Inhabitants, Climate, Products, Commerce, Laws, and Government* (London: T. Lowndes, 1774; reprint, Kingston: Ian Randle Publishers, 2003).

5. See David Henige, 'On the Contact Population of Hispaniola: History as Higher Mathematics', in *Caribbean Slave Society and Economy,* eds. Hilary Beckles and Verene Shepherd, 2–12 (reprinted from *HAHR,* 1978 and Alvin Thompson, *Colonialism and Underdevelopment in Guyana 1580–1803* (Bridgetown, Barbados: Carib Research and Publications, 1987).

6. Hilary Beckles, *White Servitude and Black Slavery in Barbados, 1627–1715* (Knoxville: University of Tennessee Press, 1989).

7. Guillaume Raynal, *A Philosophical and Political History of the Settlements and Trade of the Europeans in the East and West Indies* (1700; London: A. Strahan, 1798); Long, *History of Jamaica*; and Bryan Edwards, *The History, Civil and Commercial, of the British Colonies in the West Indies* (London: printed for John Stockdale, 1793–1801).

8. Eric Williams, *British Historians and the West Indies* (Port of Spain, Trinidad: PNM Publishing Co Ltd, 1964), 65; Thomas Carlyle, *Occasional Discourse on the Nigger Question* (London: T. Bosworth, 1853).

9. See Anthony Trollope, *The West Indies and the Spanish Main* (London: Chapman and Hall, 1860); and James Anthony Froude, *The English in the West Indies; or The Bow of Ulysses* (1888; New York: Negro Universities Press, 1969).

10. See Charles Lucas, *A Historical Geography of the British Colonies* (1888; Oxford: Clarendon Press, 1902); and A.P. Newton, *The European Nations in the West Indies, 1493–1688* (London: A. & C. Black, Ltd, 1933).

11. See Eric Williams, *Capitalism and Slavery* (Chapel Hill: University of North Carolina Press, 1944); and C.L.R. James, *The Black Jacobins; Toussaint L'Ouverture and the San Domingo Revolution* (New York: Vintage Books, 1963).

12. Long, *History of Jamaica*; Maria Nugent, *Lady Nugent's Journal of her Residence in Jamaica from 1801 to 1805* (London: West India Committee for the Institute of Jamaica, 1939); M.G. Lewis, *Journal of a West India Proprietor, 1815–17* (London: G. Routledge & Sons, Ltd, 1929); Cynric Williams, *A Tour Through the Island of*

Jamaica, from the Western to the Eastern End, in the Year 1823 (London: T. Hurst, E. Chance & Co, 1827); A.C. Carmichael, *Domestic Manners and Social Condition of the White, Coloured, and Negro Population of the West Indies* (1833; New York: Negro Universities Press, 1969); Carlyle, *Occasional Discourse;* Anthony Trollope, *The West Indies and the Spanish Main* (1859; London: Frank Cass, 1965); Froude, *The English in the West Indies;* Frank W. Pitman, *The Development of the British West Indies, 1700–1763* (New Haven: Yale University Pres, 1917), 36; and 'Slavery on British West India Plantation in the Eighteenth Century', *Journal of Negro History* 11, no.4 (1926); Lowell J. Ragatz, *The Fall of the Planter Class in the British Caribbean, 1763–1833* (New York: American Historical Association, 1928).

13. Philip Curtin, *The Atlantic Slave Trade: A Census* (Madison: The University of Wisconsin Press, 1969), 101.

14. See Richard Dunn, *Sugar and Slaves: The Rise of the Planter-Class in the English West Indies, 1624–1713* (Chapel Hill: The University of North Carolina Press, 1972), 236; See also the discussion in Ragatz, *The Fall of the Planter Class,* 85.

15. M.G. Lewis, *Journal of a West India Proprietor* (1934; London: George Routledge and Sons Ltd, 1929), 76.

16. Long, *History of Jamaica.*

17. Philip Wright, ed., *Lady Nugent's Journal* (Kingston: The University of the West Indies Press, 2003), 227.

18. Lewis, *Journal of a West India Proprietor,* 111.

19. Ibid., 90.

20. Williams, *A Tour Through the Island of Jamaica,* 18.

21. Carmichael, *Domestic Manners and Social Conditions,* 170–171.

22. Ibid.

23. Ibid., 252.

24. Trollope, *The West Indies and the Spanish Main,* 56–60.

25. Ibid., 55–56.

26. Long, *History of Jamaica;* Froude, *The English in the West Indies;* Carlyle, *Occasional Discourse.*

27. Carlyle, *Occasional Discourse,* 7–14.

28. Poem read by Lorna Goodison at the Opening Ceremony of the 2nd Conference on Caribbean Culture, University of the West Indies, Mona, January 9, 2002.

29. Froude, *The English in the West Indies* 48–50.

30. Ragatz, *The Fall of the Planter Class,* 27.

31. Pitman, *The Development of the British West Indies,* 36; and Pitman, 'Slavery on British West India Plantation', 4.

32. See Thomas Attwood, *The History of Dominica* (London: J. Johnson, 1791).

33. M.G. Smith, *The Plural Society in the British West Indies* (Berkeley: University of

California Press, 1965).

34. See Orlando Patterson, *The Sociology of Slavery: An Analysis of the Origins, Development and Structure of Negro Slave Society in Jamaica* (London: MacGibbon & Kee, 1967); and Marrietta Morrissey, *Slave Women in the New World: Gender Stratification in the Caribbean* (Lawrence, Kan: University Press of Kansas, 1989), 159.

35. Orlando Patterson, *Slavery and Social Death: A Comparative Study* (Cambridge: Harvard University Press, 1982).

36. Elsa Goviea, *Slave Society in the British Leeward Islands at the End of the Eighteenth Century* (New Haven: Yale University Press, 1965).

37. Interestingly, even though some of the enslaved arriving from West Africa were already Creoles in the sense of having mixed heritage, this fact was hardly recorded by Caribbean enslavers. For more on notions of 'Creole' in West Africa, see Paul Lovejoy, 'Identifying Enslaved Africans in the African Diaspora', in *Identity in the Shadow of Slavery*, ed. Lovejoy (London & New York: Continuum, 2000), 1–29.

38. For an elaboration of this idea, see Percy C. Hintzen, 'Race and Creole Ethnicity in the Caribbean', in *Questioning Creole: Creolisation Discourses in Caribbean Culture*, eds. Verene Shepherd and Glen Richards (Kingston: Ian Randle Publishers, 2002), 92–110.

39. Carmichael, *Domestic Manners and Social Conditions*, 252.

40. See R. Breton, *Relations de Isles de la Guadeloupe* (1647–1656) ed. J. Renard, (Paris: G. Ficker, 1929) ; du Tertre, *Histoire Général des Antilles Habitées par les Francais*; and J.P. Labat, *The Memoris of Pere Labat, 1693–1705*, trans. J. Eaden (1722; London: Constable & Co, 1931).

41. See J. Paul Thomas 'The Caribs of St Vincent: A Study in Maladministration, 1763–1773', in *Caribbean Slave Society and Economy*, eds. Beckles and Shepherd, 28–35 (reprinted from *Journal of Caribbean History*, 1984; and Hilary Beckles, 'Kalinago (Carib) Resistance to European Colonization of the Caribbean', *Caribbean Quarterly* 21, no.1 (1987)).

42. See Hilary Beckles, 1987, and H. Seaman, 'Territory and Nationhood: Colonial Dispossessions and the Resurgent Identify of the Native (Carib) Caribbean' (PhD dissertation, University of the West Indies, Cave Hill, 1999).

43. Goveia, *A Study on the Historiography of the British West Indies to the End of the Nineteenth Century* (Mexico: Instituto Pan Americano de Geographia e Historia, 1956); Kamau Brathwaite, *The Development of Creole Society in Jamaica, 1770–1820* (Oxford: The Clarendon Press, 1971; reprint, Kingston: Ian Randle Publishers, 2005); Lucille Mathurin Mair, 'Historical Study of Women in Jamaica, 1807–1834' (PhD dissertation, University of the West Indies, Mona, 1974); and Veronica Gregg, 'The Caribbean (as a certain kind of) Woman' (Paper presented at the Symposium on Engendering History, University of the West Indies, Mona, 1993);

Jean Rhys' Historical Imagination: Reading and Writing the Creole (Chapel Hill: University of North Carolina Press, 1995).

44. Beckles, 'Black Masculinity in Caribbean Slavery' (Paper presented at the Symposium: 'The Construction of Masculinity: Towards a Research Agenda', Centre for Gender and Development, University of West Indies, St. Augustine, Trinidad and Tobago, January 1–13, 1996).

45. See Brathwaite, *The Development of Creole Society in Jamaica*; Lucille Mathurin Mair, *The Rebel Woman in the British West Indies During Slavery* (Kingston: Institute of Jamaica for African Caribbean Institute of Jamaica, 1975); Barry Higman, *Slave Population and Economy in Jamaica, 1807–1834* (Cambridge: Cambridge University Press, 1976); Barry Higman, *Slave Populations of the British Caribbean, 1807–1832* (Baltimore: The Johns Hopkins University Press, 1984); Michael Craton, 'Changing Patterns of Slave Families in the British West Indies', in *Caribbean Slave Society and Economy*, eds. Beckles and Shepherd, 228–249 (reprinted from *Journal of Interdisciplinary History* X, 1979); Hilary Beckles, *Natural Rebels: A Social History of Enslaved Black Women in Barbados* (New Brunswick: Rutgers University Press, 1989); Beckles, *Centering Woman: Gender Discourses in Caribbean Slave Society* (Kingston: Ian Randle Publishers, 1999); and Barbara Bush, *Slave Women in Caribbean Society, 1650–1838* (Kingston: Heinemann, 1990).

46. See A Gautier, 'Les esclaves femes aux Antilles françaises 1635–1848', *Reflexions Historiques* (1983): 409–33; Bernard Moitt, 'Women, Work and Resistance in the French Caribbean During Slavery', in *Engendering History: Caribbean Women in Historical Perspective*, eds. Verene Shepherd, Bridget Brereton and Barbara Bailey (Kingston: Ian Randle Publishers, 1995), 155–74; Digna Castañeda, 'The Female Slave in Cuba in the First Half of the Nineteenth Century', in *Engendering History*, eds. Shepherd et al., 141–154; Félix Matos Rodrígues and Linda C. Delgado, eds., *Puerto Rican Women's History: New Perspectives* (Armonk, NY: M.E. Sharpe, 1998).

47. F. Tannenbaum, *Slave and Citizen: The Negro in the Americas* (New York: Alfred Knopf, 1946); Giberto Freyre, *The Masters and the Slaves: A Study in the Development of Brazilian Civilization* (1933; New York: A.A. Knopf, 1946).

48. See Kenneth and Virginia Kiple, 'Deficiency Diseases in the Caribbean', in *Caribbean Slave Society and Economy*, eds. Beckles and Shepherd, 173–182; Higman, *Slave Population*; Richard Sheridan, *Doctors and Slaves: A Medical and Demographic History of Slavery in the British West Indies, 1680–1834* (Cambridge: Cambridge University Press, 1985); Meredith John, *The Plantation Slaves of Trinidad, 1783–1816: A Mathematical and Demographic Enquiry* (Cambridge: Cambridge University Press, 1989).

49. Sidney Mintz, and Douglas Hall, 'The Origins of the Jamaican Internal Markey System', in *Caribbean Slave Society and Economy*, eds. Beckles and Shepherd, 319–

334; Richard Sheridan, 'Strategies of Slave Subsistence: The Jamaican Case Reconsidered', in *From Chattel Slaves to Wage Slaves: The Dynamics of Labour Bargaining in the Americas*, ed. Mary Turner (Bloomington: Indiana University Press, 1995), 48–67.

50. Nigel Bolland, 'Proto-Proletarians?: Slave Wages in the Americas', in *From Chattel Slaves to Wage Slaves*, ed. Turner; Turner, *From Chattel Slaves to Wage Slaves*.

51. Higman, *Slave Population and Economy in Jamaica*; and *Slave Populations of the British Caribbean*; Michael Craton, 'Changing Patterns of Slave Families in the British West Indies', in *Caribbean Slave Society and Economy*, eds. Beckles and Shepherd, 228– 249; 'Hobbesian or Panglossian?: The Two Extremes of Slave Conditions in the British Caribbean, 1783–1834', *William and Mary Quarterly* 25 (April 1978): 324–56.

52. Higman, *Slave Population and Economy*; *Slave Populations of the British Caribbean*; Lorna Simmonds, 'Slave Festivities and Leisure-Time Activities in Jamaican Towns' (Seminar paper, University of the West Indies, Mona 1984); Pedro Welch, *Slave Society in the City: Bridgetown, Barbados, 1680–1834* (Kingston: Ian Randle Publishers, 2002); and Beckles, 'Freedom Without Liberty: Free Blacks and Slavery in Barbados', in *Slavery Without Sugar: Plantation Society in the Americas*, ed. Verene Shepherd (Gainesville: University Press of Florida, 2002); Beckles, *Centering Woman*.

53. See Eric Williams, *Capitalism and Slavery*; C.L.R James, *The Black Jacobins*; Walter Rodney, *How Europe Underdeveloped Africa* (London: Bogle-L'Ouverture Publications, 1972).

54. See Douglas Hall, *In Miserable Slavery: Thomas Thistlewood in Jamaica, 1750–1786* (London: Macmillan, 1989); and Beckles, *Centering Woman*.

55. Brathwaite, *The Development of Creole Society in Jamaica*; Mair, 'Historical Study of Women', in *The Rebel Woman in the British West Indies*; Michael Craton, *Testing the Chains Resistance to Slavery in the British West Indies* (Ithaca: Cornell University Press, 1982); Barry Gaspar, *Bondmen and Rebels: A Study of Master–Slave Relations in Antigua, With Implications for Colonial British America* (Baltimore: The John Hopkins University Press, 1985); Beckles, *White Servitude*; *Centering Woman*; Bush, *Slave Women*; and Beverley Carey, *The Maroon Story: The Authentic and Original History of the Maroons in the History of Jamaica, 1490–1880* (Gordon Town, Jamaica: Agouti Press, 1997).

56. See Paul Gilroy, *The Black Atlantic: Modernity and Double Consciousness* (London: Verso, 1993); and Rodney, *How Europe Underdeveloped Africa*.

57. Monica Schuler, 'Ethnic Slave Rebellions in the Caribbean and the Guianas', *Journal of Social History* 3 (1970); and Douglas Chambers, 'Tracing Igbo into the Diaspora', in *Identity in the Shadow of Slavery*, ed. Lovejoy, 55–71.

58. See Ranajit Guha, *Elementary Aspects of Peasant Insurgency in Colonial India* (Delhi: Oxford, 1983), quoted in Partha Chatterjee, 'The Nation and its Peasants', in *Mapping Subaltern Studies and the Post-Colonial*, ed. V. Chaturvedi (London: Routledge, 2000), 11.

59. See Raymond Williams, *Keywords: A Vocabulary of Culture and Society* (1976; New York: Oxford University Press, 1985), 170 for views on this classic and negative interpretation of the intellectual.

60. Antonio Gramsci, *Selections from the Prison Notebooks*, trans. Quintin Hoare and Geoffrey Nowell-Smith (New York: International Publishers, 1971), 9.

61. Julien Benda, *The Treason of the Intellectuals*, trans. Richard Aldington (1928; New York: Norton, 1969), 43, quoted in Said, *Representations of the Intellectual: The 1993 Reith Lectures* (New York: Vintage Books, 1996), 5–7.

62. Said, *Representations of the Intellectual*, xii–xvi, 11.

Culture, Creolization and Marronage in the Caribbean

1. Rex Nettleford, *Caribbean Cultural Identity: The Case of Jamaica: An Essay in Cultural Dynamics* (Kingston: Ian Randle Publishers; Princeton, NJ: Marcus Wiener, 2003), xi.

2. Paul Gilroy, *The Black Atlantic: Modernity and Double Consciousness* (London: Verso, 1993).

3. Edward Long, *The History of Jamaica; or, General Survey of the Ancient and Modern State of that Island: With Reflections on its Situations, Settlements, Inhabitants, Climate, Products, Commerce, Laws, and Government* (London: T. Lowndes, 1774; reprint, Kingston: Ian Randle Publishers, 2003); James Anthony Froude, *The English in the West Indies; or The bow of Ulysses* (1888; New York: Negro Universities Press, 1969); Thomas Carlyle, *Occasional Discourse on the Nigger Question* (London: T. Bosworth, 1853); Carlyle, a leading ideologue of his class and of imperialism in the nineteenth century, was foremost among those who stereotyped the newly freed people in the British-colonized Caribbean as 'lazy'.

4. Poem read by Lorna Goodison at the Opening Ceremony of the 2nd Conference on Caribbean Culture, University of the West Indies, Mona, January 9, 2002.

5. Michael Kraus, *The North Atlantic Civilization* (Princeton, NJ: D. Van Nostrand Co Inc, 1957), 11.

6. For an elaboration of this theory see Charles W. Mills, *The Racial Contract* (Ithaca: Cornell University Press, 1997).

7. See Depestre's discussion in Kathleen Balutansky and Marie-Agnés Sourieau, eds., *Caribbean Creolization: Reflections on the Cultural Dynamics of Language, Literature and Identity* (Gainsville: University Press of Florida, 1998), as well as the editors' summary; and 'Les Aventures de la créolité', in *Ecrire la parole le la nuit: La nouvelle*

littérature antillaise, ed. Ralph Ludwig (Paris: Gallimard, 1994).

8. Immanuel Wallerstein, *The Modern World System* (New York: Academic Press, 1974), Vol. 1.

9. Nettleford, *Caribbean Cultural Identity*, xi.

10. Ibid.

11. Ibid.

12. Ibid., xii.

13. Ibid., 23.

14. Patricia Mohammed, 'The Creolisation of Indian Women in Trinidad', in *Questioning Creole: Creolisation Discourses in Caribbean Culture*, eds. Verene Shepherd and Glen Richards (Kingston: Ian Randle Publishers, 2002), 130.

15. Nettleford, *Caribbean Cultural Identity*, xiv.

16. Stuart Hall, 'The Local and the Global: Globalization and Ethnicity', in *Culture, Globalization and the World System*, ed. Anthony King (Binghamton: Department of Art and Art History, State University of New York at Binghamton, 1991), 19–41.

17. *Jamaica Times*, February 3, 1950. The leader of the Afro-West Indian League (AWIL), formed in the 1940s, was the dentist Dr M.B. Douglas who later changed his name to Abeng Doonkwa. Douglas was first a clerk in the KSAC before studying dentistry. His successor as leader of the AWIL was Millard Johnson. The AWIL existed until the 1960s. I thank Frank Gordon, Richard Hart and Ken Jones for supplying information on the Afro-West Indian League and Douglas (Doonkwa).

18. For an elaboration of this idea, see Percy C. Hintzen, 'Race and Creole Ethnicity in the Caribbean', in *Questioning Creole*, eds. Shepherd and Richards, 92–110.

19. Nettleford, *Caribbean Cultural Identity*, xiii.

20. Stuart Hall, 'The Question of National Identity', in *Modernity and its Futures*, eds. Stuart Hall, David Held and Tony McGrew (Cambridge: Polity Press in association with the Open University, 1992); See also, Robin Cohen, *Global Diasporas: An Introduction* (Seattle: University of Washington Press, 1997).

23. For an elaboration of this perspective, see Barry Chevannes, 'Those Two Jamaica's: The Problem of Social Integration', in *Contending with Destiny: The Caribbean in the 21st Century*, eds. Kenneth Hall and Denis Benn (Kingston: Ian Randle Publishers, 2000), 179–203.

22. Carol Narcisse, 'Social Integration and Disintegration: The Caribbean Experience: Jamaica', in *Contending with Destiny*, eds. Hall and Benn, 204–234.

23. Nettleford, *Caribbean Cultural Identity*, xv.

24. Ibid., 5.

25. Ibid., 45.

26. Jenny Sharpe, *Ghosts Of Slavery: A Literary Archaeology of Black Women's Lives* (Minneapolis: University of Minnesota Press, 2003).

'Sex in the Tropics'

1. *Jamaica Observer,* July 30, 2003, A1 and A4.

2. *Jamaica Observer,* July 30, 2003; *Gleaner,* July 30, 2003, A3.

3. *Gleaner,* August 2, 2003.

4. *Jamaica Observer,* July 31, 2003.

5. *Jamaica Observer,* July 30, 2003.

6. *Gleaner,* August 2, 2003, A1 and A3.

7. Ronald Hyam, *Empire and Sexuality: The British Experience* (Manchester: Manchester University Press, 1992), 2.

8. Michel Foucault, *History of Sexuality* (New York: Pantheon Books, 1978).

9. Louis Montrose, 'The Work of Gender in the Discourse of Discovery', in *New World Encounters,* ed. Stephen Greenblatt (Berkeley: University of California Press, 1993), 178–79.

10. See Douglas Hall, *In Miserable Slavery: Thomas Thistlewood in Jamaica, 1750–1786* (London: Macmillan, 1989).

11. Edward Long, *The History of Jamaica; or, General Survey of the Ancient and Modern State of that Island: With Reflections on its Situations, Settlements, Inhabitants, Climate, Products, Commerce, Laws, and Government* (London: T. Lowndes, 1774; reprint, Kingston: Ian Randle Publishers, 2003).

12. Hyman, *Empire and Sexuality,* 18.

13. Foucault, *History of Sexuality.*

14. Hyman, *Empire and Sexuality,* 92–93.

15. Hilary Beckles, 'Property Rights in Pleasure', in *Centering Woman: Gender Discourses in Caribbean Slave Society,* ed. Beckles (Kingston: Ian Randle Publishers; Princeton, NJ: Marcus Wiener, 1999), 22.

16. See Verene Shepherd, *Maharanis' Misery: Narratives of a Passage* (Kingston: The University of the West Indies Press, 2003).

17. Marina Carter and Khal Torabully, *Coolitude: An Anthology of the Indian Diaspora* (Anthem Press: London, 2002).

18. Ibid., 11.

19. Ibid., 83–85.

20. Joan Scott, *Gender and the Politics of History* (New York: Columbia University Press, 1988).

21. Sumita Chatterjee, 'Indian Women's Lives and Labor: The Indentured Experience in Trinidad and Guyana, 1845–1917' (PhD dissertaion, University of Massachusetts, 1997), 8.

22. Hugh Tinker, *A New System of Slavery: The Export of Indian Labour Overseas, 1830–1920* (London: Hansib, 1993), 266.

23. Tinker, *A New System of Slavery*, 268.
24. Public Record Office, London (hereafter PRO), Colonial Office Document (hereafter CO), 571/3, Minute Paper 54685, 'Notes on the Methods of Recruiting Emigrants in the Madras Presidency', November 6, 1915.
25. Moses Seenarine, 'The Indo-Trinidadian Family in Transition: Historical and Contemporary Perspectives' in, *Sojourners to Settlers: Indian Migrants in the Caribbean and the Americas*, eds. Mahin Gosine and Dhanpaul Narine (New York: Windsor Press, 1999), 56.
26. Madhavi Kale, *Fragments of Empire: Capital, Slavery, and Indian Indentured Labour Migration in the British Caribbean* (Philadelphia: University of Pennsylvania Press, 1998).
27. Look Lai and Parmasad.
28. Edward Jenkins, *Lutchmee and Dilloo, A Study of West Indian Life* (1877; Oxford: Macmillan Caribbean, 2003).
29. Marina Carter, *Voices From Indenture: Experiences of Indian Migrants in the British Empire* (New York: Leicester University Press, 1996), 1.
30. Chatterjee, 'Indian Women's Lives and Labor', 56.
31. Gail Pool, and Hira Singh, 'Indentured Indian Women of the Empire: Between Colonial Oppression and the Brahmanical Tradition', in *Plantation Society in the Americas* 6, no.1 (Spring 1999): 1–46.
32. Jeffery Weeks, *Making Sexual History* (Cambridge: Polity Press; Malden: Blackwell Publishers, 2000), 16.
33. Ibid., 26.
34. Chatterjee, 'Indian Women's Lives and Labor', 58.
35. Seenarine, 'The Indo-Trinidadian Family', 56.
36. Walton Look Lai, *The Chinese in the West Indies 1806–1995: A Documentary History* (Kingston: The University of the West Indies Press, 1998), 14.
37. Among the Hindus and Creoles of British Guiana (London, 1888), quoted in Jeremy Poynting, 'East Indian Women in the Caribbean: Experience and Voice', in *India in the Caribbean,* eds. David Dabydeen and Brinsley Samaroo (London: Hansib/University of Warwick, 1987), 213.
38. Jenkins, *Lutchmee and Dilloo*, 52.
39. David Galenson, ed., *Markets in History: Economic Studies of the Past* (Cambridge: Cambridge University Press, 1989); Pieter Emmer, ed., *Colonialism and Migration: Indentured Labour Before and After Slavery* (Dordrecht: M. Nijhoff, 1986); David Northrup, *Indentured Labor in the Age of Imperialism, 1834–1922* (Cambridge and New York: Cambridge University Press, 1995).
40. Joseph Beaumont, *The New Slavery: An Account of the Indian and Chinese Immigrants in British Guiana* (London: W. Ridgeway, 1871); Tinker, *A New System of Slavery;*

Rhoda Reddock, 'Indian Women and Indentureship in Trinidad and Tobago: Freedom Denied', in *Caribbean Freedom*, eds. Hilary Beckles and Verene Shepherd (Kingston: Peepal Tree Press, 1993); Jeremy Poynting, 'East Indian Women in the Caribbean'; Jo Beall, 'Women under Indenture in Colonial Natal', in *Essays on Indentured Indians in Nata,* ed. Surendra Bhana, ed., (Leeds: Peepal Tree Press, 1991).

41. Brij Lal, ed., *Bittersweet, An Indo-Fijian Experience* (Canberra: Pandanus Books, 2004); Rosemarijn Hoefte, *In Place of Slavery: A Social History of British Indian and Javanese Laborers in Suriname* (Gainesville: University Press of Florida, 1998); Verene Shepherd, *Transients to Settlers: The Experience of Indians in Jamaica 1845–1950* (Leeds: Peepal Tree, 1994); Marina Carter, *Servants, Sirdars, and Settlers: Indians in Mauritius, 1834–1874* (Delhi and New York: Oxford University Press, 1995); Seenarine, 'The Indo-Trinidadian Family'; David Trotman, 'Women and Crime in Late 19th Century Trinidad', *Caribbean Quarterly* 30, nos.3&4 (1984): 60–72.

42. Jo Beall, 'Women under Indenture in Colonial Natal', 89–115; Reddock, 'Indian Women and Indentureship', 225–237; and Jeremy Poynting, 'East Indian Women in the Caribbean, 231–63.

43. Tinker, *A New System of Slavery*, 201.

44. Reddock, 'Indian Women and Indentureship'.

45. Noor Kumar Mahabir, *The Still Cry: Personal Accounts of East Indians in Trinidad and Tobago During Indentureship, 1845–1917* (Tacarigua, Trinidad and Ithaca, NY: Calaloux Publications, 1985), 175.

46. Rosemarijn Hoefte, *In Place of Slavery: A Social History of British Indian and Javanese Laborers in Suriname* (Gainesville: University Press of Florida, 1998), 110.

47. Brian Moore, *Cultural Power, Resistance, and Pluralism: Colonial Guyana, 1838–1900* (Kingston: The University of the West Indies Press, 1995), 182.

48. Rhoda Reddock, 'The Indentureship Experience: Indian Women in Trinidad and Tobago', in *Women Plantation Workers: International Experiences,* eds. Shobita Jain and Rhoda Reddock (Oxford: Berg Publishers, 1998), 42.

49. Look Lai, *The Chinese in the West Indies*, 144.

50. Tinker, *A New System of Slavery*, 203–04.

51. Poynting, 'East Indian Women in the Caribbean', 215.

52. Reddock develops this in her article, 'Indian Women and Indentureship in Trinidad and Tobago'.

53. Jenkins, *Lutchmee and Dilloo*, 87.

54. Hyam, *Empire and Sexuality*, 94; Tinker, *A New System of Slavery,* 222.

55. Mahabir, *The Still Cry*, 101–2.

The University of the West Indies and the Decolonization Project

1. Thomas Carlyle, *Occasional Discourse on the Nigger Question* (London: T. Bosworth, 1853); James Anthony Froude, *The English in the West Indies; or The Bow of Ulysses* (1888; New York: Negro Universities Press, 1969); Edward Long, *The History of Jamaica; or, General Survey of the Ancient and Modern State of that Island: With Reflections on its Situations, Settlements, Inhabitants, Climate, Products, Commerce, Laws, and Government* (London: T. Lowndes, 1774; reprint, Kingston: Ian Randle Publishers, 2003); Maria Nugent, *Lady Nugent's Journal of her Residence in Jamaica from 1801 to 1805* (London: West India Committee for the Institute of Jamaica, 1939); Douglas Hall, *In Miserable Slavery: Thomas Thistlewood in Jamaica, 1750–1786* (London: Macmillan, 1989); A.F. Fenwick, ed., *The Fate of the Fenwicks: Letters to Mary Hays, 1798–1828* (London: Meuthuen, 1927).

2. Quoted in *Bridget Brereton*, 'Text Testimony and Gender', in *Engendering History: Caribbean Women in Historical Perspective*, eds. Verene A. Shepherd, Bridget Brereton and Barbara Bailey (Kingston: Ian Randle Publishers, 1995), 68.

3. Barry W. Higman, *Writing West Indian Histories* (London: Macmillan Education, 1999), 5–6.

4. Amy Jacques Garvey, ed., *Philosophy and Opinions of Marcus Garvey* (New York: Arno Press 1969), 1.

5. Higman, (quoting H.R. Trevor-Roper), *Writing West Indian Histories*, 118.

6. Gayatri Chakravorty Spivak, 'Can the Subaltern Speak?', in *Colonial Discourse and Post-Colonial Theory: A Reader*, eds. Patrick Williams and Laura Chrisman (New York: Harvester Wheatsheaf, 1993), 66–111.

7. Stephen Greenblatt, ed., *New World Encounters* (Berkeley: University of California Press, 1993), vii–viii.

8. Kevin Yelvington, et al., eds., 'Whose History?: Museum-Making and Struggles Over Ethnicity and Representation in the Sunbelt' (August 1999, draft paper).

9. Higman, *Writing West Indian Histories*, 98–99.

10. Alvin Thompson, *The Berbice Revolt, 1763–64* (Georgetown, Guyana: Free Press, 1999); Helen Seaman, 'Territory and Nationhood: Colonial Dispossessions and the Resurgent Identity of the Native (Carib) Caribbean' (PhD diss, University of the West Indies, Cave Hill Campus, 1999); Hilary Beckles, 'Kalinago (Carib) Resistance to European Colonization of the Caribbean', *Caribbean Quarterly* 21, no.1 (1987).

11. Barry W. Higman, *Slave Population and Economy in Jamaica, 1807–1834* (Cambridge: Cambridge University Press, 1976); Gail Saunders, *Slavery in The Bahamas, 1648–1838* (1985; Nassau: D.G. Saunders, 1995); Kathleen Monteith, 'The Coffee Industry in Jamaica, 1790–1850' (MPhil thesis, University of the

West Indies, Mona, Jamaica, 1992); Verene Shepherd, ed., *Working Slavery, Pricing Freedom: Perspectives from the Caribbean, Africa and the African Diaspora* (Kingston: Ian Randle Publishers; Oxford: James Currey Publishers, 2002).

12. Kamau Brathwaite, *The Development of Creole Society in Jamaica, 1770–1820* (Oxford: Clarendon Press, 1971; reprint, Kingston: Ian Randle Publishers, 2005); Brian Moore, *Cultural Power, Resistance, and Pluralism: Colonial Guyana, 1838–1900* (Kingston: The University of the West Indies Press, 1995); Elsa Goveia, *Slave Society in the British Leeward Islands at the End of the Eighteenth Century* (New Haven: Yale University Press, 1965).

13. Sidney Mintz and Douglas Hall, *The Origins of the Jamaican Internal Marketing System* (New Haven: Department of Anthropology, Yale University, 1960); Hilary Beckles, ed., *Inside Slavery: Process and Legacy in the Caribbean Experience* (Kingston: Canoe Press, the University of the West Indies, 1996); Woodville Marshall, 'Provision Ground and Plantation Labour in Four Winward Islands: Competition for Resources During Slavery', *Slavery and Abolition* no.1 (1991); Glen Richards, *Masters and Servants: The Growth of the Labour Movement in St. Christopher-Nevis, 1896 to 1956* (PhD dissertation, University of Cambridge, 1989).

14. Eric Williams, *Capitalism and Slavery* (London: André Deutsch 1964).

15. Lorna Simmonds, 'Slave Festivities and Leisure-Time Activities in Jamaican Towns', (Seminar paper, Mona 1984); Pedro Welch, *Slave Society in the City: Bridgetown, Barbados, 1680–1834* (Kingston: Ian Randle Publishers, 2002); Hilary Beckles, *White Power and Black Consciousness: Slave Resistance in the English West Indies During the Seventeenth Century* (Kingston: Department of History, University of the West Indies, 1981).

16. Hilary Beckles, *Natural Rebels: A Social History of Enslaved Black Women in Barbados* (New Brunswick, NJ: Rutgers University Press, 1989); Kamau Brathwaite, *Nanny, Sam Sharpe and the Struggle for People's Liberation* (Kingston: Agency for Public Information for the National Heritage Week Committee, 1977); Bridget Brereton, *Gendered Testimony: Autobiographies, Diaries and Letters by Women as Sources for Caribbean History* (Kingston: Department of History, University of the West Indies, 1994); Michelle Johnson, 'Domestic Service in Jamaica, 1920–1970' (Presented at a Symposium on Caribbean Economic History, Mona, Jamaica, 1986); Barry W. Higman, *Domestic Service in Jamaica, England and the United States, 1770–1970* (Kingston: Department of History, University of the West Indies, 1978); Lucille Mathurin Mair, *The Rebel Woman in the British West Indies During Slavery* (Kingston: Published by the Institute of Jamaica for the African–Caribbean Institute of Jamaica, 1975); Linnette Vassell, *Voices of Women in Jamaica, 1898–1939* (Kingston: Department of History, University of the West Indies, 1993).

17. Quoted in Glen Richards, 'The Pursuit of "Higher Wages" and "Perfect Personal

Freedom": St Kitts-Nevis, 1836–1956', *From Chattel Slaves to Wage Slaves: The Dynamics of Labour Bargaining in the Americas*, ed. Mary Turner (Bloomington: Indiana University Press, 1995), 275–301.

18. Verene Shepherd, *Transients to Settlers: The Experience of Indians in Jamaica 1845–1950* (Leeds: Peepal Tree, 1994); Veront Satchell, *The Jamaican Peasantry 1866–1900: Relationship Between Economic Growth and the Peasant Sector and Governmental Policies* (Kingston: Department of History, University of the West Indies, 1983); Kusha Haraksingh, 'Structure, Process and Indian Culture in Trinidad', *Immigrants and Minorities* 7, no.1 (1988); Swithin Wilmot, 'Females of Abandoned Character?: Women and Protest in Jamaica, 1838–1865', in *Engendering History: Caribbean Women in Historical Perspective*, eds. Verene Shepherd, Bridget Brereton, Barbara Bailey (New York: St Martin's Press; Kingston: Ian Randle Publishers, 1995).

19. The relevant articles can be read in Hilary Beckles and Verene Shepherd, eds., *Caribbean Freedom: Economy and Society from Emancipation to the Present* (Kingston: Ian Randle Publishers, 1993), sections 1–3.

20. Allister Hinds, 'The Political Economy of Decolonisation in the British Empire, 1939–1958' (Paper presented at the symposium to mark the 50th Anniversary of the Montego Bay Conference on West Indian Federation, University of the West Indies, Mona, November 6, 1997); and Michelle Johnson, ed., *Social and Economic Studies* (special edition of papers presented at the symposium to mark the 50th Anniversary of the Montego Bay Conference on West Indian Federation, University of the West Indies, Mona, November 6, 1997).

21. Carl Campbell, *Endless Education: Main Currents in the Education System of Modern Trinidad and Tobago, 1939–1986* (Barbados: The University of the West Indies Press, 1997); Patrick Bryan, *The Jamaican People 1880–1902: Race, Class and Social Control* (London: Macmillan Caribbean, 1991); Bridget Brereton, ed., *The Caribbean in the Twentieth Century* (Paris: UNESCO; Oxford: Macmillan Caribbean, 2004).

22. See for instance, John Campbell, 'The Emergence of the Thinker Activist: An Exploration into the Nature of Caribbean Intellectual History and the Literary Dimension of the Historical Philosophy of C.L.R. James' (MPhil thesis, University of the West Indies, St. Augustine, Trinidad and Tobago, 1997); Heather Cateau, 'Management and the Sugar Industry in the British West Indies, 1750–1810' (PhD dissertation, University of the West Indies, St. Augustine, Trinidad and Tobago, 1995); Johnson, 'Domestic Service in Jamaica'; Monteith, 'The Coffee Industry in Jamaica'; Rita Pemberton, 'The Evolution of Agricultural Policy in Trinidad and Tobago 1890–1945' (PhD dissertation, The University of the West Indies, St. Augustine, Trinidad and Tobago, 1996); and Welch, *Slave Society in the City*.

315

SECTION II
ENSLAVEMENT AND RESISTANCE

Introduction

1. For a discussion of the development of an International Economy even before the nineteenth century, see William Ashworth, *A Short History of the International Economy Since 1850* (London: Longmans, 1987), chapter 7.
2. Barbara Solow, 'Slavery and Colonization', in *Slavery and the Rise of the Atlantic System*, ed. Solow (Cambridge: Cambridge University Press, 1991), 21.
3. Franklin Knight, 'Slavery and Lagging Capitalism in the Spanish and Portuguese American Empires', in *Slavery and the Rise of the Atlantic System*, 72.
4. Immanuel Wallerstein, *The Modern World System* (New York: Academic Press, 1974), vol. 1.

Roots of Routes

1   A.P. Thornton, *West India Policy Under the Restoration* (Oxford: Clarendon Press, 1956), 1–2.
2. Lawrence A. Harper, *The English Navigation Laws: A Seventeenth-Century Experiment in Social Engineering* (New York: Columbia University Press, 1939), 30–58.
3. See Barbara Solow, 'Slavery and Colonization', in *Slavery and the Rise of the Atlantic System*, ed. Solow (Cambridge: Cambridge University Press, 1991), 29.
4. See, for example, John Thornton, 'The Birth of an Atlantic World', in *Caribbean Slavery in the Atlantic World*, eds. Verene A. Shepherd and Hilary McD. Beckles (Kingston: Ian Randle Publishers, 2000), chap. 5; and Solow, ed., *Slavery and the Rise of the Atlantic System*.
5. Cacao was a trade item between the Inca and Aztecs before the conquest.
6. David Watts, 'Caribbean Environment and Early Settlement', in *UNESCO General History of the Caribbean*, Vol. II *New Societies: The Caribbean in the Long Sixteenth Century*, ed. Pieter C. Emmer (Paris: UNESCO, 1999), 32.
7. David Watts, 'Early Hispanic New World Agriculture, 1492–1509', in *Caribbean Slavery*, eds. Shepherd and Beckles, 40.
8. O. Nigel Bolland, 'Slavery in Central America', in *Unfree Labour in the Development of the Atlantic World*, eds. Paul E. Lovejoy and Nicholas Rogers (London: Frank Cass, 1994), 11–23.
9. Ibid., 13.
10. Ibid., 15.
11. Ibid., 16.

12. Ruggiero Romano, 'The Initial Linkage with America: A General Framework', in *UNESCO General History of the Caribbean*, Vol. II, ed. Emmer, 57.

13. Thornton, *West India Policy*, 78–80. See also, National Library of Jamaica, 'Extension Treaty With Spain', Ms. 450; and 'Illicit Trade cl. 1740', Ms. 1,049.

14. Frances G. Davenport, ed., *European Treaties Bearing on the History of the United States* and its Dependencies 4 vols (Washington DC: Carnegie Institution of Washington, 1917–37, II, 1929, 1650–1697), 195.

15. Ibid.; See also Nuala Zahedieh, 'The Merchants of Port Royal, Jamaica, and the Spanish Contraband Trade, 1655–1692', *William and Mary Quarterly*, 3rd series, 43 (1986): 574; and W.A. Claypole and D.J. Buisserret, 'Trade Patterns in Early English Jamaica', *Journal of Caribbean History* 15 (1972): 1–19.

16. Davenport, ed., *European Treatises*, 195.

17. See Frances Armytage, *The Free-Port System in the British West Indies: A Study in Commercial Policy, 1766–1822* (London: Published for the Royal Empire Society by Longmans, Green, 1953) for an elaboration of the Free Port Act. See also R.B. Sheridan, *Sugar and Slavery: An Economic History of the British West Indies, 1623–1775* (Barbados: Caribbean University Press, 1974), 42, 460.

18. See Pieter C. Emmer, 'The Dutch and the Second Atlantic System', in *Slavery and the Rise of the Atlantic System*, ed. Solow, 75–96.

19. See Enriqueta Vilá Vilar with Wim Klooster, 'Forced African Settlement', in *UNESCO General History of the Caribbean* Vol. II, ed. Emmer, 166 and 172–73.

20. Nuala Zahedieh, 'Trade, Plunder and Economic Development in Early English Jamaica', in *Caribbean Slavery*, eds. Shepherd and Beckles, 178–193.

21. See Jim Ross, 'San Andres: An Islander Comeback', in *English-Speaking Communities in Latin America,* ed. Oliver Marshall (New York: St. Martin's Press, 2000), chapter 14.

22. Adolfo Meisel, 'The Continentalization of San Andrés Island, Colombia' (Thirty-Fifth Conference of the Association of Caribbean Historians, Puerto Rico, April 2003), 5.

23. James J. Parsons, *San Andrés and Providencia: English-Speaking Islands in the Western Caribbean* (Berkeley: University of California Press, 1956), 19.

24. See Parsons, *San Andrés and Providencia,* 14.

25. Peter Wilson, *Crab Antics: The Social Anthropology of English-Speaking Negro Societies of the Caribbean* (New Haven: Yale University Press, 1973), 32.

26. J. Cordell Robinson, *Providencia Island: Its History and its People* (California, MCMXCVI), 3.

27. Robinson, *Providencia Island,* 90.

28. For an elaboration of Costa Rican–Caribbean economic and social links, see Ronald N. Harpelle, *The West Indians of Costa Rica: Race, Class, and the Integration of an*

Ethnic Minority (Montreal, Ithaca: McGill-Queen's University Press; Kingston: Ian Randle Publishers, 2001).

29. Parsons, *San Andrés and Providencia*, 16.

30. Meisel, 'The Continentalization', 12.

31. Parsons, *San Andrés and Providencia*, 31.

32. Ibid., 25.

33. Edward Long, *The History of Jamaica; or, General Survey of the Ancient and Modern State of that Island: With Reflections on its Situations, Settlements, Inhabitants, Climate, Products, Commerce, Laws, and Government* (London: T. Lowndes, 1774; reprint, Kingston: Ian Randle Publishers, 2003), I. Add. Ms. 12,404, fol. 330.

34. Ibid.

35. Ibid., fol. 329.

36. Ibid.

37. Ibid.

38. Ibid.

39. Letter of Petition to His Excellency, the Duke of Effingham from the Custos, Magistrates and Vestry of St. Ann, June 29, 1790. J.A. St. Ann Vestry Minutes, 2/9/1.

40. Ibid.

41. Long, *History of Jamaica*, Add. Ms. 12, 404, fol. 330.

42. W.J. Gardner, *The History of Jamaica, 1655–1872* (London: Appleton, 1909 edn.), 325.

43. See A. Lopez and J. Petras, eds., *Puerto Rico and Puerto Ricans: Studies in History and Society* (New York: Halsted Press, 1974), 20; Fransico Scarano, *Sugar and Slavery in Puerto Rico: The Plantation Economy of Ponce, 1800–1850* (Madison: University of Wisconsin Press, 1984), 4; and M.D. Clausner, *Rural Santo Domingo: Settled, Unsettled and Resettled* (Philadelphia: Temple University Press, 1973), 71.

44. Scarano, *Sugar and Slavery in Puerto Rico*, 4.

45. For more on this, see Verene A. Shepherd, 'Pens and Pen-Keepers in a Plantation Society' (PhD dissertation, University of Cambridge, 1988).

46. Armytage, *The Free-Port System*, 51 estimated that the number of vessels entering Jamaican free ports dropped by half in 1778. In 1778, only 35 vessels entered the free ports compared to 227 in 1775.

47. CO 137/104. Enclosure in the Earl of Balcarres' Despatch to the Duke of Portland, May 25, 1800

48. Ibid. See also Armytage, *The Free-Port System*, 47, 51.

49. Lovejoy and Rogers, eds., *Unfree Labour*, 1.

50. Philip D. Curtin, *The Rise and Fall of the Plantation Complex* (Cambridge: Cambridge University Press, 1990).

'Groundings' with Tacky (Takyi) on History, Heritage and Activism

1. Most sources indicate that Tacky was a Coromantee from the Gold Coast; but Richard Hart claims that he was Ga and that the Coromantee designation was due to the misnaming of Africans according to the port or area from which they were shipped rather than from their original ethnic group. See Richard Hart, *Slaves Who Abolished Slavery Vol 2: Blacks in Rebellion*, (Kingston: Institute of Social and Economic Research, University of the West Indies, 1985), 137.

2. This date was obtained from CO 137/32, Lieutenant Gov. Henry Moore to the Lord Commissioner for Trade and Plantations, Spanish Town, April 19, 1760, fol. 1.

3. Hart, *Slaves Who Abolished Slavery Vol 2*, 137.

4. Moore to the Lord Commissioner, fols. 1–2.

5. CO 137/32, Moore to Lords of T&P, June 9, 1760 and July 24, 1760.

6. Hart, *Slaves Who Abolished Slavery*, 141.

7. Hart, *Slaves Who Abolished Slavery*, 151.

8. 1823, CO 137/157, fol. 336.

9. Ibid, fol. 336.

10. In Despatch No. 6, December 25, 1823 written by Henry Cox, Col of the St. Mary regiment to William Bullock at King's House.

11. Despatch. No. 96, The Duke of Manchester, Gov of Jamaica to the Earl of Bathurst, CO137/156, June 16, 1824.

12. CO 137/156 Campbell to Bullock, June 19, 1824.

13. For more on this emancipation war, see Michael Craton, *Testing the Chains* (Ithaca: Cornell University Press, 1982).

Revolution and Post-Revolution

1. Veronica Gregg, *Jean Rhys's Historical Imagination: Reading and Writing the Creole* (Chapel Hill and London: The University of North Carolina Press, 1995), 11.

2. Sibylle Fischer, *Modernity Disavowed* (Kingston: The University of the West Indies Press, 2004), i.

3. Ibid., 1.

4. Hilary Beckles, 'Divided to the Vein', in *Caribbean Freedom*, eds. Hilary Beckles and Verene Shepherd (Kingston: Ian Randle Publishers, 1993), 494.

5. Ibid.

6. C.L.R. James, *The Black Jacobins* (New York: Random House, 1963).

7. Claire de Bourg, 'Haitian Women at the Backbone of the Informal Economy' (Conference on 'Reinterpreting the Haitian Revolution and its Cultural Aftershocks, 1804–2004', University of the West Indies, St. Augustine, Trinidad, June 15–18, 2004), 4.

8.   Philip Curtin, *The Slave Trade: A Census* (Madison: The University of Wisconsin Press, 1969).

9.   James, *The Black Jacobins*.

10. Eric Williams, *Capitalism and Slavery* (Chapel Hill: University of North Carolina Press, 1944).

11. Jean Casimir (unpublished paper, 2004), 2.

12. Mimi Sheller, *Democracy After Slavery: Black Publics and Peasant Radicalism in Haiti and Jamaica* (Gainesville: The University Press of Florida, 2000), 5.

13. Ibid., 67.

14. David Geggus, 'The Haitian Revolution', in *Caribbean Slave Society*, eds. Beckles and Shepherd (New York: The New Press, 1993), 417.

15. Ibid.

16. Patrick Bryan, *The Haitian Revolution and Its Effects* (Kingston: Heinemann Educational Books Ltd, 1984), 30.

17. Philip Wright, ed., *Lady Nugent's Journal of Her Residence in Jamaica from 1801–1805* (Kingston: The Institute of Jamaica, 1966), xxi.

18. Ibid., 40.

19. Ibid., 198.

20. Ibid., 198.

21. Ibid., 227.

'Petticoat Rebellion'

1.   A version of this was published in Alvin Thompson, ed., *In the Shadow of the Plantation: Caribbean History and Legacy* (Kingston: Ian Randle Publishers, 2002).

2.   Bernard Martin Senior, *Jamaica As It Was, As It Is, and As It May Be* (London: T. Hurst and Grant and Son, 1835), 171.

3.   Matthew Gregory 'Monk' Lewis, *Journal of a West Indian Proprietor Kept During A Residence in the Island of Jamaica* (1834; Oxford: Oxford University Press, 1999), 87.

4.   Hilary McD. Beckles, *Centering Woman: Gender Discourses in Caribbean Slave Society* (Kingston: Ian Randle Publishers, 1999), 157.

5.   See Lucille Mathurin Mair, 'An Historical Study of Women in Jamaica from 1655 to 1844' (PhD dissertation, University of the West Indies, Mona, 1974); Mair, *The Rebel Woman in the British West Indies During Slavery* (Kingston: Published by Institute of Jamaica for the African–Caribbean Institute of Jamaica, 1975); Linnette Vassell, compiler, *Voices of Women in Jamaica, 1898–1939* (Kingston: Department of History, University of the West Indies, Mona, 1993); and Beckles, *Centering Woman*.

6. See Verene A. Shepherd, 'Locating Enslaved Women's Voices in the Colonial Caribbean: The Promises and Pitfalls of Ventriloquism' (Paper presented at the Workshop on Atlantic Crossings: Women's Voices, Women's Stories in the Caribbean and the Nigerian Hinterland Dartmouth College, New Hampshire, May 18–20, 2001).

7. See 'Rejecting Slavery: Blacks Speak Back', in *Caribbean Slavery in the Atlantic World*, eds. Verene Shepherd and Hilary Beckles (Kingston: Ian Randle Publishers, 2000), 821–67.

8. For a recent discussion of Igbo presence in the Diaspora, see Douglas Chambers, 'Tracing Igbo into the Diaspora', in *Identity in the Shadow of Slavery*, ed. Paul E. Lovejoy (Toronto: University of Toronto Press, 2000), 55–71.

9. Philip D. Curtin, *The Atlantic Slave Trade: A Census* (Madison: University of Wisconsin Press, 1969), 144.

10. Ibid., 160; and B.W. Higman, *Slave Population and Economy in Jamaica* (Cambridge: Cambridge University Press, 1976), 76.

11. David Eltis, *The Rise of African Slavery in the Americas* (Cambridge: Cambridge University Press, 2000), 85–113; Eltis 'The Volume and Structure of the Slave Trade', (Paper presented at the Conference, 'Enslaving Connections', York University, Toronto, October 2000).

12. Eltis, *The Rise of African Slavery*, 251.

13. Beckles, *Centering Woman*, 23.

14. Beckles, *Centering Woman*, 38–58; Douglas Hall, *In Miserable Slavery: Thomas Thistlewood in Jamaica, 1750–1786* (London: Macmillan, 1989); Verene Shepherd, *Contested Terrain: Cattle, Cane and Slavery in Colonial Jamaica* (Kingston: Ian Randle Publishers, forthcoming).

15. Ibid., 46.

16. Cyrus Frances Perkins, *Busha's Mistress, or, Catherine the Fugitive: A Stirring Romance of the Days of Slavery in Jamaica*. Edited and Introduced by Paul E. Lovejoy, Verene A. Shepherd and David V. Trotman (Kingston: Ian Randle Publishers; Princeton, NJ: Markus Wiener Publisher, 2003), chapter 2.

17. Cynric Williams, *A Tour Through the Island of Jamaica, from the Western to the Eastern End, in the Year 1823* (London: T. Hurst, E. Chance & Co., 1827), 339.

18. Mary Gaunt, *Harmony* (London, 1933), 19.

19. Williams, *A Tour*, 13.

20. See Mary Turner, 'Chattel Slaves into Wage Slaves: A Jamaican Case Study', in *From Chattel Slaves to Wage Slaves: The Dynamics of Labour Bargaining in the Americas*, ed. Mary Turner (Kingston: Ian Randle Publishers, 1995), 33–47.

21. Hall, *In Miserable Slavery*, 145.

22. Lewis, *Journal*, 41.

23. Perkins, *Busha's Mistress*, chapter 2.
24. Senior, *Jamaica*, 205–6.
25. Ibid., 212.
26. Ibid., 215.
27. Ibid., 216.
28. Ibid., 255.
29. Ibid., 264–65.
30. This is clear from the 'Returns of the Registration of Slaves', 1817–1832 in the Public Record Office, London.
31. See Clare Midgley, *Women Against Slavery: The British Campaigns, 1780–1870* (London; New York: Routledge, 1992).
32. See the line taken by Eric Williams in *Capitalism and Slavery* (Chapel Hill: University of North Carolina Press, 1944). For support for and opposition to Williams's view that economic forces ended slavery ultimately, see Section 17 of Shepherd and Beckles, eds., *Caribbean Slavery* (Kingston: Ian Randle Publishers, 1993).
33. See Thomas Holt, *The Problem of Freedom: Race, Labor, and Politics in Jamaica and Britain, 1832–1938* (Baltimore: Johns Hopkins University Press, 1992), 64.
34. Ibid., and Swithin Wilmot, '"Not Full Free": The Ex-Slaves and the Apprenticeship System in Jamaica, 1834–1838', *Jamaica Journal* 17, no. 3 (August–October 1984): 2–10.
35. CO 137/219, Despatch No. 111, Smith to Glenelg, May 11, 1837 transmitting 'A Return of Complaints brought before the Special Magistrates'.
36. Holt, *The Problem of Freedom*, 62.
37. See W.K. Marshall, 'We Be Wise To Many More Tings', in *Caribbean Freedom*, eds. Beckles and Shepherd (Kingston: Ian Randle Publishers, 1993), 12–20.
38. For more on the conditions of indentured Indians, see Shepherd, *Transients to Settlers: The Experience of Indians in Jamaica, 1845–1950* (Leeds: Pepal Tree Press, 1994).
39. Swithin Wilmot, 'Emancipation in Action: Workers and Wage Conflict in Jamaica, 1838-1840', in *Caribbean Freedom*, eds. Beckles and Shepherd, 48–54.
40. Wilmot, '"Females of Abandoned Character?": Women and Protest in Jamaica, 1838–65', *Engendering History: Caribbean Women in Historical Perspective*, eds. Verene Shepherd, Bridget Brereton and Barbara Bailey (Kingston: Ian Randle Publishers, 1995), 291.
41. Clinton Hutton, '"Colour for Colour, Skin for Skin": The Ideological Foundations of Post-Slavery Society, 1838–1865' (PhD dDissertation, Department of Government, University of the West Indies, 1992); See also Hutton, 'The Defeat of the Morant Bay Rebellion', *The Jamaican Historical Review*, Vol. XIX (1996): 30–38.
42. Verene Shepherd, ed., *Women in Caribbean History: The British Colonized Territories*

(Kingston: Ian Randle Publishers, 1995); See also Linnette Vassell, 'Women of the Masses', in *Engendering History*, eds. Shepherd, Brereton and Bailey, 321, 322, 327.

43.   www.ipu.org/wnm-e/world.htm; http://www.ipu.org/wnm-e/classif.htm and http://hjem.get2net.dk/Womeningovernments/Jamaica.htm

44.   See Vassell, compiler, *Voices of Women.*

45.   Peggy Antrobus, 'New Institutions and Programmes for Caribbean Women', in *Women of the Caribbean*, ed. Pat Ellis (London: Zed Books, 1986), 131–134.

46.   'The Labour Force, 1999' (Kingston: Statistical Institute of Jamaica, 2000).

47.   *Jamaica Observer*, August 2, 1999, 6.

48.   *Sunday Gleaner*, August 1, 1999, 2A.

49.   Nanny was most likely multilingual as, according to Beverley Carey, the Maroons spoke several languages, the most common being Kramanti, resembling the African form of the Twi tongue. Some Maroons spoke Arabic, others Spanish and French. As the years went by, a growing number spoke English. In order to communicate with the British, those not fluent in English used interpreters. It is also likely that a language representing a mixture of English and/or Twi/Kramanti and other African languages developed as people speaking different languages tried to communicate with one another. See Beverley Carey, *The Maroon Story: The Authentic and Original History of the Maroons in the History of Jamaica, 1490–1880* (Gordon Town: Agouti Press, 1997), 185, 446–447.

50.   Hyacinth Evans, *Gender and Achievement in Secondary Education in Jamaica* (Kingston: Planning Institute of Jamaica, March 1999), 6–7.

'Beside Every Successful Man'

1.   Jamaica Archives, *Jamaica House of Assembly Votes* (hereinafter *JHAV*), March 2, 1832, p.15.

2.   Michael Craton, *Testing the Chains: Resistance to Slavery in the British West Indies* (Ithaca: Cornell University Press, 1982); Mary Turner, 'The Baptist War and Abolition', *Jamaica History Review* 13 (1982); Barry Gaspar and Darlene Clark Hine, eds., *More Than Chattel: Black Women and Slavery in the Americas* (Bloomington: Indiana University Press, 1996); Hilary Beckles, 'Caribbean Anti-Slavery: The Self-Liberation Ethos of Enslaved Blacks', *Journal of Caribbean History* 22 (1988).

3.   For evidence of enslaved women's anti-slavery activities see Lucille Mathurin Mair, *The Rebel Woman* (Kingston: Published by Institute of Jamaica for the African–Caribbean Institute of Jamaica, 1975); Hilary McD. Beckles, *Natural Rebels: A Social History of Enslaved Black Women in Barbados* (New Jersey: Rutgers University Press, 1989); Barbara Bush, *Slave Women in Caribbean Society* (Kingston: Heinemann Caribbean, 1990); Verene A. Shepherd, Bridget Brereton and Barbara Bailey, eds.,

Engendering History: Caribbean Women in Historical Perspective (Kingston: Ian Randle Publishers, 1995); Hilary Beckles, *Centering Woman: Gender Discourses in Caribbean Slave Society* (Kingston: Ian Randle Publishers, 1999); and Verene Shepherd, ed., *Women in Caribbean History* (Kingston: Ian Randle Publishers, 1999).

4. Mair, *The Rebel Woman*; Beckles, *Centering Woman*; Bush, *Slave Women in Caribbean Society*; Stella Dadzie, 'Searching for the Invisible Woman: Slavery and Resistance in Jamaica', *Race and Class* 32, no. 2 (1990).

5. Mair, *The Rebel Woman*; Beckles, *Centering Woman*; Bush, *Slave Women in Caribbean Society*; Kamau Brathwaite, *Nanny, Sam Sharpe, and the Struggle for People's Liberation* (Kingston: Published by API for the National Heritage Week Committee, 1977).

6. Jenny Sharpe, *Ghosts of Slavery: A Literary Archaeology of Black Women's Lives* (Minneapolis: University of Minnesota Press, 2003), xiii.

7. Ashraf H.A. Rushdy, *Neo-Slave Narratives: Studies in the Social Logic of a Literary Form* (Oxford: Oxford University Press, 1999).

8. Rushdy, *Neo-Slave Narratives*, 3.

9. Sharpe, *Ghosts of Slavery*.

10. CO 137/185, 'Confession of William Binham, a prisoner under sentence of death'.

11. Verene Shepherd and Hilary Beckles, eds., *Caribbean Slavery in the Atlantic World*. See Section 11, 'Subaltern Autonomy: Social and Economic Culture', 712–83.

12. Craton, *Testing the Chains*; See also CO 137/185.

13. Turner, *Slaves and Missionaries*, 161.

14. Brathwaite, *Nanny, Sam Sharpe, and the Struggle for People's Liberation*.

15. See CO 137/185, 'A return of the number of white persons wounded and killed in the late revolt in Jamaica'.

16. CO 137/185, 'A return of every freeman tried and convicted, thereof, distinguishing in separate columns'.

17. CO 137/185. Further Confession of James Fray, a prisoner in the Savannah-la-mar gaol, January 24, 1832.

18. Confession of Robert Morris, February 1, 1832.

19. See Confession of Robert Gardner, February 11, 1832.

20. Craton, *Testing the Chains*, 315.

21. *JHAV*, February–April 1832.

22. CO 137/185, Courts Martial, St. Elizabeth, Folios 629–630.

23. Craton, *Testing the Chains*, 315.

24. Ibid.

25. See chapter 8, '"Petticoat Rebellion"?: Women and Emancipation in Colonial Jamaica'.

26. My thesis.

27. *JHAV*, April 1832, 163–67.

28. See Mary Turner, *Slaves and Missionaries: The Disintegration of Jamaican Slave Society*,

1787–1834 (Kingston: The University of the West Indies Press, 1998).

29. Ibid.

30. CO 137/185, 'Voluntary Confession of Linton, a prisoner in Savannah-la-mar gaol, under sentence of death, March 1832', Thomas Stewart, Rector of Westmoreland recorded the evidence.

31. Craton, *Testing the Chains*, 323.

32. Sharpe, *Ghosts of Slavery*, xii.

SECTION III
EMANCIPATION AND MIGRATION: NEGOTIATING FREE SOCIETY

Apprenticeship and Indentureship

1. Frank McGlynn and Seymour Drescher, eds., 'Introduction', in *The Meaning of Freedom: Economics, Politics & Culture after Slavery* (Pittsburgh: University of Pittsburgh Press, 1992), 4.

2. Patrick Bryan, 'History in the Tropics' (Inaugural Professorial Lecture), 10.

3. Woodville Marshall, 'We be Wise to Many More Tings' in *Caribbean Freedom: Economy and Society from Emancipation to the Present*, eds. Hilary McD. Beckles and Verene A. Shepherd (Kingston: Ian Randle Publishers, 1993), 12.

4. See Verene A. Shepherd, *Emancipation and Immigration: A Pan-Caribbean Overview* (Kingston: Printed by Alpha Boys' School Printery, 1999), 1.

5. See Veronica Gregg, *Jean Rhys's Historical Imagination* (North Carolina: University of North Carolina Press, 1995), 5–43.

6. Thomas Carlyle, 'Occasional Discourse on the Nigger Question', *Fraser's Magazine*, 1849; W.L. Burn, *Emancipation and Apprenticeship in the British West Indies* (London: Jonathan Cape, 1937).

7. Quoted in Patrick Bryan's Inaugural lecture, 'History in the Tropics', 4

8. Gayatri Spivak, 'Can the Subaltern Speak?', in *Colonial Discourse and Post-Colonial Theory: A Reader*, eds. P. Williams and L. Chrisman (New York: Columbia University Press, 1994), 66–111.

9. Marshall, 'We be Wise', and N.A.T. Hall (B.W. Higman, ed), *Slave Society in the Danish West Indies* (Kingston: Department of History, University of the West Indies, 1992).

10. Thomas Holt, *The Problem of Freedom: Race, Labor and Politics in Jamaica and Britain, 1832–1938* (Baltimore: Johns Hopkins University Press, 1992), 56.

11. See O. Nigel Bolland, 'Proto-Proletarians?: Slave Wages in the Americas'; and Mary

Turner, 'Chattel Slaves into Wage Slaves: A Jamaican Case Study', in *From Chattel Slaves to Wage Slaves: The Dynamics of Labour Bargaining in the Americas*, ed. Mary Turner (Kingston: Ian Randle Publishers, 1995), 123–147 and 33–47.

12. Eric Williams, *Capitalism and Slavery* (North Carolina: University of North Carolina Press, 1944); and C.L.R. James, *The Black Jacobins* (London: Secker & Warburg, 1938).

13. Jamaica Kincaid, *A Small Place* (New York: Plume, 1989), 26.

14. Diana Paton (Conference paper, 11th Berkshire Women's History Conference, Rochester, June 1999).

15. Holt, *The Problem of Freedom*, 64.

16. Hall, *Slave Society in the Danish West Indies*.

17. See Elsa Goveia's assessment of these writers in her *Historiography of the British West Indies to the End of the Nineteenth Century* (Washington, DC: Howard University Press, 1986).

18. Green, 'The Creolization of Caribbean History', in *Caribbean Freedom*, eds. Beckles and Shepherd, 28–40.

19. Bryan, 'History in the Tropics', 11.

20. Sidney Mintz and Douglas Hall, 'The Origins of the Jamaican Internal Market System', in *Caribbean Freedom*, eds. Beckles and Shepherd, 319–34.

21. Hilary McD. Beckles, *A History of Barbados: From Amerindian Settlement to Nation-state* (Cambridge; New York: Cambridge University Press, 1990).

22. For discussions of peasant development in the Caribbean see articles by Mintz, Marshall and Bolland, Section 3, of Beckles and Shepherd, eds., *Caribbean Freedom*; See also Veront Satchell, *From Plots to Plantations* (Kingston: Institute of Social and Economic Research, University of the West Indies, 1990).

23. Henry Breen, *St Lucia: Historical, Statistical and Descritptive* (London: Longman, Brown, Green and Longmans, 1844).

24. Satchell, *From Plots to Plantations*.

25. For a discussion of post-slavery immigration, see Walton Look Lai, *Indentured Labor, Caribbean Sugar* (Baltimore: Johns Hopkins University Press, 1993); K.O. Laurence, *A Question of Labour: Indentured Immigration into Trinidad and British Guiana, 1875–1917* (New York: St. Martin's Press, 1994); and Verene Shepherd, *Transients to Settlers: the Experience of Indians in Jamaica* (Leeds: Peepal Tree Press, 1994); See also Walter Rodney, *A History of the Guyanese Working People* (Baltimore: The Johns Hopkins University Press, 1983).

26. Ibid. See also, for Mauritius, Gaatan Benoit, *The Afro-Mauritian: An Essay* (Moka, Mauritius: Mahatma Gandhi Institute, 1985).

27. MS. 65, National Library of Jamaica.

28. Gregg, *Jean Rhys's Historical Imagination*, 11.

29. Thomas Carlyle, *Occasional Discourse on the Nigger Question, Fraser's Magazine*, London 1849.

30. Anthony Trollope, *The West Indies and the Spanish Main* (London: Chapman & Hall, 1860).

31. Edward Long, *History of Jamaica* 3 vols (London: T. Lowndes, 1774; reprint, Kingston: Ian Randle Publishers, 2003); Add. Ms. 12,404, British Museum, London; and James Anthony Froude, *The English in the West Indies, Or, The Bow of Ulysses* (London: Scribner, 1888).

32. J.J. Thomas, *Froudacity: West Indian Fables by James Anthony Froude explained by J.J. Thomas* (1889; London: New Beacon, 1969).

33. Rev Patrick Beaton, quoted in Benoit, *The Afro-Mauritian*, 24.

34. Gregg, *Jean Rhys's Historical Imagination*, 13, quoting Karl Marx, *Grundrisse: Foundations of the Critique of Political Economy* (Baltimore: Penguin Books, 1973), 325–26.

35. Douglas Hall, 'The Flight from the Estates Reconsidered', in *Caribbean Freedom*, eds. Beckles and Shepherd, 62–63.

36. Hugh Tinker, *A New System of Slavery* (London: Published for the Institute of Race Relations by Oxford University Press, 1974).

37. Look Lai, *Indentured Labour.*

38. Rosemarjin Hoefte, *In Place of Slavery: A Social History of British Indian and Javanese Laborers in Suriname* (Gainesville: University Press of Florida, 1998).

39. David Galenson, 'The Rise and Fall of Indentured Servitude; An Economic Analysis', *Journal of Economic History* 44, no. 1 (1984): 1–26; David Northrup, *Indentured Labor in the Age of Imperialism* (Cambridge: Cambridge University Press, 1995); and Pieter Emmer, 'The Great Escape: the Migration of Female Indentured Servants from British India to Suriname', in *Abolition and Its Aftermath*, ed. D. Richardson (London: Frank Cass, 1985).

40. For a perspective on the Morant Bay Rebellion, see Gad Heuman, *The Killing Time* (London: Macmillan, 1994). For an overview of post-slavery resistance, see Michael Craton, 'Continuity not Change: The Incidence of Unrest Among Ex-slaves in the BWI, 1838–1876', in *Caribbean Freedom*, eds. Beckles and Shepherd, 192–206; Heuman, 'Post-emancipation Resistance in the Caribbean: An Overview', in *Small Islands, Large Questions: Society, Culture and Resistance in the Post-emancipation Caribbean*, ed. Karen Fog Olwig (London: Frank Cass, 1995), 123–34; and Kusha Haraksingh, 'Control and Resistance Among Overseas Indian Workers: A Study of Labour on the Sugar Plantations of Trinidad, 1875–1917', in *Caribbean Freedom*, eds. Beckles and Shepherd, 207–14.

41. Don Robotham, 'The Notorious Riot: The Socio-economic and Political Bases of Paul Bogle's Revolt' (Kingston: Institute of Social and Economic Research, University

of West Indies, 1981).

42. Kincaid, *A Small Place*, 55.
43. Rodney, *A History of the Guyanese Working People.*

'My Feet is [sic] My Only Carriage'

1. A. Lynn Bolles, *We Paid Our Dues: Women Trade Union Leaders of the Caribbean* (Washington, DC: Howard University Press, 1996), 25; Also see Lucille Mathurin Mair, *The Rebel Woman* (Kingston: Published by Institute of Jamaica for the African–Caribbean Institute of Jamaica, 1975).
2. See Abigail Bakan, *Ideology and Class Conflict in Jamaica: The Politics of Rebellion* (Montreal: McGill-Queen's University Press, 1990); Bolles, *We Paid Our Dues.*
3. See Verene Shepherd, *Women in Caribbean History* (Kingston: Ian Randle Publishers, 1999), 88.
4. Ibid., 86.
5. Swithin Wilmot, 'Females of Abandoned Character? Women and Protest in Jamaica, 1838–65', in *Engendering History: Caribbean Women in Historical Perspective*, ed. Verene Shepherd, Bridget Brereton, Barbara Bailey (New York: St Martin's Press; Kingston: Ian Randle Publishers, 1995), 280.
6. Ibid., 282.
7. Shepherd, *Women in Caribbean History*, 87.
8. Karen Fog Olwig, 'The Migration Experience: Nevisian Women at Home and Abroad', in *Women and Change in the Caribbean: A Pan Caribbean Perspective*, ed. J. Momsen (Kingston: Ian Randle Publishers, 1993).
9. Paule Marshall, *Brown Girl, Brownstones* (Old Westbury: Feminist Press, 1959).
10. Ben Bousquet and Colin Douglas, *West Indian Women at War: British Racism in World War II* (London: Lawrence & Wishart, 1991).
11. Hugh Tinker, *A New System of Slavery; The Export of Indian Labour Overseas, 1830–1920* (London; New York: Published for the Institute of Race Relations by Oxford University Press, 1974).
12. Pieter Emmer, ed., *Colonialism and Migration: Indentured Labour Before and After Slavery* (Dordrecht: M. Nijhoff, 1986).
13. *Maharani's Misery: Narratives of a Passage to India to the Caribbean* (Kingston: The University of the West Indies Press, 2002).

The Politics of Migration

1. See K.O. Laurence, *Immigration into the West Indies in the 19th Century* (Barbados:

Caribbean Universities Press, 1974), 26; and Gisela Eisner, *Jamaica 1830–1930: A Study in Economic* Growth (Westport, CT: Greenwood Press, 1961), 144.

2. Laurence, *Immigration into the West Indies*, 26, 42.

3. Eisner, *Jamaica 1830–1930*, 147; and 1943 Population Census of Jamaica.

4. Hume Wrong, *Government of the West Indies* (New York: Negroes University Press, 1969); J. Carnegie, *Some Aspects of Jamaica's Politics, 1918–1938* (Kingston: Institute of Jamaica Publications, 1973); and Jan Ragozinski, *A Brief History of the Caribbean: From the Arawak and the Carib to the Present* (New York: Facts on File, 1992), 256–66.

5. House of Commons. Report from the Select Committee on West Indian Colonies, 1842, Resolution 11.

6. For a detailed discussion of the opposition to Indian immigration in Jamaica, see Verene Shepherd, *Transients to Settlers* (Leeds: Peepal Tree Press, 1994), 30–34.

7. Laurence, *Immigration into the West Indies*, 63–65; Shepherd, *Transients to Settlers*, 33–37.

8. Shepherd, *Transients to Settlers*, 53–62.

9. For a full discussion of the sexual disparity in Indian immigration, see Verene Shepherd, 'Gender, Migration and Settlement', in *Engendering History: Caribbean Women in Historical Perspective*, eds. Verene Shepherd, Bridget Brereton and Barbara Bailey (Kingston: Ian Randle Publishers; London: James Currey; New York: St. Martin's Press, 1995), 237–42.

10. Shepherd, *Transients to Settlers*, 65–78.

11. Ibid., 93.

12. Report of the Agent General Ewart, August 21, 1858.

13. Crossman Commission Report, 1884.

14. India Office Records, (hereafter IOR), Political (Pol.) 8189/47, Gov. Huggins to the Secretary of State, March 21, 1947.

15. Ibid.

16. Jamaica Law 23 of 1879, Clause 44 outlined the regulations surrounding the movement of Indians. The law was amended from time to time to reflect the changes in migration policies.

17. Jamaica Archives, Colonial Secretary's Office (hereafter CSO), 1b/5/18/56, Despatch No. 433, Governor of Jamaica to Secretary of State Chamberlain, July 30, 1902.

18. Jamaica Archives, Passport Register. Central Government File (hereafter CGF), 1B/9/67. PIR, 1888–1889.

19. Shepherd, *Transients to Settlers*, 182–83.

20. Ibid., 30–31.

21. CSO, 1B/5/75/59, 'Memo on the Laws Relating to East Indian Immigration in Jamaica', 1909.

22. PIR, 1879–80.

23. PIR, 1879–80.

24. H.S. Sohal, 'The East Indian Indentureship System in Jamaica, 1845–1917' (PhD dissertation, University of Waterloo, 1979), 155.

25. CGF, 1B/9/28, Lord Chamberlain to the Governor of Jamaica, December 31, 1909.

26. Ellen Davis, *Friends in Jamaica* (Richmond: American Friends Board of Missions, 1943), 12–22.

27. PIR, 1910–11.

28. Doorly to the Colonial Secretary, 1909.

29. CGF, 1B/9/47, Robert Johnstone, Acting Colonial Secretary to Mr. Reed, Director of Education, December 10, 1916.

30. *Jamaica Annual Report*, 1930, 236.

31. J.D. Tyson, *Report on the Condition of Indians in Jamaica, Trinidad and British Guiana* (Simla, 1939), 87.

32. IOR, L/P&J/8/179/108/1A, Extract from the Report of the West Indies Royal Commission, 1939.

33. Section 13 (1), Jamaica Law 22, 1896.

34. CGF, 1B/9/111/5a. The Protector of Immigrants to Messrs. Campbell and Campbell, Solicitors, November 8, 1945.

35. Ibid., Messrs Campbell and Campbell to Maragh Tewari, October 17, 1945.

36. CO, 318/445/9, H.F. Downie to Gov Richards, November 20, 1941.

37. IOR, L/P&J8/338.

38. CGF, 1B/9/111/5, Report of a meeting between the EIPS and the Privy Council, January 26, 1943.

39. For a detailed discussion of this issue see Shepherd, *Transients to Settlers*, 212–19.

40. CGF, 1B/9/104, Robinson & Lyons, Solicitors, to F.N. Isaacs, Actg Protector of Immigrants, November 22, 1928.

41. Ibid., 'Note by Ramsahai Mahara on Hindu Divorce Procedure'.

42. Ibid., Robinson & Lyons to the Protector of Immigrants, November 22, 1928 and the Protector to Sukeya, July 29, 1932.

43. L. Mansingh, 'Cultural Heritage among the East Indians of Jamaica' (Unpublished paper, September 1979), 19.

44. Tyson's Report, Appendix III, 87.

45. Ibid.

46. CO, 318/445/9, Despatch No. 2329/35, Gov Richards to H.F. Downie, January 26, 1942.

47. CO, 318/474/2, Despatch No. 232, 1946, Gov. Huggins to the Rt. Hon. A. Creech-Jones.

48. PIR, 1942/43.
49. IOR, L/P&J/8/184/108/1D, Pol. 5820. 'Review of Important Events Relating to or Affecting Indians in Different Parts of the British Empire, 1943–44'.
50. Brinsley Samaroo, 'Politics and Afro-Indian Relations in Trinidad', in *Calcutta to Caroni: The East Indians of Trinidad*, ed. J. LaGuerre (Trinidad and Jamaica, 1974), 85–97.
51. Tyson's Report, Sec. 11, 35.
52. IOR, L/P&J/8/108/17, G.S. Bozman, Joint Secretary to the Government of India to the Undersecretary of State for India, September 10, 1941.
53. Ibid.
54. Report of the Chief Electoral Officer, 1945.
55. IOR, L/P&J8/184/108/1D, Review of Important Events.

SECTION IV
SLAVERY'S LEGACIES IN POSTCOLONIAL JAMAICA

Introduction

1. Swithin Wilmot, 'Emancipation in Action: Workers and Wage Conflict in Jamaica, 1838–1848', *Jamaica Journal* 19, no.3 (1986): 55–61.

'Dear Mrs Seacole'

1. For an overview of the Battle of Trafalgar and Lord Nelson's fate, see H.L. Peacock, *A History of Modern Europe 1789–1981* (Oxford: Heinemann Educational Publishers, 1982).
2. See Rupert Lewis, 'Emancipate Yourself from Mental Slavery: Letter to Mr. Garvey' (Churches' Emancipation Lecture, Kingston, 2000).
3. Seacole's autobiography was first published in London in 1857, a year after the end of the Crimean war, and then republished in 1988 by Oxford University Press in New York.
4. Edward Long, *The History of Jamaica; or, General Survey of the Ancient and Modern State of that Island: With Reflections on its Situations, Settlements, Inhabitants, Climate, Products, Commerce, Laws, and Government* 3 vols. (London: T. Lowndes, 1774; reprint, Kingston: Ian Randle Publishers, 2003).
5. See 'Copy of the Order-in-Council of the 15th August 1805, for Prohibiting the Import of Slaves' (House of Lords, May 16, 1806).
6. See Clinton Hutton, *The Logic and Historical Significance of the Haitian Revolution: The Cosmological Roots of Haitian Freedom* (Kingston: Arawak Publications, 2005).

7. Philip Wright, ed., *Lady Nugent's Journal of her Residence in Jamaica from 1801 to 1805* (Kingston: Institute of Jamaica, 1966).

8. Mary Seacole, *Wonderful Adventures of Mrs. Seacole in Many Lands* (1857; reprint, New York: Oxford University Press, 1988), in particular chapter 3.

9. Ibid., 47.

10. Ibid., 48.

11. Ibid., chapter 5.

12. The Crimean war was fought between 1853 and 1856.

13. Sandra Pouchet Paquet, *Caribbean Autobiography: Cultural Identity and Self-Representation* (Madison: University of Wisconsin Press, 2002), 60.

14. From 'A Stir for Seacole', *Punch Magazine*, December 6, 1856.

15. For an overview of the post-slavery Caribbean, see Hilary Beckles and Verene Shepherd, eds., *Caribbean Freedom* (Kingston: Ian Randle Publishers, 1993).

16. Lucille Mathurin Mair was the first student in the Mona History Department to write a PhD thesis (in 1974) focused on the subject of women. That thesis is scheduled to be published by the University of the West Indies Press.

17. See William Andrews's introduction to the *Wonderful Adventures of Mrs. Seacole in Many Lands* (New York: Oxford University Publishers, Schomburg Library of 19th-century Black Women Works, 1988), xxvii–xxxiv.

18. Mary Prince, the daughter of enslaved parents, was born at Brackish Pond, Bermuda, in about 1788. She was enslaved in Bermuda, Turks Island and Antigua. She lived at a Moravian Mission House in England and worked for Thomas Pringle, a member of the Anti-Slavery Society. In 1831 Pringle arranged for her to publish her book, *The History of Mary Prince, A West Indian Slave. This* was the first book published in Britain about the life of a Black woman. Henry Sylvester Williams born on February 19, 1869 in Trinidad and Tobago, organized the first Pan-African Conference in 1900. He passionately believed that African people and people of African descent should not be dictated to by their colonial masters. Olaudah Equiano (c.1745–1797) was born in what is now Nigeria and was sold into slavery in childhood. On going to London he became involved in the movement to abolish the slave trade, and wrote *The Interesting Narrative of the Life of Olaudah Equiano, or Gustavus Vassa the African* (1789) which became a best selling abolitionist autobiography. Claudia Jones, born in Port of Spain, Trinidad in 1915 was a Black nationalist, political activist, communist and journalist and has been described as the mother of the Notting Hill carnival, which she helped launch in 1959 as an annual showcase for Caribbean talent. Often described as a working-class radical, Robert Wedderburn was born in Jamaica in 1762 and was instrumental in achieving the freedom of the press in Britain in the nineteenth century. His father was a White enslaver and his mother an enslaved domestic worker.

19. Tacky led the 1760 revolt of enslaved people in St. Mary in 1760. Sam Sharpe has been credited with leading the 1831–32 Emancipation War in Jamaica. See UK National Archives, CO, 137/185 and Michael Craton, *Testing the Chains: Resistance to Slavery in the British West Indies* (Ithaca: Cornel University Press, 1982).

'Up From Slavery'

1. A version of this lecture was published as 'Image, Representation and the Project of Emancipation', in *Contending with Destiny: The Caribbean in the 21st Century*, eds. Kenneth Hall, Denis Benn (Kingston: Ian Randle Publishers, 2000), 53–79.
2. 'They Called Her Moses', Jamaica *Sunday Observer*, February 11, 2001, 7.
3. Ibid.; See also Hilary Beckles and Verene Shepherd, eds., *Slave Voices: The Sounds of Freedom* (Paris: UNESCO, 1999).
4. See, for example, Michael Burke's piece in the Jamaica *Daily Observer*, August 19, 1999.
5. Jamaica Kincaid, *A Small Place* (London: Virago, 1988), 55.
6. *Jamaica Observer*, August 2, 1999, 6.
7. *Sunday Gleaner*, August 1, 1999, 2A.
8. Ricky Singh, *Gleaner*, August 3, 1999, A8.
9. Anthony Harriot, *Police and Crime Control in Jamaica: Problems of Reforming Ex-Colonial Constabularies* (Kingston: The University of the West Indies Press, 2000).
10. Veronica Gregg, *Jean Rhys's Historical Imagination: Reading and Writing the Creole* (Chapel Hill: University of North Carolina Press, 1995), 11.
11. Edward Long, *The History of Jamaica; or, General Survey of the Ancient and Modern State of that Island: With Reflections on its Situations, Settlements, Inhabitants, Climate, Products, Commerce, Laws, and Government* (London: T. Lowndes, 1774; reprint, Kingston: Ian Randle Publishers, 2003).
12. Philip Wright, ed., *Lady Nugent's Journal of her Residence in Jamaica, 1801–1805* (1805; Kingston: The University of the West Indies Press, 2002), 220.
13. Bridget Brereton, 'Text, Testimony and Gender', in *Engendering History: Caribbean Women in Historical Perspective*, eds. Verene Shepherd, Bridget Brereton and Barbara Bailey (Kingston: Ian Randle Publishers, 1995), 68.
14. See Thomas Carlyle, 'The Occasional Discourse on the Nigger Question', *Fraser's Magazine* (1849); James Anthony Froude, *The English in the West Indies; or The Bow of Ulysses* (1888; New York: Negro Universities Press, 1969); William Sewell, *The Ordeal of Free Labour* (1861; London: Cass, 1968); Anthony Trollope, *The West Indies and the Spanish Main* (1860; Gloucester: Alan Sutton, 1985); L. Hearn, *Two Years in the French West Indies* (New York: Harper & Brothers, 1890; New York: Interlink Books, 2001); Charles Stoddard, *Cruising Among the Caribbees: Summer Days in Winter Months* (New York: Charles Scribner's Sons, 1895); and William

Burn, *Emancipation and Apprenticeship in the BWI* (London: J. Cape, 1937); For Harmer's comments see Ms. 65, National Library of Jamaica.

15. Eric Williams, *Capitalism and Slavery* (1944; Chapel Hill: University of North Carolina Press, 1994; Kingston: Ian Randle Publishers, 2004).

16. Revisited in Verene Shepherd, *Maharani's Misery: Narratives of A Passage from India*; See Hugh Tinker, *A New System of Slavery: The Export of Indian Labour Overseas, 1830–1920* (London: Hansib, 1993); Pieter Emmer, ed., *Colonialism and Migration: Indentured Labour Before and After Slavery* (Dordrecht: M. Nijhoff, 1986); Marina Carter, *Servants, Sirdars, and Settlers: Indians in Mauritius, 1834–1874* (Delhi; New York: Oxford University Press, 1995); and Rosemarijn Hoefte, *In Place Of Slavery: A Social History of British Indian and Javanese Laborers in Suriname* (Gainesville: University Press of Florida, 1998).

17. Pieter Emmer, 'The Great Escape: The Migration of Female Indentured Servants from British India to Suriname', in *Abolition and Its Aftermath: The Historical Context*, David Richardson (London: Frank Cass, 1985).

18. David Eltis, *The Rise of African Slavery in the Americas* (Cambridge: Cambridge University Press, 2000).

19. Karl Marx, *Grundrisse: Foundations of the Critique of Political Economy* (Baltimore: Penguin Books, 1973), 325–26, cited in Gregg, *Jean Rhys's Historical Imagination*, 13.

20. J.J. Thomas, *Froudacity: West Indian Fables by James Anthony Froude explained by J.J. Thomas* (1889; London, New Beacon, 1969).

21. William Green, *British Slave Emancipation: The Sugar Colonies and the Great Experiment 1830–1865* (Oxford: Clarendon Press, 1976).

22. Philip Sherlock and Hazel Bennett, *The Story of the Jamaican People* (Kingston: Ian Randle Publishers, 1997). This book has the *potential* to be a good history of Jamaica but needs to be consistent with its 'Afro-centric perspective'. It also needs a good historiographical overhaul in order to include more recent works on Caribbean–Jamaican history.

23. Mark Lawson, 'Not Bigoted, Just Barking', *Guardian*, August 14, 1999, 18.

24. Stuart Hall, ed., *Representation: Cultural Representations and Signifying Practices* (London; Thousand Oaks, CA: Sage in association with the Open University, 1997).

25. Joyce Appleby, Lynn Hunt and Margaret Jacob, 'Telling the Truth About History', in *The Postmodern History Reader*, ed. Keith Jenkins (London; New York: Routledge, 1997), 216.

26. F.R. Ankersmit, 'Historiography and Postmodernism', in *The Postmodern History Reader*, ed. Jenkins, 277–97.

27. Kevin Yelvington, et al., eds., 'Whose History?': Museum-making and Struggles

Over Ethnicity and Representation in the Sunbelt' (August 1999 draft).

28. William Green, 'The Creolization of Caribbean History: The Emancipation Era and a Critique of Dialectical Analysis', in *Caribbean Freedom: Economy and Society and Emancipation to the Present*, eds. Hilary Beckles and Verene Shepherd (Kingston: Ian Randle Publishers, 1993), 28–40.

29. Patrick Bryan, 'History in the Tropics' (Inaugural Professorial Lecture, 1999), 11.

30. Gayatri Chakravorty Spivak, 'Can the Subaltern Speak?', in *Colonial Discourse and Post-Colonial Theory: A Reader*, eds. P. Williams and L. Chrisman (New York: Harvester Wheatsheaf, 1993), 66–111.

31. Stephen Greenblatt, ed., *New World Encounters* (Berkeley: University of California Press, 1993), vii–viii.

32. Donald Akenson, *If the Irish Ran the World: Montserrat, 1630–1730* (Montreal; Buffalo: McGill-Queen's University Press, 1997), 186.

33. Appleby, et al., 'Telling the Truth About History', 217.

34. Glenn Sankatsing, 'The Caribbean: Archipelago of Trailer Societies', (Seed paper of the inaugural Allan Harris Conference, Institute of Social and Economic Research, University of the West Indies, St. Augustine, November 1998), 6.

35. I recall being interviewed by the BBC Caribbean report about this issue.

36. See articles in Verene Shepherd and Hilary Beckles, eds., *Caribbean Slavery in the Atlantic World* (Kingston: Ian Randle Publishers, 2000); and in Beckles and Shepherd, eds., *Caribbean Freedom*.

37. Explored in his book, *They Came Before Columbus* (New York: Random House, 1976).

38. See Beckles and Shepherd, eds., *Slave Voices*.

39. C.G.A. Oldendorp, *History of the Mission of the Evangelical Brethren on the Caribbean Islands of St Thomas, St Croix and St John* (Ann Arbor: Karoma Publishers, 1987), 220.

The Ranking Game

1. Verene A. Shepherd and Glen L. Richards, eds., *Questioning Creole: Creolization Discourses in Caribbean Culture* (Kingston: Ian Randle Publishers, 2002) was launched at the 2nd Conference on Caribbean Culture held at the University of the West Indies, Mona, from January 9–12, 2002 in honour of Kamau Brathwaite.

2. Bernard Senior, *Jamaica As It Was, As It Is and As It May Be* (New York: Negro Universities Press, 1835), 212.

3. See for example, William Green, 'The Creolization of Caribbean History: The Emancipation Era and a Critique of Dialectical Analysis', in *Caribbean Freedom: Economy and Society from Emancipation to the Present – A Student Reader*, eds. Hilary

McD. Beckles and Verene A. Shepherd (Kingston: Ian Randle Publishers, 1993), 28–40.

4.   Edward Long, *The History of Jamaica; or, General Survey of the Ancient and Modern State of that Island: With Reflections on its Situations, Settlements, Inhabitants, Climate, Products, Commerce, Laws, and Government* (London: T. Lowndes, 1774; reprint, Kingston: Ian Randle Publishers, 2003); Anthony Froude, *The English in the West Indies; or The Bow of Ulysses* (1888; New York: Negro Universities Press, 1969); Thomas Carlyle, 'Occasional Discourse on the Nigger Question', *Fraser's Magazine* (1849). Carlyle, a leading ideologue of his class and of imperialism in the nineteenth century, was foremost among those who stereotyped the newly freed people in the British-colonized Caribbean as 'lazy'.

5.   Poem read by Lorna Goodison at the Opening Ceremony of the 2nd Conference on Caribbean Culture, University of the West Indies, Mona, January 9, 2002.

6.   M.G. Smith, *The Plural Society in the British West Indies* (Berkeley: University of California Press, 1965).

7.   Antonio Gramsci, *Selections from the Prison Notebooks*, eds. Q. Hoare and G. Smith (New York: International Publishers, 1971).

8.   Michel Foucault, 'The Subject and Power', *Critical Inquiry* 8 (1982): 777–95; and *The Archaeology of Knowledge* (London: Tavistock Publications, 1972).

9.   Stuart Hall, 'The Local and the Global: Globalization and Ethnicity', in *Culture, Globalization and the World System*, ed. Anthony King (Binghamton, NY: Dept of Art and Art History, State University of New York at Binghamton, 1991), 19–41.

10. I am currently detailing aspects of this research in a book provisionally titled *Cattle, Cane and Chattel: Contested Terrain in Colonial Jamaica* (Kingston: Ian Randle Publishers, forthcoming).

11. Kamau (Edward) Brathwaite, *The Development of Creole Society in Jamaica, 1770–1820* (Oxford: Clarendon Press, 1971; reprint, Kingston: Ian Randle Publishers, 2005); and Brathwaite, *Contradictory Omens: Cultural Diversity and Integration in the Caribbean* (Mona: Savacou Publications, 1974).

12. *Jamaica Times*, February 3, 1950. The leader of the Afro-West Indian League (AWIL), formed in the 1940s, was the dentist Dr M.B. Douglas who later changed his name to Abeng Doonkwa. Douglas was first a clerk in the Kingston and St. Andrew Corporation (KSAC) before studying dentistry. His successor as leader of the AWIL was Millard Johnson. The AWIL existed until the 1960s. I thank Frank Gordon, Richard Hart and Ken Jones for supplying information on the AWIL and Douglas (Doonkwa).

13. For an elaboration of this idea, see Percy C. Hintzen, 'Race and Creole Ethnicity in the Caribbean', in *Questioning Creole*, eds. Shepherd and Richards, 92–110.

14. Ken Post, *Arise Ye Starvelings* (The Hague: Nijhoff, 1938), 119

15. The 1943 population census used 'Indians' to refer to people born in India or those born in Jamaica whose parents were of Indian ancestry. The mixed group was called 'East Indian Coloured'. Currently the term 'Indo-Jamaicans' is widely used to describe people of Indian ancestry born in Jamaica. The use of 'Indian-Jamaicans' in the period covered by this lecture is entirely my own construction. Interestingly 'African' was (and is still) reserved for those born in Africa.

16. Verene A. Shepherd, *Transients to Settlers: The Experience of Indians in Jamaica, 1845–1950* (Leeds: Peepal Tree Press, 1994), 143.

17. For an elaboration on the 1938 labour rebellion in Jamaica see O. Nigel Bolland, *On the March: Labour Rebellions in the British Caribbean, 1934–39* (Kingston: Ian Randle Publishers, 1995), chapter 11; and Richard Hart, *Rise and Organize: The Birth of the Workers' and National Movements in Jamaica, 1936–1939* (London: Karia Press, 1989); See also *Jamaica Times,* March 4, 1950, 1 for a perspective on economic conditions in the period after the labour rebellions.

18. Shepherd, *Transients to Settlers,* 143.

19. There were several letters to the editors of the major newspapers of the day from people who competed with one another to give the 'correct' definition of a 'Jamaican'. Some supported the view that local birth was not enough.

20. Brathwaite, *The Development of Creole Society in Jamaica.*

21. Brathwaite, *Contradictory Omens,* 6.

22. B.W. Higman, *Slave Population and Economy in Jamaica, 1807–1834* (Cambridge: Cambridge University Press, 1976).

23. Long, *History of Jamaica,* 178.

24. See for example, George Beckford, *Persistent Poverty: Underdevelopment in Plantation Economies of the Third World* (Kingston: The University of the West Indies Press, 1999); Lloyd Best, 'Outlines of the Model of a Pure Plantation Economy', *Social and Economic Studies* 17 (1968): 283–326; and J.R. Mandle, *The Plantation Economy: Population and Economic Growth in Guyana, 1838–1960* (Philadelphia: Temple University Press, 1973).

25. See, for example, Beckford, *Persistent Poverty*; Higman, *Slave Population and Economy*; Verene A. Shepherd, 'Pens and Pen-keepers in a Plantation Society' (PhD dissertation, The University of Cambridge, 1988); and Shepherd, 'Questioning Creole: Domestic Producers and Jamaica's Plantation Economy', in *Questioning Creole*, eds. Shepherd and Richards, 167–80.

26. See for example, Shepherd, 'Pens and Pen-keepers', chapter 4.

27. Orlando Patterson, *The Sociology of Slavery: An Analysis of the Origins, Development and Structure of Negro Slave Society in Jamaica* (London: MacGibbon & Kee, 1970), 70.

28. W.J. Gardner, *A History of Jamaica from Its Discovery by Christopher Columbus to the*

Present Time (London: Elliot Stock, 1873), 161.

29. Shepherd, 'Pens and Pen-keepers', 346.

30. Higman, 'The Internal Economy of Jamaican Pens', *Social and Economic Studies* 38, no. 1 (1989): 61–86.

31. See correspondence between George and Peter Forbes, Jamaica Archives, Private Deposits, 4/110/17, 1811–1818; Long, *History of Jamaica*, 335; and Gardner, *A History of Jamaica*, 161.

32. *Journal of the Jamaica House of Assembly* (hereafter *JHAV*), Vol. VI (November 1783): 21 and 609.

33. Long, *History of Jamaica* (edited version), British Museum, Add. Ms. 12,404, fol. 329.

34. *The Royal Gazette*, January 27–February 3, 1821, 122.

35. 'Petition of the Stock Breeders and Graziers of St. Elizabeth' (November 27, 1816) and 'Petition of the Pen-Keepers of Manchester', *JHAV* (1816).

36. 'Petition of the Stockbreeders and Graziers of St. Elizabeth', *JHAV*, 114.

37. Ibid.

38. Brathwaite, *The Development of Creole Society*, 100; See also Shepherd, 'Questioning Creole', in *Questioning Creole*, eds. Shepherd and Richards eds, 167–180.

39. Smith, *The Plural Society*; and Elsa Goveia, *Slave Society in the British Leeward Islands at the end of the Eighteenth Century* (New Haven: Yale University Press, 1965).

40. J.B. Moreton, *Manners and Customs in the West India Islands* (London: W. Richardson, 1790), 58.

41. With 90 per cent of them resident in Jamaica in 1800, only the coffee farmers had a higher residency status than the pen-keepers, about 70 per cent of whom were residents by 1834; See Verene A. Shepherd and Kathleen E.A. Monteith, 'Non-Sugar Proprietors in a Sugar Plantation Society', in *Plantation Society in the Americas*, Vol. V, nos.2&3 (Fall 1998): 205–225.

42. Smith, *The Plural Society*.

43. George Forbes to Peter Forbes, January 12, 1811, Jamaica Archives, Private Deposits, 4/110/17.

44. Shepherd, 'Pens and Pen-Keepers', chapter 5.

45. Cynric Williams, *A Tour Through the Island of Jamaica* (London: T. Hurst, E. Chance & Co, 1827), 66.

46. The cloth was not spun locally but imported.

47. Williams, *A Tour*.

48. Ibid., 66–69.

49. Apparently, one could not be free and anti-slavery in Jamaica; See David Barclay, *An Account of the Emancipation of Slaves on Unity Valley Pen, in Jamaica* 2d edn (London, 1801).

50. National Library of Jamaica, File C, Great Houses.

51. Tweedie Family Papers, Jamaica Archives, 4/45/36–9.

52. Ibid.

53. See National Library of Jamaica, File C, Great Houses; Philip Wright, *Monumental Inscriptions of Jamaica* (London: Society of Genealogists, 1966), 2; N.B. Livingston, *Sketch Pedigrees of Some of the Early Settlers in Jamaica* (1607; Kingston: The Educational Supply Company, 1909); Journal of Henry Blagrove, 1841–42, Jamaica Archives, Private Deposits, 4/4/1–2.

54. See Sheila Duncker, 'The Free Coloureds and their Fight for Civil Rights in Jamaica, 1800–1830' (MA thesis, London, 1960).

55. 'Petitions for Privileges', *JHAV* (1827): 87.

56. Long, *History of Jamaica*, Vol. 2, 412–13.

57. Philip Wright, ed., *Lady Nugent's Journal of her Residence in Jamaica, 1801–1805* (1805; Kingston: the University of the West Indies Press, 2002), 98.

58. Island Record Office, Spanish Town, District Court Wills, Liber 55, fol. 114, 1789.

59. Ibid., Liber 61, fol. 82.

60. Bryan Edwards, *The History Civil and Commercial of the West Indies*. 2 Vols (London: J. Stockdale, 1807), Vol. 11, 248.

61. Moreton, *Manners and Customs,* 58.

62. Jamaica Archives, Tweedie Family Papers, Private Deposits, 4/45.

63. Interestingly, even though some of the enslaved arriving from West Africa were already Creoles in the sense of having mixed heritage, this fact was hardly recorded by Caribbean enslavers. For more on notions of 'Creole' in West Africa, see Paul Lovejoy, 'Identifying Enslaved Africans in the African Diaspora', in *Identity in the Shadow of Slavery*, ed. Paul Lovejoy (London & New York: University of Toronto Press, 2000), 1–29.

64. Monica Schuler, 'Ethnic Slave Rebellions in the Caribbean and the Guianas', *Journal of Social History* 3 (1970); and Douglas Chambers, 'Tracing Igbo into the Diaspora', in *Identity in the Shadow of Slavery*, ed. Lovejoy, 55–71.

65. See Ranajit Guha, *Elementary Aspects of Peasant Insurgency in Colonial India* (Delhi, 1983), quoted in Partha Chatterjee, 'The Nation and its Peasants', *Mapping Subaltern Studies and the Post-Colonial*, ed. Vinayak Chaturvedi (London: Verso, 2000), 11.

66. Cyrus Francis Perkins, 'Busha's Mistress or Catherine the Fugitive: A Stirring Romance of the Days of Slavery in Jamaica' (Unpublished novel, 1855), chapter 2. This book has since been published (Kingston: Ian Randle Publishers, 2005).

67. Maureen Warner-Lewis, 'Creolization Processes in Linguistic, Artistic and Material Cultures', in *Questioning Creole*, eds. Shepherd and Richards, 245–56.

68. Smith, *The Plural Society*; and Rex Nettleford, *Caribbean Cultural Identity: The Case*

of Jamaica (Kingston: Institute of Jamaica, 1978).

69. Partha Chatterjee, 'Nationalism as a Problem', in *The Post-Colonial Studies Reader*, eds. Bill Ashcroft, Gareth Griffiths, and Helen Tiffin (London; New York: Routledge, 1995), 164–165.

70. *Daily Gleaner*, January 10, 1957, 8, quoted in Colin Palmer, 'Identity, Race and Black Power in Independent Jamaica', in *The Modern Caribbean*, eds. Franklin Knight and Colin Palmer (Chapel Hill: the University of North Carolina Press, 1989), 113.

71. *Daily Gleaner*, August 6, 1963, 21.

72. Homi K. Bhabha, 'Cultural Diversity and Cultural Differences', in *The Post-Colonial Studies Reader*, eds. Ashcroft, et al., 206–09.

73. See Richard Burton, *Afro-Creole: Power, Opposition and Play in the Caribbean* (Ithaca, NY: Cornell University Press, 1997).

74. Speech delivered at the Cheddi Jagan Memorial Lecture, Toronto, Canada, March 2002.

75. For more on this theme of Indians and the Creole as negative, see Veronica Gregg, '"Yuh Know Bout Coo-Coo? Where Yuh Know Bout Coo-Coo?": Language and Representation, Creolization and Confusion in Indian Cuisine', in *Questioning Creole*, eds. Shepherd and Richards, 148–164; and Patricia Mohammed, 'The "Creolization" of Indian Women in Trinidad', in *Questioning Creole*, eds. Shepherd and Richards, 130–147. It should also be noted that the term 'Dougla' which is used to describe the racially mixed progenies of Blacks and Indians, is considered to be pejorative.

76. Indian men wore a 'dhoti' that covered the lower part of their bodies only, leaving the rest of the body 'exposed' according to the Presbyterians.

77. Ibid.

78. Gt. Britain. Parliamentary Papers. *Papers Relating to the West Indian Colonies and Mauritius*. Enc. Signed by J.E. Henderson in Darling to Stanley, March 29, 1848.

79. CO 142/7, *Morning Journal* (April 14–15, 1847): 3.

80. Alfred Caldecott, *The Church in the West Indies* (London: Frank Cass, 1970), 206–7.

81. *The Presbyterian*, Vol. XXVII (September 1935): 261.

82. *Daily Gleaner*, December 1, 1938.

83. Shepherd, *Transients to Settlers*, 99.

84. India Office Library, London, IOR/L/P and J/8/184/108D 'Review of Important Events Concerning Indians Abroad, 1938–39'.

85. *The Young Indian*, September 9, 1926.

86. Ibid.

87. *Jamaica Annual*, Education Departmental Report (1930): 236.

88. India Office Records, L/P and J/8/108/17, G.S. Bozman to the Undersecretary of State for India, India Office, London, September 10, 1941.

89. India Office Records, L/P and J/8/184//108/1D, 'Review of Important Events Relating to or Affecting Indians in Different Parts of the British Empire, 1943–1944', Pol. 5820.

90. India Office Records, L/P and J 8/179/108/4, Extract from J.D. Tyson's Report before the Moyne Commission.

91. Pierre van den Berghe, *Race and Ethnicity: Essays in Comparative Sociology* (New York: Basic Books, 1976); See also, Verene A. Shepherd, 'Indians and Blacks in Jamaica in the 19th and early 20th Centuries: A Micro-Study of the Foundations of Race Antagonisms', in *After the Crossing: Immigrants and Minorities in Caribbean Creole Society*, ed. Howard Johnson (London: Frank Cass, 1988), 95–112.

92. See Swithin Wilmot, 'The Politics of Samuel Clarke: Black Political Martyr in Jamaica, 1851–1865', *Jamaica Historical Review*, XIX (1996): 27.

93. See Patrick Bryan, 'The Creolization of the Chinese Community in Jamaica', in *Ethnic Minorities in Caribbean Society*, ed. Rhoda Reddock (St. Augustine, Trinidad: Institute of Social and Economic Research, The University of the West Indies, 1996), 173–271. An article on page 1 of the *Jamaica Times* of May 1, 1930 also indicated that there had been a move in Panama to repatriate even the insane on the basis that the Panamanian government was spending a lot of money on their maintenance in the asylum.

94. Bryan, 'The Creolization of the Chinese', 210–11.

95. See Howard Johnson, 'The Anti-Chinese Riots of 1918 in Jamaica', *Immigrants and Minorities* 11, no. 1 (March 1983); and Bryan, 'The Creolization of the Chinese'.

96. *Daily Gleaner,* September 5, 1930.

97. Annual Report of the Protector of Immigrants, 1933.

98. *Jamaica Times*, August 3, 1963, 12.

99. Stuart Hall, 'The Question of National Identity', in *Modernity and its Futures*, eds. Stuart Hall, David Held and Tony McGrew (Cambridge: Polity Press, 1992); See also, Robin Cohen, *Global Diasporas: An Introduction* (Seattle: University of Washington Press, 1997).

100. For an elaboration of this perspective, see Barry Chevannes, 'Those Two Jamaica's: The Problem of Social Integration', in *Contending with Destiny: The Caribbean in the 21st Century*, eds. Kenneth Hall and Denis Benn (Kingston: Ian Randle Publishers, 1998), 179–203.

101. Carol Narcisse, 'Social Integration and Disintegration: The Caribbean Experience: Jamaica', in *Contending with Destiny*, eds. Hall and Benn, 204–34.

SECTION V
'I WANT TO DISTURB MY NEIGHBOUR': ACTIVISM IN AN AGE OF INDIVIDUALISM

Introduction

1. Joyce Appleby, Lynn Hunt and Margaret Jacob, 'Telling the Truth About History', in *The Postmodern History Reader*, ed. Keith Jenkins (London: Routledge, 1997), 216.

2. F.R. Ankersmit, 'Historiography and Postmodernism', in *The Postmodern History Reader*, ed. Jennkins, 277–97.

3. Kevin Yelvington, et al., eds., 'Whose History?: Museum-making and Struggles Over Ethnicity and Representation in the Sunbelt' (Unpublished paper, August 1999).

The Emancipation Proclamation and August 1, 1838

1. Peter Howe Browne, the Marquis of Sligo, owned two properties in the parish of St. Dorothy (now a part of St. Catherine). See Thomas Holt, *The Problem of Freedom* (Baltimore: Johns Hopkins University Press, 1992), 98.

2. *Royal Gazette*, August 9–16, 1834, 817. National Library of Jamaica.

3. Holt, *The Problem of Freedom*, 56.

4. Anthony Bogues, 'The Logic of Freedom', in *August 1st: A Celebration of Emancipation*, ed. Patrick Bryan (Kingston: Department of History, University of the West Indies in association with Friedrich Ebert Stiftung, 1995), 11–22.

5. See Hilary Beckles, *Natural Rebels: A Social History of Enslaved Black Women in Barbados* (New Jersey: Rutgers University Press, 1989); Beckles, *Centering Woman: Gender Discourses in Caribbean Slave Society* (Kingston: Ian Randle Publishers, 1999; New Jersey: Marcus Wiener, 1999); and Verene Shepherd, 'Petticoat Rebellion: Women in Emancipation in Colonial Jamaica' (Churches' Emancipation Lecture, 2001).

6. William Green, *British Slave Emancipation* (Oxford: Clarendon Press, 1976), chapter 5.

7. Privy Council Minutes, June 16, 1838, Jamaica Archives, Privy Council Minutes, 1832–39, 1B/5/3/24; Jamaica Archives 7/340/1.

8. Privy Council Minutes, June 16, 1838.

9. Green, *British Slave Emancipation*, 159.

10. For varying accounts of the 1831–32 rebellion, see Mary Turner, *Slaves and Missionaries: The Disintegration of Jamaican Slave Society, 1787–1834* (Urbana: University of Illinois Press, 1982); Michael Craton, *Testing the Chains: Resistance to Slavery in the British West Indies* (Ithaca: Cornell University Press, 1982); and Philip Sherlock and Hazel Bennett, *The Story of the Jamaican People* (Kingston: Ian Randle Publishers, 1998); See also the documentary, 'Britain's Slave Trade', Programme 3.

11. Voluntary confession of Linton, a prisoner under sentence of death in the Savanna-la-Mar gaol, to Rev Thomas Stewart, Rector of Westmoreland, March 1832. Jamaica Archives, Votes of the House of Assembly, 1832, Appendix No. 1, 337–38.

'I Want to Disturb My Neighbour' and 'the Man at the Door' in an Age of Individualism

1. Tony Robinson, 'Daddy Oh', the *Sunday Observer*, June 23, 2002.
2. The *Times Higher Educational Supplement*.
3. Ibid.
4. Ibid.
5. Noise Abatement Act – report of this fine.
6. Source for literacy in 1999.

After the Exhibition is Gone

1. *Gleaner*, February 3, 2004, A4.
2. Philip Wright, ed., *Lady Nugent's Journal of Her Residence in Jamaica from 1801–1805* (1839; reprint, Mona, Kingston: The University of the West Indies Press, 2002), 165.
3. George Lamming's view of Rodney and his relationship to history and activism.
4. See Raymond Williams, *Keywords: A Vocabulary of Culture and Society* (1976; New York: Oxford University Press, 1985), 170 for views on this classic and negative interpretation of the intellectual.
5. Edward Said, *Representations of the Intellectual: The 1993 Reith Lectures* (New York: Vintage Books: 1996), xii–xvi, 11.

The Case for Reparation

1. Barry W. Higman, *Slave Populations of the British Caribbean, 1807–1834* (Baltimore: Johns Hopkins University Press, 1984).
2. Ibid.

3. See *The Trans-Atlantic Slave Trade: a Database on CD-Rom*, ed. David Eltis et al. (Cambridge: Cambridge University Press, 1999).

4. See for instance Patrick Lipscomb, 'William Pitt and the Abolition of the Slave Trade' (Phd dissertation, University of Texas, 1960).

5. Lord Anthony Gifford, 'Legal basis of the claim for slavery reparations', *Human Rights* 27, no.2 (Spring 2000).

6. Joseph Inikori and Stanley L. Engerman, eds., *The Atlantic Slave Trade: Effects on Economics, Societies, and Peoples in Africa, the Americas, and Europe* (Durham: Duke University Press, 1992).

7. See Joshua Gee, *The Trade and Navigation of Great-Britain Considered* (London: Sam. Buckley, 1729); and Malachy Postlethwayt, *The African Trade the Great Pillar and Support of the British Plantation Trade in America*, 1745.

8. Eric Williams, *Capitalism and Slavery* (Chapel Hill: University of North Carolina Press, 1944. Reprint, Kingston: Ian Randle Publishers, 2004).

9. See 'The Queen Says "No" to Rastas – But they plan appeal to United Nations', *Daily Gleaner*, January 8, 2003.

10. David Horowitz, 'Ten Reasons Why Reparations for Blacks is a Bad Idea for Blacks – and Racist Too', FrontPageMagazine.com, January 3, 2001.

11. www.cnn.com, September 7, 2001.

12. See Gad Heuman, *The 'Killing time': the Morant Bay Rebellion in Jamaica* (London: Macmillan, 1994).

13. See the *Daily Gleaner*, January 8, 2003.

14. Professor Chinweizu, 'Reparations and A New Global Order: A Comparative Overview' (Paper read at the Second Plenary Session of the First Pan-African Conference on Reparations, Abuja, Nigeria, April 27, 1993).

Challenging Masculine Myths

1. This is a shortened version of the lecture that was published. I thank Kerry-Ann Morris, Kimberly Morris, Stephen Kerr, Duane Shepherd, Shanette Geohagen and Mitzie Reid for research assistance.

2. See Delroy Chuck, 'Invest in Education', *Daily Gleaner*, Wednesday August 28, 2002, A4. Of course, neither of the major political parties has yet managed to fully realize all of these laudable objectives.

3. Charles Leslie, *A New History of Jamaica from the Earliest Accounts* (London, 1740), 36, quoted in Orlando Patterson, *The Sociology of Slavery; An Analysis of the Origins, Development, and Structure of Negro Slave Society in Jamaica* (London: MacGibbon & Kee, 1967), 40.

4.   Edward Long, *The History of Jamaica; or, General Survey of the Ancient and Modern State of that Island: With Reflections on its Situations, Settlements, Inhabitants, Climate, Products, Commerce, Laws, and Government*, vol. 2 (London: T. Lowndes, 1774), 246.

5.   Barbara Bailey, 'The Feminization of Tertiary Education', *You We*, no. 8: 3–5; *Jamaica Human Development Report, 2001* (Kingston: Planning Institute of Jamaica, 2002), 87.

6.   The G-SAT replaced the Common Entrance Exam that had been the main means of placing students at Grades 5 and 6 in public schools since 1957, in 1999. Taken over two days, the G-SAT examination is offered in mathematics, language arts, social studies, science and communication task.

7.   An article appearing in the *Jamaican Historical Review* of 1956 indicates that the name 'Mona' may have been of Roman origin and may have meant 'Isle of Man'. The name 'Mona' came into use after 1767. Before that, the property was called 'Yeamans' after a previous owner.

8.   Figueroa, 'Making Sense of Male Experience', in *You We*, no. 8 and 'Male Privileging'. Bailey reiterated this view in her speech at the 2002 Jamaica Teachers' Association retreat. See *Sunday Observer*, August 25, 2002.

9.   *CARICOM Report on the Status of Women*, 89.

10.   Odette Parry, 'Sex and Gender Constructions in the Jamaican Classroom', *Social and Economic Studies* 45, no. 4 (December 1996): 77.

11.   Antonio Gramsci, *Selections from the Prison Notebooks*, ed. and trans. Quintin Hoare and Geoffrey Nowell-Smith (New York: International Publishers, 1971); See also 'Some Aspects of the Southern Question', *Selections from Political Writing, 1921–1926*, trans. Quintin Hoare (New York: International Publishers, 1978).

12.   See summary carried in the *Daily Gleaner*, July 25, 2002, A2.

13.   *Economic and Social Survey: Jamaica 2001*, section on Education and Training (chapter 22).

14.   Kay Deaux and Brenda Major, 'A Social-psychological Model of Gender', in *The Gendered Society Reader*, ed. Michael Kimmel (New York and Oxford: Oxford University Press, 2000), 85.

15.   Elsa Leo-Rhynie, 'Gender Issues in Education and Implications for Labour Force Participation', in *Women and the Sexual Division of Labour in the Caribbean*, ed. Keith Hart (Mona: Institute for Social and Economic Research, 1989), 81–87.

16.   Joyce Cole, 'Official Ideology and the Education of Women in the English-speaking Caribbean, 1835–1945', in *Women and Education*, ed. Joycelyn Massiah (Kingston: Institute of Social and Economic Research, 1982), 2.

17.   L. Althusser, 'Ideology and Ideological State Apparatuses', in *Education Structure and Society*, ed. B.R. Cosin (Harmondsworth: Penguin, 1972) 1, quoted in Cole, 'Official Ideology', 2.

18. Parry, 'Sex and Gender', 77.

19. Figueroa, 'Making Sense of Male Experience', *YouWe*, no.8: 12.

20. At the same time, students get the distinct impression that writing history is mostly a male project.

21. William Claypole and John Robottom, *Caribbean Story Book 1* (New York: Longman, 1980), 107.

22. Michael Craton's and Barry Higman's works provide evidence of the existence of the black family. See Craton, 'Changing Patterns of Slave Families in the British West Indies'; and Higman, 'Household Structure and Fertility on Jamaican Slave Plantations: A Nineteenth Century Example', in *Caribbean Slave Society and Economy*, eds. Hilary Beckles and Verene Shepherd (Kingston: Ian Randle Publishers, 1991), 228–273.

23. J.M. Cohen ed., *The Four Voyages of Christopher Columbus* (London: Cresset Library, 1988), 139.

24. See Luis Martín, *Daughters of the Conquistadores: Women of the Viceroyalty of Peru* (Albuquerque: University of New Mexico Press, 1983).

25. Martín, *Daughters of the Conquistadores*, 2.

26. Hilary Beckles, *Black Masculinity in Caribbean Slavery* (St. Michael, Barbados: Women and Development Unit, 1996).

27. Kathleen Mary Butler, *The Economics of Emancipation: Jamaica and Barbados 1823–1843* (Chapel Hill: University of North Carolina Press, 1995).

28. Olwen Hufton, 'Women, Gender and the Fin de Siècle', in *Companion to Historiography*, ed. Michael Bentley (London and New York: Routledge, 1997), 940.

29. *Sunday Observer*, July 21, 2002, 2.

30. Oliver Clarke, Mona Academic Conference, September 2002.

31. See Richard Evans, *In Defence of History* (London: Grinta Books, 1997).

32. Ibid.

33. See Carr, *What is History* (Harmondsworth: Penguin Books, 1964).

From Redemption Song to Remembrance Walls

1. *Gleaner*, Saturday August 2, A1 and A3.

2. *Gleaner*, Saturday August 2, A1 and A3.

3. Laurence Brown, 'Monuments to Freedom, Monuments to Nation: The Politics of Emancipation and Remembrance in the Eastern Caribbean', *Slavery and Abolition* 23, no. 3 (December 2002): 94.

4. Ibid., 99.

5. www.ajc.com/opinion/content/opinion/o502/26slavery.html:21/11/03

6. This memorial opened to the public on April 29, 2004. It honours 16 million in the US armed forces in World War II and the more than 400,000 who died. See www.wwwiimemorial.com/

7. See, for example, Paul E. Lovejoy and Nicholas Rogers, eds., *Unfree Labour in the Development of the Atlantic World* (Essex: Frank Cass & Co, 1994); John Thornton, 'The Birth of an Atlantic World', in *Caribbean Slavery in the Atlantic World*, eds. Verene A. Shepherd and Hilary McD. Beckles (Kingston: Ian Randle Publishers, 2000), chap. 5; and Barbara Solow, ed., *Slavery and the Rise of the Atlantic System* (Cambridge: Cambridge University Press, 1991).

8. For a discussion of the development of an International Economy even before the nineteenth century, see William Ashworth, *A Short History of the International Economy Since 1850* (London: Longmans, 1987), chapter 7.

9. Barbara Solow, 'Slavery and Colonization', in *Slavery and the Rise of the Atlantic System*, ed. Solow, 21.

10. Franklin Knight, 'Slavery and Lagging Capitalism in the Spanish and Portuguese American Empires', in *Slavery and the Rise of the Atlantic System*, ed. Solow, 72.

11. Paul Gilroy, *The Black Atlantic: Modernity and Double Consciousness* (London: Verso, 1993).

12. Michael Kraus, *The North Atlantic Civilization* (Princeton, NJ: D. Van Nostrand Co Inc: 1957), 11.

13. For an elaboration of this theory see Charles W. Mills, *The Racial Contract* (Ithaca: Cornell University Press, 1997).

14. See Depestre's discussion in Kathleen Balutansky and Marie-Agnés Sourieau, eds., *Caribbean Creolization: Reflections on the Cultural Dynamics of Language, Literature and Identity* (Gainsville: University Press of Florida, 1998) as well as the editors' summary; and 'Les Aventures de la créolité', in Ralph Ludwig, ed., *Ecrire la parole le la nuit: La nouvelle littérature antillaise* (Paris: Gallimard, 1994).

15. Rex Nettleford pointed out in *Caribbean Cultural Identity, The Case of Jamaica: An Essay in Cultural Dynamics* (Kingston: Institute of Jamaica, 1978).

16. Hilary Beckles, 'The 200 Years War. Slave Resistance in the BWI: An Overview of the Historiography'. *Jamaican Historical Review* 13 (1982): 1–10.

17. Michael Craton, *Testing the Chains: Resistance to Slavery in the British West Indies* (Ithaca, NY: Cornell University Press, 1982).

18. John K. Thornton, 'African Soldiers in the Haitian Revolution', in *Caribbean Slavery in the Atlantic World*, eds. Verene A. Shepherd and Hilary Beckles (Kingston: Ian Randle Publishers, 2000), 933–45.

19. Craton, *Testing the Chains*.

20. Hilary Beckles, *Black Rebellion in Barbados: The Struggle Against Slavery, 1627–*

1838 (Bridgetown, Barbados: Antilles Publications, 1984).

21. Bernard Senior, *Jamaica As It Is, As It Was and As It May Be* (London: T Hurst, 1835).

22. Jamaica Archives, *Jamaica House of Assembly Votes*, March 2, 1832, 15.

23. See for instance, Craton, *Testing the Chains*; Mary Turner, *Slaves and Missionaries: The Disintegration of Jamaican Slave Society, 1787–1834* (Urbana: University of Illinois Press, 1982).

24. CO 137/185 Public Record Office, London.

25. B.W. Higman, *Slave Population and Economy in Jamaica, 1807–1834* (Kingston: The University of the West Indies Press, 1995), 12–13.

26. Turner, *Slaves and Missionaries,* 161.

27. Kamau Brathwaite, *Wars of Respect: Nanny, Sam Sharpe and the Struggle for People's Liberation,* (Kingston: Agency for Public Information for the National Heritage Week Committee, 1977), 28.

28. Craton, *Testing the Chains.*

29. See Hilary Beckles, *Bussa: the 1816 Revolution in Barbados* (Cave Hill, Barbados: Department of History, 1998).

30. Jenny Sharpe, *Ghosts of Slavery: A Literary Archaeology of Black Women's Lives* (Minneapolis: Minnesota Press, 2005).

31. Portcities, Bristol: 'Monuments to Commemorate Slavery', www.discoveringbristol. org.uk/showNarrative.php?narld=520&nacld=852

32. See interview with author on www.tonimorrisonsociety.org

Bibliography

Official Documents

Colonial Office Documents (CO)
CO 137/219
CO 137/185
CO 318/445/9
CO 318/474/2
CO 142/7, *Morning Journal*
CO 137/185
CO 137/32
CO 137/156

Colonial Secretary's Office (CSO)
CSO 1B/5/18/56
CSO 1B/5/75/59

Jamaica Archives, Passport Register. Central Government File (CGF)
CGF 1B/9/67
CGF 1B/9/28
CGF 1B/9/47
CGF 1B/9/111/5a
CGF 1B/9/104

India Office Records, (IOR)
Political (Pol.) 8189/47
IOR, L/P&J8/184/108/1D
IOR/L/P and J/8/184/108D
J/8/108/17, G.S., J/8/184//108/1D

Jamaica House of Assembly Votes (JHAV)
'Extension Treaty With Spain', Ms. 450; and 'Illicit Trade cl. 1740', Ms.
1,049 (National Library of Jamaica)
Vestry Minutes
Returns of the Registration of Slaves, 1817–1832

Island Record Office, Spanish Town, District Court Wills,
Population Census of Jamaica.
House of Commons. Report from the Select Committee on West Indian Colonies, 1842
Journal of Henry Blagrove, 1841–42, Jamaica Archives, Private Deposits, 4/4/1–2
Gt. Britain Parliamentary Papers. *Papers Relating to the West Indian Colonies and Mauritius*
Privy Council Minutes
'Copy of the Order-in-Council of the 15th August 1805, for
Prohibiting the Import of Slaves' (House of Lords, May 16, 1806)
The Labour Force, 1999' (Statistical Institute of Jamaica, 2000)
MS. 65, National Library of Jamaica

Audio Visual
'Britain's Slave Trade', Programme 3

Newspapers/periodicals
Jamaica Times
Jamaica Observer
Gleaner
Punch Magazine
Guardian
The Royal Gazette
The Presbyterian
The Young Indian
Jamaica Annual, Education Departmental Report (1930)
Delroy Chuck. 'Invest in Education'. *Daily Gleaner*, Wednesday, August 28, 2002, A4.
Jamaica Human Development Report, 2001. Kingston: Planning Institute of Jamaica, 2002.
Jamaican Historical Review
Jamaica Annual Report
CARICOM Report on the Status of Women
Economic and Social Survey: Jamaica 2001, section on Education and Training

Internet Sources

www.cnn.com
www.wwiimemorial.com
www.tonimorrisonsociety.org
www.thes.co.uk

www.elaw.org/resources/text

www.ipu.org/wnm-e/world.htm; http://www.ipu.org/wnm-e/classif.htm http://
hjem.get2net.dk/Womeningovernments/Jamaica.htm

www.ajc.com/opinion/content/opinion/o502/26slavery.html:21/11/03

www.discoveringbristol.org.uk/showNarrative.php?narId=520&nacId=852

Books, Book Chapters, Theses, Journal Articles and Unpublished Papers

Akenson, Donald. *If the Irish Ran the World: Montserrat, 1630–1730*. Montreal; Buffalo: McGill-Queen's University Press, 1997.

Althusser, L. 'Ideology and Ideological State Apparatuses'. In *Education Structure and Society*, ed. B.R. Cosin. Harmondsworth: Penguin, 1972.

Ankersmit, F.R. 'Historiography and Postmodern'. In *The Postmodern History Reader*, ed. Keith Jenkins. London: Routledge, 1997.

Antrobus, Peggy. 'New Institutions and Programmes for Caribbean Women'. In *Women of the Caribbean*, ed. Pat Ellis, 131–134. London: Zed Books, 1986.

Appleby, Joyce, Lynn Hunt and Margaret Jacob. 'Telling the Truth About History'. In *The Postmodern History Reader*, ed. Keith Jenkins. London: Routledge, 1997.

Armytage, Frances. *The Free-Port System in the British West Indies: A Study in Commercial Policy, 1766–1822*. London: Published for the Royal Empire Society by Longmans, Green, 1953.

Ashworth, William. *A Short History of the International Economy Since 1850*. London: Longmans, 1987.

Attwood, Thomas. *The History of Dominica*. London: J. Johnson, 1791.

Bailey, Barbara. 'The Feminization of Tertiary Education'. *You We*, no.8.

Bakan, Abigail. *Ideology and Class Conflict in Jamaica: The Politics of Rebellion*. Montreal: McGill-Queen's University Press, 1990.

Balutansky, Kathleen and Marie-Agnés Sourieau, eds. *Caribbean Creolization: Reflections on the Cultural Dynamics of Language, Literature and Identity*. Gainesville: University Press of Florida, 1998.

Beall, Jo. 'Women under Indenture in Colonial Natal'. In *Essays on Indentured Indians in Nata*, ed. Surendra Bhana. Leeds: Peepal Tree Press, 1991.

Beaumont, Joseph. *The New Slavery: An Account of the Indian and Chinese Immigrants in British Guiana*. London: W. Ridgeway, 1871.

Beckford, George. *Persistent Poverty: Underdevelopment in Plantation Economies of the Third World*. Kingston: The University of the West Indies Press, 1999.

Beckles, Hilary McD. 'Freedom Without Liberty: Free Blacks and Slavery in Barbados'. In

Slavery Without Sugar: Plantation Society in the Americas, ed. Verene Shepherd. Gainesville: University Press of Florida, 2000.

————. *Centering Woman: Gender Discourses in Caribbean Slave Society.* Kingston: Ian Randle Publishers, 1999.

————. 'Bussa: The 1816 Revolution in Barbados'. Cave Hill, Barbados: Department of History, 1998.

————. 'Black Masculinity in Caribbean Slavery'. Paper presented at the Symposium: 'The Construction of Masculinity: Towards a Research Agenda', Centre for Gender and Development, University of West Indies, St. Augustine, Trinidad and Tobago, January 1–13, 1996 (later published in St. Michael, Barbados: Women and Development Unit, 1996).

————. 'Divided to the Vein'. In *Caribbean Freedom*, eds. Hilary Beckles and Verene Shepherd. Kingston: Ian Randle Publishers, 1993.

————. *A History of Barbados: From Amerindian Settlement to Nation-state.* Cambridge; New York: Cambridge University Press, 1990.

————. *Natural Rebels: A Social History of Enslaved Black Women in Barbados.* New Brunswick: Rutgers University Press, 1989.

————. *White Servitude and Black Slavery in Barbados, 1627–1715.* Knoxville: University of Tennessee Press, 1989.

————. 'Caribbean Anti-Slavery: the Self-Liberation Ethos of Enslaved Blacks'. *Journal of Caribbean History* 22 (1988).

————. 'Kalinago (Carib) Resistance to European Colonization of the Caribbean', *Caribbean Quarterly* 21, no.1 (1987).

————. *Black Rebellion in Barbados: The Struggle Against Slavery, 1627–1838.* Bridgetown, Barbados: Antilles Publications, 1984

————. 'The 200 Years War. Slave Resistance in the BWI: An Overview of the Historiography'. *Jamaican Historical Review* 13 (1982): 1–10.

————. *White Power and Black Consciousness: Slave Resistance in the English West Indies During the Seventeenth Century.* Mona, Kingston: Department of History, University of the West Indies, 1981.

Beckles, Hilary, and Elsa V. Goveia. *Inside Slavery: Process and Legacy in the Caribbean Experience.* Kingston: Canoe Press, the University of the West Indies, 1996.

Beckles, Hilary McD, and Verene Shepherd, eds. *Caribbean Slavery in the Atlantic World.* Kinston: Ian Randle Publishers, 2000.

————. *Slave Voices: The Sounds of Freedom.* Paris: UNESCO, 1999.

————. *Caribbean Freedom: Economy and Society from Emancipation to the Present.* Kingston: Ian Randle Publishers, 1993.

Benda, Julien. *The Treason of the Intellectuals*, trans. Richard Aldington, 1928; reprint,

New York: Norton, 1969.

Benoit, Gaatan. *The Afro-Mauritian: An Essay.* Moka, Mauritius: Mahatma Gandhi Institute, 1985.

Best, Lloyd. 'Outlines of the Model of a Pure Plantation Economy'. *Social and Economic Studies* 17 (1968): 283–326.

Bhabha, Homi K. 'Cultural Diversity and Cultural Differences'. In *The Post-Colonial Studies Reader*, eds. Bill Ashcroft, Gareth Griffiths and Helen Tiffin. London; New York: Routledge, 1995.

Bogues, Anthony. 'The Logic of Freedom'. In *August 1st: A Celebration of Emancipation*, ed. Patrick Bryan, 11–22. Mona, Kingston: Department of History, University of the West Indies in association with Friedrich Ebert Stiftung, 1995.

Bolland, Nigel. 'Proto-Proletarians?: Slave Wages in the Americas'. In *From Chattel Slaves to Wage Slaves: The Dynamics of Labour Bargaining in the Americas*, ed. Mary Turner. Bloomington: Indiana University Press, 1995.

————. *On the March: Labour Rebellions in the British Caribbean, 1934–39.* Kingston: Ian Randle Publishers, 1995.

————. 'Slavery in Central America'. In *Unfree Labour in the Development of the Atlantic World*, eds. Paul E. Lovejoy and Nicholas Rogers, 11–23. London: Frank Cass, 1994.

Bolles, A. Lynn. *We Paid Our Dues: Women Trade Union Leaders of the Caribbean.* Washington, DC: Howard University Press, 1996.

Bousquet, Ben, and Colin Douglas. *West Indian Women at War: British Racism in World War II.* London: Lawrence & Wishart, 1991.

Brathwaite, Kamau. *The Development of Creole Society in Jamaica, 1770–1820.* Oxford: The Clarendon Press, 1971; reprint, Kingston: Ian Randle Publishers, 2005.

————. *Nanny, Sam Sharpe and the Struggle for People's Liberation.* Kingston: Agency for Public Information for the National Heritage Week Committee, 1977.

————. *Contradictory Omens: Cultural Diversity and Integration in the Caribbean.* Mona, Kingston: Savacou Publications, 1974.

Breen, Henry. *St Lucia: Historical, Statistical and Descriptive.* London: Longman, Brown, Green and Longmans, 1844.

Brereton, Bridget ed. *The Caribbean in the Twentieth Century.* Paris: UNESCO; Oxford: Macmillan Caribbean, 2004.

————. 'Text Testimony and Gender'. In *Engendering History: Caribbean Women in Historical Perspective*, eds. Verene A. Shepherd, Bridget Brereton and Barbara Bailey. Kingston: Ian Randle Publishers, 1995.

————. *Gendered Testimony: Autobiographies, Diaries and Letters by Women as Sources for Caribbean History.* Mona, Kingston: Department of History, University of the West

Indies, 1994.

Breton, R. *Relations de Isles de la Guadeloupe* (1647–1656), ed. J. Renard. Paris: G. Ficker, 1929.

Brown, Laurence. 'Monuments to Freedom, Monuments to Nation: The Politics of Emancipation and Remembrance in the Eastern Caribbean'. *Slavery and Abolition* 23, no. 3 (December 2002).

Bryan, Patrick. 'History in the Tropics'. Inaugural Professorial Lecture, 1999.

———. 'The Creolization of the Chinese Community in Jamaica'. In *Ethnic Minorities in Caribbean Society*, ed. Rhoda Reddock, 173–271. St. Augustine, Trinidad: Institute of Social and Economic Research, the University of the West Indies, 1996.

———. *The Jamaican People 1880–1902: Race, Class and Social Control.* London: Macmillan Caribbean, 1991.

———. *The Haitian Revolution and Its Effects.* Kingston: Heinemann Educational Books Ltd, 1984.

Burn, W.L. *Emancipation and Apprenticeship in the British West Indies.* London: Jonathan Cape, 1937.

Burton, Richard. *Afro-Creole: Power, Opposition and Play in the Caribbean.* Ithaca, NY: Cornell University Press, 1997.

Bush, Barbara. *Slave Women in Caribbean Society, 1650–1838.* Kingston: Heinemann, 1990.

Butler, Kathleen Mary. *The Economics of Emancipation: Jamaica and Barbados 1823–1843.* Chapel Hill: University of North Carolina Press, 1995.

Caldecott, Alfred. *The Church in the West Indies.* London: Frank Cass, 1970.

Campbell, Carl. *Endless Education: Main Currents in the Education System of Modern Trinidad and Tobago, 1939–1986.* Barbados: The University of the West Indies Press, 1997.

Campbell, John. 'The Emergence of the Thinker Activist: An Exploration into the Nature of Caribbean Intellectual History and the Literary Dimension of the Historical Philosophy of C.L.R. James'. MPhil thesis, University of the West Indies, St. Augustine, Trinidad and Tobago, 1997.

Carey, Beverley. *The Maroon Story: The Authentic and Original History of the Maroons in the History of Jamaica, 1490–1880.* Gordon Town, Jamaica: Agouti Press, 1997.

Carlyle, Thomas. *Occasional Discourse on the Nigger Question.* London: T. Bosworth, 1853.

Carmichael, A.C. *Domestic Manners and Social Condition of the White, Coloured, and Negro Population of the West Indies.* 1833; New York: Negro Universities Press, 1969.

Carnegie, J. *Some Aspects of Jamaica's Politics, 1918–1938.* Kingston: Institute of Jamaica Publications, 1973.

Carr, E.H. *What is History?* Harmondsworth, Middlesex: Penguin Books, 1987.

Carter, Marina. *Voices From Indenture: Experiences of Indian Migrants in the British Empire.* New York: Leicester University Press, 1996.

——————. *Servants, Sirdars, and Settlers: Indians in Mauritius, 1834–1874.* Delhi and New York: Oxford University Press, 1995.

Carter, Marina, and Khal Torabully. *Coolitude: An Anthology of the Indian Diaspora.* London: Anthem Press, 2002.

Castañeda, Digna. 'The Female Slave in Cuba in the First Half of the Nineteenth Century'. In *Engendering History: Caribbean Women in Historical Perspective*, eds. Verene Shepherd, Bridget Brereton and Barbara Bailey, 141–154. Kingston: Ian Randle Publishers, 1995.

Cateau, Heather. 'Management and the Sugar Industry in the British West Indies, 1750–1810'. PhD dissertation, University of the West Indies, St. Augustine, Trinidad and Tobago, 1995.

Chambers, Douglas. 'Tracing Igbo into the Diaspora'. In *Identity in the Shadow of Slavery*, ed. Paul Lovejoy, 55–71. London & New York: Continuum, 2000.

Chatterjee, Partha. 'Nationalism as a Problem'. In *The Post-Colonial Studies Reader*, eds. Bill Ashcroft, Gareth Griffiths and Helen Tiffin. London; New York: Routledge, 1995.

Chatterjee, Sumita. 'Indian Women's Lives and Labor: The Indentured Experience in Trinidad and Guyana, 1845–1917'. PhD dissertation, University of Massachusetts, 1997.

Chevannes, Barry. 'Those Two Jamaica's: The Problem of Social Integration'. In *Contending with Destiny: The Caribbean in the 21st Century*, eds. Kenneth Hall and Denis Benn, 179–203. Kingston: Ian Randle Publishers, 2000.

Chinweizu, Professor. 'Reparations and A New Global Order: A Comparative Overview'. A paper read at the second Plenary Session of the First Pan-African Conference on Reparations, Abuja, Nigeria, April 27, 1993.

Clarke, Oliver. 'From Redemption Song to War Memorials'. Mona Academic Conference, University of the West Indies, September 2002.

Clausner, M.D. *Rural Santo Domingo: Settled, Unsettled and Resettled.* Philadelphia: Temple University Press, 1973.

Claypole, W.A. and D.J. Buisserret, 'Trade Patterns in Early English Jamaica'. *Journal of Caribbean History* 15 (1972): 1–19.

Claypole, William, and John Robottom. *Caribbean Story Book 1.* New York: Longman, 1980.

Cohen, J.M. ed. *The Four Voyages of Christopher Columbus.* London: Cresset Library, 1988.

Cohen, Robin. *Global Diasporas: An Introduction.* Seattle: University of Washington Press, 1997.

Cole, Joyce. 'Official Ideology and the Education of Women in the English-speaking

Caribbean, 1835–1945'. In *Women and Education*, ed. Joycelyn Massiah. Mona, Kingston: Institute of Social and Economic Research, the University of the West Indies, 1982.

Columbus, Christopher. *The Voyage of Christopher Columbus: Columbus's Own Journal of Discovery*, trans. John Cummins. New York: St Martins's Press, 1992.

Cordell, J. Robinson, *Providencia Island: Its History and its People*. California, MCMXCVI

Craton, Michael. 'Continuity not Change: The Incidence of Unrest Among Ex-slaves in the BWI, 1838–1876'. In *Caribbean Freedom: Economy and Society from Emancipation to the Present*, ed. Hilary Beckles and Verene Shepherd, 192–206. Kingston: Ian Randle Publishers, 1993.

———. 'Changing Patters of Slave Families in the British West Indies'. In *Caribbean Slave Society and Economy*, eds. Beckles and Shepherd, 228–249. Kingston: Ian Randle Publishers, 1991 (reprinted from *Journal of Interdisciplinary History* X, 1979).

———. *Testing the Chains Resistance to Slavery in the British West Indies*. Ithaca: Cornell University Press, 1982.

———. 'Hobbesian or Panglossian?: The Two Extremes of Slave Conditions in the British Caribbean, 1783–1834', *William and Mary Quarterly* 25 (April 1978): 324–356.

Curtin, Philip. *The Rise and Fall of the Plantation Complex*. Cambridge: Cambridge University Press, 1990.

———. *The Atlantic Slave Trade: A Census*. Madison: The University of Wisconsin Press, 1969.

Dadzie, Stella. 'Searching for the Invisible Woman: Slavery and Resistance in Jamaica'. *Race and Class* 32, no. 2 (1990).

Davenport, Frances G., ed. *European Treatises Bearing on the History of the United States and its Dependencies*, 4 vols. Washington DC: Carnegie Institution of Washington, 1917–37, II, 1929, 1650–1697.

Davis, Ellen. *Friends in Jamaica*. Richmond: American Friends Board of Missions, 1943.

de Bourg, Claire 'Haitian Women at the Backbone of the Informal Economy'. Conference on Reinterpreting the Haitian Revolution and its Cultural Aftershocks, 1804–2004, University of the West Indies, St. Augustine, Trinidad, June 15–18, 2004.

Deaux, Kay, and Brenda Major, 'A Social-psychological Model of Gender'. In *The Gendered Society Reader*, ed. Michael Kimmel. New York; Oxford: Oxford University Press, 2000.

Depestre, Renee. 'Les Aventures de la créolité'. In *Ecrire la parole le la nuit: La nouvelle littérature antillaise*, ed. Ralph Ludwig. Paris: Gallimard, 1994.

du Tertre, Jean Baptiste. *Histoire Général des Antilles Habitées par les Francais 1667–1971*. Forte de France: Edition des Horizons Caraibes, 1973.

Duncker, Sheila. 'The Free Coloureds and their Fight for Civil Rights in Jamaica, 1800–1830'. MA thesis, London, 1960.

Dunn, Richard. *Sugar and Slaves: The Rise of the Planter-Class in the English West Indies, 1624–1713.* Chapel Hill: The University of North Carolina Press, 1972.

Edwards, Bryan. *The History, Civil and Commercial, of the British Colonies in the West Indies.* London: printed for John Stockdale, 1793–1801.

Eisner, Gisela. *Jamaica 1830–1930: A Study in Economic Growth.* Westport, CT: Greenwood Press, 1961.

Eltis, David. *The Rise of African Slavery in the Americas.* Cambridge: Cambridge University Press, 2000.

————. 'The Volume and Structure of the Slave Trade'. Paper presented at the Conference Enslaving Connections, York University, Toronto, October 2000.

———— et al., eds. *The Trans-Atlantic Slave Trade: a Database on CD-Rom.* Cambridge: Cambridge University Press, 1999.

Emmer, Pieter. 'The Dutch and the Second Atlantic System'. In *Slavery and the Rise of the Atlantic System,* ed. Barbara Solow, 75–96. Cambridge: Cambridge University Press, 1991.

————, ed. *Colonialism and Migration: Indentured Labour Before and After Slavery* Dordrecht: M. Nijhoff, 1986.

————. 'The Great Escape: the Migration of Female Indentured Servants from British India to Suriname'. In *Abolition and Its Aftermath,* ed. D. Richardson. London: Frank Cass, 1985.

Evans, Hyacinth. *Gender and Achievement in Secondary Education in Jamaica.* Kingston: Planning Institute of Jamaica, March 1999.

Evans, Richard. *In Defence of History.* London: Granta Books, 1997.

Fenwick, A.F., ed. *The Fate of the Fenwicks: Letters to Mary Hays, 1798–1828.* London: Meuthuen, 1927.

Figueroa, Mark. 'Making Sense of Male Experience'. *YouWe,* no. 8.

Fischer, Sibylle. *Modernity Disavowed.* Mona, Kingston: The University of the West Indies Press, 2004.

Fog-Olwig, Karen. 'The Migration Experience: Nevisian Women at Home and Abroad'. In *Women and Change in the Caribbean: a Pan Caribbean Perspective,* ed. J. Momsen. Kingston: Ian Randle Publishers, 1993.

Foucault, Michel. 'The Subject and Power'. *Critical Inquiry* 8 (1982): 777–95.

————. *History of Sexuality.* New York: Pantheon Books, 1978.

————. *The Archaeology of Knowledge.* London: Tavistock Publications, 1972.

Freyre, Giberto. *The Masters and the Slaves: A Study in the Development of Brazilian Civilization.* 1933; New York: A.A. Knopf, 1946.

Froude, James Anthony. *The English in the West Indies; or The Bow of Ulysses.* 1888; New York: Negro Universities Press, 1969.

Galenson, David, ed. *Markets in History: Economic Studies of the Past.* Cambridge: Cambridge University Press, 1989.

———. 'The Rise and Fall of Indentured Servitude; An Economic Analysis'. *Journal of Economic History* 44, no.1 (1984): 1–26.

Gardner, W.J. *The History of Jamaica, 1655-1872.* London: Appleton, 1909.

———. *A History of Jamaica from Its Discovery by Christopher Columbus to the Present Time.* London: Elliot Stock, 1873.

Garvey, Amy Jacques, ed. *Philosophy and Opinions of Marcus Garvey.* New York: Arno Press 1969.

Gaspar, Barry, and Darlene Clark Hine, eds. *More Than Chattel: Black Women and Slavery in the Americas.* Bloomington: Indiana University Press, 1996

———. *Bondmen and Rebels: A Study of Master–Slave Relations in Antigua, with Implications for Colonial British America.* Baltimore: The John Hopkins University Press, 1985.

Gaunt, Mary. *Harmony.* London, 1933.

Gautier, A. 'Les esclaves femes aux Antilles françaises 1635–1848'. *Reflexions Historiques* (1983): 409–33.

Gee, Joshua. *The Trade and Navigation of Great-Britain Considered.* London: Sam Buckley, 1729.

Geggus, David. 'The Haitian Revolution'. In *Caribbean Slave Society,* eds. Beckles and Shepherd. New York: The New Press, 1993.

Gifford, Anthony (Lord). 'Legal basis of the claim for slavery reparations'. *Human Rights* 27, no.2 (Spring 2000).

Gilroy, Paul. *The Black Atlantic: Modernity and Double Consciousness.* London: Verso, 1993.

Goviea, Elsa. *Slave Society in the British Leeward Islands at the End of the Eighteenth Century.* New Haven: Yale University Press, 1965.

———. *A Study on the Historiography of the British West Indies to the End of the Nineteenth Century.* Mexico: Instituto Pan Americano de Geographia e Historia, 1956.

Gramsci Antonio. 'Some Aspects of the Southern Question'. In *Selections from Political Writing, 1921–1926,* trans. Quintin Hoare. New York: International Publishers, 1978.

———. *Selections from the Prison Notebooks,* trans. Quintin Hoare and Geoffrey Nowell-Smith. New York: International Publishers, 1971.

Green, William. 'The Creolization of Caribbean History'. In *Caribbean Freedom: Economy and Society from Emancipation to the Present,* ed. Beckles and Shepherd, 28–40. Kingston: Ian Randle Publishers, 1993.

———. *British Slave Emancipation.* Oxford, England: Clarendon Press, 1976.

Greenblatt, Stephen, ed. *New World Encounters*. Berkeley: University of California Press, 1993, 1993.

Gregg, Veronica. "'Yuh Know Bout Coo-Coo? Where Yuh Know Bout Coo-Coo?": Language and Representation, Creolization and Confusion in Indian Cuisine'. In *Questioning Creole: Creolisation Discourses in Caribbean Culture*, eds. Verene Shepherd and Glen Richards, 148–164. Kingston: Ian Randle Publishers, 2002.

———. *Jean Rhys' Historical Imagination: Reading and Writing the Creole*. Chapel Hill: University of North Carolina Press, 1995.

———. 'The Caribbean (as a certain kind of) Woman'. Paper presented at the Symposium on Engendering History, University of the West Indies, Mona, 1993.

Guha, Ranajit. *Elementary Aspects of Peasant Insurgency in Colonial India* (Delhi: Oxford, 1983), quoted in Partha Chatterjee, 'The Nation and its Peasants'. In *Mapping Subaltern Studies and the Post-Colonial*, ed. V. Chaturvedi. London: Routledge, 2000.

Hall, Douglas. 'The Flight from the Estates Reconsidered'. In *Caribbean Freedom: Economy and Society from Emancipation to the Present*, ed. Beckles and Shepherd. Kingston: Ian Randle Publishers, 1993.

———. *In Miserable Slavery: Thomas Thistlewood in Jamaica, 1750–1786*. London: Macmillan, 1989.

Hall, Kenneth, and Denis Benn, eds. *Contending with Destiny: The Caribbean in the 21st Century*. Kingston: Ian Randle Publishers, 2000.

Hall, N.A.T. (B.W. Higman, ed), *Slave Society in the Danish West Indies*. Mona, Kingston: Department of History, University of the West Indies, 1992.

Hall, Stuart. *Representation: Cultural Representations and Signifying Practices*. London; Thousand Oaks, CA: Sage in association with the Open University, 1997

———. 'The Question of National Identity'. In *Modernity and its Futures*, eds. Stuart Hall, David Held and Tony McGrew. Cambridge: Polity Press in association with the Open University, 1992.

———. 'The Local and the Global: Globalization and Ethnicity'. In *Culture, Globalization and the World System*, ed. Anthony King. Binghamton: Department of Art and Art History, State University of New York at Binghamton, 1991.

Haraksingh, Kusha. 'Control and Resistance Among Overseas Indian Workers: A Study of Labour on the Sugar Plantations of Trinidad, 1875–1917'. In *Caribbean Freedom: Economy and Society from Emancipation to the Present*, ed. Beckles and Shepherd, 207–214. Kingston: Ian Randle Publishers, 1993.

———. 'Structure, Process and Indian Culture in Trinidad'. *Immigrants and Minorities* 7, no.1 (1988).

Harpelle, Ronald N. *The West Indians of Costa Rica: Race, Class, and the Integration of an*

Ethnic Minority. Montreal, Ithaca: McGill-Queen's University Press; Kingston: Ian Randle Publishers, 2001.

Harper, Lawrence A. *The English Navigation Laws: A Seventeenth-Century Experiment in Social Engineering.* New York: Columbia University Press, 1939.

Harriott, Anthony. *Police and Crime Control in Jamaica: Problems of Reforming Ex-Colonial Constabularies.* Mona, Kingston: The University of the West Indies Press, 2000.

Hart, Richard. *Rise and Organize: The Birth of the Workers' and National Movements in Jamaica, 1936–1939.* London: Karia Press, 1989.

————. *Slaves Who Abolished Slavery Vol 2: Blacks in Rebellion.* Mona, Kingston: Institute of Social and Economic Research, University of the West Indies, 1985.

Hearn, L. *Two Years in the French West Indies.* New York: Harper & Brothers, 1890; New York: Interlink Books, 2001.

Henige, David. 'On the Contact Population of Hispaniola: History as Higher Mathematics'. In *Caribbean Slave Society and Economy,* eds. Beckles and Shepherd, 2–12. Ian Randle Publishers, 1991 (reprinted from *HAHR*, 1978).

Heuman, Gad. 'Post-emancipation Resistance in the Caribbean: An Overview'. In *Small Islands, Large Questions: Society, Culture and Resistance in the Post-emancipation Caribbean,* ed. Karen Fog Olwig, 123–134. London: Frank Cass, 1995.

————. The *"The Killing Time": The Morant Bay Rebellion in Jamaica.* London: Macmillan, 1994.

Higman, Barry. *Writing West Indian Histories.* London: Macmillan Education, 1999.

————. 'Household Structure and Fertility on Jamaican Slave Plantations: A Nineteenth Century Example'. In *Caribbean Slave Society and Economy,* eds. Beckles and Shepherd, 228–273. Kingston: Ian Randle Publishers, 1991.

————. 'The Internal Economy of Jamaican Pens'. *Social and Economic Studies* 38, no.1 (1989): 61–86.

————. *Slave Populations of the British Caribbean, 1807–1832.* Baltimore: The Johns Hopkins University Press, 1984.

————. *Domestic Service in Jamaica, England and the United States, 1770–1970.* Mona, Kingston: Department of History, University of the West Indies, 1978.

————. *Slave Population and Economy in Jamaica, 1807–1834.* Cambridge: Cambridge University Press, 1976

Hinds, Allister. 'The Political Economy of Decolonisation in the British Empire, 1939–1958'. Paper presented at the symposium to mark the 50th Anniversary of the Montego Bay Conference on West Indian Federation, University of the West Indies, Mona, November 6, 1997.

Hintzen, Percy C. 'Race and Creole Ethnicity in the Caribbean'. In *Questioning Creole: Creolisation Discourses in Caribbean Culture,* eds. Shepherd and Richards. Kingston: Ian Randle Publishers, 2002.

Hoefte, Rosemarijn. *In Place Of Slavery: A Social History Of British Indian And Javanese Laborers in Suriname*. Gainesville: University Press of Florida, 1998.

Holt, Thomas. *The Problem of Freedom: Race, Labor, and Politics in Jamaica and Britain, 1832–1938*. Baltimore: The Johns Hopkins University Press, 1992.

Horowitz, David. 'Ten Reasons Why Reparations for Blacks is a Bad Idea for Blacks – and Racist Too'. FrontPageMagazine.com. January 3, 2001.

Hufton, Olwen. 'Women, Gender and the Fin de Siècle'. In *Companion to Historiography*, ed. Michael Bentley. London and New York: Routledge, 1997.

Hutton, Clinton. *The Logic and Historical Significance of the Haitian Revolution: The Cosmological Roots of Haitian Freedom*. Kingston: Arawak Publications, 2005.

—. 'The Defeat of the Morant Bay Rebellion'. *The Jamaican Historical Review*, Vol. XIX (1996): 30–38.

—. '"Colour for Colour, Skin for Skin": The Ideological Foundations of Post-Slavery Society, 1838–1865'. PhD dissertation, Department of Government, University of the West Indies, 1992.

Hyam, Ronald. *Empire and Sexuality: The British Experience*. Manchester: Manchester University Press, 1992.

Inikori, Joseph, and Stanley L. Engerman, eds. *The Atlantic Slave Trade: Effects on Economies, Societies, and Peoples in Africa, the Americas, and Europe*. Durham: Duke University Press, 1992.

James, C.L.R. *The Black Jacobins; Toussaint L'Ouverture and the San Domingo Revolution*. New York: Vintage Books, 1963.

Jenkins, Edward. *Lutchmee and Dilloo, A Study of West Indian Life*. 1877; Oxford: Macmillan Caribbean, 2003.

John, Meredith. *The Plantation Slaves of Trinidad, 1783–1816: A Mathematical and Demographic Enquiry*. Cambridge: Cambridge University Press, 1989.

Johnson, Howard. 'The Anti-Chinese Riots of 1918 in Jamaica'. *Immigrants and Minorities* 11, no.1 (March 1983).

Johnson, Michelle, ed. *Social and Economic Studies*. Special edition of papers presented at the symposium to mark the 50th Anniversary of the Montego Bay Conference on West Indian Federation, University of the West Indies, Mona, November 6, 1997.

—. 'Domestic Service in Jamaica, 1920–1970'. Presented at a Symposium on Caribbean Economic History, Mona, Jamaica, 1986.

Kale, Madhavi. *Fragments of Empire: Capital, Slavery, and Indian Indentured Labour Migration in the British Caribbean*. Philadelphia: University of Pennsylvania Press, 1998.

Kincaid, Jamaica. *A Small Place*. New York: Plume, 1989.

Kiple, Kenneth, and Virginia Kiple. 'Deficiency Diseases in the Caribbean'. In *Caribbean Slave Society and Economy*, eds. Beckles and Shepherd, 173–182. Kingston: Ian

Randle Publishers, 1991.

Knight, Franklin. 'Slavery and Lagging Capitalism in the Spanish and Portuguese American Empires'. In *Slavery and the Rise of the Atlantic System*, ed. Solow. Cambridge: Cambridge University Press, 1991.

Kraus, Michael. *The North Atlantic Civilization*. Princeton, NJ: D. Van Nostrand Co Inc, 1957.

Lal, Brij, ed. *Bittersweet, An Indo-Fijian Experience*. Canberra: Pandanus Books, 2004.

Laurence, K.O. *A Question of Labour: Indentured Immigration into Trinidad and British Guiana, 1875–1917*. New York: St. Martin's Press, 1994.

———. *Immigration into the West Indies in the 19th Century*. Barbados: Caribbean Universities Press, 1974.

Leo-Rhynie, Elsa. 'Gender Issues in Education and Implications for Labour Force Participation'. In *Women and the Sexual Division of Labour in the Caribbean*, ed. Keith Hart, 81–87. Mona, Kingston: Institute for Social and Economic Research, the University of the West Indies, 1989.

Leslie, Charles. *A New and Exact History of Jamaica*. London: Printed for J. Hodges, 1739, 1740.

Lewis, M.G. *Journal of a West India Proprietor, 1815–17*. London: G. Routledge & Sons, Ltd, 1929.

Lewis, Rupert. 'Emancipate Yourself from Mental Slavery: Letter to Mr. Garvey'. Churches' Emancipation Lecture, Kingston, 2000.

Ligon, Richard. *A True and Exact History of the Island of Barbados 1647–1650*. 1657; reprint, London: Frank Cass & Co, Ltd, 1970.

Lipscomb, Patrick. 'William Pitt and the Abolition of the Slave Trade'. PhD dissertation, University of Texas 1960.

Livingston, N.B. *Sketch Pedigrees of Some of the Early Settlers in Jamaica*. 1607; Kingston: The Educational Supply Company, 1909.

Long, Edward. *The History of Jamaica; or, General Survey of the Ancient and Modern State of that Island: With Reflections on its Situations, Settlements, Inhabitants, Climate, Products, Commerce, Laws, and Government*. London: T. Lowndes, 1774. Reprint, Kingston: Ian Randle Publishers, 2003.

Look Lai, Walton. *The Chinese in the West Indies 1806–1995: A Documentary History*. Mona, Kingston: The University of the West Indies Press, 1998.

Lopez, A., and J. Petras, eds. *Puerto Rico and Puerto Ricans: Studies in History and Society*. New York: Halsted Press, 1974.

Lovejoy, Paul. 'Identifying Enslaved Africans in the African Diaspora'. In *Identity in the Shadow of Slavery*, ed. Lovejoy. London & New York: Continuum, 2000.

Lovejoy, Paul, and Nicholas Rogers, eds. *Unfree Labour in the Development of the Atlantic*

World. Essex: Frank Cass & Co, 1994.

Lucas, Charles. *A Historical Geography of the British Colonies.* 1888; Oxford: Clarendon Press, 1902.

Mahabir, Noor Kumar. *The Still Cry: Personal Accounts Of East Indians In Trinidad And Tobago During Indentureship, 1845–1917.* Tacarigua, Trinidad and Ithaca, NY: Calaloux Publications, 1985.

Mandle, J.R. *The Plantation Economy: Population and Economic Growth in Guyana, 1838–1960.* Philadelphia: Temple University Press, 1973.

Mansingh, L. 'Cultural Heritage among the East Indians of Jamaica'. Unpublished paper, September 1979.

Marshall, Paule. *Brown Girl, Brownstones.* Old Westbury: Feminist Press, 1959.

Marshall, Woodville. 'We Be Wise To Many More Tings'. In *Caribbean Freedom: Economy and Society from Emancipation to the Present,* ed. Beckles and Shepherd, 12–20. Kingston: Ian Randle Publishers, 1993.

——————. 'Provision Ground and Plantation Labour in Four Windward Islands: Competition for Resources During Slavery'. *Slavery and Abolition* no.1 (1991).

Martín, Luis. *Daughters of the Conquistadores: Women of the Viceroyalty of Peru.* Albuquerque: University of New Mexico Press, 1983.

Marx, Karl. *Grundrisse: Foundations of the Critique of Political Economy.* Baltimore: Penguin Books, 1973.

Mathurin Mair, Lucille. *The Rebel Woman in the British West Indies During Slavery.* Kingston: Institute of Jamaica for African Caribbean Institute of Jamaica, 1975.

——————. 'Historical Study of Women in Jamaica, 1807–1834'. PhD dissertation, University of the West Indies, Mona, 1974.

McGlynn, Frank, and Seymour Drescher, eds., 'Introduction'. In *The Meaning of Freedom: Economics, Politics & Culture after Slavery.* Pittsburgh: University of Pittsburgh Press, 1992.

Meisel, Adolfo. 'The Continentalization of San Andrés Island, Colombia'. Thirty-Fifth Conference of the Association of Caribbean Historians, Puerto Rico, April 2003.

Midgley, Clare. *Women Against Slavery; The British Campaigns, 1780–1870.* London; New York: Routledge, 1992.

Mills, Charles W. *The Racial Contract.* Ithaca: Cornell University Press, 1997.

Mintz, Sidney, and Douglas Hall. 'The Origins of the Jamaican Internal Markey System'. In *Caribbean Slave Society and Economy,* eds. Beckles and Shepherd, 319–334. Kingston: Ian Randle Publishers, 1991.

Mohammed, Patricia. 'The Creolisation of Indian Women in Trinidad'. In *Questioning Creole: Creolisation Discourses in Caribbean Culture,* eds. Shepherd and Richards. Kingston: Ian Randle Publishers, 2002.

Moitt, Bernard. 'Women, Work and Resistance in the French Caribbean During Slavery'. In *Engendering History: Caribbean Women in Historical Perspective*, eds. Verene Shepherd, Bridget Brereton and Barbara Bailey, 155–74. Kingston: Ian Randle Publishers, 1995.

Monteith, Kathleen. 'The Coffee Industry in Jamaica, 1790–1850'. MPhil thesis, University of the West Indies, Mona, Jamaica, 1992.

Montrose, Louis. 'The Work of Gender in the Discourse of Discovery'. In *New World Encounters*, ed. Stephen Greenblatt, 178–79. Berkeley: University of California Press, 1993.

Moore, Brian. *Cultural Power, Resistance, and Pluralism: Colonial Guyana, 1838–1900*. Mona, Kingston: The University of the West Indies Press, 1995.

Moreton, J.B. *Manners and Customs in the West India Islands*. London: W. Richardson, 1790.

Morrissey, Marietta. *Slave Women in the New World: Gender Stratification in the Caribbean*. Lawrence, Kan: University Press of Kansas, 1989.

Nabudere, Dani. 'Development Theories, Knowledge Production and Emancipatory Practices'. 50th Anniversary Conference Reviewing the First Decade of Development and Democracy, South Africa, Durban, October 2004.

Narcisse, Carol. 'Social Integration and Disintegration: The Caribbean Experience: Jamaica'. In *Contending with Destiny: The Caribbean in the 21st Century*, eds. Kenneth Hall and Denis Benn, 204–234. Kingston: Ian Randle Publishers, 2000.

Nettleford, Rex. *Caribbean Cultural Identity: The Case of Jamaica: An Essay in Cultural Dynamics*. Kingston: Ian Randle Publishers; Princeton, NJ: Marcus Wiener, 2003.

Newton, A.P. *The European Nations in the West Indies, 1493–1688*. London: A. & C. Black Ltd, 1933.

Northrup, David. *Indentured Labor in the Age of Imperialism, 1834–1922*. Cambridge and New York: Cambridge University Press, 1995.

Nugent, Maria. *Lady Nugent's Journal of her Residence in Jamaica from 1801 to 1805*. London: West India Committee for the Institute of Jamaica, 1939.

Oldendorp, C.G.A. *History of the Mission of the Evangelical Brethren on the Caribbean Islands of St Thomas, St Croix and St John*. Ann Arbor: Karoma Publishers, 1987.

Palmer, Colin. 'Identity, Race and Black Power in Independent Jamaica'. In *The Modern Caribbean*, eds. Franklin Knight and Colin Palmer. Chapel Hill: The University of North Carolina Press, 1989.

Paquet, Sandra Pouchet. *Caribbean Autobiography: Cultural Identity and Self-Representation*. Madison: University of Wisconsin Press, 2002.

Parry, Odette. 'Sex and Gender Constructions in the Jamaican Classroom'. *Social and Economic Studies* 45, no.4 (December 1996).

Parsons, James J. *San Andrés and Providencia: English-Speaking Islands in the Western*

Caribbean. Berkeley: University of California Press, 1956.

Paton, Diana. Conference paper, 11th Berkshire Women's History Conference, Rochester, June 1999.

Patterson, Orlando. *Slavery and Social Death: A Comparative Study*. Cambridge: Harvard University Press, 1982.

————. *The Sociology of Slavery: An Analysis of the Origins, Development and Structure of Negro Slave Society in Jamaica*. London: MacGibbon & Kee, 1967.

Peacock, H.L. *A History of Modern Europe 1789–1981*. Oxford: Heinemann Educational Publishers, 1982.

Pemberton, Rita. 'The Evolution of Agricultural Policy in Trinidad and Tobago 1890–1945'. PhD dissertation, the University of the West Indies, St. Augustine, Trinidad and Tobago, 1996.

Perkins, Cyrus Frances. *Busha's Mistress, or, Catherine the Fugitive: A Stirring Romance of the Days of Slavery in Jamaica*. Edited and introduced by Paul E. Lovejoy, Verene A. Shepherd and David V. Trotman. Kingston: Ian Randle Publishers; Princeton, NJ: Markus Wiener Publisher, 2003.

Pitman, Frank W. 'Slavery on British West India Plantation in the Eighteenth Century'. *Journal of Negro History* 11, no.4 (1926).

————. *The Development of the British West Indies, 1700–1763*. New Haven: Yale University Press, 1917.

Pool, Gail, and Hira Singh. 'Indentured Indian Women of the Empire: Between Colonial Oppression and the Brahmanical Tradition'. *Plantation Society in the Americas* 6, no.1 (Spring 1999): 1–46.

Postlethwayt, Malachy. *The African Trade the Great Pillar and Support of the British Plantation Trade in America*, 1745.

Post, Ken. *Arise Ye Starvelings*. The Hague: Nijhoff, 1938.

Poynting, Jeremy. 'East Indian Women in the Caribbean'. In *India in the Caribbean*, eds. David Dabydeen and Brinsley Samaroo. London: Hansib/University of Warwick, 1987.

————. 'East Indian Women in the Caribbean: Experience and Voice'. In *India in the Caribbean*, eds. David Dabydeen and Brinsley Samaroo. London: Hansib/University of Warwick, 1987.

Ragatz, Lowell J. *The Fall of the Planter Class in the British Caribbean, 1763–1833*. New York: American Historical Association, 1928.

Ragozinski, Jan. *A Brief History of the Caribbean: From the Arawak and the Carib to the Present*. New York: Facts on File, 1992.

Raynal, Guillaume. *A Philosophical and Political History of the Settlements and Trade of the Europeans in the East and West Indies*. 1700; London: A. Strahan, 1798.

Reddock, Rhoda. 'The Indentureship Experience: Indian Women in Trinidad and Tobago'.

In *Women Plantation Workers: International Experiences*, eds. Shobita Jain and Rhoda Reddock. Oxford: Berg Publishers, 1998.

Richards, Glen. 'The Pursuit of "Higher Wages" and "Perfect Personal Freedom": St Kitts-Nevis, 1836–1956'. In *From Chattel Slaves to Wage Slaves: The Dynamics of Labour Bargaining in the Americas*, ed. Mary Turner, 275–301. Bloomington: Indiana University Press, 1995.

————. 'Masters and Servants: The Growth of the Labour Movement in St. Christopher-Nevis, 1896 to 1956.' PhD dissertation, University of Cambridge, 1989.

Robotham, Don. *The Notorious Riot: The Socio-economic and Political Bases of Paul Bogle's Revolt*. Mona, Kingston: Institute of Social and Economic Research, University of West Indies, 1981.

Rodney, Walter. *A History of the Guyanese Working People.* Baltimore: The Johns Hopkins University Press, 1983

————. *How Europe Underdeveloped Africa*. London: Bogle-L'Ouverture Publications, 1972.

Rodrígues, Félix Matos, and Linda C. Delgado, eds. *Puerto Rican Women's History: New Perspectives*. Armonk, NY: M.E. Sharpe, 1998.

Romano, Ruggiero. 'The Initial Linkage with America: A General Framework'. In *UNESCO General History of the Caribbean*, Vol. II *New Societies: The Caribbean in the Long Sixteenth Century*, ed. Pieter C. Emmer. Paris: UNESCO, 1999.

Ross, Jim. '"San Andres: An Islander Comeback'. In *English-Speaking Communities in Latin America,* ed. Oliver Marshall, chapter 14. New York: St. Martin's Press, 2000.

Rushdy, Ashraf H.A. *Neo-Slave Narratives: Studies in the Social Logic of a Literary Form.* Oxford: Oxford University Press, 1999.

Said, Edward. *Representations of the Intellectual: The 1993 Reith Lectures.* New York: Vintage Books, 1996.

————. *Orientalism*. London: Penguin, 1992.

Samaroo, Brinsley. 'Politics and Afro-Indian Relations in Trinidad'. In *Calcutta to Caroni: The East Indians of Trinidad*, ed. J. LaGuerre. Trinidad; Jamaica, 1974.

Sankatsing, Glenn. 'The Caribbean: Archipelago of Trailer Societies'. Seed paper of the inaugural Allan Harris Conference, Institute of Social and Economic Research, the University of the West Indies, St. Augustine, November 1998.

Satchell, Veront. *From Plots to Plantations*. Mona, Kingston: Institute of Social and Economic Research, the University of the West Indies, 1990.

————. *The Jamaican Peasantry 1866–1900: Relationship Between Economic Growth and the Peasant Sector and Governmental Policies*. Mona, Kingston: Department of History, University of the West Indies, 1983.

Saunders, Gail. *Slavery in The Bahamas, 1648–1838*. 1985; Nassau: D.G. Saunders, 1995.

Scarano, Fransico. *Sugar and Slavery In Puerto Rico: The Plantation Economy of Ponce, 1800–1850*. Madison: University of Wisconsin Press, 1984.

Schuler, Monica. 'Ethnic Slave Rebellions in the Caribbean and the Guianas'. *Journal of Social History* 3, (1970).

Scott, Joan. *Gender and the Politics of History*. New York: Columbia University Press, 1988.

Seacole, Mary. *Wonderful Adventures of Mrs. Seacole in Many Lands* (1857; with an introduction by William L. Andrews). New York: Oxford University Press, 1988.

Seaman, Helen. 'Territory and Nationhood: Colonial Dispossessions and the Resurgent Identify of the Native (Carib) Caribbean'. PhD dissertation, the University of the West Indies, Cave Hill, 1999.

Seenarine, Moses. 'The Indo-Trinidadian Family in Transition: Historical and Contemporary Perspectives'. In *Sojourners to Settlers: Indian Migrants in Caribbean and the Americas*, eds. Mahin Gosine and Dhanpaul Narine. New York: Windsor Press, 1999.

Senior, Bernard. *Jamaica As It Was, As It Is and As it May Be*. 1835; New York: Negro Universities Press, 1969.

Sertima, Van. *They Came Before Columbus*. New York: Random House, 1976.

Sewell, William. *The Ordeal of Free Labour*. 1861; London: Cass, 1968.

Sharpe, Jenny. *Ghosts Of Slavery: A Literary Archaeology of Black Women's Lives*. Minneapolis: University of Minnesota Press, 2003.

Sheller, Mimi. *Democracy After Slavery: Black Publics and Peasant Radicalism in Haiti and Jamaica*. Gainesville: The University Press of Florida, 2000.

Shepherd, Verene. *Contested Terrain: Cattle, Cane and Slavery in Colonial Jamaica*. Kingston: Ian Randle Publishers, forthcoming.

————. *Maharanis' Misery: Narratives of a Passage*. Mona, Kingston: The University of the West Indies Press, 2003.

————, ed. *Working Slavery, Pricing Freedom: Perspectives from the Caribbean, Africa and the African Diaspora*. Kingston: Ian Randle Publishers; Oxford: James Currey Publishers, 2002.

————. 'Questioning Creole: Domestic Producers and Jamaica's Plantation Economy'. In *Questioning Creole: Creolization Discourses in Caribbean Culture*, eds. Richards and Shepherd, 167–180. Kingston: Ian Randle Publishers, 2002.

————. 'Petticoat Rebellion: Women in Emancipation in Colonial Jamaica'. Churches' Emancipation Lecture, 2001.

————. 'Locating Enslaved Women's Voices in the Colonial Caribbean: The Promises and Pitfalls of Ventriloquism'. Paper presented at the Workshop on Atlantic Crossings: Women's Voices, Women's Stories in the Caribbean and the Nigerian Hinterland Dartmouth College, New Hampshire, May 18–20, 2001.

————. *Emancipation and Immigration: A Pan-Caribbean Overview.* Kingston: Printed by Alpha Boys' School Printery, 1999.

————, comp and ed. *Women in Caribbean History: The British Colonized Territories.* Kingston: Ian Randle Publishers, 1995.

————. 'Gender, Migration and Settlement'. In *Engendering History: Caribbean Women in Historical Perspective*, eds. Shepherd, Brereton and Bailey, 237–242. Kingston: Ian Randle Publishers; London: James Currey; New York: St. Martin's Press, 1995.

————. *Transients to Settlers: The Experience of Indians in Jamaica 1845–1950.* Leeds: Peepal Tree, 1994.

————. 'Pens and Pen-keepers in a Plantation Society'. Phd dissertation, University of Cambridge, 1988

————. 'Indians and Blacks in Jamaica in the 19th and early 20th Centuries: A Micro-Study of the Foundations of Race Antagonisms'. In *After the Crossing: Immigrants and Minorities in Caribbean Creole Society*, ed. Howard Johnson, 95–112. London: Frank Cass, 1988.

Shepherd, Verene, and Glen L. Richards, eds., *Questioning Creole: Creolization Discourses in Caribbean Culture.* Kingston: Ian Randle Publishers, 2002.

Shepherd, Verene, and Kathleen E.A. Monteith, 'Non-Sugar Proprietors in a Sugar Plantation Society'. *Plantation Society in the Americas* V, nos. 2&3 (Fall 1998): 205–225.

Sheridan, Richard. 'Strategies of Slave Subsistence: The Jamaican Case Reconsidered'. In *From Chattel Slaves to Wage Slaves: The Dynamics of Labour Bargaining in the Americas*, ed. Mary Turner, 48–67. Bloomington: Indiana University Press, 1995.

————. 'Pens and Pen-Keepers in a Plantation Society'. PhD dissertation, University of Cambridge, 1988.

————. *Doctors and Slaves: A Medical and Demographic History of Slavery in the British West Indies, 1680–1834.* Cambridge: Cambridge University Press, 1985.

————. *Sugar and Slavery: An Economic History of the British West Indies, 1623–1775.* Barbados: Caribbean University Press, 1974.

Sherlock, Philip, and Hazel Bennett. *The Story of the Jamaican People.* Kingston: Ian Randle Publishers, 1997.

Simmonds, Lorna. 'Slave Festivities and Leisure-Time Activities in Jamaican Towns'. Seminar paper, the University of the West Indies, Mona 1984.

Smith, M.G. *The Plural Society in the British West Indies.* Berkeley: University of California Press, 1965.

Sohal, H.S. 'The East Indian Indentureship System in Jamaica, 1845–1917'. PhD dissertation, University of Waterloo, 1979.

Solow, Barbara. 'Slavery and Colonization'. In *Slavery and the Rise of the Atlantic System*, ed. Solow. Cambridge: Cambridge University Press, 1991.

Spivak, Gayatri Chakravorty. 'Can the Subaltern Speak?'. In *Colonial Discourse and Post-Colonial Theory: A Reader*, eds. Patrick Williams and Laura Chrisman, 66–111. New York: Harvester Wheatsheaf, 1993.

Stoddard, Charles. *Cruising Among the Caribbees: Summer Days in Winter Months*. New York: Charles Scribner's Sons, 1895.

Tannenbaum, F. *Slave and Citizen: The Negro in the Americas*. New York: Alfred Knopf, 1946.

Thomas, J.J. *Froudacity: West Indian Fables by James Anthony Froude explained by J.J. Thomas*. 1889; London: New Beacon, 1969.

Thomas, J. Paul. 'The Caribs of St Vincent: A Study in Maladministration, 1763–1773'. In *Caribbean Slave Society and Economy*, eds. Beckles and Shepherd, 28–35. Kingston: Ian Randle Publishers, 1991 (reprinted from *Journal of Caribbean History*, 1984).

Thompson, Alvin, ed. *In the Shadow of the Plantation: Caribbean History and Legacy*. Kingston: Ian Randle Publishers, 2002.

————. *Colonialism and Underdevelopment in Guyana 1580–1803*. Bridgetown, Barbados: Carib Research & Publications, 1987.

Thompson, Alvin. *The Berbice Revolt, 1763–64*. Georgetown, Guyana: Free Press, 1999.

Thornton, A.P. *West India Policy Under the Restoration*. Oxford: Clarendon Press, 1956.

Thornton, John. 'The Birth of an Atlantic World'. In *Caribbean Slavery in the Atlantic World*, eds. Shepherd and Beckles. Kingston: Ian Randle Publishers, 2000.

————. 'African Soldiers in the Haitian Revolution'. In *Caribbean Slavery in the Atlantic World*, eds. Shepherd and Beckles, 933–945. Kingston: Ian Randle Publishers, 2000.

Tinker, Hugh. *A New System of Slavery: The Export of Indian Labour Overseas, 1830–1920*. London: Hansib, 1993.

Trollope, Anthony. *The West Indies and the Spanish Main*. 1859; London: Frank Cass, 1965.

Trotman, David. 'Women and Crime in Late 19th Century Trinidad'. *Caribbean Quarterly* 30, nos. 3&4 (1984): 60–72.

Turner, Mary. 'Chattel Slaves into Wage Slaves: A Jamaican Case Study'. In *From Chattel Slaves to Wage Slaves: The Dynamics of Labour Bargaining in the Americas*, ed. Mary Turner, 33–47. Bloomington: Indiana University Press; Kingston: Ian Randle Publishers, 1995.

————. *Slaves and Missionaries: The Disintegration of Jamaican Slave Society, 1787–1834*. Mona, Kingston: The University of the West Indies Press, 1998.

————. 'The Baptist War and Abolition'. *Jamaica History Review* 13 (1982).

Tyson, J.D. *Report on the Condition of Indians in Jamaica, Trinidad and British Guiana.* Simla, 1939.

van den Berghe, Pierre. *Race and Ethnicity: Essays in Comparative Sociology.* New York: Basic Books, 1976.

Vassell, Linnette. 'Women of the Masses'. In *Engendering History: Caribbean Women in Historical Perspective*, eds. Shepherd, Brereton and Bailey. New York: St Martin's Press; Kingston: Ian Randle Publishers, 1995.

————. *Voices of Women in Jamaica, 1898–1939.* Mona, Kingston: Department of History, University of the West Indies, 1993.

Vilar, Enriqueta Vilá with Wim Klooster. 'Forced African Settlement'. In *UNESCO General History of the Caribbean*, Vol. II *New Societies: The Caribbean in the Long Sixteenth Century*, ed. Pieter C. Emmer. Paris: UNESCO, 1999.

Wallerstein, Immanuel. *The Modern World System.* New York: Academic Press, 1974.

Warner-Lewis, Maureen. 'Creolization Processes in Linguistic, Artistic and Material Cultures'. In *Questioning Creole: Creolisation Discourses in Caribbean Culture*, eds. Shepherd and Richards, 245–256. Kingston: Ian Randle Publishers, 2002.

Watts, David. 'Early Hispanic New World Agriculture, 1492–1509'. In *Caribbean Slavery in the Atlantic World*, eds. Shepherd and Beckles. Kingston: Ian Randle Publishers, 2000.

————. 'Caribbean Environment and Early Settlement'. In *UNESCO General History of the Caribbean*, Vol. II *New Societies: The Caribbean in the Long Sixteenth Century*, ed. Pieter C. Emmer. Paris: UNESCO, 1999.

Weeks, Jeffery. *Making Sexual History.* Cambridge: Polity Press; Malden: Blackwell Publishers, 2000.

Welch, Pedro. *Slave Society in the City: Bridgetown, Barbados, 1680–1834.* Kingston: Ian Randle Publishers, 2002.

Williams, Cynric. *A Tour Through the Island of Jamaica, from the Western to the Eastern End, in the Year 1823.* London: T. Hurst, E. Chance & Co, 1827.

Williams, Eric. *Capitalism and Slavery.* Chapel Hill: University of North Carolina Press, 1994; Kingston: Ian Randle Publishers, 2004.

————. *British Historians and the West Indies.* Port of Spain, Trinidad: PNM Publishing Co Ltd, 1964.

Williams, Raymond. *Keywords: A Vocabulary of Culture and Society* 1976; reprint. New York: Oxford University Press, 1985.

Wilmot, Swithin. 'The Politics of Samuel Clarke: Black Political Martyr in Jamaica, 1851–1865'. *Jamaica Historical Review*, XIX (1996).

————. 'Females of Abandoned Character?: Women and Protest in Jamaica, 1838–1865'. In *Engendering History: Caribbean Women in Historical Perspective*, eds. Shepherd, Brereton and Bailey. New York: St Martin's Press; Kingston: Ian Randle

Publishers, 1995.

————. 'Emancipation in Action: Workers and Wage Conflict in Jamaica, 1838–1848'. *Jamaica Journal* 19 no.3 (1986): 55–61.

———— '"Not Full Free": The Ex-Slaves and the Apprenticeship System in Jamaica, 1834–1838'. *Jamaica Journal* 17, no.3 (August–October 1984): 2–10.

Wilson, Peter. *Crab Antics: The Social Anthropology of English-Speaking Negro Societies of the Caribbean.* New Haven: Yale University Press, 1973.

Wright, Philip, ed. *Lady Nugent's Journal.* Mona, Kingston: The University of the West Indies Press, 2003.

Wrong, Hume. *Government of the West Indies.* New York: Negroes University Press, 1969.

Yelvington, Kevin, et al., eds. 'Whose History?: Museum and Struggles Over Ethnicity and Representation in the Sunbelt'. Unpublished paper, August 1999.

Zahedieh, Nuala. 'Trade, Plunder and Economic Development in Early English Jamaica'. In *Caribbean Slavery in the Atlantic World*, eds. Shepherd and Beckles, 178–193. Kingston: Ian Randle Publishers, 2000.

————. 'The Merchants of Port Royal, Jamaica, and the Spanish Contraband Trade, 1655–1692'. *William and Mary Quarterly*, 3rd series, 43 (1986).

Index

Printed in the United States
64698LVS00003B/76-198

9 789766 372552